International Construction Project Management: General Theory and Practice

John Bennett

BUTTERWORTH
HEINEMANN

Butterworth-Heinemann Ltd
Linacre House, Jordan Hill, Oxford OX2 8DP

PART OF REED INTERNATIONAL BOOKS

OXFORD LONDON BOSTON
MUNICH NEW DELHI SINGAPORE SYDNEY
TOKYO TORONTO WELLINGTON

First published 1991

1 0 3 7 6 8 6 0

British Library Cataloguing in Publication Data
Bennett, John
    International construction project management:
    General theory and practice.
    I. Title
    692.068

ISBN 0 7506 1330 0

Library of Congress Cataloguing in Publication Data
A catalogue record for this book is available from
the Library of Congress

Printed and bound in Great Britain by Billings Ltd, Worcester

14/01/92

Contents

Preface

Construction project management is important for two main reasons. First, construction shapes the majority of mankind's immediate environment. As a consequence, it has a tremendous capacity to contribute to people's wealth, health and happiness. However, faced with a world population likely to reach ten billion by the middle of the twenty-first century, construction projects must be managed efficiently if the industry's potential for good is to be realized for the majority of mankind. The world simply is not rich enough to squander natural resources through inefficient construction project management. It is therefore a tragedy that, in recent decades, construction products have become relatively more expensive in almost every country in the world. Construction's failure to match the productivity gains achieved by other major industries must be put right. This book makes a contribution to that crucial task by providing prescriptions for practitioners to follow in managing construction projects.

The second way in which construction project management is important is as an academic subject. This is because it cuts through the barriers which too often separate the arts, humanities and sciences. The subject brings together academics concerned with the practical application of these three great bodies of human knowledge in design, management and engineering. Their joint work has the potential to provide new theories about human behaviour within a cultural and physical world which draw on an unusually broad body of knowledge. This book makes a contribution to this work by describing a theory which explains the behaviour of construction projects.

The book's contributions to practice and theory reflect its two main sources. They both spring from my earlier book (Bennett, 1985). Since it was published, I have used the ideas which it describes in working with practitioners, in undertaking research and in teaching.

My work with practitioners has been undertaken within the Centre for Strategic Studies in Construction at the University of Reading. I am the Director of the Centre, which was set up in 1986 to make the University's knowledge and skills easily available to construction practitioners on a commercial basis. My own work within the Centre is mainly concerned with studies designed to help construction firms develop their own strategies in a changing world; consultancy aimed at helping major customers make effective use of the construction industry; and teaching on training courses for experienced construction project managers. As a matter of policy, in its formative years, the Centre has worked only with excellent practitioners and very experienced customers. This is to ensure that the Centre's staff learn the patterns of behaviour which go with success. In this spirit I have used the Centre's work to create opportunities to study good construction practice at first hand in the USA, Japan and Europe, to distil the main lessons and to help practitioners to apply them in the UK. The Centre's work provides a rigorous test for my theoretical ideas; either they are seen to provide benefits in practice or the Centre goes out of business. This book describes the ideas that work in practice.

I have also used the ideas in Bennett (1985) in my research and teaching. This work has been undertaken as Professor of Quantity Surveying within the Department of Construction Management and Engineering, University of Reading, a post I have held since 1975. My academic research has been funded by the Science and Engineering Research Council and I gratefully acknowledge the value of their support. The principal aim of my recent research has been to define the concepts which must be included in any general theory of construction project management. In particular I have sought ways of measuring project success and the factors which determine it. My teaching has also helped in the search for fundamental concepts. In particular, teaching management to first-year undergraduates has caused me to understand general management theory well enough to reduce the subject to its basic concepts and the relationships between them. The challenge of thinking sufficiently clearly to create a first-year subject out of the great diversity of ideas which make up the management literature has helped to define the theoretical basis for my work with practising construction project managers and their customers. This book describes the set of ideas which I have found to be helpful in formulating an academic basis for research, teaching and consultancy.

The opportunity to write this book arose from the generosity of the University of Reading in releasing me from my duties as Director of the Centre and Professor in the Department for six months, sabbatical leave in mid-1990. I gratefully acknowledge the value of this time in bringing together my theoretical ideas and practical experience in a way which I hope will be of value to both fellow academics and fellow practitioners. In the preface to Bennett (1985) I acknowledged my debt to the many people who had helped to shape my ideas. Those acknowledgements stand and I must add to them all the people referred to throughout this book and listed at the end in the References. The book draws freely on their ideas and I am pleased to have this opportunity of acknowledging my intellectual debt to them all.

I must also thank Heather O'Connor who word-processed the manuscript for the book from my scribbled, altered and amended drafts. Finally, and above all,

I thank my wife Sue and my children Stephen and Kate for providing the encouragement and support needed to write this book.

I must add one important explanation to the book. The English language does not yet have a satisfactory way of including both sexes when referring to individuals. The common form is almost always masculine. This weakness often applies also to collective nouns. Hence, whenever I have used the masculine form to describe individuals generally or to describe groups of people, I intend it to refer to women and men equally. I recognize that this is unsatisfactory and look forward to the day when the language develops a good way of avoiding what remains an insidious prejudice. Meanwhile, I hope, notwithstanding this defect, that the book helps construction project managers of both sexes to make confident decisions which lead on to successful projects.

John Bennett
University of Reading

1 Buildings, bridges and brain-waves

Construction provides the stage on which almost all human activity takes place. Creating this stage is a major activity. As a consequence, construction forms a large part of the gross national product of practically every nation on earth. The organizations which carry out the activities of producing, repairing and maintaining the products which make up the built environment are collectively called the construction industry.

The construction industry includes a rich variety of firms and individuals. Sharp financiers, idiosyncratic artists, scientists, technologists, production engineers, street-wise managers, factory workers, skilled craftsmen, machine drivers and labourers all work together to create new construction products. These products are normally large, heavy and expensive and most are custom-made to an individual specification. Generally each product is fixed in one location although, in total, construction is geographically widely distributed. As a consequence of these characteristics and of the uneven pattern of demand for particular types of construction in any one geographical location, the industry organizes its work as a series of individual projects.

Project organizations are assembled by drawing teams from a multitude of firms to design, manufacture and construct a building, bridge or other new construction product or to alter or repair an existing one. As their individual contributions to the whole are completed, the teams leave the project organization to work on another new project.

The complete design, manufacture and construction process is long, involved and often clumsy and inefficient. Its success depends on bringing together the right teams of people and establishing the right relationships between them. Doing this requires an understanding of management theory and practice. This book describes a framework of ideas designed to help provide that understanding.

Two fundamental ideas underlie this book. The first is that the appropriate choice of project organization is crucial to the success of construction projects. The importance of this choice is best described by an analogy. A motorist setting out on a journey must choose which road to take. Provided he chooses an appropriate road, even if he drives slowly and somewhat carelessly, he is likely to reach his intended destination. However, if he chooses a wrong road, no matter how fast and brilliantly he drives, he will never complete his journey.

The same problem faces construction projects; if they have an inappropriate organization, they flounder. Costs escalate, completion dates are missed, quality deteriorates and the people involved are damaged by stress. There are a number of books about construction projects which include the word disaster in the title. They describe many projects which set off with an inappropriate organization and then staggered from crisis to crisis until the project organization was changed to a more appropriate form. Hall (1980) provides the most interesting of the project disaster books and he leaves little doubt about the importance of an appropriate choice of project organization.

The second idea which is fundamental to the rest of this book is based on the contingency theories of management. Thus, the book owes an intellectual debt to the pioneering work of Woodward (1965) and Lawrence and Lorsch (1967). Simply stated, the second fundamental idea is that the choice of an appropriate project organization depends on the nature of the product, its environment and the overall objectives of the customer who commissions the project.

The relationships between objectives, environment, product and organization do not form a simple sequence. In most construction projects there is a rich interaction between these key elements. In practice, the appropriate organization is designed in parallel with the product. As this process is worked through, it may cause the customer's objectives to be modified. All of these interacting decisions and the resulting actions are influenced by the environment, which in any case is itself subject to change. To some extent changes in the environment are a response to the evolving project. Consequently, all four elements interact with each of the others. Figure 1.1 illustrates the structure of the interactions

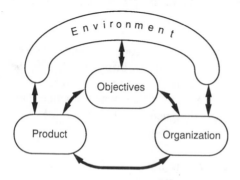

Figure 1.1   *Key factors in designing construction project organizations*

between the key elements which shape the choice of appropriate construction project organizations. However, Figure 1.1 is static and an important issue for managers is that, as projects move through time, each of the elements in Figure 1.1 may alter. Consequently, the design of a construction project organization cannot be the result of a once and for all decision. Organization design needs attention throughout the life of projects if the people involved are to be allowed to give of their best.

To design effective construction project organizations, we first need a language which helps us to think about the important management concepts. The first five chapters of this book are used to identify and name these concepts. Since the nature of its products is fundamental to the work of the whole industry, we begin with the buildings, bridges and other brain-waves which are the end-results of construction projects.

Function and quality

The construction industry produces a vast range of products which serve an even wider variety of functions. The usual way of describing these products is in terms of their dominant function. Thus we speak of churches, offices, libraries, schools, factories, bridges, roads, sewers, power stations and many other dominant functions. This focus is important for the designers of the end product. They must understand the functions to be performed by a new product and it is helpful to have information about particular functions grouped together. Consequently it is useful, for example, to have a word for buildings which are dominated by the teaching function. We call such products schools, and this helps us to think about, communicate about and store information about buildings dominated by the teaching function. However, this is primarily a designers' classification. Managers need different concepts. Before we turn our attention directly to management, it is helpful to consider the designer's concepts of function and quality.

Function and quality define the objectives of projects which relate directly to their physical end products. They provide the framework within which designers must make their decisions. They also shape the work of managers and contractors. Managers therefore have a substantial interest in ensuring that function and quality are fully considered and agreed before major resources are committed to any new project. This is important because, as Duffy and Henney (1989) conclude in their well researched study of modern office buildings, the design of buildings has too often suffered from oversimplified generalizations by architects, developers and customers. They have, in too many cases, preferred to use a *rule book* for providing easy answers, rather than thinking problems through. This criticism can legitimately be levelled at the past. Obviously there are exceptions, but too much of our built environment is mediocre in terms of the way it performs in use.

As an example of what is needed for the future, Duffy and Henney consider that the starting point for developing better office buildings has to be a careful analysis, for every new project, of the needs of the users. The analysis should look at the nature of the work to be accommodated and pay particular attention to the way it changes. It should get inside the culture of the users and so understand the needs which the new building must satisfy in terms of: support for individual members of staff; reinforcement of the overall organization; flexibility; ease of communication; comfortable conditions; image; and security. The analysis should also consider information technology issues. These include: the need for workstations and networks; the incidence of environmentally demanding equipment; the need to protect the operation of equipment; its demand for power and cooling; and the demands of telecommunications from and to the users.

Duffy and Henney see modern office buildings as comprising four main elements which need to be analysed separately because the needs of users in respect of each are likely to be different. The four elements are: the shell, which has a life of fifty years or more; the services, which can be readily attached to and detached from the shell and have a life of ten to fifteen years; the scenery, comprising the partitions, finishes and furniture, which have a short life of no more than five to seven years; and the sets, which are rearrangements of the scenery to meet the daily or weekly exigencies of office life. Duffy and Henney use this analysis to identify a series of generic office building types for the future to which they give descriptive titles, including *big city high spec, city fringe medium spec, highly serviced towers, smaller city high identity, high-tech*, and *utility*.

This kind of well informed and analytical thinking forces customers into relating their own needs to important general developments in office building. It does not provide any form of straightjacket, but instead it provides a basis for purposeful feedback and learning from others' experience. The outcome is a well considered statement of the function and quality to be provided by a new project.

Function of course means all the activities, whether carried out by people or machines, which are to be accommodated by the end product of a construction project. Quality needs slightly more consideration because in practice the term is used to describe two distinctly different concepts. The sense in which it is used here is to describe the initial choice of the level of quality required by a customer in the various parts of a new construction. Thus, it is closely related to the image, status, performance and life expectancy of the parts.

Unfortunately, quality is also used to describe the actual standard of construction work. Construction workers commonly speak of good or bad quality workmanship. This concept is closely linked to quality control, that is, ensuring that customers are provided with the standard of work they have specified. The distinction will probably be clearer with the aid of an example. Marble floor finishes are widely accepted as being of a higher quality than, say, vinyl floor finishes. However, either of these levels of quality may be constructed to a proper standard, a poor standard, a very good standard or even excellent standard. So the concepts of quality and of work standard are closely related but it is important to distinguish between them.

With this early diversion into terminology complete, we can return to the manager's role in helping to produce a well considered statement of the function and quality to be provided by a new project. Producing such a statement is primarily the responsibility of the designers. Managers are responsible for ensuring that sufficient time and resources are allocated to this important stage of their projects. They need to recognize that producing a statement of function and quality may need a great deal of study, it may require new research, seminars or workshops where the customer and the users work with experts and designers to explore possible answers. In these circumstances, producing the statement is essentially a learning process for everyone involved so that they are aware of the significance of the choices which they make. It may be that the right answers are well established, and the customer is experienced and understands his own needs thoroughly; or it may be that pressures of time or resources necessarily limit the process of producing a statement of a project's objectives to selecting the best from those immediately available.

Whatever circumstances exist, managers are responsible for ensuring that a statement of function and quality is produced efficiently and deals with all the central, crucial issues. As much as anything, this means ensuring that the necessary knowledge and experience is assembled and directed to the customer's real needs. Thus we see that producing a statement of function and quality is a project responsibility in which managers are acting in support of the designers. Managers themselves need to take a different view of the end product and use different concepts in undertaking their own primary responsibilities.

Complexity

Managers' primary responsibility is to ensure the efficient execution of the processes necessary to produce the end products of their projects. Their interest in any specific end product therefore centres on the way in which it determines the actions necessary to produce it. It is this set of actions which project organizations are designed to facilitate. It is this set of actions which managers need to think about, in a systematic way, in order to manage their projects efficiently.

To enable them to think about their work in this way, managers need concepts which identify the key differences between the sets of actions which make up separate projects. The first and fairly obvious difference, from a management viewpoint, is that projects differ in terms of the number of different actions needed to produce the end product. The number of different actions determines the complexity of the project.

Practitioners frequently describe their projects as simple or complex when they are discussing management issues. This indicates a practical acceptance that complexity makes a difference to the management of projects. However, for complexity to have other than a theoretical value, we need to be able to identify actions which should be regarded as separate as opposed to those which can be grouped together. Miller (1959) first identified the factors which cause work to become differentiated in this way.

Technology is the starting point for identifying separate groups of actions. Technologies are distinct bodies of knowledge and sets of skills and the related tools, plant and equipment needed to apply them. Technologies help us to process materials, energy and information. Those which directly serve the basic, direct work of producing constructions are usually clustered around the use of particular materials or components, or else they relate to specific systems or elements of the end products. There are many differences between all the technologies which construction project managers must take into account. However, at the present stage of the discussion, these differences can be put to one side. What is important to an initial management overview is the existence of distinct technologies within projects. The more technologies, the more complex the project. However, technology is not the only factor at work.

Groups of actions undertaken in separate and distinct physical locations also add to the complexity of projects. In the early stages of projects, design is commonly undertaken in several separate offices and studios. In the main, this physical separation of the project work coincides with and merely reinforces differences in the knowledge, skills, tools, plant and equipment, that is, in the technology being used. Consequently, it does not add to the complexity of the project. However if, for example, structural design was being undertaken in several different offices, the project would be more complex. Similarly, if the flow of components needed for a project exceeded the capacity of any available manufacturing plant, so that several factories were used, the project would be more complex than if all the components were produced in one factory. Equally, the physical arrangement of work on site may dictate that separate physical locations are managed and staffed independently. Individual buildings within a multi-building project, distinct sections of a long road or pipeline, the abutments at either end of a bridge or groups of floors in a high-rise building, all provide a basis for territory to add to the complexity of projects.

In addition, projects may be made more complex because groups of actions must be undertaken at different times. A straightforward example is where shift working is adopted so that two or even three separate teams work at different times of the day. Each shift takes up the work where the previous one left off. Such a project is clearly more complex than one in which only one work shift is employed.

Differences in technology, territory and time are the three bases for regarding groups of actions as being separate and distinct from the point of view of project managers. These three factors, in other words, determine the degree of complexity in construction projects.

Size

The second major factor that managers must consider is the size of the projects. There is overwhelming evidence in the management literature that size is a crucial factor in organization design. It is self-evident that construction projects differ from each other in terms of size. It is also clear that construction firms and their customers recognize the significance of these differences. General contractors commonly have a small works division to deal with small projects. Public authorities who maintain lists of approved contractors classify them in various ways, but the one characteristic common to all such lists is the size of the projects which each contractor is competent to undertake. It is widely understood that mega-projects need to be handled by one of a relatively tiny number of international contractors. On the other hand, there are dozens of local firms in most towns and cities throughout the world capable of handling small projects.

Size is usually measured in terms of value. This is convenient but inevitably leads to inconsistencies. A small, complex, high quality project will be classified as the same size as a large, simple, low quality project simply because their costs happen to be similar. Another common approach is to measure the physical size of the end product. Thus, public sector buildings in many countries are described in terms of the number of cubic metres of space they provide, commercial buildings are commonly described in terms of square feet of lettable floor area, and motorways in terms of kilometres of highway of various widths, expressed in terms of the number of traffic lanes. Another approach is to describe the capacity of a project in terms of its primary function. Thus we may speak of a school for 500 pupils, a 250-bed hospital or an oil refinery which processes 10 000 barrels of oil per day. This gives us a broad measure of relative size for projects of one particular type. It does not of course tell us anything about the relative size of the school, hospital and oil refinery. In management terms they may be the same size or very different; the numbers do not tell us.

As far as size is concerned, the most important fact for managers to know is the number of units of activity they must manage. The total size of the project organization has a major and direct influence on the manager's task and this is directly determined by the number of separate units of activity necessary to complete the project. Rather than attempt to count all the individuals likely to be involved in a project, which would be difficult and too detailed to be useful, it is more accurate to use technologically distinct teams to calculate the number of units of activity. The reason for this is that managers of whole projects, other than very small projects, have no choice but to leave the organization of teams to first-line managers. Therefore the smallest organization unit which they can take into account is teams.

The use of teams rather than individuals undoubtedly leads to inaccuracies in judging the size of projects because the size of teams varies. Teams may consist of one individual, more usually two or three, or they may be much larger. In the general management literature, it is widely reported that the size of teams found in different situations varies considerably. However, teams in construction tend to be fairly small. Their size is determined in the long run by economic considerations. In each sector of the industry, teams will tend over time to move towards the size which experience shows is most efficient. However, the size of efficient construction teams in general is fairly consistent. To a large extent this is because the nature of much construction work requires teams to rely on solving day-to-day problems for themselves. The first-line manager is often a working foreman who spends a significant proportion of his time resolving minor issues relating to the organization, arrangement or working practices of his team. A further consistent feature of the general management literature is that, where there is a need for much work-related communication, teams tend to be small. So, although there is some variation in the size of construction teams, it is not sufficient to invalidate the use of teams as a measure of project size.

There is, however, one important caveat which must be stated. This is that there exists a systematic relationship between the size of projects and the size of teams. As projects get bigger, teams also get bigger. This is simply because there are more workplaces available on a large project and so the efficient size for any given technology tends to increase. This systematic relationship does not invalidate the use of teams as a measure of overall project size. It does mean, however, that the relative size of large projects will be understated but in a consistent manner. A project measured as bigger will in fact be bigger. It will comprise more teams and so will require more management. Size measured in terms of teams is, in other words, a useful measure for managers. That is, it is when we have added one further dimension to the basic concept of the team.

Teams work through time. A team which completes its work on a project in two days poses a different management task from one that takes two months or another that takes two years. Each of the three cases is likely to be part of very different sized projects. It could happen of course that all three cases occur on the same project. It would be a very arbitrary measure which counted all three teams, taking two days, two months and two years, as contributing equally to a measure of project size.

I am grateful to my colleague at Reading, Colin Gray, for the insight that the basic unit for managers of construction sites is one day's work for one team. There are many reasons for this judgement which will become apparent later in this book. However, in straightforward terms, most construction activities require certain actions at the start and finish of each day. Machinery must be started up or closed down, materials need to be distributed to workplaces, workers must be briefed, loose objects may need to be secured and so on. There is a distinct pattern to a day's work for a construction team. Experienced foremen are reasonably good at looking at moderately sized elements of their work and predicting how many days it will take to complete. Also, work of any magnitude tends to be fitted into whole days. Work will be dragged out to the end of a day if it looks like finishing early. That is, of course, unless workers have the discretion to choose their own working hours. Equally, work which can just about be finished before the end of a day will tend to be speeded up so as not to leave a tiny amount of unfinished work for the next day. At least, when workers are well managed this effect is common. There is in other words wide practical recognition of the concept of a day's work on construction sites.

However, construction projects comprise much more than work on site. Construction work takes place, and to an increasing extent, in factories, drawing offices, industrial laboratories and design studios. As we work through that list, the concept of a day's work for a team becomes progressively harder to relate to practical reality. As work becomes more concerned with thinking than with physical actions, the boundaries of work become blurred. Designers think about their designs when they are in the bath, driving to their studio or playing golf. Creativity is unpredictable. A new design problem may take an hour or six months to solve. Nevertheless, work does tend to take place in day-long chunks. So although the earlier, creative stages of construction projects are less predictable, teams do in fact undertake a day's work. We can therefore theoretically accept that the size of a construction project is most usefully measured in terms of days-work for teams.

Repetition

The next characteristic of end products which is of interest to managers is the extent to which they allow patterns of work to be repeated. It is well known that repetition of an activity, usually called practice, improves performance. We rightly expect a well practised worker to produce more work of a better standard than one who is rusty at a particular activity. What is true for individuals also appears to be true for organizations.

When the work of an organization provides consistent repeating patterns of reasonably similar work for a series of teams, productivity increases. The organization as a whole, comprising the series of teams, learns how to work together. The teams adjust their membership and methods to create a steady rhythm of work. All strive to complete their tasks to the same time-scale so that no team is delayed by the unfinished work of any preceding team. When the resulting improvements in productivity are plotted they produce a learning curve or experience curve, as it is sometimes called. Such curves for construction work typically have a slope of between 95 and 85 per cent. This means that, for each doubling of the number of repetitions, the labour content falls to between 95 and 85 per cent of the previous productivity level. Figure 1.2 provides a typical picture of a learning-curve in construction. It is taken from a major United Nations (1965) study of the effect of repetition on building operations and processes on site. The data illustrated in Figure 1.2 relates to the building of 45 houses in Finland. The houses were constructed in two phases separated by a gap in time. The learning curve is initially steep, but after the eighth house

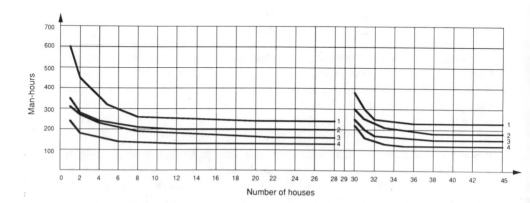

Figure 1.2   *Typical learning curve in the construction of 45 one-family houses in Finland: 1, outer wall elements; 2, ceilings; 3, wooden partitions; 4, services (Source: United Nations Committee on Housing, 1965)*

productivity settled into a shallow learning curve. However, a break in the work after house 29 caused a rise in labour consumption for the first three houses in the second series. Thereafter the workforce settled back into the previous shallow learning curve.

The United Nations study examined the pattern of productivity in many building projects which provided repetition in various ways. It concluded that, for repetition to have its full benefits, the design should ensure the maximum identity of operations, and projects should be of sufficient size to provide for specialization and they should provide space for teams to work independently. In addition, the work must be planned and organized properly and supported by adequate day-to-day supervision of the work.

Given these circumstances, a successive improvement in labour productivity is achieved in all kinds of building operations carried out consecutively and continuously in series. The benefits are inhibited by breaks in time, including those caused by late deliveries of materials and bad weather conditions. Changes in the composition of teams reduce output. Also, where output is closely linked to the capacity of machinery or equipment or constrained by the output of other workers, the benefits of repetition may not appear. However, where reasonably identical operations carried out by the same teams of workers in identical sequences are undertaken without breaks, productivity improves over time.

The United Nations study identified three phases in the pattern of productivity produced by repetitive operations. The first is an *operation-learning phase* during which workers acquire sufficient knowledge of the task to be performed. Labour productivity increases rapidly during the operation-learning phase. Second, there is a *routine-acquiring phase* during which a gradual improvement of labour productivity is achieved through growing familiarity with the work and through small changes in work method and organization. In practice, approximately stable operational times are ultimately achieved. Finally, there is often an *end phase*, during which productivity reduces as the work nears its final completion. In most cases this is due to modifications and additions to the operation which come at the end. This stage is often associated with failures of planning and supervision. The end phase is usually relatively short and so does not entirely negate the earlier improvements in productivity.

The study found that the productivity benefits translate into lower costs. The cost benefits are of two kinds. First, the direct costs of undertaking the work are reduced and, second, the time on site is reduced and so site overhead costs are lower because the site organization is needed for a shorter period. For the maximum cost savings to be obtained, it is usually necessary to ensure that the workers share in the benefits of increased labour productivity. Thus, repetition leads to higher wages and lower costs. These are important benefits and so it behoves managers to search actively for ways of creating the conditions that allow productive repetition to occur.

Uncertainty

The next characteristic of concern to construction project managers is the level of uncertainty inherent in the work they must manage. When work is predictable, that is certain, management faces a very different task from that on projects where the work is uncertain.

There are a multitude of sources of uncertainty. Figure 1.3 lists some of the more important ones. There is also a substantial literature on the management

Customer/government/regulatory agencies

Funding/fiscal

Definition of project

Project organization

Design

Local conditions

Permanent plant supply

Construction contractors

Construction materials

Construction labour

Construction plant

Logistics

Estimating data

Inflation

Exchange rates

Force majeure

Figure 1.3   *Sources of uncertainty (Source: Hayes, et al., 1986)*

of uncertainty or risk in construction. Hayes *et al.* (1986) and Marshall (1988) provide good introductions to the subject. The substantial literature is evidence that it is commonly accepted that construction is inherently risky. However, not all construction is equally uncertain and managers of individual projects need to consider the actual level of uncertainty they may expect to face.

There are two distinct categories of uncertainty. First, there is that which derives from the nature of the work required to produce the end product. This we shall call variability. Second, there is uncertainty which derives from the environment of projects. This we shall call interference.

Variability

It is part of the human condition that we do not achieve exactly what we set out to achieve. Sometimes we do better but often we produce less than we had hoped for. It is also part of the human condition that we feel good if we do better than we expect. Equally we tend to experience some sense of failure if something takes longer or costs more than we had expected. One consequence of this is that once we have accepted a target we strive to meet it. In other words, our expectations exert a positive influence in moderating the range of variability in human performance. Nevertheless, the productivity of any one team does vary from day to day and productivity varies even more when we consider the work of different teams.

Managers considering the design of a construction project organization do not know exactly which teams will be employed to do the work. Consequently, they face a degree of uncertainty over the levels of productivity which they can realistically assume. It is nevertheless important to have some idea of the variability in productivity which managers will have to deal with as their projects proceed.

There are many causes of variability. However, in general terms, work which can be carried out by one team independently of other teams, which is well understood and is comfortably within the competence of the local construction industry will be relatively certain. On the other hand, work that requires teams to work interdependently, which is ill-defined and is outside the range of experience of the local construction industry will be relatively uncertain in its performance.

Projects that demand new answers lead to uncertain work. New designs, new techniques, new uses of materials, new materials, new plant or equipment or new ideas all make actual levels of productivity difficult to predict. This is not to argue that innovation should be avoided. It is merely to note that initially it creates uncertainty, which requires additional management. In addition to the uncertainty inherent in individual actions, the nature of the interdependencies between separate teams also influences variability. Walker (1989) describes a series of case studies of construction projects which classify the interdependencies between teams as pooled, sequential or reciprocal.

Pooled interdependency occurs when teams share an independent resource. An example is a tower crane which provides otherwise independent teams with materials. Equally, a number of design teams may all use the same offices. All rely on the effective management of the offices and the facilities they provide but otherwise they work independently, probably on different projects. Interdependency arises because a failure in any one of the teams using the pooled resource can affect the work of the other teams.

Sequential interdependency arises when a series of teams each pass work on to the next one in a single, straightforward sequence. Each team is dependent on the preceding one for the timing and standard of the input to their work. A simple example which is relevant to construction is the need to design, manufacture and construct in that sequence. The manufacture of many prefabricated construction products cannot begin until the design is substantially complete. Equally, the products cannot be installed on site until they have been manufactured. Thus, there is sequential interdependency.

Reciprocal interdependency arises when work moves backwards and forwards between a number of teams. The work moves forward in time as a series of short steps in which the outputs from each team become the inputs for the others in a largely unpredictable sequence. Much design work is of this nature. A reasonably typical situation would see an architect making a decision which influences the work of structural engineers and services engineers. Their parallel decisions influence each other and cause the architect to rethink. A new decision is passed to the engineers, who have to rethink their designs. The resulting new decisions are passed to the structural steelwork contractor and the electrical contractor. They in turn produce new input for the structural engineer and his subsequent new decision influences the next step in the architect's work. Many such sequences have been recorded in the literature of construction management. Figure 1.4 provides a greatly simplified representation of the general nature of much design work. Walker (1989) found that reciprocal interdependencies are the dominant type in construction projects. These are the most difficult to manage, requiring close contact and good communications between the interdependent teams. This is one of the main reasons why construction work is subject to high levels of variability.

Variability arises, by definition, from inside construction projects. Its level is determined by the nature of the work of the separate teams, the extent to which they are practised in their work; and the nature of the interdependencies

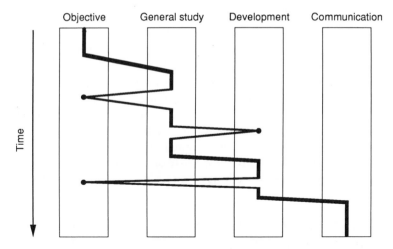

Figure 1.4 *The general nature of design development (Source: Bennett, 1985)*

between them. These are all factors which to a large extent lie within the direct responsibility of project management. There is therefore a need for managers to think about and make some prediction of the variability likely to arise in any new project. This requires data on the levels of variability associated with different kinds of construction in different circumstances. In an extensive search for sources of good data to measure the variability in productivity, Bennett and Ormerod (1984) found that researchers and practitioners collect data which identifies variability. However, in many cases, especially with practitioners' data, the fact of variability is ignored. The data is reduced to a single mean value which is then used in planning future construction projects. This is to ignore vital information and suggests that much construction management relies on oversimplistic models of their projects.

Bennett and Ormerod identified sufficient data to provide the raw material for a model of the construction stage of projects which takes explicit account of variability. They also identified the existence of lead activities which enjoy relatively stable conditions and so are less variable than other work. Brickwork is one example in projects which use load-bearing brickwork to provide the main structure. Similarly, the structural steelwork in projects with a steel frame is often used to set the tempo and general style for all of the site work. Bennett and Ormerod found that the lead activity experienced variability of ±30 per cent of its mean value, while for other activities variability is of the order of ±50 to ±60 per cent. These figures relate to work in the UK in the 1970s and there is little doubt that other values apply in other countries and at other times. It is an important responsibility of managers to organize their work from project to project, so that they are provided with relevant data on variability.

Interference

The second major cause of uncertainty comes, by definition, from outside projects. The environment of construction projects has a considerable capacity to spring surprises. Delays are commonly caused by severe weather conditions, late delivery of materials or components, a shortage of labour, machines which fail, a refusal to grant a necessary authorization or to provide essential information, and a multitude of other factors. The common effect is to cause the planned progress of a project to be interrupted. It is therefore wise for construction project managers to make some assessment of the potential for externally generated interference, since it has a direct effect on the difficulty of their own task.

The first important fact which needs to be understood in considering interference is that all construction projects are influenced by a number of distinctly different environments. To some extent each team operates within an environment which has unique characteristics. For example, there will be a distinct market for each of the separate resources required for a project. Each will have its own conventions, ways of doing business, levels of supply and demand, and potential for interference with projects. Many of these separate environments will be influenced in a broadly consistent manner by general political, economic, social and technical factors. Nevertheless, managers need to be aware of the possibility that individual teams in the context of a particular project may face specific and unusually difficult environments.

It is also necessary to recognize that the effective environment changes as projects move through their major stages. Initially, construction projects face a world dominated by powerful people. Hall (1980) reviewed projects drawn from several industries, including construction. He found that the early stages are influenced by three distinct groups of people. These are politicians, government bureaucracies and special interest groups within the local community. Hall provides numerous examples of how major projects have been shaped, interrupted and delayed by the interplay of conflict, compromise and confusion among powerful politicians, bureaucrats and special interest groups. Each have their own objectives and these are likely to alter over time as personalities and power bases change. Which objectives dominate, and therefore which decisions are made about the future of any one project, depends on the relative power of the key actors at the decisive points in a project's history.

Managers need to develop a feel for the human environment of their projects. They need to know who are their friends, who are their enemies and who will simply sit on the fence when support is needed. They should make a judgement about the best, worst and most probable progress of their project given the likely aims of powerful politicians, bureaucrats and special interest groups.

As projects move from these initial stages, different factors come into play. During construction on site the weather must be considered. Trade unions may exert an influence. A neighbouring large project could alter the market for labour or basic materials. A major accident in a factory producing components could halt production for weeks. Obviously, managers cannot anticipate all these events. However, there is good data about some of the factors, notably about the weather. Also it is possible to make an informed judgement about the general level of interference likely to be experienced by examining records from previous similar projects in the same geographical location.

Bennett and Ormerod (1984) identified a few sources of live data which describes the incidence of delays caused by external factors. Their data suggests that, depending on the project and its particular environment, up to 20 per cent of the total available time may be lost through interference. In a series of simulations of live projects, Bennett and Ormerod modelled the effects of weather using data provided by the Meteorological Office. They produced good predictions of actual progress by using a figure of seven per cent time delays for interference other than that caused by weather in simulations of general building projects in southern England in the early 1980s.

We may conclude, therefore, that construction projects may face significant uncertainty generated by variability and interference. Although, by definition, uncertainty cannot be predicted exactly, managers can and should review such data as exists and form a judgement about the likely incidence of both internally and externally generated delays.

Speed and economy

Having established the complexity, size, potential for repetition and probable uncertainty of the tasks inherent in a construction project, the remaining issue for managers is to establish the levels of speed and economy which they will aim to achieve. Figure 1.5 illustrates a range of choices. It is based on the important idea that for any project there is a normal speed and level of costs. That is, the local construction industry, in the absence of pressures to perform differently, will approach projects in a manner largely shaped by habit and convention, and we can usefully regard the resulting performance as normal. It produces the levels of speed and economy at which designers, manufacturers and constructors feel comfortable.

The actual level of performance which can properly be accepted as normal varies with geographical location and time. However, the existence of a normal level of performance relating to a specific place and time and the existence of performances both better and worse than this norm are widely reported in studies of construction costs and times.

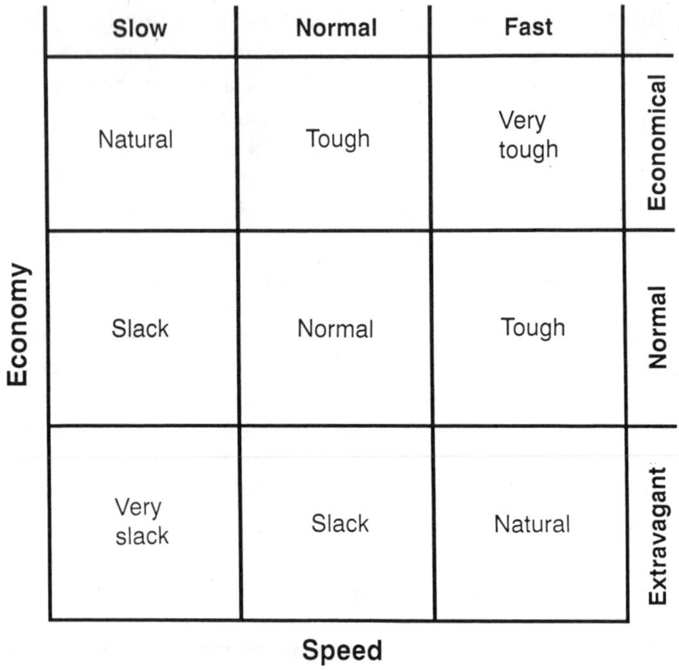

	Slow	Normal	Fast	
	Natural	Tough	Very tough	Economical
Economy	Slack	Normal	Tough	Normal
	Very slack	Slack	Natural	Extravagant

Speed

Figure 1.5   *Range of project performance options*

A nice illustration of the potential variation in costs is provided by a well researched series of articles by Davis, Belfield and Everest (1977). The first article in the series deals with the likely costs of new warehouses. It provides a basis for designers to calculate a realistic first estimate. The costs included in the article all relate to warehouses in Outer London at June 1977 price levels. The following quotation illustrates the existence of a range of costs: 'there can be a substantial range of costs for each element and these we have chosen to illustrate by means of histograms. Absolute precision in the determination of these histograms is not possible, so a degree of judgement is called for in their application.' The histograms for foundations, for example, range from £50 to less than £10 per square metre of gross floor area. Similarly, those for external cladding range from £46 to £4 per square metre of gross floor area. Even taking one single level of quality for external cladding and one size of building produces a price range of £46 to £32 per square metre of gross floor area. Similar evidence of a range of potential costs is provided by all good construction cost guides.

Thus, for any specific level of quality there is a normal price and a range of achievable options around it. Customers and their project teams may decide to adopt the normal level of costs as the target for their project. However, they may decide to aim for greater economy by setting a cost target below the normal price. They may on the other hand decide to be extravagant with money, perhaps because speed or certainty of completion on a specific date is all important, and so set a high cost target.

Similar considerations apply to speed, as is very clearly shown by a thorough study of project times for commercial buildings included in a NEDO (NEDC Construction Industry Sector Group, 1988) report, *Faster Building for Commerce*. It is based on a detailed analysis of 60 commercial projects built between 1984 and 1986 in the UK. It examines the total time between the start of a project and its completion and also the time on site. The study confirms the well known effect that, although larger projects take absolutely longer than smaller ones, they are constructed relatively much faster. Figure 1.6 illustrates this

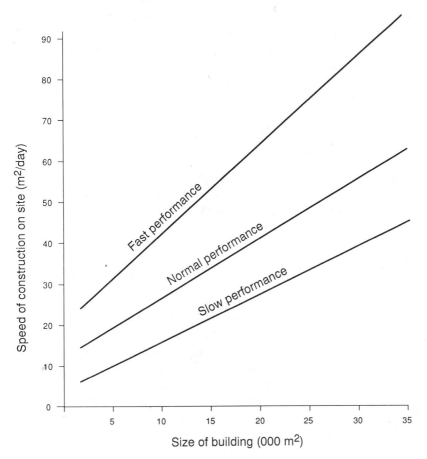

Figure 1.6 *Speed of construction on site for commercial building in the UK in the 1980s (Sources: Flanagan, et al. 1986 and NEDC Construction Industry Sector Group 1988)*

effect. However, more importantly, the study found that the range of times for buildings of the same size and general type varied enormously. 'The slowest projects had durations twice as long as average and the very fastest took one quarter the average time. It was not unusual between similar projects for one to take a year longer to build than the other.' Equally interesting is the finding that projects with a short construction time tended also to have a short pre-construction time. 'Concern and pressure for speed led to fast progress in both the presite and site phases.' Consequently, the range of total time for complete projects was as wide as that for time on site.

It is clear from these examples, which are representative of many similar studies, that customers and their project organizations need to make a clear choice of the level of speed and economy they will seek to achieve. Managers have a responsibility for taking the lead in establishing these key objectives and for ensuring that the choice is based on good, up-to-date data and a detailed analysis of the new project. Figure 1.5 illustrates a range of choices which may be made and which will face project organizations with very tough, tough, natural or normal, slack or very slack objectives. The particular choices made will have a direct effect on all the management tasks, whether the project aims to produce a building, a bridge or some other brain-wave.

Construction project manager's role

As we discussed at the beginning of this chapter, the appropriate form of project organization depends on the nature of the project, its environment and the overall objectives of the customer. The concepts described in this chapter provide a basis for taking these factors into account.

The statements of function, quality, speed and economy define the customer's objectives. These are expanded, in management terms, by making an experienced judgement or estimate of the likely complexity, size, repetition and uncertainty of the project. The judgement about the level of uncertainty requires the probable influence of the environment to be considered. Thus, all the factors which determine the appropriate form of project organization are taken into account. The general nature of the relationships between these key factors and the management tasks is illustrated in Figure 1.7. Management is made more difficult as projects become more complex, larger, include more variety, face more uncertainty, and have tougher objectives in respect of speed and economy. As the management of any one project is made more difficult, more management is likely to be required for the efficient execution of that project.

It follows that the intended message of this first chapter is that the managers of a construction project should work with the customer and designers to produce an

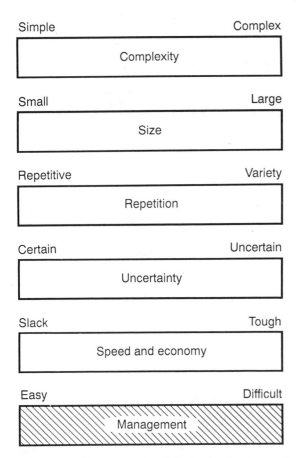

Figure 1.7 *Management and the key factors in construction projects*

agreed statement of the values for each of the key factors. Such a statement needs to be produced early in the life of a project. It helps to lay the essential ground-work for decisions about the form of project organization which will be adopted. The statement will need to be modified as the project progresses. Certainly it will become very much more detailed, even if its broad outlines remain reasonably true to the original version. Consequently, it is a continuing part of managers' responsibilities to maintain an up-to-date statement of the current values of the key factors. This is necessary because decisions about the form of an appropriate organization are needed throughout the life of all projects.

However, before we can deal with the way that these decisions are made, we must consider the nature of the people construction managers must use in forming their organizations. This is the subject of Chapter 2.

2 Customers, consultants, contractors and critics

The construction industry comprises millions of people throughout the world. It usually forms about 10 per cent of the working population in developed countries and a considerably higher proportion in developing countries. The construction industry includes, as an interesting and important example, about 20 per cent of Japan's hard-working and productive labour force. Within the global construction industry, and indeed within each local construction industry, is a huge variety of workers organized into separate legal entities. These comprise many types of organization but they will henceforth in this book be referred to collectively as firms. The firms that make up the construction industry act either as consultants or as contractors. The practical distinction between these two modes of working is that consultants provide resources which they agree to devote to customers' projects, while contractors agree to deliver specific parts of specified end products. Consultants' contracts are therefore fundamentally concerned with inputs to projects, while contractors' contracts are fundamentally concerned with outputs from projects. Whichever of these two roles a firm plays, it is made up of teams of people knowledgeable and skilled in some specific aspects of construction work. It is these teams which are brought together to form project organizations.

Construction project managers need a structured way of thinking about these potential members of their project organizations. They must also bring into their frame of reference the industry's customers, regulators and powerful critics. These all exert significant influences on construction projects and so cannot be ignored by effective managers.

The central focus for construction project managers, as far as the need to understand people is concerned, is the team rather than the individual. As we describe in Chapter 1, the reason for this emphasis is purely practical. It is simply that many of the most important tasks facing construction project managers involve judgements about work which will be carried out by teams who will be appointed to the project organization at some time in the future. Therefore there is no opportunity to discover the nature or character of specific teams, still less of individuals. Consequently, much of construction project managers' work relies on understanding the general nature or character of teams.

The need to focus on teams rather than on individuals greatly simplifies the task of management. This is because the actions and thought processes of teams are necessarily more open to public inspection than is the case with individuals. Construction teams are formed to undertake some kind of construction work which they have jointly agreed they will undertake. The agreements that provide the basis for teams are often explicit and formal. They usually relate to publicly defined categories of work. Indeed, many construction teams advertise the kinds of work they are prepared to undertake as a means of obtaining work. Such advertisements necessarily rely on widely understood descriptions of the kind of work which is on offer.

The decision-making processes of teams are also much more public than those of individuals. This is because the thought processes, the inner workings of the *mind of a team*, necessarily take place through interactions between people. Thus there is usually some clear, external, physical evidence of a team's thinking. This is in stark contrast to the workings of the minds of individuals, where most thought remains for ever hidden from everyone, except the individual himself.

It follows that construction project managers need a relatively coarse level of understanding of human behaviour. This is not to argue that a subtle and deep understanding is not to be preferred. Certainly it will help managers to understand their own interactions with others. This obvious truth applies to everyone, not just to managers. However, construction project management can be pursued successfully, indeed often there is no choice but to pursue it, on the basis of an understanding of the general nature and character of the behaviour of teams. The purpose of this chapter is to provide a basis for that understanding.

Having argued that construction project managers need to understand the behaviour of teams rather than individuals, we begin, apparently perversely, by considering certain characteristics of individuals. More particularly we shall consider features of the human nervous system. There are two main reasons for this. First, we all have extensive and privileged knowledge of the workings of one human nervous system, our own. Second, as Beer (1972) argues cogently, the human nervous system is by far the most highly developed and relevant model of the behaviour of human organizations, including teams, available to us. Both the nervous system and human organizations exist to direct humans towards patterns of successful behaviour. However, the human nervous system is the result of several million years of trial and error and selection based on survival of the fittest. Formal human organizations are a relatively recent phenomenon. So the human nervous system provides an unusually well developed model for managers to use in thinking about the behaviour of construction teams.

Control in humans

The reason for considering the human nervous system is to use those features which illustrate important principles of efficient human organization, to provide a model which will help managers understand their own roles. No attempt is made to produce a complete description of the human nervous system, nor is any attempt made to be anatomically correct. The aim is solely to identify a model of efficient organizations. The following brief description draws freely on the excellent and much fuller description provided by Beer (1972).

The main physical features of the human nervous system, shown in Figure 2.1, are well known. There is a spinal cord, which runs through the backbone, from which nerves run both to and from all parts of the body, and at the top of which is the brain. The spinal cord in fact consists of two curved plates which together form a tube. Inputs, providing information about the state of the body, enter at the back of the tube, and outputs, providing instructions about actions to be taken, leave from the front. Thus information about the state of the various parts of the body flow up the rear plate to the brain. Similarly, instructions flow

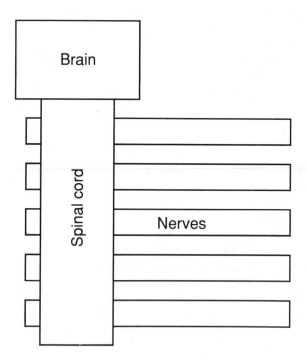

Figure 2.1   *Human nervous system*

down the front plate from the brain and thence to the nerves linking it to the parts of the body which are to take action.

Decentralized decision-making

The human nervous system operates at two distinct levels. Decisions are made locally where nerves run into and out of the spinal cord. A well known example of local decisions is what are commonly called *reflex actions*. The knee-jerk reflex results from a local decision. Decisions are also made in the brain, using information which flows up the spinal cord combined with information already in the brain. These high level decisions are passed down the spinal cord to the parts of the body that need to be informed.

There are thirty-one pairs of nerves connected to the spinal cord, each serving specific parts of the body. In addition, the brain has 12 pairs of cranial nerves which provide direct connections to all parts of the body. They mainly deal with the senses, providing instructions to seek information about the world outside or the state of some part of the body and passing information gathered by the senses back to the brain. However, one of the cranial nerves, the vagus, has a different and important role. It descends from the brain in two great branches, to the right and left, to all parts of the body. It gives the brain the power to override local decisions when rapid action is needed.

We see then that the various parts of the body are controlled by instructions about how to act made locally and also by instructions passed down from the brain. The top level decisions are normally passed down the spinal cord and so involve the local decision-makers. However, in an emergency the brain has a fast track, through the vagus nerve, to issue instructions directly to the distributed parts.

The dual control of all the parts of the body appears to be achieved chemically. Local decisions are transmitted using adrenergic impulses, and the direct messages from the brain are cholinergic. In any given situation, they produce counter effects. For example, the adrenergic impulses increase heart activity but the cholinergic impulses decrease it. The body functioning normally provides each part with the balance of chemicals needed for survival. However, a decision, made either locally or at the top, changes the chemical composition and so changes the actions of the parts affected by the decision. The great beauty of this procedure is that it deals automatically with the common problem of decentralized systems; that is, receiving instructions from the top and from the local decision makers, which conflict. Because each part of the body reacts to the actual chemical composition provided to it, depending on the strength of the message, reflected in the amount of chemical transmitted, a local decision may override a top level decision or vice versa. This, for example, allows a casual decision by the brain to stretch out a hand to be overridden by a local reaction to the fact that the hand has strayed into a fire. However, if the hand is stretched into a fire to rescue a child, the message from the brain will be much stronger and so will override the local reflex action which seeks to withdraw the hand from the fire.

At any one time, the chemical composition controlling the actions of any one part of the body has just one value. The fact that the chemical mix results from two distinct decision centres is irrelevant to the part of the body receiving instructions as to how to act. At any one point in time it receives only one instruction, which it therefore obeys. The decision may be reversed seconds later and altered again after a few more seconds. The part simply acts on the current single chemically transmitted instruction and never has to deal with the problem of receiving conflicting instructions.

Coordination

The separate parts of the body do not, however, act independently. There is coordination, otherwise we would all be far clumsier than we actually are. The coordination is provided by two separate systems shown in Figure 2.2. The first prevents actions based on local decisions being taken without regard to their effects on nearby activities. It connects together the separate reflex arcs at points remote from the spinal cord; that is, the points where actions take place. The connections are provided by paravertebral ganglionic chains which regulate and integrate feedback about the current state of each part of the body. This is fed back to the brain but, before it reaches the top levels of the system, it is in effect reviewed by each of the local action points to ensure that the separate parts of the body take mutually consistent actions. This is equivalent to the application of a set of low level procedures to deal with minor, routine conflicts between various parts of the body. In the management literature such arrangements are usually referred to as a grapevine; that is, local, often informal communications between first-line managers who need to know what is happening elsewhere in the organization faster than the official channels are able to tell them. So they create their own local network of contacts. The human nervous system has its own grapevine but unlike its human organization equivalents it is a normal, formal part of the system and it is used by both local decision-makers and the top sections of the brain.

The second source of coordination is situated at the top of the spinal cord. It is the lowest section of the brain. It comprises four distinct parts with somewhat different functions. Lowest is the medulla, where information from the spinal cord about local decisions and direct feedback about the current state of each part of the body from the paravertebral ganglionic chains are brought together.

The medulla provides much of the coordination of reflex actions. The second part of the lowest section of the brain is the pons. It is responsible for filtering the information passed on to the upper parts of the brain and also for connecting two halves of the third part of this section of the brain. This is the cerebellum, which is situated to the side of the main line from the spinal cord to the brain. It receives information from both above and below necessary for its function of controlling skilled acts. This requires the coordination of muscles. Information about the current state of the body's muscles passes up and instructions to them pass down the spinal cord. To this is added information from the cranial nerves about conditions both outside and inside the body. Also, if conscious attention and an effort of will are required, this is provided as input from the highest section of the brain. All of this information is used by the cerebellum to coordinate the actions needed to perform skilled acts. Finally, the fourth part of the lowest section of the brain is called the mesencephalon where

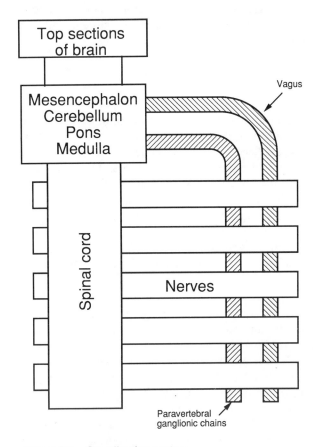

Figure 2.2   *Coordination system*

the *righting reflexes* which keep the body in equilibrium are monitored and coordinated.

Thus we see that the four-part, lowest section of the brain provides coordination primarily based on autonomous decisions. That is, apart from the coordination of skilled acts, they do not require conscious, intellectual effort from the highest section of the brain. It is rather as though the body comes complete with a set of middle management procedures for dealing with potential conflicts between the various parts of the body. These are in addition to the procedures applied at a low level in the paravertebral ganglionic chains. The middle management procedures are applied autonomously by the lowest section of the brain unless they are consciously overridden by a decision from higher up.

The lowest section of the brain, the spinal cord and the reflex arcs, together with all their interconnections, ensure the autonomic internal stability of the human body. Before we move up to the high level command system, we must consider the kinds of information handled by the human nervous system and the important role of information filters.

Control information

The body is studded with receptors which gather information. Some of this information is about the outside world. This is provided by a variety of exteroceptors. The first of these are teleceptors, which collect information about distant objects. The eyes and ears are the body's teleceptors. Then there are chemical receptors which serve the senses of taste and smell. Third, there are cutaneous receptors, those in the skin, of which there are many types. Touch, for example, is sensed in three distinct ways; nerve endings just below the surface respond to slight pressure, others much deeper respond to heavy pressure, and hairs on the surface which detect the lightest touch. There are other receptors in the skin which react to external cold and others which detect external heat.

The body also has many interoceptors which capture information about the internal states of the body. The afferent nerves provide information about muscles, visceroceptors report to the brain about the interior organs residing in the great cavities of the body, and proprioceptors serve the kinaesthetic sense, which tells the body where it is relative to everything around it. Proprioceptors behind the ear sense the position and movement of the head in space and enable us to keep our balance. All these receptors and many more carry information back to the spinal cord and up to the brain. However, the nerves which carry the information are complex. Every millimetre or so along their length is a node which is linked to other nerves in a confusion of connections. Hence information about the body and its environment is richly distributed throughout the entire nervous system.

Local decisions

The system does not simply transmit information; it acts on it, filters it and stores it. These functions are carried out by a series of what we can usefully think of as specialized computers. There is one at each point where the 31 pairs of lateral nerves join the spinal cord and one in each of the four parts of the lower section of the brain. It is interesting that these specialized computers are not dotted around the system relatively isolated from each other. Nor does each require its own information capture procedures or produce its own localized output. The specialist computers in the human nervous system are highly integrated. They all act on the same stream of information passing up the spinal cord and into the brain.

Each of the specialized computers carries out three tasks on the information flowing up the spinal cord. First, it inspects the information coming up to decide whether it should be dealt with at the local level. If so, a command is sent to the appropriate part of the body instructing it to take action. The second task of the specialized computers is to pass on upwards a modified version of the information that has been operated on. Part of the modification is a message to the effect that action has been taken. If, on the other hand, the specialized computer is not competent to command action based on the information coming up the spinal cord, it has two options. One is to pass on the information untouched, the other is to filter it.

Information is passed straight on when it is urgent or of special interest. It may be that some danger threatens and so the sense data is not filtered. It is passed on in a fast one-way track to the brain. The responsibility for activating this arousal mechanism is widely distributed throughout the nervous system. There are no special purpose parts for arousal; it appears to be a general function of the spinal cord at large.

Non-urgent information to be passed up the spinal cord is filtered. This is similar to the kind of filtering carried out in statistical analysis. Thousands of pieces of information can be compressed into a few vital statistics which fully describe all the relevant characteristics of a whole set of information, including the existence and character of time trends. These few statistics are transmitted rather than bombarding the brain with all the detailed sensory input received throughout the whole body. The filtered information provides just sufficient information for the brain to recognize anything of significance which requires action.

This is not to suggest that the human nervous system does in fact work statistically; but the effect is as if it did. We all know from our experience of our own bodies that we are not conscious from second to second of all the mass of information available to our bodies. We should be completely unable to think if our conscious brain were bombarded by so much information. Most is suppressed, not brought to our attention, yet if a crisis occurs the information about it is rushed straight to the top of our consciousness and receives our full attention. If we are suddenly faced by a mad dog, a splinter in one of our fingers or a serious error in our firm's financial accounts, the specific problem has our full attention. None of the relevant information is suppressed. We search our brain for an answer and undoubtedly our brain searches the rest of the nervous system in the concentrated effort of finding a way out of the crisis.

This brings us to the third task of the specialized computers which sit in line on the spinal cord and the lower brain. It is to keep a record of the basic unfiltered information in case it needs to be referred to later. Thus we see that memory is widely distributed in the human body, just as it is in human organizations.

Top management

The integrated series of specialized computers working on information flowing through the spinal cord feeds highly digested and selected information up to the highest sections of the brain. The top management of the human nervous system can usefully be thought of as two distinct sections. The lower of these two provides the great linking mechanism between conscious and autonomous control. It consists of many distinct parts whose separate functions are very difficult to identify. However, in total, this section of the brain appears to have three important roles.

First, it acts as an intelligent switch. In this role it passes instructions about the decisions made by the brain downwards to the lower levels of the nervous system. It also passes upwards all of the information needed by the top section of the brain to run the body. The information flowing upwards includes that requested by the top section and that which the autonomous lower levels of the system decide to pass up. The second function of the section of the brain next to the top is to capture all available information about the environment through whichever are the appropriate senses. This is filtered and distributed both upwards and downwards for use by all other decision-makers. Third, it operates the body's arousal mechanisms. That is, it selects between pain or pleasure and waking and sleeping.

Staff functions

This section of the brain plays many of the roles which in human organizations are called staff functions. They control the flow of information to top management about both the lower levels of the organization and the environment. So we see that top management acts, not so much on the *facts*, as on the *facts as given*. It is interesting to note that in the human nervous system the staff functions are clearly and unambiguously in the main line of command. Here there is no pretence that staff functions have no responsibility. The role of selecting, filtering and reprocessing information before it is passed on is simply and naturally an integral part of the main line of command. In the human nervous system the handling of information by this staff function has two distinct aspects.

There is first the information itself which, as in the lower sections of the system, is transmitted chemically. However, the way in which it is handled depends on the general state of the body. We are not considering a simple go/no-go switch. Information enters, which at one time is passed on but at another is retained in this *intelligent switch*. The specific decisions appear to depend on the level of electrical activity in this section of the brain. There clearly are electrical thresholds which change the state of the body from, for example, sleep to waking. The level of electrical activity relative to these thresholds determines what information is passed on. When the top section of the brain does not wish to be disturbed, information is toned down, much of it to the point of extinction. When the top section of the brain wishes to be stimulated, which, for example, may result from the early effects of alcohol or perhaps from the recognition of a great opportunity, the information is toned-up and the whole body experiences a sense of heightened awareness. It seems likely that it is one of the roles of top management to set the tone for the staff functions.

Beer (1972) suggests that a useful way of thinking about the intelligent switch, which determines what facts are given to top management, is to see it as four richly interconnected major areas of concern. Figure 2.3 illustrates this idea. The intelligent switch contains models of the current state of each part of the internal body and of its perception of its environment. It also contains a model of the current internal actions of the body and of actions intended to influence the world outside. These four models are richly interconnected in such a way that the intelligent switch can maintain them all in balance. It appears that this is achieved by the brain knowing the states of each model which will ensure survival of the nervous system and therefore of the body it controls. When one of the models strays outside its range of acceptable states, the other three change, within their own acceptable limits, in a search for a new set of interconnections which will bring the deviating model back into a safe state. As the models themselves change so the intelligent switch sends instructions to the relevant parts of the body to take actions which correspond to those being modelled. The intelligent switch keeps searching for a new homeostasis until it has brought all four models, and therefore the body itself, into an acceptable state. The searching for a new homeostasis is not entirely random. This brings us to a very important human characteristic, which is the ability of the nervous system to learn.

Learning

Each of the four models in the intelligent switch can take up any one of billions of different states. These potential states are very richly interconnected both inside each model and between the separate models. That is, there is a huge number of possible routes inside the switch. Where a route connecting two possible states is used and results in a more satisfactory condition, it is reinforced or deepened. This means it is more likely to be used in the future. Where a connecting route produces a worse condition it is weakened and so is less likely to be used in the future. As the brain gets older, and with repeated use, some channels become very deep and others which are unused disappear altogether. In this way the brain learns successful strategies. Eventually the brain becomes very set in its behaviour and it is virtually impossible for it not to

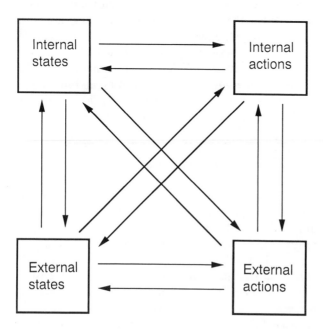

Figure 2.3 *Major areas of concern interconnected in the intelligent switch* *(Source: Beer 1972)*

keep using the well worn channels which it knows result in satisfactory behaviour.

This process of learning is not restricted to the brain. It appears that the whole body reinforces successful links and inhibits unsuccessful ones. So when we speak of someone as having green fingers, we are referring to the practised habits which actually reside in his fingers and which make him an exceptionally skilful gardener. The same is true of all experienced craftsmen and artists. They can practise their skills subconsciously. A pianist will often speak of letting his fingers play over the keyboard. This is exactly what they are doing, making their own decisions with very little conscious direction.

The great seat of conscious learning is, of course, the cortex, the highest level of the brain. Our description thus far has avoided any discussion of the conscious mind. This is partly because it is extremely complicated, very little is understood about how it works, and because as far as construction project management is concerned all the rest of the book is in a sense about activities in this top section of the brain.

There are, however, a few characteristics of the cortex which need to be understood in order to complete our model of human organizations. The first feature of the cortex which we should note is that it has no direct connection with the outside world or with the inside world. It is reliant on the filtered and selected information which the intelligent switch, or staff function, chooses to provide.

The second interesting feature of the cortex is that it can usefully be thought of as consisting of billions of neurons which are richly interconnected. Neurons can store and process information. The brain appears to work by looking for patterns in this information. Understanding which is the highest achievement of the human nervous system, is equivalent to being able to anticipate patterns. We have understanding when we can, having identified one pattern, accurately predict the existence of others. If they in fact appear, then we feel a sense of satisfaction in that we have understood something about ourselves or the world around us. In this way we imbue messages, which change the information patterns in the cortex, with meaning.

Meaning

We all accept that words, numbers and symbols have meaning. We decide the meaning for ourselves but because humans are social animals we reach agreements with other people about meanings. The process of deciding meanings works something like this.

As information enters the cortex it is searched for patterns. Patterns which recur form reinforced connections between the neurons that identify them. Thus the pattern is remembered. If the pattern keeps recurring it becomes deeply embedded in our memory. If it fails to recur, it will fade away and be forgotten. Next the brain looks for patterns of patterns; that is, for connections between things remembered. So when a child is repeatedly told that an object, which has formed a pattern in his brain, has a name, the sound of which forms a second pattern in his brain, he connects the two patterns. Thus he learns that a particular object is, for example, called *door*. Initially he is likely to associate the word with one specific example, perhaps the door of his bedroom. Subsequently he learns that several objects are called door. Some are very similar to his bedroom door but a glazed front entrance door, a car door, the automatic door to a supermarket or an up-and-over garage door are all very different. So the child learns to abstract patterns from dissimilar objects and learns what we can properly regard as higher level meanings. Faced with the great variety of real world doors, the single word door develops a complex meaning in the child's brain.

Meaning is developed and clarified by experimenting. When he first hears the word door and thinks he understands it, a normal, healthy child will use it at every opportunity. In this way, by pointing at things and calling them door, he learns which are doors and which not. In doing so he is likely to learn about windows, screens, partitions and many other large non-door, rectangular objects. He learns through a process of feedback. The feedback he gets from his experiments with the word door is a sense of pleasure aroused by his parents' approval when he correctly identifies a door or a sense of pain aroused by his parents' disapproval when he uses the word for something which is not a door. As the child becomes more experienced he also learns to connect meanings; that is, to play with meanings and to imagine things which have never existed. Thus he can envisage a circular, red door even though he has never seen one. This of course is the beginning of creativity, forming new and original associations.

So we see that, when we say that the human brain searches for meaning, we mean it looks for patterns already stored inside itself. We look for similarities. Thus our image of door may be conjured up by a door-shaped hole or a noise which sounds like a door being slammed shut. There is a marvellous unpredictability about the connections made in any one human brain. Indeed it is the rich and wide-ranging relationships which grow up in human brains that provide the basis for mature creativity and inspired problem solving. These talents arise out of a search for meaning within a brain already richly endowed with patterns or, as we commonly call them, concepts. As new information enters the brain we attempt to match the patterns it forms with ones already stored. Humphrey (1983) suggests that our concepts of beauty are based on the mind's habit of searching for consistency and its desire to classify, together with its reaction to minor discrepancies which signal something new and interesting and so arouse pleasure. So information entering our brains may merely reinforce what we already know. For a while this is satisfying but, quite soon, simply experiencing familiar objects becomes boring. Alternatively, new information may very largely match a recognizable pattern which calls up remembered concepts but also provides a slight deviation which adds something new and interesting to our knowledge. To return to our example of doors, if we see a door with an arched top when we have previously seen only rectangular doors, this is interesting. It gives us pleasure to be able to extend our knowledge of the world.

There is of course also a third possible situation. This is that the information entering our brains does not match any existing patterns. It is meaningless *noise* and so we cannot learn anything new. We tend to find this irritating and generally seek to avoid noise. Of course, if the meaningless noise recurs, we may begin to detect patterns and so build new concepts. Thus, as with repeated experiences with a foreign language, we gradually learn the meanings.

This helps us to understand Humphrey's point about pattern and beauty. Great architecture, for example, creates consistent rhythms which we recognize but also introduces variations which surprise and delight us. Architecture of course uses well established symbols to provoke predictable responses, but the mere repetition of established symbols does not produce great architecture. It is a subject of some controversy as to whether a complete departure from these familiar symbols can be regarded as great architecture. The problem of course is that it will take time before a judgement can be made. Like learning a foreign language, understanding and appreciating modern architecture take time. Thus immediate and critical judgements about new buildings are often revised decades later when the new symbols have become accepted as a proper part of our culture.

The human nervous system's ability to develop highly abstract concepts such as beauty and culture, while at the same time dealing with all the minute-to-minute actions needed to stay alive, mark it out as the most powerful and successful model available to us of how to arrange human organizations. At the centre of this great strength is the ability to develop appropriate levels of language for each separate part of the system.

Levels of language

We have already seen how the cortex is provided with highly digested and selected information. It does not deal with the same information as lower levels in the system. The process of filtering and selectively compressing information takes place throughout the entire human nervous system. Consequently, each level is dealing with different information and therefore needs its own specific language; that is, a language appropriate for dealing with the level of abstraction in the information available to that level. The language must also enable each level to communicate with the immediately adjacent levels both above and below. Also, where a higher level is provided with the ability to override formal channels of communication in a crisis, its language must include a command facility well understood by the lower levels.

The central purpose of each higher level language is to provide an overview of the behaviour of the parts in the next level down. Therefore it does not need to consider all of the minute-to-minute, routine behaviour of all of these parts. Nor indeed could it do so. In the same way that, in a management hierarchy, each level of managers is equipped with brains of approximately the same size and capacity, so each part of the human nervous system has the same kind of capacities as the parts below. Therefore in neither case is it practical to provide *managers* with all the information. They need sufficient to provide a picture of the overall pattern of behaviour of the parts for which they are responsible, uncluttered by all the detail. Indeed it is all the detail which prevents the parts at lower levels from recognizing clear warning signs of potential crises. So we say they cannot see the wood for the trees. It is the prime responsibility of managers to recognize when a warning signal threshold is reached and step in to take the actions necessary to avoid a problem developing into a crisis. Obviously, as in the human nervous system, the lower levels have a responsibility to look out for problems and, if they are competent to do so, to deal with them. Or, if the problem falls outside the range of their own capabilities, the lower levels must send a warning signal to their managers. Often it is the combination of a few small warning signals and small changes in the overall pattern of behaviour, perhaps also combined with changes in the environment, which enable a higher level manager to see a problem before it becomes obvious to the local managers.

So the purpose of higher level languages is not to provide a better way of thinking about all the detail of lower level activities. It is to think about different things. Obviously there must be a clear relationship between the different levels of language. There must be points of overlap so that vertical communication is effective. But there is no way of avoiding the need for each level to have its own specific language and therefore its own way of looking at the world.

There is one further important difference between the levels of language; they deal with different timescales. We all know that the cortex is capable of thinking about the future, of living in the past and, in some people, of appearing to pay attention to every time except the present. Obviously it can and does deal with immediate issues, but for much of the time it concentrates on events in the past or possible events in the future. On the other hand, the senses, in for example our hands, must deal with the current state of the body. If our hand has strayed into a fire, it would be of no use to the body if the senses choose that moment to remember and concentrate on the sensations caused by a cool breeze. The body would rapidly be destroyed if the lower levels dealt other than with real time. The differences in timescale are built into the levels of language. So the lower levels simply do not have the language to consider long term plans, neither in fact do they have the information necessary to begin to develop such language skills.

There is of course a very important difference between the human nervous system and human organizations. The separate parts in the human nervous system are content with their role in life. The nerves in our hands do not harbour a secret desire to become the cortex. People, however, often are ambitious. The carpenter may well wish to become a project manager. This is good and should be encouraged but, from the viewpoint of the project, the message from our model is that it is essential that the carpenter is, first and foremost, a competent carpenter. As we have seen this includes taking account of the wider interests of the project in taking responsibility for looking out for potential problems and in a crisis acting on higher level instructions. But primarily and centrally we want the carpenter to concentrate on the important task of building the wooden parts of the end product in accordance with the drawings and specifications and in accordance with the practice of good craftsmanship. We expect him to bring with him to the project a well developed understanding of the language of carpenters.

Models of construction project organizations

The preceding description provides the five level model of human organizations shown in Figure 2.4. Clearly, in terms of this model, a construction project manager is directly responsible for the top level, 5. He relies on good staff, at level 4, to provide him with all relevant information. They operate on a management-by-exception principle, reporting problems to the project manager which cannot be handled lower in the organization. They respond also to direct requests from the project manager for particular information. Their normal manner of working is to draw in information from the autonomic controlled levels 1, 2 and 3 and from the environment, monitor it, deal with problems within their own competence and report exceptions up to level 5. The two top levels, following the logic of the model, rely to a great extent on the separate teams which make up the project organization undertaking local control on their own initiative.

Team managers at level 2 make their own local decisions on the basis of instructions from the higher levels and their own knowledge and experience of relevant answers. They take account of the effect of their own decisions on adjacent actions by using the grapevine. Their team also collects information about its own local environment and this too is considered in making local decisions.

Information about local actions and progress is passed up to the autonomic control at level 3. Here managers concerned with the day-to-day coordination of the whole project keep the work of the separate teams in balance. The level 3 managers supplement the formal feedback of information by plugging straight into the grapevine and also by monitoring information about the environment. This helps to ensure that they have early warnings of potential problems and so

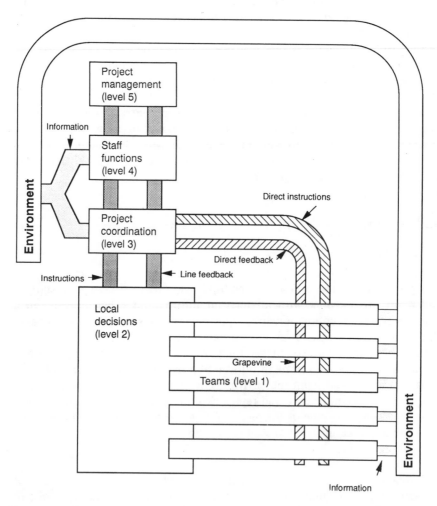

Figure 2.4 *Model of human organizations based on the human nervous system*

can take remedial actions. By these means the work of levels 1, 2 and 3, for so long as the project is proceeding according to plan, is largely self-regulating or autonomic as far as levels 4 and 5 are concerned. Obviously this is not how it appears to those working at the lower levels. They face daily problems. But they deal with them and so leave top management with the time to focus on longer-term issues.

It is worth recalling from the model of the human nervous system some of the conditions for this happy state of affairs. First, the whole organization must learn from its successes and failures, so that it concentrates on actions that work. Second, the system is rich in information; there is systematic monitoring of internal and external states, and there are duplicated sources of feedback. Third, responsibility for identifying potential crises is widely distributed, so whoever first sees a problem must solve it or send an urgent message to inform top management. Finally, there needs to be an unambiguous system which enables each team to know when to follow instructions from top management, when to act on local decisions, and when to take their own initiatives. This must be achieved without causing chaos or irritation.

The links between the autonomic lower three levels and top management are the filtered and selected feedback about lower level actions and the progress of the whole project which are passed upwards to the project manager. Also, warnings of major crises are fed straight to him on a fast track through all the lower levels. Then there is a set of links which pass instructions or requests for information downwards. These give expression to the project manager's responsibility for taking the major, strategic decisions which provide direction for the whole project. In doing this he is responsible for setting the tone or style of the project. In terms of the human nervous system, this is equivalent to ensuring that the project is awake when it should be working, that it has sensible rest periods, that it feels pleasure when it is being successful and pain when it needs a reminder about correct behaviour. Finally, we must remember that the success of the project organization represented by our model depends on an adequate range of languages. It will not do for everyone to speak the same language, attractive though that idea is at first thought. It is necessary for each level of manager to have a language, and therefore a view of the project, appropriate to his particular responsibilities. It is worth noting at this point that the main purpose of this book is to give construction project managers a language appropriate to their roles.

Construction teams

It is now time to recall that our purpose in developing a model based on the human nervous system was to provide a language or way of thinking about construction teams from a management viewpoint. The model does identify for us three crucial attributes of teams. Kuhn (1976, 1982) argued that just these three general characteristics of organizations provide sufficient depth of analysis to construct a theoretical framework for the whole of the social sciences. Be that as it may, they certainly provide sufficient detail for the work of a construction project manager.

The first important characteristic of teams is that they have knowledge. We saw from our model that teams learn from their experience and develop concepts which they imbue with meaning in order to retain and communicate useful knowledge. Of course much knowledge comes from the experiences of others, which they have communicated. This learnt knowledge is added to and considerably enriches a team's own direct experiences. From the mix of first and second-hand knowledge, all teams bring to projects a wide range of information. Obviously, construction project managers are primarily interested in knowledge about construction; so the first important characteristic of the teams which we are interested in is that they have knowledge of construction.

We know from the way in which knowledge is richly interconnected in the human brain that other, non-construction, knowledge may unexpectedly also prove to be of use. So, especially if we want teams to take responsibility for solving the day-to-day problems which arise in their work and to develop a wide commitment to their projects, it is an advantage if teams have a wide education and a broad knowledge of the world. However, the central point is that the first important characteristic of construction teams is that they have relevant knowledge.

The next suggestion from our model is that teams make decisions. They do so on the basis of their own preferences or values. Thus, for example, teams, like all normal, healthy humans, prefer pleasure to pain. Generally teams are likely to prefer more money to less, more leisure time to less, and work which they can feel proud of producing rather than work which is second-rate and banal. However, the situation is never as clear cut as these examples once we are faced with more complex choices, based on valuing different things. Some teams will prefer more money to more leisure time, others the reverse. Some will prefer interesting work to more money, others the reverse, and so on. Thus each team has its own value system.

A useful way to think of value systems is as a list of possible choices arranged in order of priority. Things which are preferred are higher on the list than those which are valued less. Teams have different value systems; even those within the construction industry have different priorities from each other. Indeed, over time any one team's values will change. At one period, money will be important, later leisure or interesting work may be more attractive, and so on. What is consistent is that all teams have values on the basis of which they make decisions. This is the second important characteristic of teams.

Finally we can deduce from our model that teams should be able to take specific actions; that is, actions in which they are skilled or practised. In Chapter 3 we shall consider in more detail the vast range of things which construction teams are able to do. What is important for the moment is that construction teams are able to take some actions relevant to construction projects. They would, of course, be of little value to managers if this were not so.

Feedback

The three important general characteristics of teams are illustrated in Figure 2.5. This shows also one combination of the basic characteristics which is sufficiently important for it to be given a separate name. The additional concept is feedback. It consists of the team taking an action which changes its environment and then having knowledge of the effect of its action. Control, of course, comes from the team using feedback to guide its actions towards desired results. This is achieved by comparing feedback with the original intention and, depending on the outcome of that comparison, deciding to continue with the same action because it has produced an acceptable result or, when the feedback deviates significantly from what was intended, changing that action in some way which brings the feedback into the range of acceptable answers.

We saw that the human nervous system is provided with many sources of feedback. These are essential for its survival. Similarly, teams need to know the effects of their actions if their work is to match the overall needs of projects.

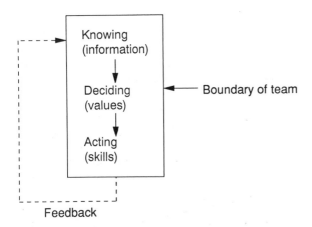

Figure 2.5 *Basic characteristics of teams*

There is, however, an important difference between the model we have constructed and construction projects. This is that there are considerable differences in the time-scale of construction feedback. The human nervous system at the level at which we have considered it receives very fast feedback on its actions. Construction projects have to be managed with feedback of very variable time-spans. There is of course a great deal of immediate feedback. The craftsman working with a material obtains second-by-second feedback on the effect of his actions. He can see the effect of his actions on the material and he can feel the effect through his hands as he works. However, feedback on the performance in use of the part he is making will necessarily take time to become available. Similarly, an architect sketching the first designs for a building may have to wait years before his actions are joined in a feedback loop by knowledge about the appearance of the actual building.

Construction teams are generally concerned with short term feedback; that is, feedback which arrives in time for it to influence their behaviour while they are still working on the project. Longer term feedback is valuable in that it provides knowledge which helps future projects. It is, however, of less interest than short term feedback in managing any specific project. The fact that some important parts of construction project feedback are very long term means that managers must often make decisions without all the relevant information.

The fact that feedback is less than complete is an important problem for construction project managers. It means they must build into their project organizations additional controls to, as it were, take the place of the feedback which is too long term to be used. Indeed society at large recognizes this and imposes planning and building regulations to control what may and may not be built.

The position of any individual human is of course the same as that of the project manager in terms of long term feedback. It is simply that our model, which concentrates on lower level control from the viewpoint of the level 5 manager, does not deal with long term feedback; that is an issue for later chapters. Meanwhile, there is one further step we can take in building the project manager's language for thinking about construction teams.

Team interactions

We have now constructed a basic model of construction teams and we shall use it to identify the types of interactions between teams which are of interest to construction project managers. Therefore the first type of interaction must have to do with knowledge. That is with knowledge which originally resides with one team being given to a second team. We call this type of interaction *communication*.

Successful communication requires a concept to be identified by one team and translated by them into words, numbers or symbols which other teams are likely to understand. These signs that stand for the concept which is to be communicated must be transferred into some communication medium. This may be spoken words, drawings, a written document or electronic impulses in an information system. Then the medium must be transferred to the second team. They in turn must identify the words, numbers or symbols and interpret them. All five of the components source, coding, medium, detection and decoding are essential for communication to take place.

The second type of interaction between teams has to do with decisions about values. These are called *negotiations*. The aim of negotiations is to reach a joint decision about an exchange of things of value. Typically in construction projects there are many negotiations between teams about money, working hours, the quality of work, safety, welfare, and many other issues. The common aim is to find a basis for agreement about a transaction in which each team gives up something of value in return for something else of value. In a good negotiation all the teams believe they have received more value than they have given up. In other words everyone thinks they have obtained a good deal.

Construction teams normally join a project organization on the basis of a negotiated agreement. This negotiation may include a process of competitive tenders in which many of the details of the agreement are resolved. However, there are always some further details to be resolved before the initial or major bargain is settled. Once it is agreed, the major bargain is usually embodied in a formal contract but, no matter how detailed, this can provide only a general framework of agreement. There are inevitably many further matters which have

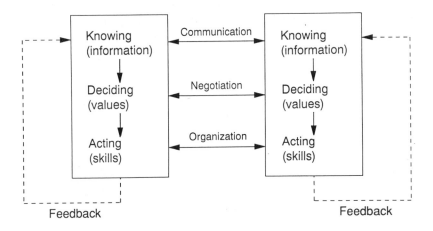

Figure 2.6 *Basic interactions between teams*

to be settled as the work progresses. These may include the exact date on which work will start, the milestones in its progress, the exact sequence and arrangement of the work, its precise quality, and how specific problems are to be resolved. These and many other similar matters typically require subsidiary transactions based on day-to-day negotiations. So the second type of interaction, in practice, comprises major bargains and subsidiary transactions.

The third class of interactions between teams is concerned with coordinating their separate actions. As we saw from our model, coordination is provided locally through the grapevine and also by means of decisions by senior managers. However, irrespective of its source, the actual coordination is provided by communications and negotiations. The concept of organization is useful to describe the coordinated actions of teams but it does not identify an additional form of interaction. Therefore, although Figure 2.6 shows the logically complete set of three kinds of interaction, in practice managers and their teams interact by either communicating or negotiating. In fact, of course, nearly all interactions are a mixture of communication and negotiation. In negotiating we give information in order to structure the expectations of the other party and we often propose bargains in order to alter the pattern of communications. When we are communicating, we do the same things. We offer information in the hope that it will evoke some particular response from the recipient, as well as provide him with additional knowledge. Nevertheless it is helpful to think about all interactions in terms of the characteristics of communication and also to consider them separately as negotiations. The two approaches provide a clearer and richer analysis of what is happening in any particular interaction than if it were seen from just one of these viewpoints.

The final important point we need to make in considering team interactions is that construction project managers are faced with the same limited range of interactions as all the other teams within projects. Consequently, they must work entirely through communications and negotiations with the customers, consultants, contractors and critics who are involved with their projects. They have no other weapons in their armoury.

3 *Systems in construction*

Systems thinking has revolutionized science. In many separate fields new ideas and new ways of thinking about subjects have followed from the adoption of a systems approach.

In essence the difference between systems thinking and earlier scientific approaches is that it focuses on the whole rather than on separate elements. Classical science works by taking a subject and dividing it into ever smaller elements. Each is studied in isolation and knowledge is built up step by step. This has been very successful and the understandings derived from an elemental approach have led to many important discoveries. It is, however, an approach, that works best with inanimate objects. Living and moving things need to be studied as a whole if we are to understand important features of their behaviour. It is no coincidence that systems thinking emerged from biology and not the more fundamental sciences of physics and chemistry.

Systems give us a way of thinking about complete subjects so that we can study their separate elements in context. Systems force us to consider the interactions between elements. The approach is valuable because generalizations developed by observing one kind of system often have applications for other, often very different, kinds of system. Also, systems occur widely in many different fields and many different forms. Hence ideas from other subjects have the potential to help us understand construction systems.

We used this approach in Chapter 2. The human nervous system was used to help us understand the systems of construction project organizations. We assumed that some characteristics of the first system are also to be found in the second. We focused on control and the flows of information and in doing so ignored many other characteristics of the human nervous system. We ignored its weight, energy consumption, life expectancy and physical appearance. These characteristics are likely to be important to scientists working in other subjects. They may choose to study the human body as a structural system, a fuel-production system or a waste-management system. The starting point for all such studies is the same as our own, the human body. What is different is our purpose, and because of that, the way we choose to look at the body. In other words, systems exist in our minds; they are a way of looking at the world. They help us answer specific questions or to think about specific subjects. They allow us to understand very complex subjects by systematically ignoring most of their characteristics. By concentrating on specific aspects of the subject, as we did in Chapter 2 on just control and information flows in the human nervous system, we can identify and so focus our attention on just those characteristics which are relevant to our chosen interest.

Systems thinking is specifically designed to help us understand complex subjects. There is no doubt that construction project organizations are extremely complex and, as we have seen in Chapter 2, a systems approach helps us to think about them constructively. We now need to consider the idea of systems in greater depth so that we can use this powerful approach more confidently.

Characteristics of systems

Systems are any collection of elements which interact in a sufficiently regular manner to be of interest. This means, for example, that a collection of waste material thrown into a rubbish skip is not a system. The separate parts of the collection do not interact in any regular or interesting manner. It means also that a number of things which are often referred to as systems are in fact not. The so-called number systems or language systems are, by our definition, not systems. Their elements, numbers or words, do not interact. The meaning attached to them is influenced by adjacent numbers or words but that interaction takes place in a human brain not between the actual numbers or words themselves. Our definition does mean however that there are many aspects of construction projects which can legitimately be regarded as systems. Before we identify examples, it will be helpful to describe some of the general characteristics of systems so that we are aware of the implications of describing a collection of separate elements as a system.

Kuhn (1974, 1982) based his fundamental theory of social science on a systems approach. In doing so he undertook an extensive search of the systems literature to identify the characteristics of systems which are important for understanding human organizations. The following description draws freely on his scheme.

Controlled systems

As we have already noted, systems consist of interacting elements. The elements of systems at different times take distinguishably different states. These states are the system variables. A controlled system is one in which the elements continue to interact and change but at least one variable remains within a specified range. There are many obvious examples in construction projects. Buildings are designed to maintain the temperature within specified ranges in particular spaces. Similarly, processing plants are designed to maintain specified ranges of temperature in the various chemicals flowing through them. Project organizations are given cost targets and time targets and are expected to complete the various stages of their projects inside these targets. So there are many controlled systems in construction projects and it is this type of system which construction project managers need to understand.

Environments

A major theme of systems thinking is the importance of the interactions between systems and their environments. This is echoed in much of the established management theory. Lawrence and Lorsch (1967), for example, considered that organizations are very largely shaped by their environments. We need, therefore, to draw a distinction between a system and its environment. A system can be defined by identifying all its elements. Anything not so listed is outside the system and therefore forms part of its environment. However, we are interested only in those parts of the environment which exert a significant effect on the system. So whether something is regarded as part of the environment or simply ignored depends on its relevance to the problem under consideration. The boundaries of a particular system have to be chosen by whoever wishes to use a systems approach. This choice can be made only with reference to a particular problem. A key decision for construction project managers arises in the definition of their projects. The choice of which elements to include inside a construction project and which to regard as part of the environment is important. The practical implication is that managers are deciding to take direct responsibility for managing everything inside their project. On the other hand, they are also accepting that things in the environment are outside their direct control. Nevertheless, they must allow for the behaviour of some of these things in making their plans.

The interactions between systems and their environments fall into two categories which arise from the fact that all controlled systems process inputs and produce outputs. Inputs to a system are any movement of information, matter or energy from the environment, through the system boundary into the system. An input alters the system in some way. Outputs from systems are any movement of information, matter or energy from the system, through its boundary into the environment. An output alters the environment in some way.

Construction project managers need to identify the inputs and outputs of their projects. They need to consider how the inputs are influenced by the environment and the effects of the outputs on the environment. Any of these interactions may create problems. Good managers consider the possibilities, weigh up the risks, and review and rehearse contingency plans to deal with any which may pose a major threat to their proposed courses of action. Indeed, good managers form their plans in ways that minimize the maximum threats to their project's success. This is the *minimax* strategy, which game theory tells us is the right approach to complex situations in which we are unable to calculate an optimum answer.

Managers have another fundamental reason for identifying the inputs and outputs of their projects. They provide the only robust and mature basis for measuring the success of construction projects.

Construction project success

The performance of a system, for example the success or otherwise of a construction project, is measured most comprehensively in terms of an output : input ratio. Since money is the only practical common measure for all the outputs and inputs of construction projects, it follows that their success in practice is most comprehensively measured in terms of the value : cost ratio; that is, the value of the end product compared with the costs of all the inputs used in producing it. Certainly this measure of success begs a large number of questions. It assumes that valuation techniques are reliable and consistent and can, for example, fully take into account the aesthetic merit of different buildings. It also assumes that all costs can be identified, including, for example, both capital and revenue costs. There are a multitude of other reservations about adopting the value : cost ratio as the measure of a construction project's success. However, if some other less comprehensive measure is adopted, no matter how subtle or complicated it may be, then success is being measured in a limited, partial manner. There are often good reasons for adopting a less than comprehensive measure. For example, construction projects are normally directed towards the customer's stated objectives. Success then is in meeting the objectives. Another common criterion for success is that the customer is happy with the project. This of course may be achieved other than by meeting his stated objectives. For example, a shrewd and less than honest construction project manager may persuade customers to concentrate on minor or superficial aspects of their projects which happen to be going well. As a result they may be happy, at least for a while, with a project which in fact fails to meet some of their real needs.

In addition to considering the success of whole projects, construction project managers must establish specific and limited criteria for the success of each separate part of their project organizations. Each team needs to have clear, short term targets for their current activities couched in easily and unambiguously measured terms. These are most unlikely to be couched in terms of the value : cost ratio.

All this is true but, nevertheless, it is the case that the only objective, comprehensive, practical criterion for the success of construction projects is the value : cost ratio. Therefore construction project managers should, at the very least, use this ratio in making their own judgements about projects.

Feedback and control

Figure 3.1 illustrates the view of systems developed thus far in this chapter. It contains one addition which we encountered earlier, in Chapter 2, when we were identifying the key characteristics of construction teams. This is feedback, which was defined as a system having an effect on its environment and being aware of that effect. The effect is some form of output and the awareness is an input in the form of information. Feedback is essential for control. Its existence as one of the features of construction teams is sufficient for us to decide that such teams are capable of acting as controlled systems.

Control also requires that the system has some objective or goal. Controlled systems are not indifferent about outcomes; they have preferences about specific variables or outputs. It is an important part of a construction project manager's role to define clearly the objectives for the controlled systems which make up his project organization. Controlled systems also need the ability to take corrective actions. That is, to identify deviations between feedback and objectives, select among possible responses, and direct behaviours towards bringing the system variables back to within the preferred range. Whoever or whatever takes these decisions forms the control subsystem. In the case of construction teams,

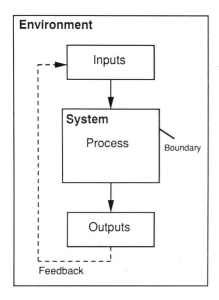

Figure 3.1 *Controlled systems*

identifying deviations and selecting responses is a function of knowledge and values, while directing behaviours is an important form of action. We can therefore extend our earlier model of construction teams to include the control subsystem. This is illustrated in Figure 3.2.

Much of the literature on systems draws a distinction between negative feedback and positive feedback. The distinction being made, which is useful, is concerned with the nature of the reaction to feedback, not with a characteristic of the feedback itself. Negative feedback occurs when a system's response to feedback varies inversely with deviations in the variables which are the subject of control. The result is that, if a variable moves from an initial satisfactory state, the system's reaction to the feedback moves it back towards its initial state. So the feedback is negative in the sense that the reaction to it negates the

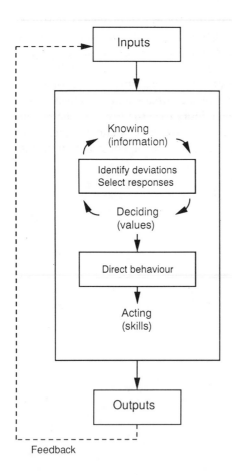

Figure 3.2 *Construction teams as controlled systems*

effect of the actions which caused the original deviation from the preferred system state. Positive feedback on the other hand reinforces any deviation in a variable and moves the system even further from its initial state. Positive feedback therefore does not form the central part of control subsystems which seek to maintain given variables within a defined range. It does, however, form part of control subsystems which seek to maintain a given variable within a single limit. In many management situations, this is exactly the situation. Budgets set limits to costs and programmes set limits to the times teams have available to complete their work. Control in these situations is based to some extent on positive feedback. When a team is doing better than its target, managers need to reinforce this behaviour. They need, in other words, to provide positive feedback; this may take the form of praise or some more tangible reward. However, if the target is not being met, the team needs negative feedback to guide them back to within their budget or programme.

Hierarchy of systems

In the discussion to this point we have described construction projects, construction teams and a number of parts of each of these as systems. We have also identified control subsystems. So there are hierarchies of systems within construction project organizations. They consist of subsystems, which are systems which form part of a larger system, sub-subsystems, which form part of a larger subsystem, and so on through as many levels as is useful. When a level is reached at which, from the particular current viewpoint, a part is not usefully regarded as a system, the part is an element. Logically there should also be supersystems and indeed many construction projects do form part of mega-projects or, in our present terminology, supersystems. As we have already established, the use of these terms depends on the viewpoint of the user. Thus, for a team manager, the team organization can properly be viewed as a system, the project organization as a supersystem, members of the team as subsystems, and specific skills of those members as elements. But for the project manager teams may be seen, for at least some purposes, as elements; groups of teams responsible for stages of the project may be seen as subsystems, and the project organization as a whole as a system.

Hierarchies of distinct levels occur in all successful controlled systems, the most ubiquitous being molecules, cells, organelles, organs, organisms and organizations. Each level has distinct properties, not possessed by lower levels. Each level is fundamentally more complex than lower levels. Each level requires a distinct language to enable us to understand and deal with its distinct characteristics. All of these features necessarily occur in successful construction project organizations. Chapter 2 describes a model which suggests that such organizations comprise hierarchies consisting of five distinct levels.

Propositions about systems

We have now described the important general characteristics of controlled systems. We will end this review of the characteristics of systems by stating a few propositions about the behaviour of successful systems. These propositions occur extensively in the systems literature and they describe important features of the behaviour of the systems that occur in construction projects. All successful controlled systems receive inputs from their environments. For a controlled system to continue to operate, its inputs must include negative feedback relevant to its control variables or positive feedback where there exists a limit on at least one control variable.

Some oscillation in the value of the control variables is inevitable unless feedback can be activated simultaneously with the environmental changes which it measures. Thus the oscillations or, in more practical terms, deviations from the plan will vary inversely with the speed and also with the sensitivity and accuracy with which relevant feedback operates.

All successful controlled systems operate through the differentiation of their subsystems and the coordination of the work of these subsystems. Differentiation develops to enable systems to deal with variations in their environment. That is, specialized subsystems develop to deal with significant categories of inputs. These may be important resources or information about potential threats to the system's performance. We have already seen that a differentiated subsystem is needed to deal with feedback. This is the control subsystem. In construction projects there may also be subsystems to deal with buying materials and components, forming contracts with consultants and contractors, providing for welfare and safety on site, dealing with industrial relations issues, and undertaking each different type of basic work. The relative strength of these subsystems and the extent to which they are specialized and therefore differentiated from each other depend on the nature of the opportunities and threats provided by the environment. They depend also of course on the nature of the work required by the project. Lawrence and Lorsch (1967) in their influential study of organization structures and processes, defined differentiation as differences in cognitive and emotional orientation among managers in different functional departments. It arises because managers have to deal with problems which are shaped by different technologies and environments. It means that managers have different goals and a different time orientation, adopt different reporting procedures, view rewards differently, exercise control in different ways, and generally behave differently and develop different attitudes. For example, some managers are primarily concerned with their task while others are more concerned with people. Some are rewarded for the specific measured output of their own team while others are rewarded on the basis of a general perception of how well the whole project organization is performing. Some managers operate under close and detailed control while others have great freedom to decide how they work. All of this is likely to be reflected in differences in the formality of the structure of different parts of project organizations. Some will have several levels of management; others will have broad organizations with few managers.

Differentiation, or at least appropriate differentiation, is necessary for successful projects. Projects in which everyone had the same attitudes and behaved in the same manner would be incapable of dealing with the variety of problems that arise. However, differentiation must be matched by appropriate coordination. Lawrence and Lorsch (1967) define this as the state of collaboration that exists among departments that are required to achieve unity of effort. Coordination is one of the main responsibilities of construction project managers and the various means available by which managers carry out this task are described in Chapter 5.

A further feature of the behaviour of controlled systems is that any given end result may be achieved by different routes. This is often called the principle of equifinality. However, for all except the very simplest of systems, it is impossible to identify the route which optimizes the performance of the system and of all its subsystems. Since construction projects are complex, managers cannot hope to optimize the performance of construction project organizations. They must settle for satisfactory answers. The reasoning behind this judgement is discussed in depth by March and Simon (1958). The distinction they draw is between an optimum answer and a satisfactory answer. An optimum answer exists if there is a set of criteria which enable all possible answers to be examined and the selected answer is preferred by all these criteria to all other options. A satisfactory answer exists if there is a set of criteria which describes a minimally satisfactory answer and the selected answer meets these criteria. We can see that to optimize, necessarily requires processes several orders of magnitude more complex than those required to satisfice and therefore requires far more management resources.

There is an important implication for construction project managers arising from the practical impossibility of identifying the optimum form for complex systems. It is that managers have a continuing responsibility to search for better ways of doing things. They should however do so cautiously. This is because the behaviour of controlled systems as complex as construction projects cannot be fully understood. A change to one element is likely to have unexpected repercussions elsewhere, which may or may not be beneficial. Wise managers therefore work with elements and groups of elements which they know work well. They change only a few things, perhaps one or two, at a time and do so only after wide discussion and agreement. Having made a change, they pay a great deal of attention to its effects and work hard to try to ensure that it produces real improvements in performance. If it does, it is adopted and used on the present and on future projects until a further change, at some time in the future, provides even more benefits. However, if after a sensible period of time the change is not working, then it must be reversed and the old, established methods reinstated. Good managers keep searching, year after year, in this steady cautious manner for improvements. Perhaps the most important message from systems thinking is that this is the only way to create world-class project organizations.

Systems in construction projects

We have identified a number of systems within construction projects. There are two distinct categories. First, there are those which directly form a part of the end product. Second, there are systems which form part of the project organization and are therefore concerned with the processes by which the end product is produced.

This distinction is of considerable significance. The systems which form a part of the end project can be fully designed and specified before they are created. The systems which form part of the project organization cannot be completely predetermined. Their general structure can be defined in terms of the responsibilities of each part. However, construction is too complex, too variable and too beset by interference from project environments for any design or specification of a project organization to be complete. There are always unanticipated situations which must be dealt with by some form of organizational change. Teams have to be induced to enter project organizations, and the negotiations needed to persuade a team to accept any given role are likely to alter the role description to some extent. Also, of course, the team appointed may in practice behave in a manner which is different from that agreed. Similar difficulties may arise with parts of the end product; bricks may crumble, beams may sag under their load and pipes may leak. Teams may fail in somewhat similar ways, but beyond this they may decide to move outside their agreed role. Such initiatives may be helpful or unhelpful. Bricklayers may decide to help unload bricks because the materials manager is busy elsewhere. On the other hand, they may devote their efforts to provoking an industrial dispute in the hopes of gaining some financial, political or other advantage. Bricks, beams and pipes do not behave in such ways. Therefore, although systems in the end product may be, and indeed usually have to be, fully specified in advance, the systems in project organizations cannot be fully prespecified. There has to be a division between the initial or major bargain, which provides a formal role description embodied in some form of legal contract, and the subsidiary negotiations and transactions which fill out and modify that initial description.

The primary concern of construction project managers is the management of the systems that form the processes which produce the end product. We need therefore to turn our attention at this point to the general nature and character of the processes through which construction projects produce their end products.

Processes in construction

The total set of processes by which construction products are produced is marked by distinct stages separated by major events. An obvious example, and perhaps the most dramatic of such events, is the start of work on site. Walker (1989) proposed a hierarchy of stages marked by events which he called decision points. At the highest level are what Walker has called primary decision points. He considered that there are only two primary decision points to be found in all construction projects. These are first, the decision that additional real property is required and second, the nature of the real property to be provided. These two primary decision points divide projects into three primary stages: the project conception, project inception and project realization. At the next level of detail are key decision points made by the customer. Walker gives as examples: approval of design, budget and programme proposals, decisions to delay the project, and decisions to change the nature of the project. A third level of detail is provided by operational decision points. These are decisions which the project organization is left to make without needing to refer them to the customer. Walker gives as examples: settling the details of project programmes, a decision to use bills of quantities as the basis of competitive tenders, and detail design decisions.

This is a useful framework for thinking about the stages of projects. The distinction between key decisions and operational decisions is especially important. It provides, as we shall see in Chapter 5, the basis for major elements of project coordination. However, the immediately important point is that construction projects move through stages. Certainly, in discussions with experienced designers and experienced construction managers, there is a wide recognition that projects move through distinct stages marked by distinct events. Indeed experienced customers often ask for a formal report at key decision points. They define the issues to be dealt with in such reports and are unwilling to give authority to proceed further with a project until all these issues are dealt with to their satisfaction.

Key decision points usually mark the need for some change in the project organization. New participants need to be brought into the project, different procedures need to be applied, a different style or nature of work needs to be adopted, different sub-objectives become important or different features of the project's environment demand attention. Experienced practitioners can predict these change points with a fair degree of accuracy for projects which are similar to others on which they have worked. In the very least, they can predict the character of the work necessary to reach the next key decision point. They know the resources, costs and time necessary to complete that work. This is because there are distinct families of projects which broadly move through the same sequence of decision points. Practitioners working on projects within that family become familiar with the pattern of work which they need to undertake. However, not all projects are the same; for example, the pattern of work in simple, small, repetitive and certain projects differs from that on complex, large, non-repetitive and uncertain ones. Both differ from that to be found on a moderately complex, medium sized, somewhat repetitive and reasonably certain project. Similarly, differences in customers' objectives generate further distinct categories of projects. Practitioners experienced in each of these families of projects know the likely overall pattern of work. They can make good and detailed predictions about the work leading up to the next key decision point for any such project on which they are working.

It is difficult to generalize about the stages of projects in any detail. However, there are distinct categories of work which tend to dominate the key stages of construction projects. We will consider each of these in turn, in order to build an overall picture of the construction process. The ensuing description is based on current good practice and draws on research into the various ways in which construction project management is practised throughout the developed world. Practising managers, in reading the next sections, could therefore bear in mind their continuing responsibility to search for better answers, and treat the descriptions of the main stages of construction projects as an opportunity to review their own approach. The descriptions also provide the basis for identifying the major elements of project organization systems.

Development and finance

The first stages of construction projects are dominated by decisions relating to development and finance. Indeed, unless someone recognizes a development need or opportunity and assembles the finance necessary to satisfy the need or realize the opportunity, there will be no construction project.

Needs and opportunities arise from many sources. Much construction exists to serve basic human needs for shelter and security. Many public sector projects fall into this category. These needs arise from increases in population but also from changes in the composition of a population over time. Thus a growing proportion of young people or of old people commonly creates a need for new construction. A different category of development needs arises from decisions to improve standards by, for example, providing better care for the old or sick, expanding educational opportunities or improving the environment.

Changes in other sectors of the economy frequently trigger the need for new construction. Thus increases in leisure time have resulted in a wide range of new construction, especially in the field of transport. Similarly, changes in retailing fashion and habits have led to major construction projects. Deregulation in the City of London led to the so-called 'Big Bang' and to some of the largest and most important construction projects of the 1980s.

On occasions, organizations have little choice but to acquire new property if they wish to stay in existence. This may be because a lease is due to run out and it is impossible to renew it. It may be because existing property is inadequate or is beyond repair. Or it may be that competitors have invested in new technology which provides a decisive advantage and the remaining firms must respond or go out of business.

Many construction projects aim to improve the efficiency of the organizations who use them. A new factory usually allows a more efficient layout of plant and equipment to be adopted. New constructions can be designed to reduce running costs. A new office building may allow staff previously scattered in different buildings to be brought together. This may in turn produce faster and cheaper communications and even, perhaps, better decisions. A new building is often used to provide better accommodation so that staff are happier. This in turn can produce economies due to reduced staff turnover and less absenteeism.

Many construction projects exist to provide for expansion either to meet increases in demand or to provide new services or products. Similarly, organizations moving into a new area of operation, a new business, a new location or a new way of delivering a service usually need new construction. A further factor in much construction is a desire on the part of the developer to use the new facility to enhance the image or perceived status of his organization.

A different and very important source of new construction projects is direct speculative investment. A developer sees an opportunity arising from any one of the primary sources described above and decides to take the opportunity of profit. He may build in order to sell the end product or he may retain it for the rent it will produce.

New construction projects usually spring from a mixture of these possible sources. The need or opportunity usually exists for some time before it is recognized clearly and defined. However, defining a development need or opportunity is not sufficient to create a construction project. There must also be sufficient finance to fund all the inevitable costs. There are many categories of costs to be covered which may include land, rights over land, professional advice in obtaining permits, design, manufacture, construction, management, finance and profit.

There are many sources of finance for construction projects. A customer may use his own funds; he may qualify for a grant or soft loan of some kind from government, a quasi-government body or a charity; he may look outside for other investors through a joint venture, a share issue or bonds; or he may seek a loan. Possible sources of loans include banks, large financial institutions and major companies. The financing of construction projects has become very sophisticated and has given rise to the expression *financial engineering* to describe the activities of innovative financial experts. At the heart of the financial equation, which all successful developers must solve, is the fact that construction ties up large sums of money before the investment provides any return. In the very early stages of a project, before there is any physical construction to attract and impress investors, finance tends to be expensive because of the risks that one or other of the multitude of things which can stop or delay a project will in fact occur. As projects get nearer to completion finance becomes easier to arrange. The risks are less, most of the costs are known, in a speculative development tenants may have signed agreements to rent, and of course the end product substantially exists. Because of these differing financial environments many projects are financed in distinct stages. For example, short term finance is normally used to cover the costs incurred during the design, manufacture and construction of speculative developments. This money usually attracts high interest rates because of the uncertainties associated with incomplete constructions. Then, as the picture becomes clearer, long term finance is sought from investors more interested in security than in high return. The second loan is used to pay off the first and to cover the continuing costs of running the project until the rents or other income reaches a level where it becomes self-financing and hopefully profitable.

Brownlie and Harris (1987) describe the results of a study of sources of finance for construction projects. They concluded that banks remain the primary source of finance and, for projects overseas, government loans or guarantees. Capital and money markets are not generally used for construction projects, largely because construction is too uncertain and is regarded as risky by the financial markets. A growing source of funds is that provided by large, cash-rich contractors. As they become involved in property development, there could well be greater demand for bonds or revolving credit facilities to replace traditional overdraft facilities.

In all the financial decisions needed to enable construction projects to be undertaken, the inherent risks, general interest rates, inflation rates, business confidence, tax regulations and costs will be the subject of judgement, expert advice, calculation and simple instinct. Given all the factors which could work against any construction project, it is perhaps surprising that so many are undertaken. Yet the urge to build, to leave something of oneself behind which may last for centuries, is very deep in the human nature. Consequently, throughout the world many development needs and opportunities are recognized and finance is assembled so that new construction projects may begin.

Design

A second distinct stage of construction projects is dominated by design decisions. Design today is a team activity. Even simple constructions need to draw on a range of knowledge and experience greater than is commonly found in one person's mind. Modern design teams are likely to include a variety of engineering specialists, including structural engineers, services engineers, civil engineers and process engineers. They include architects, builders, specialist contractors of many kinds, managers and of course the customers. Nevertheless, there is nearly always a single driving force behind the design of successful construction projects. This is usually a single powerful personality or at the most two people whose combined talents gell into a creative partnership. The single driving force is the primary designer. That is, the individual or partnership who conceived the overall design concept, which may, depending on the nature of the project, be based on aesthetic, scientific or technological criteria. However it is formed and whatever its inspiration, the key role of the single driving force is to maintain the original vision throughout the whole design process. The driving force gives the end product a sense of integrity and coherence which cannot come from widely dispersed, democratic, team decisions. The old joke about a camel being a horse designed by a committee, although unkind to camels, does apply to construction. It may seem unfair to the many people involved with a major new building that history will attribute it to a single designer or pair of designers. But history, in attributing St Paul's Cathedral to Sir Christopher Wren or the Pompidou Centre to Renzo Piano and Richard Rogers, is recognizing an important truth about design.

The need for an individual, central, coherent vision is entirely consistent with the idea that design nowadays is necessarily a team effort. Modern constructions draw on a vast range of technologies and it is part of the skill of great designers to be able to conduct a vast orchestra of specialists and for the resulting product to be harmonious.

Design moves through a number of distinct stages, all of which are called by the single name, design. This creates confusion. There is merit in having clear labels for the main stages of the total design process.

Broadbent (1973) proposes a systematic approach to design in architecture based on six stages. The stages derive from his view of the fundamental purposes of buildings. These are that they are designed to contain human activities; they must modify climate in order to provide comfortable and stimulating conditions internally whatever the weather outside; and in addition they are cultural symbols into which people read meanings. This last point is true whether or not the designer sees his building as a cultural symbol. People will make judgements about new buildings; they are seen as conveying powerful messages about style, status, power, prestige, social responsibility, environmental concern and taste. Also, buildings add value, both to the materials of which they are built and to the land on which they stand. Broadbent's analysis of the purposes of buildings is equally true of all constructions provided we interpret the term, human activities, widely so that it includes the activities of machines, plants and animals. Given that modification, his six stage approach to design applies, not just to buildings, but to all constructions.

Broadbent's approach is based on three interrelated systems: human, building and environment. When the human system wishes to perform activities in a particular place and the environmental system in that place is incompatible with these activities, a building system is designed to reconcile the other two. Each of these systems has two main elements. Thus, there are six main elements in the total system. Each must be considered and taken into account by designers and thus each provides a distinct stage of design. Figure 3.3 shows the six main elements in Broadbent's scheme. Since the design process is a system, as we defined it earlier, it can be entered at any point and the elements considered in any sequence. What is crucial to good design is that all six elements are considered. They are considered, in the following sections, in what might be regarded as the conventional sequence.

Customer objectives

The first stage covers the development and finance issues described earlier. Broadbent brings a great concern with image to his own description of this

Environment system	Building system	Human system
Cultural context Physical context	Building technology Internal ambience	User requirements Customer objectives

Figure 3.3 *Main elements in the design system*

stage. Indeed he implies that the prime motivation for much building is to give expression to otherwise hidden motives of the customer. He describes building as a means of exciting envy in one's competitors, establishing confidence in one's customers, advertising one's wealth, demonstrating social responsibility or showing love for one's country.

This emphasis does not deny the importance of customers' single and direct objectives, such as creating comfortable and stimulating spaces to house specific activities. It does, however, recognize that the environment to be modified has political, social, cultural and aesthetic dimensions as well as the more obvious physical, technological and economic ones. This produces a rich mix of objectives which need to be drawn out of customers and made explicit in an agreed statement or brief. However, there is also a need for a functional brief. This takes us into the second stage of the design system.

User requirements

We must first recognize that the user requirements may conflict with the customer's objectives. An extreme example is provided by prisons. However, much the same type of dichotomy arises in most public sector building and indeed the distance between senior management and junior staff in almost all organizations makes a separate study of user requirements necessary.

The aim of such a study is to produce a complete list of all the activities to be accommodated. For each we need to know the physical space required, the necessary environmental conditions, the relationships with other activities and the effects on the physical structure of the end product. Given a detailed statement for the individual activities, they can be grouped together in several ways: in terms of physical movements between activities, in terms of common environmental needs (e.g. air-conditioning, quiet, good light) or in terms of social needs. Once the clusters of activities have been identified, attention can be directed towards spatial sequences and circulation patterns. These define the processes to be accommodated. Obtaining an agreed statement of the processes is just as important as the definition of the individual activities. Just as chemicals are processed and transformed as they pass through the various elements of a processing plant, so people are processed as they move through buildings. The effects may be less dramatic but they are real and form an important part of the function of buildings. Thus it is helpful to agree a chart which illustrates the sequences by which various categories of users move into, through and out of a building.

Taken together the statements of customer objectives and user requirements constitute what is usually called the customer's brief.

Physical context

The next step is to analyse the proposed site for the new construction. We need to know what designs will be permitted within laws governing the public interest in health, safety, convenience and amenity. We need to study the physical characteristics of the site. These include its climate, geology and topography. We need to identify sources of noise, smell, visual attraction or pollution. We need to understand the social, historical, cultural and religious context of the site. We need to know if it has major political or economic significance to the local community. We should consider the opinions of neighbours as well as looking at the actual surrounding buildings and other constructions, including particularly those which accommodate or generate traffic. We need to identify existing vegetation and available services. We need to give particular consideration to views from the site and also to views of the site. The aim of all this data is to help the designers produce the outline of a desirable and permissible construction envelope. This may take the form of drawings, computer generated graphics, models or a formal report on the overall size and shape of the proposed construction.

Internal ambience

The next step is to fit the clusters of activities, spatial sequences and circulation patterns agreed in the brief into the outline construction envelope. Many of the decisions will be simple and obvious. For example, the main entrance may be determined simply by ease of access, the directors' suite may well be situated to enjoy the best views, a drawing office needs north light, production facilities may require heavy duty access for large volumes of input materials, and so on. However, as more activities are plotted into the outline construction envelope so clashes occur. Two or more activities will compete for the same physical location. At this stage there needs to be agreement on priorities in terms of comfort and stimulation for individual activities and in terms of the relationships between them. High priority activities will get the best locations. Low priority activities may have to accept poor views, noisy conditions and relatively long journeys through or around the new construction.

Having located activities within the overall construction envelope in abstract terms, it is time to consider their physical containment. This is done first in terms of the size and performance requirements of each space. We need to consider how much or how little the various activities should be separated from each other by physical walls and so on, and how far they should be open. Circulation counts as an activity and must be allocated space accordingly.

The design now consists of spaces surrounded by surfaces. The surfaces exist to contain and provide support for all the activities identified and defined in the brief. At this stage the design may still be relatively abstract or it may be recognizable as a model of a real physical construction.

Cultural context

The next step is to produce a design for a physical three-dimensional form. The translation from the detailed and abstract analysis which has preceded this stage to the choice of physical form will be accomplished using one of four types of design process.

Broadbent makes it clear that the choice of physical form inevitably carries with it large cultural connotations, hence the title of this stage. He also provides us with detailed descriptions of four types of design process.

First, there is pragmatic design. That is, working through trial and error and using knowledge about the properties of materials and the way they have been used in the past to design the form of all the parts of the end product. Materials are used to provide structural forms in mass, planar or frame constructions and space divisions in mass, planar and skin constructions. Relating these uses to the earlier analysis may be sufficient to suggest a satisfactory shell to which will need to be added services to create the required internal environments.

Second, designers may adopt an iconic design approach. This consists of using tried and accepted forms. They are repeated because they are known to work in terms of construction and the performance of the end product.

Third, designers may use analogical design. Analogy is the central mechanism of creativity. It is the process of creating a new form by using one which already exists as a starting point and playing with it. Le Corbusier's use of a crab shell in designing Ronchamp, Frank Lloyd Wright's use of water lilies in the design of the Johnson Wax Factory, and John Utzon's use of the sails of yachts in his design for Sydney Opera House provide famous examples of analogical design. It is perhaps more common to take an existing building or style of building as a starting point, but to use the earlier forms in an original, interesting, beautiful manner.

Fourth, designers may rely on canonic design. That is, using a given pattern, a grid of fixed proportions or some other geometric system. Such an approach is evident in the earliest architecture and remains important today in schemes for the modular coordination of prefabricated components. Many of the schemes adopted in the past were based on the proportions of the human body, others are based on the geometric properties of ideal shapes, while others merely provide a regular grid or more usually a series of regular grids superimposed on each other. Designers use these to guide their choice of the sizes and shapes of all the parts of the end product.

Having, by some combination of these four design processes, produced a number of possible building forms, it is wise to apply some basic checks. These can be very simple: can it be made to stand up, what will it cost, how will it behave environmentally, will it be easy to maintain and alter, will it meet the legal requirements, how long will it take to construct, and does it satisfy the brief? The answers to these questions should be ranked against the customer's objectives and priorities to select the agreed conceptual design. This will almost certainly be described in some combination of drawings, models and reports, although computer graphics technology is beginning to provide attractive ways of presenting design proposals to customers.

Building technology

All that remains, once the conceptual design is agreed by the customer, is to design the specific technological answers for each part of the end product. That is, to design the structural systems, the space dividing systems, the services systems and the fitting-out systems. This is commonly called the detail design stage and it produces the working drawings and specifications.

Nowadays detail design inevitably draws on the knowledge and experience of specialist contractors. Although it is sensible as far as possible to use tried and tested methods, where new answers are needed the contractors provide a source of both good ideas and deep understanding of the behaviour and performance of available technologies.

Working together, designers and contractors complete the final stage of what is conventionally described as design in construction projects. Although the six stages are distinct, it is important to understand that they are elements in a richly interconnected system. Design does not move through a simple, linear sequence. The stages interact and apparent progress in one stage is frequently invalidated by a subsequent stage. Also, the stages can be tackled in any sequence. Many designers begin with a clear idea of form and mould the other stages to this predetermined vision, which is itself subsequently influenced by the more practical analysis of, for example, the user requirements and the physical context.

It is also important to understand that design is not complete at the end of the six stages described thus far. There is still more detail to be added, but this takes us into what is normally considered to be the next main stage of construction projects.

Manufacture and construction

The next main stage of construction projects is dominated by decisions about manufacture and construction. That is, with making and assembling all the physical parts of the end product. This activity is divided between the site and a large number of factories which may be located anywhere in the world. The distributed nature of this total activity means that transport often plays a significant part in the manufacture and construction processes.

The managers of construction projects have an influence over only parts of this total system. Much of the relevant manufacturing industry operates independently of any one construction project. Indeed, a significant proportion serves other industries in addition to construction. Also, many of the companies producing basic construction materials are very large compared with the consultants and contractors responsible for most construction projects. This arises because many basic materials and components are standard or at least relatively homogeneous. Hence international demand provides considerable scope for economies of scale. Consequently, product manufacturers operate in markets where there is a tendency for monopoly or oligopoly conditions to prevail. Obvious examples include cement, common bricks, timber, steel bars and rolled sections, paint, plastic pipes, roofing felt, flat glass, concrete roofing tiles, sheet insulation, plasterboard, basic sanitary fittings and so on. There are also local concentrations of supply in respect of heavy materials such as aggregates and ready mixed concrete. Managers of individual projects need to be aware of the nature of the various material supply industries. However, except in the case of mega-projects or projects which form part of a significant and continuing programme of work, they are unlikely to be able to do other than merely accept the performance of the various construction materials industries. Or, where their supply, delivery or price performance is unacceptable, simply avoid using particular materials by having them designed out of the project. In general, it must be said that despite their relatively weak position, designers can specify basic construction materials and expect them to be supplied reasonably reliably throughout the developed world. The situation in developing countries can be very different. In such countries, there is often no reliable local construction materials supply industry and so managers need to buy overseas and arrange international transport, import, storage, protection, and local transport. All of these stages must be planned and taken into account in the overall programmes and budgets for construction projects in many of the developing countries.

The situation is different in all parts of the world when project-specific components are used. Construction project managers have considerable responsibilities arising out of the manufacture of such components. They need to understand the character of the various bespoke manufacturing industries on which their projects draw so that they can plan and control an integrated manufacture and construction process. This is necessary mainly because the manufacture of some products takes a surprisingly long time. Unless this time-scale is taken into account, projects can be badly delayed.

The manufacture of bespoke products begins with a design process. Working drawings and specifications produced by design consultants provide insufficient information for manufacture. They normally provide a general picture of the appearance of the required components and specify the materials and finishes to be used. In order to organize their manufacture, every separate part must be drawn to a large scale and all the joints and connections detailed. The result is what has become known as the shop drawings. These are the detailed manufac-turing drawings. They are produced by the manufacturer's own production engineers and draughtsmen. It is normal for shop drawings to be checked and approved by the design consultants. They, quite reasonably, wish to ensure that manufacturers have interpreted their design intentions correctly. It is not uncommon for designers to want to improve the manufacturer's first proposals and even their second and third. Indeed, some of the world's very best architects take this stage of design so seriously that they insist on working in manufac-turers' drawing offices alongside the production engineers while the shop drawings for key components are produced. The resulting designs are the product of joint work which therefore, potentially at least, combines highly developed aesthetic sensitivity with deep technical competence. Before full design approval is given, it may well be necessary for a number of prototypes to be produced and tested. It may be necessary to commission original research and development work to solve unusual detail design problems. This in turn may require the resources of a wide variety of firms, including some from entirely outside the construction industry. Particularly in high-tech buildings, the manufacture of bespoke components often draws on sophisticated, purpose designed materials. As an example, Norman Foster's design for the Renault Centre in Swindon, UK included a detail in which the structural steel frame passed through the external envelope. Since the two elements behave very differently, the junction posed a problem. It was solved with the help of a firm whose normal business is manufacturing neophrene skirts for hovercraft. This type of interaction between construction design and ideas borrowed from other industries is becoming increasingly common. It raises new issues for construc-tion project managers who find they have to coordinate working styles and customs, some of which may be quite alien to construction's normal methods. It is often the production and agreement of the shop drawings which provides an early test of a construction project's coordination devices.

The shop drawing stage provides detailed agreement on exactly what is to be manufactured. It is a major activity in which for example a medium sized (20 000 m² floor area) modern shell and core office building is likely to require between 3000 and 4000 shop drawings. Once they are agreed by the architect, the next step in the manufacturing process is to assemble all the necessary materials and bought in subcomponents. For even a moderately sophisticated building, these are likely to come from many different parts of the world. Gray and Flanagan (1989) report, as an example, the purchase of polished granite which was to form a major part of the cladding for a building in the City of London. It was quarried in Africa, cut and polished in Italy, and the first delivery was made, almost exactly to the day, one year after the order was placed. Only then could the prefabrication of the cladding begin. This is not an entirely unrepresentative example; indeed, the sequence of events for sophisticated bought-in subcomponents can be even more tortuous and lengthy.

The actual manufacturing of bespoke products for the construction industry tends to be organized in a manner which is more concerned with flexibility and minimizing capital investment than with speed or efficiency. This is largely a response to unpredictable patterns of demand and the extreme variety of the products ordered. The way many buildings are designed generates small variations in otherwise standard components. So manufacturers incorporate large time buffers between separate manufacturing processes and rely extensively on subcontracting to smooth out peaks in demand. This enables them to schedule for an almost constant workflow through their factories, which keeps their manufacturing costs to a minimum. It does, however, tie up capital in buffer stocks of partly manufactured components between each separate process. Overall it is slow, inefficient and expensive, but as long as all bespoke manufacturers rely on the same technology it can be, and indeed is, profitable.

However, the cosy world of small craft-based manufacturing is being challenged. Just-in-time techniques have begun to demonstrate that the old philosophy is all too often based on very poor economics. Some construction manufacturers have recognized this and can deliver individually designed products quickly and reliably. However, for the foreseeable future, managers of construction projects will be faced with a component supply industry of very variable performance.

Construction managers have more direct control over activities on site. This control nowadays often begins early in the life of a project. Construction managers need to work with customers and designers in establishing a project brief and overall design criteria which take account of the needs of construction. This means that construction managers must ensure that the site is evaluated from a construction viewpoint; that their project organizations incorporate up-to-date knowledge and experience of the local construction industry; and that clear construction criteria are established in agreement with designers. By establishing the overall method of construction early, construction managers help ensure that designs do not create unexpected problems on site. By

identifying the separate construction work packages and defining the boundaries between them, determining the overall construction sequence and the
general pattern of the flow of materials and components around the site and
into their final positions, construction managers help ensure efficient site
construction. The preliminary construction strategy is embodied in drawings
and statements describing the construction method at a strategic level, an
overall project programme and a budget. The programme and budget need to
deal with the whole of the detail design, shop drawings and manufacturing
stages, in addition to the construction stage. At this stage, they do so at the level
of work packages which are equivalent to the work of separate construction
teams.

The overall construction strategy, embodied in the method statement, programme and budget, needs to be agreed and understood by all the designers and
the customer. It has implications for their work. For example, the sequence of
construction work often influences the design of junction and fixing details and
the timing of payments by the customer. For these kinds of reasons, the
development of the construction strategy involves discussions among the whole
project organization.

The construction strategy provides one of the two key starting points, conceptual design is the other, for specialist contractors' work. They must each work
within the framework so formed and undertake the same kind of strategic
planning for their own work as the construction manager does for the whole
project. All the specialist contractors must divide their own work into its major
stages and produce their own strategic method statement, programme and
budget. These cover the production of shop drawings, agreement of the design,
production engineering, procurement of materials and components, manufacturing, delivery, storage, distribution around the site, and final construction.
They deal with major items of plant and equipment on site, essential temporary
works, on-site and off-site storage, safety, welfare, major labour relations issues,
and the removal of rubbish and waste materials. All of these plans must take
account of the needs of other adjacent specialist contractors.

It is normal for specialist contractors to be responsible for coordinating their
work, both in design and organizational terms, with that of other specialist
contractors. They do so within an overall, strategic framework provided by the
designers and construction managers. It is also the responsibility of designers
and construction managers to check and agree the specialist contractors'
proposals. They need to ensure that these proposals are in accordance with the
overall framework or, where problems are thrown up so that new strategic
decisions have to be made, that these are fully considered, agreed and
communicated to the whole project organization. These tasks have become very
onerous with today's fast-track construction methods, because it is likely that to

some extent the development of the set of coordinated method statements, programmes and budgets will still be underway after construction on site has started.

Any project's information systems will be severely tested when detail design, shop drawings, manufacturing and construction on different work packages are all underway simultaneously. Consequently, creating an efficient and fast information system is a crucial responsibility for managers. This needs to provide clear objectives for all project participants in a form which allows their performance to be measured. It must also provide feedback on quality, times and costs so that throughout the project people know what is happening and have the confidence to make local decisions. Finally, the project information system needs to provide designers, managers and the customer with regular reports on progress. We shall discuss the use of information systems again in Chapter 5.

When the strategic planning of construction is well done and the plan is fully implemented in manufacturing, construction on site still requires hard work and good management. Construction is essentially a sequential process of assembling components which provide the support for subsequent components. Support at intermediate stages is provided by temporary works, plant, equipment and the muscle power of workers. Constructions have always been constructed in this way and, where projects use well established technologies and craft skills, regular patterns of working have emerged. In these circumstances construction managers and specialist contractors know the sequences of work, the types of plant and equipment needed at each stage, and the nature of the temporary works needed to support the workers and their work. There are few surprises and there is relatively little need for formal management.

However, where projects use new technologies, new materials and new skills, construction throws up many problems and needs much management. The difficulties arise from the absence of directly relevant experience. Partly because of this, one of the important implications of innovation is that design has to be very detailed in order to provide precise details for the construction of every component. It is not possible to rely on craft knowledge to make good any deficiencies in the design information. The construction workers may well not fully understand the detail design philosophy, and therefore any modifications or adaptions on site can all too easily cause failures. The result is a multitude of drawings which must not only be checked and agreed by designers, construction managers and specialist contractors, but must also be understood by the workers on site so that construction follows the designer's intentions exactly.

Many modern projects in fact combine traditional work with new technologies. This complicates the design and construction tasks even further. There is not only the very different management approach required by the two forms of construction, but the work itself is also very different. For example, prefabricated components are normally produced to tolerances of the order of ± 1mm, while traditional work normally works to tolerances of at least ± 10mm. Forming connections between the two is as difficult as creating an efficient project organization which combines the two distinct philosophies of site based craftwork and factory based prefabrication.

Modern construction can be managed efficiently only by dividing the process into a hierarchy of self-contained and self-sufficient stages. These begin with the major stages of establishing the site organization systems, substructure, structure, external envelope, internal subdivisions, concealed fittings and services, finishes, exposed fittings and services and decoration, and commissioning. Each of the main stages needs to be divided into self-contained and self-sufficient substages. Depending on the size of the project there may need to be two levels of substages. Then finally the work is divided into one day units. Management's aim is to contain variability within the work of one day. When this proves impossible effort is concentrated on directing the project back onto the planned progress by the end of the current substage or, for larger projects, the current sub-substage. This is normally one week's work. When this is not achieved, a crisis situation is signalled and all efforts need to be directed towards achieving the next milestone. On smaller projects this is the planned end date for a major stage, and on large projects for a substage. Thus there is a clear systematic focus of workers' attention on putting the overall plan into effect. When this is achieved and the construction of a new facility is complete, projects enter their final stage.

Facilities management

Construction projects usually end with the completion of construction. However, some continue into a further stage which is dominated by decisions about facilities management. Usually this comprises establishing or helping to establish a facilities management system to run the end product; the aims of which are to help the owner use and operate his new facility efficiently and to provide comfortable and stimulating environments within which people can live and work both happily and efficiently.

Facilities management requires staff who are well trained in the proper operation of the facilities under their control. They need to be supported by systems which monitor the performance of the facilities themselves and also the behaviour of users. The systems need to be able to identify significant changes and trends so that problems and new opportunities can be identified. In many cases these systems need to be built into the fabric of the facilities themselves. In processing plants, for example, sensing devices distributed throughout the facility provide managers with up-to-the-minute information about the behaviour of every key part. The facilities managers can sit in a computerized control room and monitor the behaviour of the entire plant. As operating problems arise, the managers adjust the plant to keep it running efficiently at the required rate. Increasingly, however, these routine adjustments are built into computerized expert systems, which take the place of human control. Human intervention is then restricted to strategic changes; that is, to finding ways of improving the performance of the whole plant by, for example, spotting bottlenecks and altering the plant to remove them; planning and implementing major maintenance activities; and dealing with failures of components or systems.

Many large modern buildings have similarly sophisticated monitoring and control systems. Armed with the comprehensive information they provide, facilities management can make a very significant difference to the performance of the organizations who occupy their buildings. This is especially true where the work of the organization using the building is subject to frequent unpredictable changes. In these circumstances, facilities managers need to be fully involved in the senior management of the user organization. They have a major role to play in helping to maintain employees' satisfaction by using the inherent flexibility and adaptability of their buildings to create environments which support each new pattern of work. Thus we see that construction project systems should flow through into the facilities management systems if customers are to receive the best possible value from their investments.

Ubiquitous systems

Many aspects of construction projects can usefully be treated as systems. This allows us to apply general knowledge about systems in managing construction projects. As we have described in this chapter, construction projects as a whole can be looked at, from many viewpoints, as collections of elements which interact sufficiently regularly to be of interest. Therefore the general propositions about systems described at the start of the chapter apply to these systematic features of construction projects. As the implications of this are being worked out in construction management research and practice, so we are steadily improving our ability to plan and control ever larger and more complex projects, in ever more rapidly changing environments, and to do so faster and more efficiently than ever before. In other words, systems thinking has the potential to provide important new insights into construction project management, just as it has in other subjects.

As with all new knowledge, systems thinking can be used for good or bad ends. This thought should serve to remind us of the crucial importance of objectives or goals in determining the behaviour of construction teams. Establishing the objectives for a construction project is a major responsibility which has a direct and significant effect on the nature of our built environment. Objectives cannot be perfect or exact; they must leave room for local decisions, but they must provide sufficient constraint to ensure responses to problems. Objectives depend on value judgements which ought to be the subject of wide debate and consensus. To a large extent, widely agreed objectives are embodied in the standards and norms which society imposes on construction work and which teams bring with them when they join a new project organization. This important category of project objectives is the subject for the next chapter.

4 *Standards in construction*

The previous chapter described the important ideas that systems provide for construction project managers. It is likely, in due course, that the new scientific approach to chaos will provide yet deeper insights into the behaviour of construction projects. It is understandable that managers should be interested in new ideas, but it is important also to remember the role of established ideas in managing construction projects. Methods which have existed for decades and been found to work well, so that they are embodied in standards, deserve careful attention.

There are two distinct categories of standards which deserve attention. The first and most obvious is public standards; that is, published and widely known standards used by many firms. In addition, there are standards which grow up within individual organizations, which are also important in managing construction projects. As we shall see, some of these become public standards, but organization standards which remain private also play a key role in construction, which managers need to understand.

Public standards

The construction industry has many well established public standards. One major reason for this chapter is to serve as a reminder of the important role of public standards in managing construction projects. No attempt is made to describe individual standards in any detail because by definition that would merely duplicate material already in the public domain.

Standards are central to the successful management of construction projects. It is therefore important for managers to understand how and why they came into existence. Standards provide agreed answers to commonly occurring problems. They came into existence in one of two main ways; either one answer is clearly identified as the best and widely adopted, or, a committee of experts is set up to decide on the best answer and then it is published as a standard.

Informal standards

Historically the first of these methods of creating standards was much the more important. As buildings were built and roads and services constructed, so workers tried various methods of using construction materials. Some of these methods worked well and others failed in some way. The best methods were repeated and passed on from craftsman to apprentice. These best methods became the standard approach and were used widely. In this way standards were established for the size of bricks, the size of roof and floor timbers, the slopes and laps in roofing tiles, the ways of providing damp-proof courses, and the construction of roads.

The standards were gradually recorded so that new entrants to the industry could supplement their practical training by referring to textbooks. These became much more important with the growth of the construction professions. Architects and engineers needed some knowledge of a range of building construction details without going through all the practical training which provided the basis of craftsmen's knowledge. So very detailed building construction textbooks became widely available in the nineteenth century. Architects and engineers used the textbook details in designs for new constructions. Gradually they began to influence the details on the basis of their experience and, even more gradually, also on the basis of formal research.

Another source of informal standards, which has become increasingly important over the past century, is provided by trade literature issued by manufacturers of building materials. It is obviously in their own best interests that their products should be used successfully. They therefore produce descriptions of how to use their materials in various situations and circumstances. Much of this literature is excellent, being both well researched and well presented. Where a monopoly or near monopoly situation exists, the literature produced by the one dominant firm becomes the effective standard. Where a sector of the market is served by many firms, it is common for them to form a trade association to produce agreed descriptions of good practice. These are often based on long and careful research of the behaviour of materials and components in particular situations. They are used widely as *de facto* standards.

A classic example of a manufacturer creating a standard comes from the world of computers, where IBM have established *de facto* standards which have a wide influence. In this case the major reason why these particular standards have become established is that users have every confidence that IBM will provide reliable support for their systems long into the future. Other technically superior answers appear but, without the assurance of long term back-up and support, they have no choice but to become IBM compatible if they are to survive in the marketplace. In construction there is nothing which matches the worldwide influence of IBM. However, as was described in Chapter 3, there are many examples of monopoly or oligopoly conditions in local markets for basic construction materials. Lowe (1987) identified two broad categories of mechanisms which enable a firm or a small number of firms to enforce a monopoly or oligopoly: legal and economic. Legal mechanisms include the use of patents, copyrights and trademarks to give protection. Another mechanism founded on legal rights is where a firm has secured key mineral rights to a critical raw material. Also a state franchise may be awarded to a firm operating in a particular sector and competitors may be legally banned from operation. Economic mechanisms include: cost advantages, where perhaps because of a technological lead one firm can produce more cheaply than competitors; economies of scale, where perhaps the capital investment needed to enter a market are high so that the number of firms able to operate profitably is restricted; and brand loyalty, where a firm has succeeded in associating desirable qualities exclusively with their own brand-named products.

Lowe used this framework to examine the UK market in basic building materials. He identified: London Brick Company's monopoly of the fletton brick market; a classic oligopolistic situation in grey cement where three firms share 85 per cent of the market; Pilkingtons' domination of the production of flat glass; British Gypsum's monopoly in the market for plaster and plasterboard; British Steel Corporation's neo-monopoly of heavy rolled steel products and reinforcing bars; an oligopolistic market in basic sanitary fittings where four firms, Armitage Shanks, Twyfords, Doulton and Ideal Standard control 85 per cent of the market; and similar concentrations in the markets for concrete roofing tiles, insulating materials, plumbing, heating and ventilating, and electrical equipment, plastic products, paint and many other sectors of the construction materials marketplace. Similar situations exist in many other countries. Wherever there is a concentration of market share and for whatever reason it came about, the dominant firms have the power to create informal standards.

Formal standards

It is not at all uncommon for informal standards to be adopted as formal national standards. In general this comes about because of the operation of self-interest. A simple and obvious example is provided by a committee of experts assembled to produce a national standard specification for a material manufactured by a monopoly firm. That firm will own much of the relevant practical expertise. Therefore the firm's own approach is likely to provide the basis of the resulting national standard. There are a number of obvious temptations for firms in such a position. They may seek to embody wide tolerances and low standards in the formal specifications in order to avoid creating problems for themselves in meeting national standards. Another firm operating in a different market may seek to incorporate high standards or distinctive, arbitrary features of their own products in order to make life difficult for potential competitors.

It is in practice impossible to produce standards which are free from any form of bias. Representatives of professional bodies will seek to ensure that standards do not prejudice the interests of the members of their own profession. Government representatives will have one eye on what they perceive to be the public interest; but this will be viewed from the perspective of their own departments. A representative from Greenpeace or Save the Children will inevitably seek an opportunity to further the interests of their own cause. Consequently, it is right that the use of standards is voluntary except where issues of public health or safety arise. In the UK, for example, there are British Standard Specifications for many kinds of building materials. However, there is also a National Building Specification promoted by the Royal Institute of British Architects. This provides for the use of British Standards, but also provides alternative specification clauses for architects who wish to use a different quality or achieve a different performance from the one laid down in the British Standard.

A distinctive feature of British practice is the existence of major negotiated standards. These include standard forms of contract for building work produced by the Joint Contracts Tribunal (JCT). The JCT has eleven constituent bodies representing customers, architects, contractors, engineers, surveyors and government. It is not surprising, with so many interests to be taken into account, that JCT forms of contract are long and complicated. However, having numerous constituent bodies is not the only reason why formal committees produce lengthy standards. The UK Standard Method of Measurement of Building Works is produced by a Joint Committee of just two bodies, the Building Employers Confederation and the Royal Institution of Chartered Surveyors. It has long been criticized for producing sets of rules for measuring building work which are too detailed. The reason in this case is not the range of interests to be served but the age of the convention. The Joint Committee was set up in 1912 and produced its first Standard Method in 1922. Since that date, in each new edition of the Standard Method, additional rules have been added to deal with problems encountered on individual building projects and reported to the Joint Committee. It was not until the seventh edition of the Standard Method, published in 1988, that any serious attempt was made to halt the accretion of rules dealing with minor items of work and the creation of ever longer and more complex classifications of measured items. The tendency for British Standards to become over-complex and over-long has its roots in the way the committees that produce them are organized.

The committees that produce the various British Standards are made up of volunteers who are prepared to spare time from their normal work. As Hillebrandt (1984) observed, the members of these standard-setting committees act without pay and are usually successful and therefore busy in their own specialist fields of operation. As a result the meetings of the committees are held at long intervals and the process of producing a new standard tends to be lengthy and cumbersome. The slow pace of committee work is compounded by the constituent bodies insisting on individually examining and usually altering every new standard and every revision of existing ones before giving them their formal approval.

As a consequence of the way they are produced, formal standards tend to describe a conservative view of current good practice. They do not represent the best; instead they provide a middle-of-the-road, majority view. This, of course, is their strength. It means that they are safe to use. A practitioner using a formal standard to solve a problem of the type for which it was produced is unlikely to be regarded as acting negligently. Standards, however, have other important benefits, besides providing a defence against charges of negligence. Before we examine these benefits, we must consider the internal standards that develop in individual organizations.

Organization standards

Organizations develop standards for many purposes. They adopt standard approaches to the design of their products. Although most organizations produce a variety of different products, many successful firms adopt a distinctive style which marks out the things they produce from those of their competitors. Certainly the work of many of the world's greatest architects is immediately recognizable because of distinctive ways of using particular details or forms. They develop personal vocabularies of materials and styles which are refined in successive new designs but which essentially remain standard.

Organizations also develop standards for their production processes. So, faced with a particular manufacturing or construction task, they will adopt a standard answer. This may or may not be explicit. The standard answer may be recorded in detail and embodied in formal rules or procedures. Alternatively, it may simply be used and reused as workers base each new decision on what was done last time. In this way standard repertoires of joints, junctions and fixings gradually evolve. Particular ways of forming shapes, creating distinctive colours, achieving specific performances and handling the multitude of day-to-day problems of making things are all repeated as long as they are successful. Over time they become either formal or informal organization standards.

In much the same way, organizations develop standards for the behaviour of their staff. In addition to the obvious need for standards describing direct work processes, organizations tell workers how to behave towards each other, how to behave towards customers, suppliers and subcontractors, how to act in a crisis and what to do if an accident occurs, and commonly provide rules for every situation in which the efficiency or survival of the organization may be affected. In many cases rules also exist to provide and reinforce the authority or sense of power of senior managers. Rules telling workers how to dress sometimes fall into this category. Often, of course, dress restrictions are necessary for health or safety, and they are also legitimately used to reinforce a company image. In other cases, rules about individual behaviour can become petty and counterproductive. Good managers, knowing this, will review company rules at regular intervals and prune any which are not serving the company's main objectives. In doing this, managers should consider the unwritten as well as the formal written rules. These are often equally powerful and managers can influence the unwritten rules by the example of their own behaviour.

Organizations need standards for dealing with matters of discipline, for specifying the criteria for testing their products, for keeping records (particularly financial accounts), for collecting and handling information, for allocating responsibilities, and for many other matters. This has been understood for as long as men have written about management. Much of Taylor's (1903, 1911) influential work was concerned with establishing standards. His primary concern was to make management scientific; that is, to analyse work in order to find the best way of carrying out each essential task. His method was to study the methods used by experienced workers, step by step, in minute detail, decide which steps in a process were essential, and identify the most efficient method of doing each of these small pieces of work. Taylor believed that, among hundreds of experienced workers all doing the same task, one or two would have found the best way of doing each small part of their total task. However, it was unlikely that any worker would have found the best ways for all the separate steps. By long and careful study and analysis Taylor could identify the best method for the total task: the best material to use, the best tools and machines, the most efficient way to manipulate the tools or machines, the best flow of work and the best sequence of work. This was then established as the standard and taught to all the workers. Teaching was reinforced by a bonus scheme which rewarded workers for working in the standard way.

Taylor worked for 26 years perfecting his methods, which succeeded in raising productivity, reducing the size of work forces, increasing wages and raising profits in a number of different activities. Taylor found that good men, suited to the particular work, will produce two to three times as much as the normal average for between 30 and 100 per cent more pay than the average for their trade. Taylor demonstrated that the extra productivity can be maintained over many years without damaging the health of the workers. Taylor, however, warned against underpaying men: 'they will become dissatisfied and look for easier work.' This was ignored by many greedy men who subsequently tried to apply his methods and failed because workers were not allowed to share in the benefits of greater productivity. On the other hand, Taylor also warned against overpaying men 'it does not do for most men to get rich too fast.'

Taylor's work was done as a practising manager in the Midvale Steel Company and the Bethlehem Steel Company, both in the USA, and later as a consultant, at the end of the nineteenth century and the early years of the twentieth century. His approach to labour reflected the attitudes of his time. He accepted that much work is boring and warned against employing intelligent men to do repetitive work. 'The lower mental calibre of the labourer renders him more fit than the mechanic to stand the monotony of repetition.' Taylor believed that workers achieve less than first-rate output because they have a natural instinct to take it easy. Workers slow down to the pace of the poorest and least efficient of their fellow workers. Managers encourage this by using any fast work as the basis of piece work rates which tend to cut wages. So workers learn not to work fast. Taylor believed that 'workmen cannot be induced to work extra-hard without extra-pay.' He also believed that managers must determine all aspects of working methods independently because 'when workers have a say in determining how they are to work they will deceive their employers about possible rates of output.' For Taylor the scientific approach is for management to direct and control, on the basis of exact information as to how much work a first-class man can do in a day.

In today's developed world, Taylor's ideas apply directly only to the work of machines. We now know that we cannot afford to ignore the total input of a healthy, educated, well informed workforce. However, his ideas have been enormously influential far beyond his own direct applications of scientific management. They led directly to the great benefits of mass production and can be discerned in the consistent analytical approach which underlies modern Japanese manufacturing methods.

Although Taylor tells us how to establish efficient mechanical standards, it is March and Simon (1958) who provide the classic description of the way organization standards are necessary to enable organizations to function reasonably reliably and reasonably consistently. They observed that most problems within organizations are resolved by selecting the appropriate standard and applying it. Organizations develop complex patterns of standards which continue to operate virtually independently of the idiosyncratic concerns of individual workers.

March and Simon found that considerable effort is devoted to forcing problems into existing standard answers. In applying standards to new situations, managers and workers are much more likely to change the selection criteria than to change the standard. So, in effect problems are classified into broad categories which ignore minor, though sometimes important, variations. In general, faced with a problem which does not quite fit any of the existing standards, an individual will first review the variables under his own control.

Then he will consider how he can influence other variables, so that an existing standard can be used. Next he will consider changing the criteria which use of particular standards should satisfy, to see whether an existing category can be expanded to accept the troublesome situation. Only when all else fails will he consider devising a new answer. In the main, new standards are modifications of or new combinations of parts of existing standards. In searching for new answers, individuals tend to search, not for the best answer, but for one which is good enough. In March and Simon's terminology people satisfice rather than optimize.

One of the important ways in which standards persist is by relying on generalized skills which are learnt by people or built into machines and which can be applied to a wide variety of situations. Typing, drilling holes, cutting metal and a charming manner are examples of generalized skills. They have the advantage that they are robust; they do not depend on specific people or specific machines. People and machines with generalized skills are generally widely available. As a consequence, standards do not need to be changed because of changes in personnel.

Organizations systematically simplify the information they use in order to allow standards to be applied easily. For example, organizations filter raw data into summarized information which is then used to make decisions. Also, workers tend to report progress which is steadier and consistently closer to their managers' expectations than is justified by actual performance. So all the interesting blips and exceptions of the real world are ignored and decisions are made on the basis of deceptively smooth records of reality, which facilitates the use of standards.

In a similar way, individuals tend as far as possible to make decisions one at a time, sequentially, and thus ignore the rich interactions between the resulting actions. So managers work with models which greatly simplify the complexity of the real world. Each standard is regarded as being independent and is used without explicit consideration of its effects on others. This simplification enables organizations to decide and to act. The real world is too complex to comprehend and so we trade the certainty of established but inevitably somewhat inappropriate standards against the great costs of developing unique but probably better answers.

We find in successful organizations a robust and stable set of standards guiding the basic, direct work. These standards tend to use interchangeable parts, generalizable skills and simple materials of known properties, and to work with plans that incorporate buffers and safety margins. In addition, special units are created for those parts of the work which face uncertainty and need time to make new decisions. These units include research and development, planning and estimating departments, and senior management. It is an important part of their work to protect the basic operating core of their firm from uncertainty and so enable it to concentrate on achieving higher productivity and quality.

Standards in construction projects

There are few opportunities to develop project specific standards except on very large construction projects. In any case, as we now know, individuals persist in using established standards and there is rarely sufficient time or resources to change these in the context of an individual project. Instead, managers need to form their project organizations from selected firms which bring with them appropriate standards. This is important because standards provide many potential benefits for construction project managers.

Both public and organization standards reduce the need for project specific information to be produced and communicated. The savings in time and resources are enormous. The costs of construction projects that use well established standards at every stage of their design, manufacture and construction are significantly lower than those of equivalent projects undertaken without the benefit of standards. The ratio of total costs are likely to be of the order of 1 : 2 or 3 or even more for projects that use very new and original methods. Also, a standard project will be completed much faster than an equivalent non-standard one. The benefits of using standards arise at every stage of the process.

A standard design reduces the need for project specific design work to just deciding the position of the new construction on the site and designing the work in the ground. When all the superstructure is standard it is usually easy to obtain official approvals quickly. The exact materials and components required are predetermined and so can be ordered early. The programme of work can be based on direct experience of producing an identical product. Manufacturers can reuse their shop drawings and may even have a dedicated production line for the standard components. Construction on site begins some way down the learning curve and so is immediately more productive than the construction of a new non-standard design. Work on site will experience few problems arising from design details that do not work or components that do not fit properly. All these inevitable teething troubles, which come with any new design, will have been identified and eliminated on previous projects. Waste from mistakes and the need to redo work are all eliminated or at least greatly reduced. As a consequence of the greatly reduced uncertainty, the management of the whole project is relatively easy. There is every incentive for managers to plan for fast accurate work so that, throughout their projects, resources are tied up for the minimum length of time. The great benefits of standards come from the accumulated effects of all these savings.

Standards make it sensible to invest in work-study in order to find the most efficient ways of working. They make it sensible to invest in training so that workers know the most efficient methods. They make it sensible to invest in dedicated plant and equipment so that manual work is reduced. They make it sensible to invest in research and development to find more efficient answers. In other words, the wide use of standards provides a basis for construction to behave like other manufacturing industries and invest in the quality of its products and the productivity of its workforce.

There is of course a legitimate concern that a wide use of standards will result in dull, repetitive environments lacking necessary variety and interest. The modern approach to standards avoids this trap. It standardizes small parts and subcomponents, it standardizes procedures so that workers are faced with familiar tasks, and it makes use of flexible machines and computers which control production in real time to mass-produce a variety of products. These methods have all been brought together in what the Japanese call *just-in-time* production. Although just-in-time techniques are still very much in an experimental stage in construction, they are much more developed in other industries. Just-in-time provides many important lessons for construction in the effective use of modern standards.

Just-in-time

Before the emergence of just-in-time production philosophies, engineers concentrated directly on maximizing the output of capital equipment and its attendant labour. The obvious way to achieve this is to organize work to provide long runs of identical products. The way to do that is to minimize variety, store orders for each separate product until sufficient for an economic run are assembled, and create buffer stocks of partly finished products between each separate process. The results are high utilization of capital equipment but a slow response to orders and little variety in products. That is, all the things that give standards a bad name. Figure 4.1 illustrates a typical factory layout using traditional methods of organization. The figure makes it obvious that, although the capital equipment involved in the direct production processes may well be utilized to a high level, there is considerable capital tied up in storage space, the buffer stocks held there and the labour and equipment needed to move and keep track of all the partially finished products.

Just-in-time seeks not to maximize capital utilization, but to minimize the throughput time of each product. Its approach is to identify slack resources or waste and eliminate them. The buffer stocks of partially finished products between the separate processes shown in Figure 4.1 are a slack resource. They are also a source of waste because parts get damaged or mislaid as they wait for the next stage in the production process. Just-in-time therefore eliminated buffer stocks. This typically identified a new problem. The processing plant and equipment now had to deal not with long runs of identical products carefully assembled in the buffer stocks, but with a stream of different products. Traditional processing plant takes a long time to re-tool for each different product. Therefore it was necessary to design new plant which could be re-tooled quickly. Once this was in place, it could be seen that a great deal of time was spent in transporting partially finished products between the separate processes. This was solved by classifying products on the basis of the sequence of processes required to manufacture them. Then separate manufacturing lines each designed to produce one of these categories of products were created by bringing all the related plant close together in the correct sequence. Figure 4.2 illustrates a production line capable of producing the product used as the basis of Figure 4.1. The great simplicity is immediately obvious. A just-in-time factory has several production lines. This may well require additional plant and equipment to ensure that each line is fully self-sufficient. Each line is staffed by a group of workers each trained to operate several adjacent machines in the line, to monitor them for wear, to undertake preventative maintenance on them and to re-tool them for different products. Thus there are more machines than workers. Machines run only when they are needed, but the workers are each

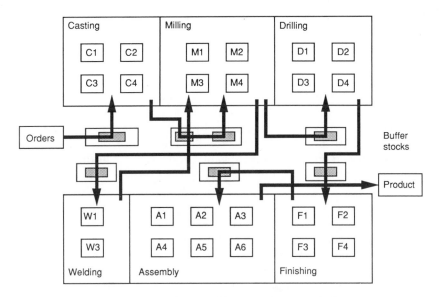

Figure 4.1   *Traditional factory layout with route of one product*

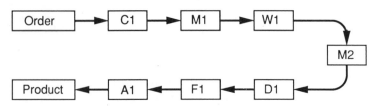

Figure 4.2   *Just-in-time production line*

supplied with a steady stream of work. Parts of products which do not fit conveniently into the pattern of work on any of the production lines are subcontracted out to other firms. Products which do not fit any of the production patterns are redesigned or simply no longer manufactured.

The common result is that production times for any one product are reduced from weeks to hours. Orders can be dealt with immediately, so that customers are not held up and, because of the fast re-tooling capability, it is feasible to provide a greater variety of products. Total costs are also reduced because the capital costs of extra machines is more than offset by a greater throughput per worker and the savings in capital previously tied up in buffer stocks and storage space.

Having created a highly geared production system, waste or re-working because of defective products becomes very disruptive. It interrupts the flow of products down each production line. Therefore the next step is to concentrate on achieving a consistently high standard of work. Management does this by placing great emphasis on the need to get products *right-first-time*. Every worker is given direct responsibility for the standard of his work. They inspect their own work and do not pass it on to the next stage in the production process until it is complete and accurate. It is also common in measuring workers' performance to inversely relate production to levels of scrap, faulty work and machine breakdown in order to reinforce the importance of all aspects of quality. The common results are more reliable products and a further reduction in costs.

Just-in-time does not, however, stand still. As each problem is solved, the search begins for the next bottleneck or source of waste or inefficiency. The continual aim is to find permanent solutions to problems so that they do not recur. This requires the products, as well as the process, to be questioned and if necessary redesigned to be easier to manufacture. The whole workforce is encouraged to search for better ways of working and improvements to their products. This philosophy may appear to be the antithesis of standardization. It is important, therefore, in drawing out the lessons for the construction industry, to identify which parts of the whole product and process system are standardized and which are flexible.

The overall production process, that is the technology and sequence of the required actions, is standardized. There are in fact usually a number of production lines in any one factory, each of which provides a different sequence of processes. However, each product must fit into one or other of these standardized production lines. The products emerging from each line will vary, but the technology and sequence of actions needed to produce them are standard. The variations in products come from differences in the shape or colour of parts, the number of parts, and often from differences in bought-in components. The variety, however, must be contained within one consistent production method and sequence. This commonly requires careful attention to the design of robust standardized connections between the separate parts. Thus a modern motor car production line produces a great variety of models but uses a single sequence of consistent assembly techniques. Differences in the mix of models required are programmed into the supply to the production line of different components and subassemblies. So the production line is supplied with the parts it needs to create the required variety of models in the right sequence. Each variant of any one component or subassembly is fixed in the same standard manner. Hence technology, sequence of production and the form of connection details are all consistent or standard but the products vary considerably in almost every respect except the reliability and speed with which they are produced.

These, then, are the kind of standards which the construction industry should seek to adopt. By standarizing production engineering, the whole industry will have a basis for improving its productivity, reliability, speed and economy. It will have a focus for research and development. All this can be achieved without denying customers and designers the variety of products and range of quality they legitimately demand.

Hutchins (1988), however, provides a powerful description of the care and attention needed from everyone involved before these benefits can be achieved. For Hutchins, just-in-time is as much an attitude of mind as a set of production techniques. It requires deep and sustained commitment to achieving ever better performance, by all levels of management and all workers. When a problem arises, it should always be taken seriously and regarded as an opportunity of finding a permanent improvement. The whole team responsible for the work where the problem has arisen should focus their attention on searching for a long term answer. Nothing should be left unplanned and every deviation from the plan should be regarded as a problem worthy of study. Problems should be tackled immediately, when and where they occur. In this way the source and causes of each problem are likely to be identified accurately. Any temptation to blame individual workers for problems should be resisted. It is management's responsibility to remove the causes of problems and everyone's responsibility to find a permanent solution.

Workers need to be trained in statistical control techniques so that they can analyse and improve their own work. They should be encouraged to discuss their work by being provided with comfortable and stimulating social areas. These need to be attractive places with good lighting and soft furnishings. They can usefully have charts and diagrams around the walls illustrating features of the workers' performance and important aspects of their work. Managers should be active in encouraging workers to search for a steady stream of well thought-out innovations to improve both the product and the process. Workers should be encouraged to maintain a smart appearance, to wear appropriate clothes, to keep their workplace clean and free of rubbish and waste material, and generally to maintain their environment in a condition which encourages productivity and quality. They should be encouraged to set ever tougher targets for themselves, to question everything about their work with a view to finding better answers. The aim always needs to be better control and greater certainty in performance. All too often managers react to problems by increasing their efforts to estimate the costs or times of poorly managed work or by adding extra inspectors or controllers. This merely institutionalizes problems, it does nothing to remove them. Just-in-time is about finding the real causes of problems by analysing them in detail one at a time and finding irreversible answers. The aim is to get work right-first-time and so achieve *zero defects*.

All of this indicates the kind of commitment needed from construction project managers in order to exploit the power of excellent standards. When this is done well, the results, as Hutchins (1988) describes, are remarkable improvements in productivity, quality, market-share and profitability. We shall consider more of the implications of just-in-time and its dependence on standards in Chapter 7, when we review the Japanese approach to construction project management.

5 *Management in construction*

We have now mapped out the key dimensions of the construction project manager's task. We considered first the key factors of the work which must be managed and then the important characteristics of the people who do the work or who influence its management in some other way. We then looked at the systems and standards that bring people and work together in various ways. Now, before we are ready to consider current practice in construction project management, we must identify the management devices used to form construction project organizations.

We recognized in Chapter 1 that construction work is undertaken by differentiated teams and in Chapter 3 we learnt that effective systems provide sufficient coordination to balance the level of differentiation. Our concern in this chapter is to identify the various ways in which coordination is provided. Galbraith (1973) provides a comprehensive scheme which has stood the test of time. He identifies five coordination devices, implies a sixth and describes two further design strategies which serve to reduce the need for coordination. Figure 5.1

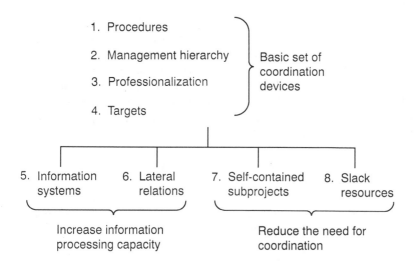

Figure 5.1   *Coordination devices*

illustrates his complete scheme. It is based on the idea that organizations exist to process information. Teams need information to tell them what work they should do. In so far as they do not bring the necessary information with them, the project organization must provide it. Coordination, then, consists of ensuring that teams have sufficient information to know what work to do. This is provided by some combination of six coordination devices.

Procedures

Procedures are standards; they specify the actions necessary when specified work-related situations occur. In so far as project situations can be anticipated and the appropriate actions predetermined, procedures provide an effective way of achieving a coordinated pattern of work.

The work of the Coordinating Committee for Project Information (1987) in the UK provides a good example of how procedures provide coordination. The Committee was sponsored jointly by the Association of Consulting Engineers, representing structural engineers and building service engineers, the Building Employers Confederation, representing general contractors and specialist contractors, the Royal Institute of British Architects, representing architects, and the Royal Institution of Chartered Surveyors, representing building surveyors and quantity surveyors. Its task was to produce and publish a set of procedures which, if followed, would ensure the coordination of the working drawings, specifications and bills of quantities produced by separate, independent professionals for individual building projects. The Committee published separate sets of procedures for drawings, specifications and bills of quantities in 1987. Each procedure laid down rules governing the content and arrangement of project information and provided for cross-references between separate documents to facilitate searches for specific pieces of information. At the same time the Committee published a classification scheme to provide a consistent structure and to establish the cross-references. The classification scheme is based on differences in technology and so identifies categories of building work. The Committee also published a guide to the use of the procedures. The complete set of procedures provides comprehensive general guidance on the production of building project information. However, it inevitably leaves many decisions of detail to individual project organizations.

The code of procedure for production drawings provides many examples. The general procedure identifies six techniques for coordinating service installation drawings: copy-negatives, overlay checking, overlay draughting, combined services drawings, detailed drawings, and photo-drawings. The building services coordination for any one project will make use of one or perhaps two of these techniques. They may be applied only in particularly complex situations such as plant rooms and service ducts or, if the services are complex throughout, they may be applied to complete buildings. These decisions must be made by the responsible managers and communicated to everyone involved in producing and checking the production drawings.

The code of procedure also describes four types of drawing arrangement: office of origin, type of information, parts of buildings and location. The choice of arrangement, according to the code, depends on the size, complexity and variability of the end product. Further project decisions, on which the code provides general guidance, are the sizes of the sheets of paper to be used, the choice of scale for the various categories of drawings, and the method of drawing, numbering and titling. These are all matters on which project managers need to make decisions so that one consistent coordinated approach is used throughout a project irrespective of which team produces individual production drawings.

Procedures provide coordination by predetermining decisions. Given the discretion to make their own choices, separate teams will decide, often arbitrarily, on different approaches. The result is extra work in: learning several different approaches; reconciling information from different sources which is inconsistent; searching for information when it is unclear whether it does or does not yet exist; and generally wasting time dealing with information, rather than being able to concentrate on designing, manufacturing or constructing the end product. Procedures, however, can go only so far; they deal with situations which can be anticipated and which recur sufficiently frequently to justify producing and learning a predetermined answer. Other situations need other coordination devices.

Management hierarchy

The second coordination device is to create management roles. Managers are responsible for the work of those below them in a management hierarchy. Figure 5.2 illustrates a simple management hierarchy comprising seven basic work teams plus two levels of management. As problems arise which a basic work team lacks the information to resolve, they refer it to the manager immediately above them in the hierarchy. Provided that he is competent to deal with the problem, he makes a decision taking account of its effects on other teams. However, if the problem falls outside of his competence, he refers it to his manager for decision and so on until a level in the hierarchy is reached where a manager has responsibility over all the teams involved in the particular problem. Thus, using Figure 5.2 to illustrate the operation of management hierarchies, a problem in shop drawings caused by detail design can be resolved by the design manager. However, a problem in construction caused by detail design cannot be resolved by the construction manager so he must refer it to the project manager. He is competent to make a decision which takes account of design and construction interests. The decision is communicated to the design manager and the construction manager and they in turn inform detail design and construction and any other of their teams affected by the project manager's decision. Managers delegate responsibility for specified parts of their work to their subordinates. However the managers also remain responsible. Thus in Figure 5.2 the project manager is responsible for the work of all seven basic work teams and of the two managers. To discharge their own responsibilities, managers must either trust their subordinates or check their work. In making this choice they need to bear in mind that the more they check the work, the less the subordinate will feel responsible for it. Creating responsible subordinates requires trust not checking. The effective way to ensure that subordinates will act responsibly is for their managers to agree with them the required end products of their work. It is then best if they are free to decide how they will work, within whatever constraints are necessary to allow the rest of the project organization to work effectively. Then manager and subordinate should discuss at regular intervals the actual progress, any problems which have arisen, possible answers and plans for the next stage of the work. These discussions should take place daily at the level of basic work and less frequently at higher levels of the hierarchy.

Managers have authority over their subordinates. That is, an implicit agreement exists that subordinates, within limits identified as legitimate, will do what their managers instruct them to do. It is also part of this implicit agreement that organizations will provide subordinates with specified rewards for as long as they continue to accept legitimate authority. It is often suggested that authority has several possible sources, including expert knowledge, formal position or

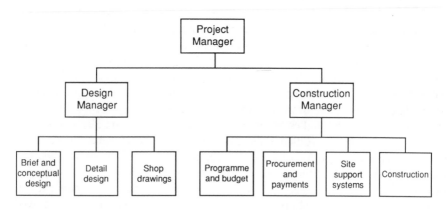

Figure 5.2 *Management hierarchy*

charisma. It seems more likely that authority depends on the ability to give or withhold rewards. Certainly, within construction projects, authority depends on managers' control over payments to the teams under them. Without that they would, in the final analysis, have no effective power to persuade teams to undertake work on their projects.

The structure of management hierarchies is shaped by the tasks to be undertaken. The overall structure is defined in terms of the number of levels of management and the size of the teams or, as this second dimension is usually referred to, the managers' *span of control*. For any given task, the two dimensions, in theory, have a simple relationship. Given a project comprising the work of 100 teams, a span of control of ten will produce three levels of management (1, 10, 100). However, a span of control of six would require one extra level of management (1, 3, 17, 100) and at least ten additional managers. Similarly, the complexity of projects influences the dimensions of the management hierarchies responsible for it. With a span of control of six, three projects of different degrees of complexity will have management hierarchies of (1, 2, 10), (1, 3, 17, 100) and (1, 5, 29, 167, 1000). Although the span of control is equal, or as near equal to six as the numbers involved will allow, the ratio of managers to teams in the three cases is 1 : 3.3, 1 : 4.8 and 1 : 5.0. In practice, as management hierarchies grow larger the spans of control tend to increase. The effect is that the number of levels in the hierarchy increases rather more slowly than the growth in complexity theoretically implies. The reason is almost certainly that, faced with growth, most managers prefer slightly bigger teams to creating an extra level of management with its attendant increase in bureaucracy and formality.

Mintzberg (1979) reports an interesting series of laboratory experiments designed to compare the performance of tall and flat management hierarchies. The tall hierarchy had four levels and a span of control of two while the flat hierarchy had one manager controlling the work of 14 individuals. The hierarchies, shown in Figure 5.3, were given identical marketing and production information and required to produce a business plan which was agreed throughout the organization. There was no significant difference in the time taken to complete the task. However, the working methods were different. The greater number of levels in the tall hierarchy interrupted the vertical flow of information frequently. On the other hand, the flat hierarchy needed more time for discussion and consultation. The greater time for information to pass through more levels of a tall hierarchy was offset by time taken up in resolving differences and coordinating the work of more subordinates. However, the tall hierarchy consistently produced better results. This came about because the tall hierarchy created greater formality, so that subordinates were more careful about the way they collected information to be passed up to their managers. Also, managers had more time for analysis and the middle managers in particular provided the means for repeated evaluations of decisions. In addition, the narrow span of control permitted a much more orderly decision and communication process than was evident in the flat hierarchy. Freed from the burdens of having many subordinates, managers had time to develop a better understanding of the problems involved in creating a business plan. The effect of managers being swamped by large spans of control and so having insufficient time for analysis and decision-making has been confirmed in studies of real management hierarchies.

The shape of management hierarchies also influences the behaviour of those at the bottom level undertaking basic work. A tall hierarchy and small spans of control engender a feeling of security because there is always a manager available to consult. A flat hierarchy and wide spans of control encourage workers to make their own decisions, to take risks, to be creative, to make mistakes; in short, to develop their own abilities and confidence or to fail.

Managers need to take into account the nature of the work they supervise in selecting the appropriate span of control or, in other words, the size of their teams. The more interdependent the work of subordinates and the greater their need for direct supervision, the smaller the appropriate span of control. This means that competent, experienced teams operating under pooled interdependency can be relatively large, but teams who are learning a new task within a structure dominated by reciprocal interdependencies, in other words the common construction industry situation, need to be relatively small. These factors are unlikely to remain consistent throughout all levels of a management hierarchy. We might envisage a large construction project in which the work of

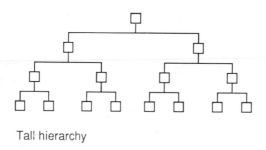

Tall hierarchy

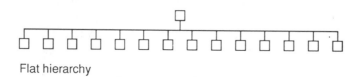

Flat hierarchy

Figure 5.3   *Tall* versus *flat management hierarchies*

top management is divided on a functional basis of design, manufacture, construction and commission. Their work is reciprocally interdependent and the top team is small. At the next level each manager is responsible for one of 20 independent buildings and the surrounding landscaping and services. The work is subject only to pooled interdependency and the teams can be large. At the basic working level the teams are inexperienced in the particular work required by the project. Also, the work at this level is sequentially interdependent and so the teams are relatively small. The overall result is a management hierarchy which is made up of large teams in the middle and smaller ones at the top and bottom.

Woodward (1965) in a major and important study of industrial organizations found that the shape of management hierarchies in successful firms depends on the nature of their work. She identified three distinct categories of work. The following descriptions of these categories bring out their essential character in order to show their effect on appropriate management hierarchies.

Unit production

Firms who manufacture individual items or prototypes, where the work is non-standard, rely on competent craftsmen to undertake the basic work. First-line managers work closely with them in small teams. These first-line managers tend to have high-technical competence based on long practical experience. The non-standard work makes it more economical to use flexible craftsmen and general machinery rather than invest in specialized machines which may be rendered obsolete by changing patterns of customers' orders. The flow of work through the manufacturing process tends to be slow and to use buffer-stocks of materials and partially finished products to create a steady supply of work.

Since most control is exercised by the first-line managers, there is little scope for formal planning or specialized middle managers. Therefore there are relatively few managers and there are wide spans of control in the middle of the management hierarchy. However, at the top, the need to deal with individual customers in order to secure a steady stream of orders leaves top managers with little time for supervision. Consequently, the span of control at the top of unit production firms tends to be narrow.

Woodward found little differentiation among the managers. They all needed to be able to deal with customers and craftsmen, and to understand product design and production technology sufficiently to match customers' demands to crafts-men's capabilities. Coordination arises out of frequent direct personal contacts in solving day-to-day problems and crises. Unit production clearly has many of the characteristics of small scale, one-off, traditional construction.

Mass production

Firms who manufacture standard products use mass production technology. The basic work is coordinated by detailed procedures. It is subdivided into small routine tasks which can be undertaken by unskilled, and therefore easily replaceable, workers. Such work requires little direct supervision and spans of control for first-line managers are very wide.

Middle management is widely differentiated, with design and development, production and sales people having little or no direct contact. Communication is largely of a formal, written nature. The links between separate departments take the form of sequential interdependencies which are substantially decoupled by differences in the timing of their work and the creation of large buffer stocks of completed products. Thus design and development takes place relatively independently of production and sales. When a new product is to be introduced, it is usual for a taskforce comprising staff from both development and production to plan its introduction. Once that is successfully achieved, production continues with the production staff actively discouraging any interference from design and development or sales people. The salesforce works independently, concentrating on understanding the marketplace and seeking to sell whatever is produced. Production itself, at middle management levels, is obsessed with control. The direct line management is supported by many specialists. It is the specialists' job to plan the mass-production system. They search for faster methods of production, smoother flows of components and products and more productive machines, and generally seek to fine-tune their mass-production 'machine'. As we saw in Chapter 4, at its most highly developed, mass production is becoming more flexible by standardizing the production processes in a manner which allows the products themselves to vary. The development of just-in-time technologies is primarily the work of the specialists. Their approach is based on questioning every aspect of work. It leads to numerous taskforces which cut across the rigid structures of design, development and production. Consequently, as the technology changes the organization has to change to accommodate new tasks and new ways of working.

In the classical mass production organization, middle management is highly differentiated with each separate department adopting a management hierarchy best suited to its particular work. Thus design and development have small spans of control because of the close interdependence of their work. On the other hand a geographically based sales force, with only pooled interdependencies, has wide spans of control. In efficient firms, each department finds a structure that matches its own specific tasks.

Woodward found that top management in mass production is characterized by spans of control in the five to seven range. They took a long range, strategic view of their firm, in sharp contrast to the day-to-day concerns on the production floor. Consideration of the introduction of new products typically spans years and represent major decisions in the life of mass production firms. New products frequently require massive capital investment in plant, equipment, design, development and training. These are top level decisions which vitally affect the overall health of the firm. They are taken in boardrooms which are often organizationally very remote from the drawing-offices, production lines and showrooms which have to implement the strategic decisions.

The overall pattern of management hierarchies in mass-production firms is shaped by small spans of control at the top, variable spans in the middle and wide spans at the base. Because mass production provides economies of scale in production, successful firms are large and classically have many levels of management. However, modern information technology is replacing middle managers with computerized information systems and so the number of levels is tending to reduce. Peters and Waterman (1982) found fewer than average numbers of levels in the companies they regarded as excellent. They instance Toyota which has five levels between the Chairman and first-level managers, while Ford, for example, has at least fifteen. This is one of the factors that enable Toyota to produce 40 motor cars per employee per year, while the big US motor car firms produce about 10 per employee.

One of the main factors causing change in classical mass production is that it is riddled with hostility and distrust. Woodward identified three major points of conflict: between the demands of rigidly standardized and tightly controlled production work and workers' need for social interaction; between the short term focus of the lower levels of management and the long term focus of top management; and between the middle managers directly involved in production, who are concerned with short term efficiency and so need consistency and long uninterrupted runs, and the specialists, who are seeking for improvements to production methods. As a result mass production in, for example, the motor car industry historically had awful industrial relations. The newer production and management technologies are gradually reducing the causes of conflict and creating more satisfactory work situations.

Turning now to construction, the essential approach of classical mass-production firms is to be found in those parts of the industry producing standard products. An obvious example is firms specializing in mass housing. They produce standardized products using semi-skilled workers trained to undertake a narrow range of carefully predetermined tasks. They require few direct managers once the roads, underground services and foundations are in place. Consequently, spans of control are wide in the production divisions. The design and development of new house types is undertaken remote from the production division. Indeed, Leopold and Bishop (1983) found that in many cases experienced house builders subcontracted the design of new house types to consultants. Similarly, sales is highly differentiated from production and has its own distinctive management hierarchy. Top management is concerned with strategic issues, including demographic changes, interest rates, inflation levels, changing lifestyles, political battles to obtain more land for development, and many other issues remote from the day-to-day production work. The industrial relations conflicts that characterize other mass-production industries have largely been avoided in construction. This is mainly due to the geographically fragmented and relatively slow sequential production process, which prevents any concentration of large numbers of workers. There is certainly a latent potential for conflict. Leopold and Bishop (1983) were particularly interested in the work of architects in mass housing. This is seen as least satisfying where mass-production philosophies are most rigorously applied. In the preliminary design stages the architect's role is to produce, at extremely short notice, a layout for a potential site which incorporates the maximum number of specified standard houses chosen primarily to maximize sales potential. In the detail design stages, the architect's role is dictated by site management and the sales force. They may decide to use an alternative material because it will save money or improve sales potential. Often the change is dictated by material supply problems or the need to take advantage of an opportunity of obtaining a specially low price. The architect's role is merely to produce a new detail drawing, incorporating the new material. Leopold and Bishop found little scope for traditional architectural values, and commercial criteria dominated architectural issues once the standard house designs were established. As in manufacturing industry, this bias is changing and customers are demanding more variety in new houses. We can expect to see the same kind of developments in mass housing as are evident in mass production elsewhere. These changes will in turn alter the management hierarchies which are appropriate in this sector of the construction industry in much the same ways as they have in manufacturing industry.

Process production

Firms who use continuous automated production have substantially replaced the need for a basic workforce by using machines. A modern oil refinery for example runs itself, and its tiny operating workforce merely monitors production. Process production firms comprise highly educated and trained specialists who design the technical system and then maintain it.

At the base of the management hierarchy are small teams of skilled workers who maintain the plant. In the middle are small specialized teams who research, develop and design new products and new processing plants. Direct line, middle managers responsible for production are indistinguishable from the specialists in terms of their knowledge and experience; in fact, it is common for them to interchange jobs regularly. Sales is a highly sophisticated marketing exercise designed to ensure that products, produced in a continuous stream, are sold as consistently as they are produced.

Top management in process production tends to have wide spans of control, consisting of broadly based committees. The middle level managers are competent to make many key decisions. Consequently, top management can supervise relatively large numbers of people. This is essentially achieved by a management committee authorizing decisions made lower down.

The overall picture is of a management hierarchy in which the production system is fully automated and completely regulated. Since machines do not have the same social needs as people, the conflicts of mass production do not arise. Instead, the management hierarchy, which sits on top of the automated production process, relies on small teams and direct contact between experts to provide coordination.

The robots and automated controls on which process production depends are still in an experimental or at best a development stage in the construction industry. It is nevertheless helpful to have models of management hierarchies from other industries as a guide to likely developments in construction. Figure 5.4 illustrates the three idealized types of management hierarchy found by Woodward. They provide a framework for us to consider the other four coordination devices.

Professionalization

When a management hierarchy becomes overloaded with demands for information, it is sensible to consider the possibility of allowing subordinates to have more authority to make their own decisions. It is safer to do this if the subordinates are professionals, that is, if they have been educated and trained to apply a specific body of established knowledge and techniques to practical problems. Simon (1972) believes that all professional practice is concerned with the process of changing existing situations into designed and preferred ones. Schon (1983), in his brilliant analysis of professional practice, identifies two distinct types of activity. The first he calls *technical rationality*. That is instrumental problem solving made rigorous by the application of scientific theory and technique. It is the application of general principles to specific problems. So professionals have two primary bases for their work: the field of knowledge the profession commands and the techniques of production or application of knowledge over which the profession claims mastery. Professionals also learn diagnosis, that is, fitting knowledge and techniques to specific

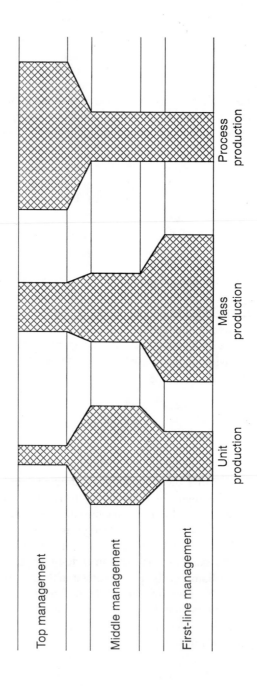

Figure 5.4   *Spans of control in management hierarchies*

problems. Professional problems are not unique; there are sufficient uniformities in problems and in the devices for solving them to enable useful categories of problems to be identified. Professionals learn these categories of problems and the associated standardized answers through education and training.

Throughout the world, the development of professions is closely associated with the universities. Researchers in universities provide the basic and applied science from which techniques for diagnosing and solving the problems of practice are derived. Practitioners provide researchers with problems for study and with the criteria for testing the utility of the research results. The universities teach new entrants to the professions the basic science followed by the applied science. The professional skills of applying this knowledge to practical problems may be learnt at university simultaneously with the applied science component, or they may come later in professional training. This varies from profession to profession and depends on the availability of live problems or the ease of simulating the realities that the professional will face in practice.

The technical rationality model of professional practice regards it as a process of pigeon-holing problems. Each specific individual problem is put into a pigeon-hole which represents one of the standard categories of problems which the professional has learnt. The same set of standardized techniques is then applied to all the problems in any one pigeon-hole. This view allowed Mintzberg (1979) to liken employing professionals to buying and installing machines, in that both reduce the number of rules required in any organization. The rules are built into the machines and the organization pays for the rules in the price of the machines. A similar way of reducing the number of written rules is to employ professionals who have complex rules inculcated into them by education and training. They bring these into the organization and are expected to act on them without further reference to senior management.

This narrow view of professionalization encompasses a great variety of skilled activities. Importantly, from the viewpoint of construction project managers, it includes the work of craftsmen. Galbraith (1973) uses the work of construction craftsmen to illustrate the way in which professionalization provides information for organizations. He contrasts the centralized planning of mass production with construction craftwork. In mass-production, the characteristics of work processes which are planned in advance include: the location at which a task will be performed; the movement of tools, materials and workers to this workplace; the most efficient arrangement of the workplace; the particular movements to be performed in getting the task done; the schedules and time allocations for particular operations; and the inspection criteria for each operation. In construction, all these characteristics of the work process are governed by the craftsman in accordance with established craft standards. Thus craftsmen bring important information to the organizations in which they

work, as do technically rational professionals, and thus are themselves important coordination devices.

There is, however, another kind of professional work. This was recognized by
both Mintzberg (1979) and Schon (1983). Mintzberg described it as work in
innovative organizations or 'adhocracies'. These are organizations set up to
provide sophisticated innovation which requires professionals not to apply their
standardized answers, but to treat existing knowledge and skills as bases on
which to build new answers. Schon describes the second type of professional
practice as reflection-in-action. It recognizes that some professionals are faced
not with neat categories of problems, but with messes. The professional who
reflects-in-action is skilled at reducing messes to manageable problems. He
makes sense of uncertainty, instability, uniqueness and value conflicts, and then
defines the problems. This provides a basis for choosing among competing
professional paradigms in order to find an appropriate answer. This second type
of professional practice emerges from a long process of taking actions and
thinking about these patterns of actions and their consequences. It is developing
an instinct for what works and what does not. Every experienced professional
can recognize situations, for example peculiarities of a certain kind of building
site or irregularities of materials or structures, for which he cannot give a
reasonably accurate or complete description but which provide a reliable guide
to action. He makes judgements of quality for which he cannot state adequate
criteria, and he displays skills for which he cannot state the rules and
procedures. As professionals experience many variations of problems, they
develop repertoires of expectations, images and techniques. These come from
thinking about cases. In effect, the professional reflecting-in-action has become
a researcher in the context of his own practice. He does not depend on the
categories of established theory and technique, but constructs new implicit
theories. He does not separate means and ends but deliberates about them
interactively as he considers a problematic situation. He will try something to
see if it has the expected results. If it does not, this new knowledge will aid the
selection of the next trial-in-action. He does not separate thinking from doing;
his implementation is built into his inquiry. As they reflect-in-action, professionals build and store deep in their memory many complex patterns of problems
and answers. Faced with a new problem, they play through their repertoire of
patterns to find those which are triggered by the characteristics of the problem
situation. The patterns that come to the surface of consciousness become the
basis for action. The process of pattern matching takes place rapidly and
enables experienced professionals to act quickly and confidently. As we say,
they have seen it all before. Yet the results can be new and unique.

The mystery of how creativity emerges from learned patterns lies in the
complexity of the human brain and the complexity of professional problem-
solving work. Schon (1983) provides a fascinating description of an architect
designing. There are two characteristics of this process which are important.

First, design takes place as a series of small trial answers. The architect selects one part of the total problem to tackle first. He selects an answer and judges it. He may reject his first attempt and try another answer or, more likely, he will pursue the first answer by selecting a new part of the problem to tackle. His answer for this must respect the implications of his own earlier decisions. He continues in this way, tackling problems one at a time and building a complex tree of decisions. As he does so the answers talk back to him, suggesting new problems and new opportunities. These new and unexpected phenomena cause him to evaluate the actions that created them. As he evaluates his stream of answers in terms of established design practice, in terms of their conformity to or violation of earlier answers, and in terms of how interesting he finds the problems or potentials they have created, he builds his understanding of the nature of the problem and of possible answers. On this basis the experienced designer moves confidently back and forth between considering parts of the problem and reviewing the whole of his current answer. All the while he is drawing on his learned repertoire of patterns but using them creatively.

The second important characteristic of architects' design is that it gives rise to a high level language. The language about design uses rich analogies and metaphors to describe the architect's feel for the problem and potential answers. He will talk about characteristics of the site, and will describe parts of the building as moving from one location to another and in doing so creating spaces which themselves have particular characteristics. Schon's architect talks of 'a kind of garden' which is not literally a garden and 'the soft back areas' which are not literally soft. The metaphors of garden and soft are used to convey particular values. Schon identified 12 categories of words which make up the architect's language of designing. These include: the functions of buildings, components and external works; the characteristics of building sites; building elements; kinds of spaces and the relationships between spaces; the form of buildings and elements of buildings; structures and technologies; the scale of buildings and their elements in relation to each other and their surroundings; costs; the style or mode of buildings; historical precedents for styles or architectural modes; models used to represent the design solutions; and methods of explaining designs to customers and users. This language allows others, who understand it and are in sympathy with it, to be drawn into the design process. In this way good architects coordinate the work of all the designers involved with their projects. They describe the kind of building they want to create in evocative, ambiguous terms which encourage others to work in sympathy with the overall design intentions but allow them to be creative.

It is the existence of high level languages and the step-by-step nature of professional work which enables multidisciplinary teams to be creative. As Mintzberg (1979) explains, the building of new answers often requires the combination of different bodies of knowledge and skills. Rather than allowing the specialization of individual professionals to determine the boundaries of problems, problem-solving organizations must break through the language barriers. This allows an electrical engineer, for example, to spot an answer to a difficult architectural problem, simply because he does not know the conventional wisdom and sees the problem in a different way. To achieve this high level of creativity requires time to build a common language and time to allow the step-by-step process to be brought into the open. Multidisciplinary teams who have worked together on several projects begin to develop a kind of team instinct for the next move. Each member of the team can, to some extent, anticipate the actions of the others. Gradually a good team begins to achieve the effortless confidence of the individual professional. When it does so, of course, it is able to draw on a much richer set of patterns than can ever be available to any one individual. However, there is rarely sufficient time or resources to build a new and creative team within one construction project. This is why wise customers allow the key members of their project organizations to bring their own networks of professional collaborators with them.

The existence of two distinct types of professional practice, technical rationality and reflection-in-action, provides a great temptation for professionals. For many good practitioners, reflection-in-action is more interesting and rewarding than technical rationality. Yet many problems and many customers need a simple application of technical rationality. They do not need a new answer, they are best served by the application of a standard, established answer. The existence of the temptation to turn simple problems into complex ones, to search for new answers when a perfectly good one already exists, gives rise to the need for the next coordination device.

Targets

Targets or goals are a way of giving pre-eminence to customers' objectives. They focus the attention of individual teams on the needs of projects rather than allowing them to pursue their own professional interests. They also allow teams to work independently and their work to be coordinated provided they all meet their targets. This is difficult to achieve without some degree of waste. The waste arises because inevitably, if tough targets are set which demand consistently high levels of efficiency, some teams will fail to meet their targets. This is likely to have a disruptive effect on the work of other teams and also require additional management effort to re-establish a coordination framework. Therefore, to enable targets to achieve coordination, some degree of slack or waste must be allowed, so that all teams can achieve their targets. Slack targets may be justified if, for example, speed is important. They allow all teams to work simultaneously, safe in the knowledge that their work will fit with that of the other teams. Slack targets may also be justified if the extra cost of the waste they imply is less than that of the additional management efforts required to deal with failures to meet tight targets. So slack targets allow control to be achieved and enable teams to enjoy the feeling of success that comes from meeting targets. Having achieved control and a satisfied organization, management can use that as a basis for seeking more efficient performance without losing control. Indeed, that is how all efficient organizations are developed. By seeking better performance, year after year, organizations gradually become world-class.

Targets need to be comprehensive if they are to allow completely independent work. This view may be seen as being in conflict with the modern management principle of concentrating on a few key objectives. As Peters and Waterman (1982) said, 'more than two objectives is no objectives'. To resolve this apparent conflict we must distinguish between targets which are constraints and those which are to be the focus of an organization's efforts to improve its own performance. The second category of targets are what Peters and Waterman are referring to as objectives. Constraints are targets which must be met in order for the end product to function satisfactorily.

A structural engineer designing a structural steel frame may have a set of targets which include the nature of the loads transmitted onto the frame by other elements, the loads transmitted by the frame onto the foundations, a maximum size for columns and beams, a minimum column spacing, the maximum deflection in beams, a maximum cost, the timing of design, manufacture and construction processes, and the planned life of the frame. It may be decided, on a particular project, to concentrate on reducing the total weight of the structural frame by 10 per cent compared with normal current practice and halving the normal deflection in beams. These targets then become the objectives. The rest are constraints which must be met by the structural engineer's design. As long as the constraints are based on the engineer's own performance norms, he can concentrate most of his efforts on the two key objectives.

Targets as a whole, objectives and constraints, need to be comprehensive in order to allow teams to work independently. They need to deal with all technological and organizational interactions between teams. They also need to specify the key characteristics of each separate element, in so far as they affect the essential performance of the total product. This, for all practical purposes, is impossible for a new design. It would be necessary virtually to design, manufacture and construct the complete product in order to establish totally comprehensive and realistic targets. Consequently, the wide use of targets as a means of coordination is feasible only in respect of repeat or standard projects. In other situations an evolutionary, step-by-step approach to setting targets must be adopted. To some extent this reflects professionals' step-by-step methods, but it is more formally structured and predetermined.

Project cost control provides an important example which is of direct relevance to construction. Figure 5.5 illustrates the procedure recommended by Bennett

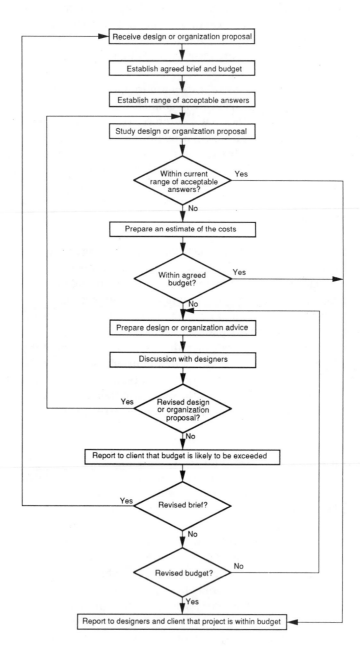

Figure 5.5   *Cost planning standard procedure (Source: Bennett et al., 1981)*

et al. (1981) for setting and achieving cost targets throughout construction projects. It assumes an agreed budget, which is subdivided into sufficient detail to enable design and management proposals to be reviewed one at a time, as they emerge. Bennett *et al.* also suggest a structure for cost data which reflects the professional's normal step-by-step approach to design. A section of this data structure is shown in Figure 5.6.

The overall approach to cost control using the procedure of Figure 5.5 and the data structure of Figure 5.6 is to set an overall budget based on tight, challenging targets for each separate element, plus a separately identified contingency element to provide a carefully considered degree of slack in the overall target. The allocation of the contingency element in response to cost problems is carefully managed to encourage designers and managers to search for better answers. At the same time it provides a safety net to cope with really difficult problems without damaging the overall quality of the end product. The same approach of setting tight individual targets for subelements plus a contingency to provide a degree of slack is recommended by Bennett *et al.* when main elements are subdivided to provide more detailed cost targets. The approach continues throughout the cost control process as finer and finer cost targets are set to whatever level of detail is sensible and appropriate for a particular project. By this means design and management decisions can be reviewed one at a time, so that separate professionals can work independently, yet the overall cost consequences of their decisions are coordinated in accordance with the budget agreed with the customer.

Similarly well developed methods exist to coordinate the planning of design, manufacture and construction programmes. They too provide a structure of an overall completion date, medium term targets and short term targets. Within each of these separate elements, experienced managers employ a combination of

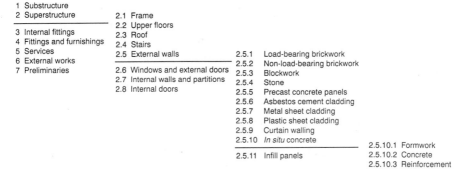

Figure 5.6 *Section of cost data structure (Source: Bennett* et al., *1981)*

tight individual targets and a degree of slack to provide a safety net. This improves their chances of achieving the overall agreed programme without having to deal with major crises.

Targets should be set in agreement with the teams responsible for achieving them. There is a great deal of evidence from practice that targets set in agreement with the team who will carry out the work are far more likely to be achieved than those which are imposed. This is true even when the targets are identical. The sense of commitment engendered when a team feels that it has set its own targets has a direct beneficial effect on subsequent performance. Indeed, teams tend to set tough targets for themselves when challenged by their managers armed with hard evidence from relevant practice that better performance is being achieved by competitors.

A good approach is for managers to explain the overall project objectives, show each team how their work fits into this framework and how the required performance relates to their own previous achievements, and then ask them to propose how they can meet the required targets. In the ensuing discussions, team and manager should be able to agree tough targets which the team is committed to achieving. Then, as work proceeds, good managers remind teams of their targets. They do this frequently, with enthusiasm and good humour. Finally, when targets are met, good managers provide immediate, tangible rewards so that their teams feel like winners.

Information systems

The basic coordination devices of procedures, management hierarchy, professionalization and targets are sufficient for many straightforward projects. However, where the teams undertaking the basic work of a project are likely to need more information and decisions than managers can sensibly provide, thought must be given to increasing the information processing capacity of the project organization. The first option available is the use of an information system; that is, the formal collection of information and its distribution to those in the project organization who need to know, in a convenient form and at an appropriate time.

It is obviously essential for information about the project objectives, design and management to be widely distributed. Every team needs to know what they are required to do in sufficient time to plan and organize their work. It is beneficial if they also know how their work fits into the project as a whole. The UK procedures for coordinated project information, described earlier in this chapter, provide a good illustration of the care and detail needed to ensure that essential project information is provided. Increasingly this is being achieved, at least on large construction projects, with the aid of computer-based three-dimensional models of the end product linked to expert systems and databases of specification and management information.

At present the use of computers in construction is too often fragmented. It is not uncommon to find that in one office a designer uses a powerful computer-aided design and drafting system to produce project drawings and then, in another office, a construction estimator or planner uses a digitizer to put the information from these same drawings back into another computer. The reasons are partly to do with incompatibilities between separate systems, but have even more to do with individual firms' concern to limit their own liabilities. Firms worry that if they provide basic data generated in their own computer systems, which may well contain errors, for another firm's computer system, over which they have no control, to work on directly, the results may well be unpredictable and expensive. They may be held liable for their own internal errors. Consequently, many designers refuse to make their basic computer data available to others. They insist on relying on the centuries old methods of exchanging design data and decisions in the form of paper drawings and reports. Managers need to devise ways of overcoming these worries, perhaps by providing some form of indemnity, to encourage the use of faster and more efficient automatic data exchange.

There are, however, substantial technical problems still to be solved in creating completely automatic distributed construction project information systems. The essential problem is the scale and complexity of large construction projects. The data to be handled and the multitude of relationships simply overwhelm CAD/CAE/CAM systems developed in other industries for product design, engineering and manufacture. Work has started in solving the immense challenges to theory and technology, most importantly at Stanford University's Centre for Integrated Facility Engineering. At Stanford a bold programme of work aims to integrate four emerging technologies. The first of these is artificial intelligence or expert systems, which will capture and make readily available the best current practice in design and management tasks. Second, Stanford will use both graphic and non-graphic databases to provide the most effective techniques for representing all the kinds of data which must be handled. Third, they aim to integrate process automation and robotics into project information systems so that intelligent automated machines are embedded in the design, manufacturing and construction processes. Fourth, Stanford will draw on modern information communication technology to coordinate information produced and used by distributed teams. All of this requires massive research and development investment. There is no doubt that, in the long run, answers will be found. Managers can look forward to the day when essential project information is automatically available. In the meantime they must decide how best to use the normal information processing methods, computer or manual, available to the teams who make up their project organizations to create a coordinated basic information system.

In addition, where the four basic coordination devices are likely to be overwhelmed, managers should consider using a control information system. The aim of such systems is to provide managers with an early warning of problems, so that they know where to concentrate their efforts. A control information system requires a clear definition of measurable targets, accurate and timely feedback which is compared with the targets, and action to alter the situation when a deviation is signalled. Each of these steps is difficult, which provides an important practical reason for managers to concentrate their efforts on a small number of absolutely key objectives.

Peters (1988) emphasizes the importance of identifying a few simple, measurable targets which are of central importance to the success of the organization. He suggests many targets which can usefully be considered by managers. Some of special relevance to construction project managers are: the number of real innovations introduced; the cost of remedying defective work; the customer's satisfaction; speed of getting back on programme after a delay; time spent by managers talking directly to basic teams; number of awards given for meeting targets; hours devoted to training; quality of welfare and safety provisions; time spent by managers each day on key objectives; number of first-line managers at meetings; number of revised design drawings issued; and proportion of rejected materials or components delivered to site. Peters further suggests that each team be assigned the task of developing rough, unconventional, paper-and-pencil measures of their own performance. This is a further refinement of the principle of establishing effective targets by joint agreement, which was described earlier in this chapter. The measures should be living things, subject to constant discussion, rather than infrequent formal review. They should be visible, shared with everyone and supported by training, so that everyone understands how they are produced and what they mean for the success of the project. Where the measures require clerks, accountants or computers to collect and process data, these should be a part of the teams and not form a remote, centralized department. Peters places considerable emphasis on the crucial importance of setting conservative financial objectives and providing all the support needed to ensure that only very occasionally will any manager fail to meet them. Finally, he places absolute importance on total integrity. 'A deal made on a milestone which is subsequently missed is grounds for dismissal.' Having agreed a key objective and been provided with the support needed to meet it, there are very, very few excuses for failure.

All of this means that managers must act to solve problems. When a key objective is in danger of being missed, this must be treated as a crisis and clear, effective action taken quickly to get the project back on target. A central information system which is not used to provide control is simply a waste of resources. Once it is discredited by being ignored, nobody will bother to provide the system with accurate or up-to-date information. It will become totally useless. On the other hand, a system which is taken seriously will increase managers' capacity to handle information and make decisions. It does this by moving routine information processing from managers to clerks, accountants and computers. So it releases managers to concentrate on important issues, that is, threats to planned progress.

The information processed by control information systems begins as raw data collected from the basic working level of the project. It is analysed and summarized as it passes up through the management hierarchy. The aim is to give each manager feedback relevant to his own responsibilities and key objectives expressed in an appropriate level of language. In general this means that project managers require data describing the pattern of medium-term trends. This will tend to be fuzzy information which recognizes risks and uncertainties. It will focus on the variability of teams' performances and levels of interference from the project's environment. At the level of first-line managers, information needs to relate directly to the short term performance of each manager's own team. It will tell them, for example, how their quality or safety record compares with targets and with the project norms, their chances of meeting the next programme milestone or budget, or their team's training record. At this level, information will be clear and certain. In similar ways, throughout project organizations, managers need to be provided with information relevant to their own direct responsibilities.

Managers should not rely solely on a formal information system. As we learnt in Chapter 3, the human nervous system has rapid warning channels as well as slower, formal information channels. Managers also need both. Good managers frequently walk the places where their teams are working. As they do so, they talk to the teams about their work. They check that teams know their targets, know how well they are doing, know how their work is measured, know who their managers are and generally are well informed and well motivated. Good managers also work with an open door, in the sense that they will talk to anyone who comes to their office with a problem. On large projects, the equivalent of a suggestions box or a minister's red box is useful. This is a place where anyone can put a note, a copy of a document, a comment, a suggestion or anything they think the manager ought to see. Such action does not remove the responsibility of subordinates to deal with the problems they find, but it does provide a random picture of a project or part of a project for the responsible manager. Managers should browse through their red boxes every day and use them to supplement formal information and to guide their own walking-the-job. In total, these separate, independent sources of information provide managers with a good chance of having a reliable basis for action.

Lateral relations

An alternative way of increasing a project organization's information processing capacity is to add additional management roles which provide lateral relations between teams at the same level in the management hierarchy. Figure 5.7 illustrates such a role added to the management hierarchy shown in Figure 5.2. The role illustrated provides coordination between the shop drawings team and the programme and budget team. In other words, when problems involving the two teams arise, they do not have to be referred up through the management hierarchy but can be resolved locally. There are a number of ways in which lateral relations can be provided. The arrangements appropriate for any particular project depend on the amount of information to be communicated and the number and difficulty of the problems likely to arise. Therefore the ways of providing lateral relations are considered in the sequence of increasing capacity to deal with communications and negotiations.

Direct contact

First, the team leaders can meet regularly to keep each other informed and to deal with any joint problems which have arisen. This coordination device is used widely in construction. Design team meetings are used on building projects to coordinate the work of architects, engineers and specialist contractors. On large processing plants it is now common for the specialist contractors working in each separate area of the construction site to meet each week to agree which team will have priority in access to workplaces during the following week. The construction management approach to construction projects relies on each specialist contractor coordinating their work technically and organizationally with that of the others. Much of this is achieved through direct lateral meetings between the responsible managers at the same level in the management hierarchy.

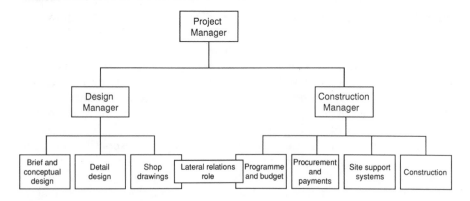

Figure 5.7 *Lateral relations role within the management hierarchy*

Direct meetings are generally effective in providing coordination. The managers directly involved know the relevant information and generally have a real interest in sharing it with others working at the same level in the same project. Equally, when problems arise, there is generally a common interest in finding good answers quickly. Indeed, when no formal arrangements are built into a project organization, informal lateral meetings spring up. This phenomenon is so common it has been given a name: the grapevine. Direct meetings do however take managers away from their direct team management responsibilities, which may suffer as a consequence. Also, it is by no means certain that they will find an answer which is in the best interests of the project as a whole. Even at low levels of interaction, the costs of relying on direct contact can easily exceed the benefits. Then it is worthwhile to consider the creation of separate roles to provide lateral relations.

Liaison roles

Liaison roles provide the simplest form of dedicated lateral relations roles. A common example occurs in the design stages of major processing plants. It is normal for the programme and budget teams to be represented in design teams. This is achieved by creating a liaison role occupied by one person who is a member of two teams. He is responsible for ensuring good communications between the two teams. He is expected to recognize problems early and persuade the two teams to confront the issues involved and find answers. The role carries no formal authority. However, because it sits in the interaction channel and often provides the role occupant with a unique and important body of knowledge, an energetic and talented person in a liaison role can acquire considerable influence. He can, by consistently representing the project objectives, come to be regarded as the unofficial spokesman of the customer or project manager. This is a difficult role to undertake. It requires someone who is trusted by both teams, who understands the technology of both teams and who can persuade others to address key issues without stepping in and actually making decisions. So it requires an individual who gets on well with people and who has a broad technical competence. It also requires an individual who can live with the fact that, if they do their job well, it is quite possible that nobody will notice this fact and the managers with direct-line responsibility will get the credit for the project's success. Liaison roles provide an excellent training for those who aspire to top management, and many of the outstanding leaders in the industry have spent a year or two, at a formative stage in their careers, in such positions.

Integrating managers

The third way of providing for lateral relations is to create an integrating management role. This is similar to a liaison role but with some authority over the decisions made by the teams it is responsible for coordinating. The role does not necessarily carry direct authority over the members of the teams, but has the right to be involved in their decisions. The role can work in one of three different ways which provide different degrees of authority. First, such roles can simply have the responsibility of authorizing or rejecting proposals put forward by the basic teams. Second, the integrating manager can take the initiative in proposing answers for the teams to consider and agree. Third, they can have authority to make decisions which the basic teams must accept. In practice all three approaches tend to result in similar behaviour most of the time. This is because good integrating managers work through discussion and agreement as far as possible. So, whichever pattern of formal authority is in existence, there will usually be real efforts to reach agreement on decisions. It is only when negotiation and persuasion have failed to produce a consensus that the differences between the three patterns of authority become significant.

The authority carried by an integrating manager is essentially that of the customer or project manager in respect of specific aspects of the project. The customer or project manager would carry out the role himself if he had the time. Creating a separate role relieves him of a mass of detailed work. Typically, integrating managers have authority over specific, defined aspects of the basic teams' work. These may include quality, programmes, budgets, productivity levels and resource usage. As the overall task of managing a project becomes more demanding, more aspects of coordination are delegated to more integrating managers. The allocation of authority should be considered carefully because it can serve to reinforce project objectives. Subjects made the responsibility of powerful integrating managers will be taken seriously.

The introduction of integrating managers raises problems of overlapping authorities. The basic team managers and integrating managers may disagree. They may disagree over possible answers to problems. More damagingly, they may disagree over the nature of a problem and therefore over who has authority. Integrating managers therefore need to be tough. They must stand between teams without being absorbed by them. They need to be problem-solvers rather than dogmatic personalities wedded to established answers. They need to be good communicators and good negotiators. They need, for example, to be able to present engineering problems in programme and budget terms and vice versa without distortion, so that different disciplines develop a common view of the questions to be answered. The aim must be to achieve coordination without eliminating the differences in attitudes, language and style that make for good performance in different types of basic work.

It is easy to see how an integrating manager's role can become overloaded. When this happens some authority must be given back to the teams. There are two ways of doing this. The first is short term, while the second goes to the heart of the way a project is organized. The short term approach to difficult coordination problems is to set up a taskforce.

Taskforces

A taskforce is a group of individuals drawn from several teams brought together to solve a difficult problem arising from the interactions between their teams. Taskforces may include full-time members or only people who share their time between team and taskforce. A taskforce works best when it is set up to solve one problem, is given a relatively short time to find an answer, and is disbanded when its work is done. The members should be sufficiently experienced in the subject of the problem to understand its causes and possible answers.

Taskforces are often used to solve difficult design problems. A good example is the external cladding of the Lloyds Building in London. The external cladding is part of the building's heating system. Warm air is circulated through triple-glazed window units. Taskforces of architects, structural engineers, services engineers, cladding specialists and heating specialists tackled various problems which arose out of the close interlocking of external cladding, structure and services. Similar short term, specific problems arise in many projects, and taskforces provide an effective way of finding answers which are likely to be accepted throughout a project organization.

Matrix structure

When the need for lateral relations exceeds the capacity of integrating managers aided by taskforces, the use of a matrix structure should be considered. This in effect combines the management hierarchy and the integrating managers into a single structure. Figure 5.8 illustrates a matrix structure for a multi-building project. The project manager has subdivided his organization into two overlapping categories of roles. The first is a functional division which provides managers who are responsible for design, manufacture and construction. In practice, other functional roles may be created to deal with quality, programme, budget, training, welfare, safety and other specialist functions. In each case the manager is responsible for establishing the overall strategy, maintaining professional standards, establishing professional procedures and generally ensuring coordination of all aspects of the particular function throughout all the separate buildings and external works which make up the complete project. The second main division of the project organization provides managers who are responsible for each subproject. Their role is to coordinate the work of the separate teams responsible for each separate function on their building or part of the external works. Both types of manager are equal. All are responsible directly to the project manager.

At first sight the matrix structure looks confusing. It breaks the well known principle of unity of command; that is, that a man should have one boss. It undoubtedly creates problems. However, before we discuss these, it is worth remembering that duality of command is much commoner than the classical management theorists recognized.

We all have two natural parents and most people are raised in the dual authority structure of the family. This goes very deep into human nature. Our brains, which are clearly divided into two halves which serve different functions, tend to divide the world into pairs of opposites. We speak of day and night, black and white, right and wrong, pleasure and pain, and many other dualities. As Townsend (1971) argues, two-man teams provide the most effective form of top management. It is extremely valuable to work with one other person who asks the awkward, obvious, crucial questions that we may otherwise have overlooked. Traditional forms of construction project organization can be regarded as having a dual authority structure. They require construction teams to be

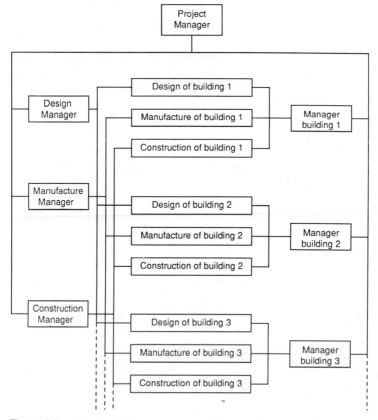

Figure 5.8 *Matrix structure for multi-building project*

responsible to the site manager for most matters, but they also have to satisfy the architect or engineer over standards of materials and workmanship. This does not in fact usually create a formal matrix structure, but the work of the construction teams would be little changed if it did. This is exactly what is done on major projects handled by the construction management procurement approach. The teams undertaking basic work are managed by the designer and the construction manager. This creates problems, especially in the early stages of projects. However, as we consider the potential problems, it is worth remembering that a matrix structure may well cause less uncertainty for teams on difficult construction projects than any of the alternative forms of project organization.

The first and most obvious problem with a matrix structure is that teams are responsible to two different managers who have different interests and therefore different objectives. This can easily generate a sense of confusion and conflict. The matrix structure does not cause this, but it does tend to highlight conflicting objectives. Although such conflicts should be resolved in meetings between the project manager and his immediate subordinate managers, not all managers will be able to resist the temptation to pursue what they see as their own legitimate responsibilities into the work of teams. Managers used to having undisputed control over a specific work area may well find it uncomfortable to have to argue their case, to defend their decisions and to be unable to allocate blame or credit unambiguously to individual teams. This can create severe stress for managers more used to unitary control structures. Matrix structures tend to generate more meetings, more paperwork and more interactions of all kinds than other organizational forms. The need to communicate and negotiate widely can easily create too many demands on managers' time. This adds to the stress which is often observed in practice to be a characteristic of matrix structures.

A further problem is the difficulty of maintaining a balance between the different interests within the matrix. A strong emphasis by the project manager can cause a reversion to a traditional single chain of authority. On the other hand, an exact balance of interests could easily produce complete stalemate with no decisions being made. In practice, effective power changes with the subject under discussion. A balance is achieved by the different interests each winning arguments on the issues of greatest concern to them. It requires considerable maturity for managers to recognize when to lose gracefully and when to insist that their own view should prevail.

Matrix structures are expensive in management time and effort. There tend to be more managers, more time spent discussing work and more negotiations between specialist teams than in single-authority structures. This is often erroneously seen as a symptom of inefficiency. Matrix structures provide the right answers for problem-solving projects. They tend to force important questions to the surface where they must be tackled. The structure provides a balance of points of view and a balance of authority. This means that all decisions are open to challenge and so need to be robust if they are to be accepted. It is also common for decisions which are widely debated and emerge from a consensus, rather than being imposed by a solitary manager, to be widely understood and implemented effectively. In practice, wide ranging multidisciplinary decision-making is necessary early in construction projects, but during the later stages needs to give way to a clear line of command, as the decisions are put into action. This is achieved in the construction management procurement approach, for example, by giving the construction manager pre-eminence during the construction stages of projects. This kind of stage-by-stage fine tuning is entirely consistent with the principles of matrix structures and of course makes good practical sense.

Design strategies

We have now considered the six coordination devices shown in Figure 5.1. Construction project managers need to select an appropriate combination of them in order to ensure that everyone in their project organizations has all the information they need to carry out their work. While they are making these organizational design decisions they need also to consider two strategies which reduce the need for information to be communicated throughout individual projects.

Self-contained subprojects

The first way of reducing the demands for information is to divide projects into self-contained subprojects. In effect this creates a number of separate smaller projects. This is worth doing if the cost of managing the subprojects plus any essential coordination between them is less than the cost of managing the total project as a whole. This can happen because management costs tend to increase geometrically with increases in the difficulty of the task being managed. As we discussed in Chapter 1, the difficulty of managing projects tends to vary directly with size. Therefore, as suggested by Figure 5.9, which illustrates the general character of management costs, the management cost of four subprojects is likely to be much less than the management cost of a bigger project, equal in size to the four subprojects. Provided that the costs of coordinating the sub-projects are relatively low, which is likely if they are substantially self-contained and independent, there are benefits in subdividing the big project into separately managed units.

There are a number of ways in which this can be done in construction projects. It is reasonably common to separate the design stages from the manufacturing and construction stages by arranging for them to take place at different times. When this is done so that the stages are completely separate and design is absolutely complete before manufacturing or construction begins, the management task is far simpler than when these stages are allowed to overlap in time. Projects are commonly subdivided on a geographical basis. Sections of a motorway project are allocated to separate managers, each of whom is provided with all the resources required to complete his work independently of the other sections. Large low-rise housing projects are commonly divided into self-contained subprojects of about 30–40 houses. High-rise buildings are subdivided into independent zones of two or three floors during the fitting-out stages. Major shopping centres almost invariably separate the design, manufacture and construction of the main structure from the fitting-out of individual shops. So

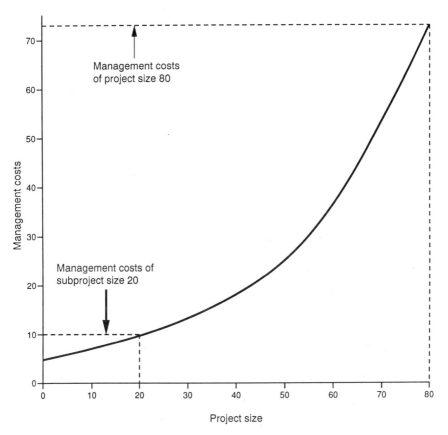

Figure 5.9 *Management costs*

there are many examples in practice, where construction project managers decide to simplify their overall management task by creating self-contained subprojects.

The creation of subprojects which have all the resources they need may imply a trade-off between specialization and coordination. The refurbishment of a large hotel, for example, could be organized as one integrated project. It would use specialist contractors for each separate trade. Their work would be coordinated by careful programming to give each specialist, at any one time, control of a reasonable number of clear work spaces. Alternatively, the hotel could be subdivided into small zones, each made the responsibility of a single team of multi-skilled generalists. They would place concrete, lay blocks, plaster, lay floor screeds, fix tiles, install sanitary equipment, fix pipes and plumbing fittings, and make connections to main services. Their work would not have to be coordinated with that of other similar teams and so management costs would be lower. However, the team is likely to be less productive at each separate type of work than a team which specializes in that work. Therefore their direct costs are higher. Construction project managers must decide the balance of advantages between higher direct costs and lower management costs on a case-by-case basis. In many projects the simplification of the management task resulting from the creation of subprojects will provide overall benefits.

Slack resources

The second way of reducing the demands for information is to provide slack resources. These are extra resources provided to a manager to help ensure that he meets his targets. By meeting targets, managers avoid the need for their superiors to deal with problems. Thus the senior managers' work is simplified and their costs are reduced. Project managers must balance these reduced costs against the additional costs of providing the slack resources.

Construction provides many examples of slack resources. A construction project manager may calculate that a project requires two tower cranes to provide a high probability that no team will have to wait more than fifteen minutes for craneage. He may nevertheless decide to provide three tower cranes to make virtually certain that no team is ever delayed. In other words, he may decide to provide slack resources to obtain greater certainty in performance.

Slack resources are often provided because it is difficult to organize work so that all teams are fully occupied. For example, a large multi-storey reinforced concrete frame may justify separate teams for vertical formwork, horizontal formwork, bar bending, vertical reinforcement, horizontal reinforcement, making concrete, transporting concrete and placing concrete. It may require concrete mixing plant, dumper trucks, tower cranes, hoists, bar bending equipment, concrete pumps and a carpenter's workshop to prefabricate and modify the formwork. To calculate the optimum size of teams for such a complex set of activities to ensure that all are working efficiently is, for all practical purposes, impossible. The number of possible combinations of resources is far too large for them all to be considered. Yet in practice managers decide such matters routinely. This is possible because, since it is not possible to calculate a perfect answer, all managers in practice settle for answers which do not utilize resources efficiently. They may adopt some kind of decision rule. For example, a manager may rank teams in order of their direct unit costs and plan the work of the most expensive first, aiming for high efficiency. Then the work of the second most expensive is planned to fit in with the plan for the first team as efficiently as possible and so on. A conscientious manager may try several sequences of teams to see if he can improve on the first attempt. In general, this search will not be pursued very far and once an answer which meets the manager's key targets is found it is very likely to be adopted. As March and Simon (1958) suggest, managers generally satisfice not optimize. In doing so they are accepting the necessity of providing slack resources.

The marketplace dictates acceptable levels of slack resources. Individual managers need to find answers that match the performance of their competitors. All can remain profitable, despite under-using resources, as long as the market-determined norms are accepted by all. Managers generally work in ignorance of the actual level of slack resources they are authorizing. They accept the norms of their local construction market and believe that they are being efficient as long as they achieve that level of performance. The results of this introverted approach can be seen by comparing the performance of different construction markets. Bennett *et al.* (1979) found that in the late 1970s the construction cycle per floor for reinforced concrete buildings was 3 days in the USA and, at best, 21 days in the UK. They found also that buildings in the USA used less resources than similar ones in the UK. In other words, the UK building industry was providing more slack resources. It was doing so not as a conscious decision, but simply in response to a market-determined norm. Since the 1970s, performance in the UK has improved and Flanagan *et al.* (1986) found that costs and times closer to those in the USA are being achieved. Partly as a result of these international studies and other similar work, the building productivity norms in the UK have changed over time and now provide much higher efficiency than was widely accepted in the 1970s.

Slack resources, however, are not simply an unconscious response to norms. The provision of slack resources can be a conscious and rational decision to aim for greater certainty in the performance of basic work, in order to reduce the flow of information about problems. This in turn reduces the need for management and so may result in greater overall efficiency.

Finally, we should remember that, if managers fail to select appropriate combinations of coordination devices for their projects, slack resources will arise by default. Teams will not have the information they need to work efficiently, they will be kept waiting for decisions by overloaded managers who, under stress, will often make hurried and poor decisions. Projects will be delayed, use extra resources, incur extra costs and generally perform badly. All of which are signs of unplanned slack resources.

6 *Practice in the USA*

The next three chapters describe important aspects of contemporary practice in each of the three great trading blocks of the World: the USA, Japan and Europe. The three have different construction strengths and they achieve them by methods which in many respects are distinctive and which in each case provide important lessons for construction project managers. The following descriptions concentrate on the distinct strengths of each member of the trading triad because these provide the clearest guidance to successful practice.

We begin with the USA, which has provided a source of ideas for improving the efficiency and speed of building in other countries for several decades. This deserved reputation is based largely on an ability to deliver large high-rise buildings faster and at lower costs than is achieved elsewhere. Figure 6.1 illustrates examples of the products of this distinct strength. The US approach to building is crucially dependent on very competent specialist contractors and the widespread use of procedures and standards. Together they provide the

Figure 6.1 *Chicago looking towards Lake Michigan from the Sears Tower*

basis for a very effective, essentially simple approach to the design, manufacture and construction of buildings.

The US approach is very much based on letting the market do its work. Major developers see buildings as financial investments first and as architecture second. Both are important, but the most beautiful building will remain on the drawing board if the money does not work out. This priority flows through the whole design, manufacture and construction process. Designers, construction managers and specialist contractors are selected on the basis of the lowest price for a specified product. For example, it is usual in appointing specialist contractors for the product to be specified initially only in general terms so as not to inhibit the search for economy. The specification is developed in subsequent meetings which steadily define the exact scope of the work to be performed and its programme. An important aim of these meetings is to produce a generic specification which can be satisfied by several competing specialist contractors. Consequently, competition on design and price are fierce and only the shrewdest firms survive. The overall benefit is that major US developers are able to choose from a large number of efficient specialist contractors in assembling their project teams.

To take advantage of this strength, the US approach divides buildings into distinct work packages. Each is the work of one specialist contractor who designs, manufactures or arranges the supply of materials or components and constructs a distinct part of the whole building. The contractors' design work is coordinated by the architect; and their manufacturing and construction work is coordinated by a general contractor or, more usually on large projects, by a construction manager. Although this coordination provides detailed descriptions of the work to be done, it leaves specialist contractors with a great deal of responsibility for solving the day-to-day problems that arise in all projects. Especially during the construction stage, they are expected to ensure that their work fits in with that of all the other specialist contractors in terms of both design and management. This dual level coordination depends on everyone involved in a project conforming to established procedures. These are based on standards which are used nationally but which are refined by local custom and practice. At the local level the procedures form a detailed, practical and tightly interrelated system.

Each firm of architects, engineers, construction managers and specialist contractors has its own procedures. These establish a pattern of roles and responsibilities for their own staff at each clearly defined stage of a project. Generally, the stages are consistent in all the firms working on any one family of projects in any given locality. Also, the definitions of roles and responsibilities are generally consistent with each other. However, at the start of any project, stages within that project, and individual meetings within stages, the whole of the team involved carefully establishes that there is a common understanding of the immediate objectives, the scope of the current activity, and each individual's responsibilities. The consistent checking that everyone knows what they and everyone else is supposed to be doing at every stage is called *kick-off*. There are kick-off meetings at the start of each stage and an implicit kick-off agenda item at the start of each meeting. This serves to identify any incompatibilities between separate firms' procedures, and allows any necessary project rules to be established early. The overall effect is that misunderstandings are uncommon and projects are imbued with a team spirit which ensures that everyone is striving wholeheartedly for the common objectives.

The overall sequence of distinct project stages is shown in Figure 6.2. It begins with the brief (called the program in the USA). The customer is leader of the project team at this stage. The brief establishes the physical context, the user requirements and the customer's objectives. The second stage is concept, and the architect becomes leader of the project team. It is concerned with the cultural context and the internal ambience of the building. The third stage is engineering (called design development in the USA) and the leading role is taken by the engineers. It defines the building's technology. The fourth stage is shop drawings, in which the specialist contractors are the dominant influence. It provides the final definition of every part of the building. The final stages of manufacturing and construction are the direct responsibility of the specialist contractors. The customer, architect and engineers retain a monitoring responsibility throughout the whole process to ensure that their decisions are respected in subsequent decisions.

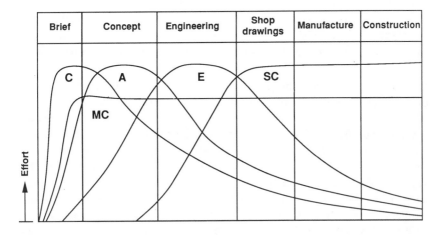

Figure 6.2 *Stages in US building projects: C, customer; A, architects; E, engineers; SC, specialist contractors; MC, construction managers*

The sequence of stages forms one half of a matrix organization. The other half is management. The construction manager is the leader of this second' main responsibility, which runs as a continuous thread through all the other stages. The construction manager becomes the *de facto* project leader during the shop drawing, manufacturing and construction stages. His role is primarily concerned with methods, programme, budget and forming contracts with the specialist contractors. These responsibilities are fully interrelated with each other and with the mainline decisions made during brief, concept, engineering, shop drawings, manufacture and construction processes. The actual management links between all the separate activities are formed by project coordinators (called project managers in the USA). Every separate firm involved with the project has a project coordinator. They are responsible for ensuring that their own firm carries out all its responsibilities in accordance with the programme. They are also responsible for communications between their firm and everyone else involved in the project. This does not prevent individuals dealing directly with people in other firms, but when they do so they tell their project coordinator that the direct communication has occurred. The project coordinators together, under the overall leadership of the architect's and construction manager's project coordinators, coordinate the whole project.

The efficient and systematic US approach depends on the use of well understood technologies. This is recognized and considerable effort is devoted to ensuring that projects do not reinvent the wheel. Consequently, specialist contractors use methods with which they are familiar, and to a large extent rely on materials and components which can be called up at short notice. Yet customers and architects have a reasonable degree of freedom to produce interesting and imaginative buildings. Provided they stay within the constraints of the established approach, they can confidently develop and design whatever the local planning, zoning and building controls will allow. They know that they will be able to find specialist contractors who will work together effectively to turn the architect's ideas and the customer's schedule and budget into reality.

The US approach relies on the professionalism of architects, engineers, construction managers and specialist contractors to coordinate their own work. The US approach does not rely on excessive amounts of paperwork to ensure that every eventuality is explored before work begins on site. Time is vitally important to many developers and so the fast-track approach to projects has been devised to allow construction to start at the earliest possible date. With the fast-track approach, design and construction overlap and inevitably unforeseen problems arise. The US philosophy to building requires day-to-day construction problems to be solved by the specialist contractors as a normal part of their work. Certainly when difficulties arise there is a very healthy concentration on the search for a solution. However, the fast-track approach appears to have pushed the level of problems on many projects beyond what can be accepted as normal. The result has been an unhealthy growth in claims and counter-claims. This has brought lawyers and claims consultants into the industry and these developments threaten to strangle the US approach in over-complicated contracts and defensive attitudes. The best developers recognize this and continue to provide room for normal human errors. Some, for example, agree not to bring any action against the project team provided that total costs remain within a predetermined percentage of the agreed budget. However, generally, claims and over-legalistic attitudes provide a damaging complication for the inherently simple US approach to building.

This chapter concentrates on the construction management approach to large-scale development in the USA. There are several reasons for this. First, the US construction management approach to procurement provides a very clear picture of the fundamental responsibilities which arise in all construction projects. Also, at its best, it provides very efficient and fast design, manufacture and construction. Finally, its failures provide important insights into the essential character of the construction industry.

Developers

The best US developers are among the most experienced customers of the building industry to be found anywhere in the world. They take an active interest in all aspects of their projects. They determine the financial viability of each project, assemble the necessary finance, take the final decisions on what will be built, choose the main features of the project organization, select the principal designers, managers and specialist contractors, and take the major risks on the final outcome of the project.

Developers work on long time-scales. They are always looking for development opportunities because it may take them many years to assemble all the ingredients for a viable project. The developer needs to own or to have agreements with the owners of all the land and air-space needed for any new project. He needs an understanding with the local authorities who control what may be built. They have become very sophisticated in demanding public benefits in return for permissions to build. The developer must also understand the local market for the buildings he intends to have built. All these factors must be brought into balance, and good developers hope also that the interplay of market forces will allow the creation of fine buildings which enhance the local environment. So both pride in the end product and a relentless commitment to achieving a successful commercial outcome are important ingredients for US developers.

Major developments often need a consortium of large companies to provide the necessary financial muscle. These may include several developers, possibly construction companies and potential tenants and financial institutions. However, most if not all successful major projects have a single main driving force. This is the developer who pushes the project forward, deals with influential groups who may oppose his ideas, acts as a champion for the project when others waiver, and generally provides leadership. It is the developer who decides that a construction project will start.

The beginning of a construction project is marked by the production of the developer's brief. Experienced developers work with a designer and construction manager to explore the potential of their development opportunity. They look at alternative schemes and test the trade-offs between functions, quality, time and cost to produce a very detailed project brief. This states the size and performance of the spaces to be provided, specifies the quality and form of major elements of the finished building, and stipulates the budget and programme. The brief establishes a datum which shapes subsequent design and management proposals. It sets the initial tone and establishes the general character of the project.

The other important style setting role of the developer, usually aided either by a small, directly employed staff or by consultant advisers, is to provide the source of authority at all major progress meetings. He will be involved in all decisions which influence total value, time or costs. He makes the detailed trade-offs between the budget and the programme which are necessary on every building project as its design is fully worked out. In doing this, experienced developers will actively seek to minimize their own risks.

The risks involved in construction are very real. In 1981 two walkways in the lobby of the Hyatt Regency Hotel in Kansas City collapsed killing 113 people and injuring almost 200. As Sabbagh (1989) reports: the steel fabricator said the structural engineer made changes from his own original design, the structural engineer said it was the fabricator's idea, the steelwork subcontractor blamed the engineer, the construction manager blamed the steelwork subcontractor and the steel fabricator, and the architect blamed the structural engineer and the steel fabricator. In the US marketplace a developer faced with these conflicts has no choice but to sue everyone and leave the courts to allocate damages.

In theory the developer's position in respect of design responsibilities is straightforward. He contracts directly with the architect who then subcontracts to all other design consultants. Hence when problems arise due to design faults, the developer's recourse is to the architect. However in practice, design, especially with a fast-track approach, is a team task. All the consultants make decisions, many of which the architect is not competent to check. If he were, there would be no point in employing the consultant. The position is further complicated by the involvement of specialist contractors in design. It is rendered almost impenetrable by the role of construction managers in the design stages. Consequently there are few clear responsibilities when design problems arise.

In response, US developers went through a period of relying on tougher and ever tougher contracts. This in turn, combined with an over-willingness to sue, made professional indemnity insurance cover very expensive. More recently the most experienced developers are relying more on careful selection of their project teams, monitoring their work and creating a contingency reserve fund of up to 5 per cent of the construction costs of projects. The new philosophy is to see contracts as a safety-net above which good designers, managers and subcontractors will strive to provide an excellent service to the developer. Only in the case of serious and expensive errors will the contract and its supporting legal processes be used.

These problems highlight one of the key features of the US approach. It operates within a very fragmented industry. Therefore one of the main issues in construction project management in the USA is providing a system of coordination to weld together all the separate firms who make up a construction project organization. Two sets of actions need to be coordinated. These are, first, design; that is, the selection of all the parts of the finished product. Second, the manufacture and construction of projects must be coordinated. In addition the project as a whole, design plus manufacture and construction, must be coordinated. In the US construction management approach, coordination of design is made the primary responsibility of the architect, and coordination of manufacture and construction are the primary responsibility of the construction manager. He is also normally made responsible for controlling the programme and budget. Beyond that, however, overall coordination effectively remains with the developer and is exercised through his attendance at key meetings. Figure 6.3 illustrates the overall management structure in US style construction management. Within the formal structure shown in Figure 6.3, day-to-day leadership of project teams, in practice, rests with the architect and engineers during the concept and design development stages and with the construction manager during the shop drawings, manufacturing and construction stages. The construction manager also takes the lead in buying the work packages. This may be done at various points in the overall design process, depending on the level of detailed constraints which the designers wish to place on specialist contractors' subsequent development of their design. However, whenever the project team is unable to reach agreement on a decision, the developer will decide quickly on the direction he wants his project to follow, to avoid any delay. In this and indeed all other respects, the typical US developer is very willing to undertake the role of leading his projects.

Architects and engineers

Architects in the USA understand the realities of the development marketplace. They see their designs both as architecture and as a major component in determining the success or otherwise of a financial investment. US architects know how floor area, rental values, building costs, interest rates and inflation rates interact to impose constraints on design. They recognize the cost and value of time and accept the need to be involved in negotiating trade-offs between these factors with developers and construction managers. In the US approach, as in most of the rest of the world, the architect's firm is employed, project by project, by the developer under a contract which makes him responsible for designing the complete building. Yet in the USA the architect is directly responsible for only the feel and the face of the building as it is experienced by the general public and the building's users. All the rest, the structure and the environmental services, is designed by engineering consultants. They may be employed in the same firm as the architects, or the engineers may work in

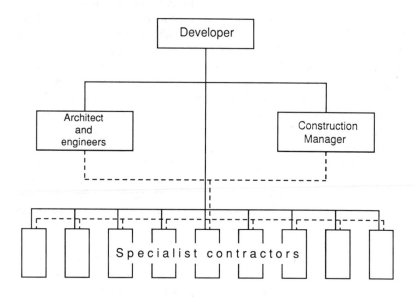

——————— Contractual and coordination links

------- Coordination links

Figure 6.3   *Construction management project organization structure in the USA*

separate firms and act as subcontractors to the architect. Under either arrangement, it is the architect's responsibility to ensure that all the design decisions fit together to describe a building which is visually satisfying and works properly.

Design is inevitably a team effort between the main design disciplines. On all except the very smallest projects, it is also a team effort within each discipline. A typical architectural organization for a major project is likely to be run by a top level team comprising: the conceptual designer who creates the overall image of the building; a senior designer who deals with the design issues which arise in the day-to-day running of the project; a project manager who ensures that the work of all the designers is heading towards the same one building and who, for example, chairs regular (usually weekly) design coordination meetings; and a technical coordinator who keeps track of the status of all the drawings to ensure that changes are communicated to everyone involved in case they cause consequential changes to other parts. He also deals with the local authorities whose approval is needed before certain work can be carried out. Finally, the technical coordinator ensures that the design architect's concepts are translated into practical details for the specialist contractors who will actually build each detail of the building.

The four principal architects (conceptual designer, senior designer, project manager and technical coordinator) are backed up by an army of designers, draughtsmen and specifiers. Important among these is the manager of the computer-aided design system. His job is to take the earliest hand-drawn sketches and translate them into computer drawings that can be gradually refined and changed in a controlled manner. The computer version of the drawings provides the design database for the whole project. Nowadays computer-based drawings are an indispensable tool for technical coordination on major building projects. There is no other economical means of ensuring that design changes in a fast-track project are traced through all of the hundreds of drawings needed to record the designers' decisions.

This task is made particularly onerous by the close interaction of the work of architects, structural engineers and services engineers. Although the architect is responsible for the overall performance and appearance of the building, it is the structural engineer who ensures that it forms a safe and efficient structure. The structural stability of buildings is essential for them to function properly. Buildings must not only stand up, they must be stable because other than very slight movements are disturbing for users. So the structural engineer must work with the architect's conceptual designs and ensure that the overall size and shape of the building and the choice of materials and the way these materials are joined together can withstand the expected forces. These forces include wind pressure, movements due to changes in temperature, the weight of the building itself and, most unpredictable of all, the loads imposed by the users and all the furniture, equipment and other effects they may bring with them. The structural engineer must design a structure which accommodates all these forces and fits in with the architect's overall concept and the needs of the environmental engineers. In the case for example of a steel framed building, this means producing drawings which will allow the steelwork contractor to identify every one of thousands of separate pieces of steel. All this must be achieved rapidly and accurately while the rest of the design, which potentially influences all of the structural calculations, is being worked out.

The role of environmental engineers is even more demanding. They are responsible for the heating, cooling, lighting, power, information and communication systems, plumbing, sewerage, sprinkler systems and lifts and elevators of the building. Every separate space must provide a comfortable and convenient environment for its users. To some extent this is provided by the fabric of the building. So the environmental engineer's job is to add sufficient systems to make up the difference between the conditions created by the fabric and those needed for comfortable and efficient use. Inevitably this task is tightly interdependent with the work of the architects and structural engineers.

The environmental engineer's job is to make the building work as a total environment for whatever activities its users may engage in. The environmental systems must work reliably, be easy to maintain, and be easy to replace as they wear out or are superseded by future developments, and should use as little energy and produce as little waste matter as possible. Keeping track of all the systems throughout a large building and predicting how they will work individually and in combination with the rest of the building is very difficult. The primary performance of individual components is usually well understood and documented. However, the side-effects of these same components often produce surprises. These may become very significant when the components are combined into complete systems which interact with other systems. Over time the environmental systems can be tuned so that they achieve a reasonable balance between all the competing criteria. This tuning process is known as commissioning the systems, and can only take place when the building is virtually complete. It is common to appoint one specialist contractor to manufacture and construct the services and another to commission them. The environmental engineers retain a general responsibility for checking that the specialist contractors' work conforms to their design intentions. The engineers must carry out all of this complex work speedily while ensuring that their services take up the minimum possible building space so that the maximum amount is left for the users.

A further important responsibility is to ensure that the building is properly connected to the public utilities: water, sewerage, power, fire protection, information and communication services, and possibly also distinct heating systems. Any one of these may be overloaded by a new construction project. So the environmental engineers need to agree the demands their new building will make with a multitude of responsible authorities.

In the US approach to building design, the consultants produce a complete design but do not develop it into the fine detail of selecting every part. This is left to the specialist contractors. It is they who produce the shop drawings which describe every part which is to be manufactured for the building. Alternatively, the design consultants may select standardized components which can usually be bought from stock. These are specified sufficiently to enable the specialist contractors to identify the selected component or one that is equal to it. So, in both the approaches used by designers, the specialist contractors have a degree of discretion over the exact materials and components they will use. This allows them to search for the lowest priced parts which meet the designers' requirements.

It is normal for the architect to have a contractual obligation to check specialist contractors' shop drawings. These may include suggested design changes, different materials and different types of fixings, as well as ideas which will not work or are incompatible with the design concepts. The architect must check all the shop drawings to ensure that the building will be safe, work properly and look good. This must be achieved quickly in what is, in any case, a rapidly changing situation. For example, in a fast-track project, one set of shop drawings may be based on the architect's design which was current at the time they were produced but be outdated by a new version by the time the architect checks them. The change may have resulted from a good idea by another specialist contractor, or a design consultant may have seen the need for some alteration. In either event, the need to produce new shop drawings can be expensive, it can lead to mistakes and it tends to demotivate the project team. There is therefore great pressure on the architect to make design decisions quickly and then not to change them. On the other hand, designers always want to produce the best possible answers and most find it difficult to resist a chance to improve their building. This is one of the major reasons for the introduction of construction managers into the US approach. It is an important part of their role to keep a check on the time and cost implications of all design decisions. In practice this discipline, especially where it is fully supported by the developer's own direct authority, serves to concentrate designers' attention on a few really important design issues and to accept specialist contractors' ideas for the rest.

The speed and certainty of design decisions required by fast-track methods is achieved by using standard details for almost every element. These are stored in computer-aided design systems or a manual equivalent called *sticky-backs*. These are transparent self-adhesive sheets of alternative standard design details. Designers simply select a detail and fix it onto their project drawings. The details are generic standards; that is, they allow specialist contractors a degree of freedom to select specific materials and components which meet the performance defined in the standard.

The benefits of the standard design details are, first, ease of quality control by designers in checking their drawings. Second, the standards allow very fast design. For example, on a building project value $50 million (1990 prices) of 15 storeys, with limited use of standard details and much one-off design, the production of working drawings of sufficient detail to invite bids for all the work packages took 18 months. In a building of similar size and configuration using all standard details stored on a CAD system, the equivalent process of producing working drawings ready to invite bids took 1 month. Third, standard details allow specialist contractors to work efficiently. This is because they become familiar with the approach of individual design firms and so know at the bid stage exactly what work they will have to do. This allows prices and programmes to be submitted with great confidence. However, this great strength now, depends on construction managers, with the support of developers, exercising considerable discipline over designers.

Construction managers

The traditional US approach was based on design consultants producing a complete design. This formed the basis for competitive bids from general contractors. One of these, usually the lowest bidder, was awarded a contract to construct the building in accordance with the design. From this point on, the project was in the hands of the general contractor. It was his task to select the most appropriate construction methods, resolve construction problems and deliver a complete building. The architect's role during construction was to check that the design was being correctly interpreted. There were few design changes after the contract was awarded because there was time for problems to be spotted and sorted out before construction began.

With fast-track methods, design and construction decisions must be made at the same time. This requires the general contractor's construction expertise to be available during the design stages. This is achieved by employing the contractor as a consultant and paying him a fee to provide construction advice and to manage the construction process. The term *construction management* is used to describe this role.

Two distinct approaches have emerged. In the first the construction manager employs the specialist contractors. He is paid his fee, plus the direct costs of the specialist contractors' work. This approach is most usually offered by firms who were originally general contractors. In the UK, this approach is called *management contracting* to distinguish it from the second approach, which is called construction management on both sides of the Atlantic. In this approach the developer employs the specialist contractors direct. He also pays them direct. The construction manager is employed as a consultant, usually on a fixed fee basis. The second approach is most usually offered by firms who have grown out of a combined architect/engineer firm. Seeing the need for construction advice during design, they have developed this expertise in order to be able to offer developers a complete construction consultancy service. In most cases the construction management division is now constituted as a separate firm and is not tied to the work generated by the architectural and engineering divisions. As a consequence, in the USA there are few practical differences between the two approaches and the term construction management is used for both. Indeed, depending to some extent on market conditions, most US construction management firms are willing to adopt either approach.

The construction manager is responsible for ensuring that the building is constructed in accordance with the design, the programme and the budget. His main central responsibility is to establish the overall construction method; that is, to create an efficient production process on the construction site. This means identifying all the work which must be carried out to realize the design. Next the construction manager must decide the sequence in which the work is to be done. Then competent, properly equipped people must be employed to undertake the work. They must be provided with all the support needed to enable them to work effectively. This includes the technological support of plant and equipment, as well as quality control, safety, industrial relations and welfare systems. It also includes a management system which ensures that everyone involved in the project is provided with all the information and instructions they need to do their work. In addition, the construction manager must establish an efficient supply, distribution and if necessary storage system to ensure that the construction workers have the materials and components they need to do their work.

The construction manager manages the total construction process plus all the necessary preceding steps. His aim is to ensure that each day the workers on site know exactly what they are to do and have available everything needed to achieve their defined tasks. However, US construction managers concentrate on establishing a well thought-out construction strategy. They delegate detailed decisions to specialist contractors. So US construction managers rely to a large extent on employing experienced specialist contractors and requiring them to provide for themselves much of the support they need to do their work. Similarly, as described earlier in this chapter, design consultants are self-sufficient and very professional in terms of their own specialisms. So construction managers can concentrate on creating an overall technical and management framework which coordinates the separate activities of the designers and specialist contractors. Beyond this, good construction managers maintain pressure on the project team to search for efficient answers.

The most important weapons in the construction manager's relentless search for efficiency are the programme and budget. These provide a disciplined framework for the whole project team. They are prepared early in the life of projects on the basis of much debate and discussion between the developer, designers and construction managers. They are developed in step with the briefing and early design processes. Then, as project decisions are made by designers, construction managers and specialist contractors, the effects on time and costs are calculated and related to the current programme and budget. If all is going well, the figures match reasonably closely. However, if the construction manager identifies significant deviations, this becomes the signal for an often frantic search for a quicker or cheaper answer. All members of the project team, including the developer, may well be drawn into brainstorming sessions aimed at bringing the project back onto programme and budget. These can be very exciting and productive times in the life of projects. Good, new answers often emerge in response to problems first identified as a cost or time failure. Recognizing this, US construction managers have formalized the process of searching for better answers. This is now called *value engineering*.

Value engineering provides a powerful tool in the search for efficiency. It also nicely illustrates the active role of construction managers in seeking to ensure that projects provide developers with good value for money.

Value engineering was developed in various manufacturing industries and has subsequently become a common feature of major US building projects. Its formal procedures often provide benefits beyond those arising from traditional design and cost control methods. At the heart of these formal procedures are workshops which bring together the developer, designer and construction managers for between eight and 40 hours of intensive work. They may be assisted by specialists in value engineering techniques. Value engineering is most effective in the conceptual design stage, the stage at which detail design is first considered, and immediately after each specialist contractor is appointed. A typical value engineering workshop includes the following stages:

1 *Selection* The value to the developer and the costs of each major part of the project are related to each other to identify those which provide poor value for money. They are selected for study.

2 *Information* Each part selected is examined to establish what it does, what essentially it must do, to confirm its costs and value and to identify any constraints.

3 *Speculation* By using creative techniques, including brainstorming, analysing the function of the part, comparing its design with that of similar projects, developing and building on new ideas, a number of alternatives that will do the required job are identified. In a formal workshop, typically between three and ten alternatives are proposed.

4 *Evaluation* Each idea generated in the speculation stage is evaluated to determine which offers the best value for money.

5 *Development* The most promising ideas are developed further to ensure that they will work, meet all the requirements and do not give rise to problems. Any required approvals or tests are identified and the costs, savings and benefits calculated.

6 *Presentation* When a formal value engineering workshop is used, the results are presented to the developer to decide which he wishes to adopt. In all cases, of course, it is good practice to involve the developer when substantial improvements or economies are proposed.

7 *Implementation* The changes accepted by the developer are put into effect.

8 *Audit* Feedback on costs and performance is obtained and reported to the developer.

When these stages are carried out systematically, they usually provide real improvements in value for money for developers, over and above that provided by the project team's initial ideas. Thus value engineering provides a nice illustration of the benefits of bringing specialist, professional management, with its concern for efficiency, into the normal work of the construction industry.

However, important as value engineering is, it provides only one of the tools which construction managers call on in support of their work of ensuring the systematic application of agreed procedures within the overall framework of stages illustrated in Figure 6.2. The construction managers act, in effect, as guardians of the agreed programme. To reinforce this the stages are marked by formal decision points, at each of which the developer commits himself to the expenditure needed for the next stage. Figure 6.4, which is an extension of Figure 6.2, illustrates the four key decision points.

The first decision point is marked by the production of the brief. This can usefully be seen as the agreed *definition of the problem*, which the project is to solve. The second decision point is at the end of conceptual design and can usefully be seen as the agreed *definition of the solution*. It describes what is to be built and records the definitive project programme and budget. The subsequent engineering and shop drawings stages are essentially a systematic development of the agreed conceptual design. At some point within these further design stages, the specialist contractors for each of the work packages are selected. This is the third key decision point for the developer. It can usefully be described as producing the agreed *definition of the manufacturing and construction work*. It is not one single decision point in respect of the whole project, as there are likely to be at least 40–50 work packages on major building projects. There is, however, one such decision point in respect of each of the work packages. As Figure 6.4 indicates, the stage at which the definition of the manufacturing and construction work occurs, varies in respect of separate work packages even within one project. When designers wish to leave detail design to the specialist contractor, the decision point is early in the overall process. When designers wish to define all the details of the design, the specialist contractor is selected later on the basis of fully detailed drawings which contain all the information normally shown on shop drawings. The final key decision is that the work is complete. This fact is certified by the architect and construction manager, work package by work package, and in addition a Certificate of Occupancy must be issued in respect of the whole project by the local authority before the developer can begin to use his new facility.

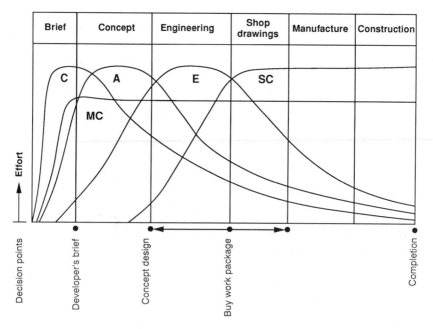

Figure 6.4   *Key decision points: C, customer; A, architects; E, engineers; SC, specialist contractors; MC, construction managers*

Construction managers drive their projects to the four key decision points by means of regular coordination meetings. These take place every week and, if a project is in difficulties, more frequently. Each is attended by representatives of all the firms directly involved with the current stage of the project. Each meeting begins with a kick-off item to check that everyone understands the purpose of the meeting and their current responsibilities and objectives. Then each firm reports its progress. A useful form of reporting is based on three categories of situation. Category A means the firm is on programme and has no problems. Category B means the firm has problems but can deal with them within its own resources. Category C means that the firm has problems which require help from others. Absolute honesty is encouraged by using the coordination meetings to find answers and not to allocate blame. However, a more powerful incentive derives from all firms knowing that, if they are discovered hiding the true state of their progress, they face the real possibility of being dismissed from the project, being replaced by one of their competitors and having to meet a substantial claim for damages from the developer. This ever-present threat forces every firm's project coordinator to know his project thoroughly, to be active in anticipating problems, and to try very hard to avoid them. This work relies a great deal on direct discussions between the project coordinators of separate firms. The informal coordination takes place between the formal coordination meetings so that most project coordinators are able to report category A or B situations. This approach allows the formal meetings to concentrate on any major problems that informal discussions have been unable to resolve.

The formal coordination meetings lead up to the review meetings which mark each of the key decision points. These are attended by the developer, architect, construction manager and any other members of the project team centrally involved in the decision point. Typically, before the meeting, a formal report on the proposals to be reviewed is circulated by the construction manager. The meeting begins by agreeing the scope of the meeting and checking that there is a common understanding of the nature of the decision to be made. This is followed by a formal presentation of the proposals and then a decision is made. Usually this confirms everyone's agreement to the proposals since they will have been widely discussed in the weeks leading up to the review meeting. However, the meeting is the developer's last opportunity to make changes without disrupting the formal project procedures. Consequently, he may ask for changes or he may delay his formal agreement to the next stage in order to spend more time deciding whether or not to continue with the project. These however are unusual responses, especially once a project has moved past the earliest stages. In general, the review meetings provide fixed points in time by which defined sets of information must be completed and then agreed as the basis of the next stages of the project. They provide a strategic framework for the construction managers' work.

Construction management is carried out by surprisingly small teams. A $50 million (1990 prices) high-rise office block will have a construction management team comprising an office-based project manager, one manager and one assistant project manager. It is their responsibility to provide construction expertise, produce the schedule and budget, buy all the work packages and manage the project. Construction management on site is the responsibility of a superintendent and four or five assistant superintendents. It is their responsibility to manage the construction work. The team of project managers and superintendents is supported by administrative and secretarial staff. In addition, they may draw in expert colleagues to provide advice on specialized or unusual tasks. For example, many construction management firms have project managers who are also specialists in value engineering, equal opportunity laws or contractual issues. They can be consulted by colleagues working on other projects as specific problems arise in these subjects.

The use of small teams places great personal responsibility on every individual construction manager to work hard for the success of their projects. US construction managers are unwilling to accept any delays to their projects if they can possibly be avoided. They regard finishing a project either on time or better still early as *winning* and, as with all Americans, they like to win. This winning or *can-do* attitude is an important ingredient in the US construction management approach. Figure 6.5 illustrates the can-do attitude in action on the roof of a new high-rise building.

US construction managers are one of the key strengths of the modern US approach. They provide developers with very professional construction advice, which is aligned with their own interests. They have made it possible to deliver large high-rise building projects significantly faster than with the traditional general contractor approach and faster than is normal anywhere else in the world.

Specialist contractors

The remaining crucial role in the US approach to building is that of the specialist contractors. The US building industry is blessed with many competent, efficient, street-wise specialist contractors. They know their own business very well and are used to competing for new work in terms of design, time and cost.

Specialist contractors exist in many forms and sizes. Many are major industrial companies, others comprise the relatively small central core of a network of independent firms linked by technological interdependencies, while yet others are small independent firms who have developed specialist skills and knowledge.

In total, they provide the wide variety of technologies required by modern building. Although these range from traditional craftsmanship to very high technology, the typical US specialist contractor on large scale development projects deals with moderately sophisticated manufactured components. Although market forces are causing a steady increase in the amount of prefabrication, there remains a significant amount of hand work on site as components are cut and fitted and pushed and pulled into position. Figures 6.6 and 6.7 illustrate a typical range of components.

The task of US specialist contractors is defined in the design and management information provided for them. This tends to be a combination of detailed information for elements which influence the appearance, performance or safety of the finished building and statements of performance requirements for other elements. Much is left to good trade practice and to the specialist contractors' own detail design. The information provided also defines key dates in the construction process and the specialist is expected to programme his own work to meet these. The specialist contractor works with the design team, construction manager and other specialist contractors to reach agreement on everything needed to deliver the construction work on time. Overall the specialist contracting system is efficient and reliable.

There are distinct features of the US marketplace which help to create this situation by facilitating efficient specialist contracting. First, there is considerable certainty for specialist contractors about what they are required to produce. The majority of buildings in the USA are characterized by standardization: repetition and the use of off-the-shelf components. This creates considerable certainty for each specialist contractor about the actual work to be done. This is further reinforced by certainty about the boundaries between the work of separate specialist contractors. Lines of demarcation established in negotiations between trade unions exert a widespread influence. Although there is a strict division between union and non-union contractors and projects, the negotiated agreements establish a common understanding about the proper work for individual trades.

Second, key design decisions are delegated to the specialist contractors. They normally have tremendous freedom to adapt designs to suit their own particular products and skills so that they have the opportunity to use well known, efficient methods and so achieve the lowest possible prices. This allows specialist contractors to trade-off design, manufacturing and construction considerations to maximize productivity and thereby enhance their competitive position. Engineering and construction demands tend to dominate detail design, probably because specialist contractors are required to produce such a high proportion of the detail design information. Certainly designers are responsible for reviewing specialist contractors' shop drawings to ensure compliance with their design intentions. However, in many projects, the developer exerts considerable pressure on the whole project team to complete their work quickly so that he can begin to earn a return on his investment. This makes it difficult for all except the most dedicated of designers to reject specialist contractors' shop drawings except on the basis of serious technical errors. The overall effect is that specialist contractors have considerable discretion over what they build. This design freedom is possible, to a large extent, because the official regulation of aesthetic considerations in the USA generally is minimal. So, provided a detail is technically adequate and generally conforms to the design concept, it is difficult for designers to find reasons or excuses for rejecting specialist contractors' proposals.

(*a*)

(*b*)

(c)

(d)

Figure 6.5: *(a) The reinforced concrete contractor's team discovers a problem with the reinforcement. (b) The reinforced concrete contractor's team and the construction manager's site superintendent search for a solution over the drawings. (c) The site superintendent telephones the structural engineer to get his agreement to the proposed solution. (d) The site superintendent tells the reinforced concrete contractor's team how they can proceed. The whole sequence of events took less than ten minutes from the initial discovery of the problem*

(a)

(b)

Figure 6.6:   *(a) Aluminium sections are preassembled into cladding units on the floor they will enclose. (b) The resulting panels are fixed to the floor edge*

The third feature of the US marketplace which helps to ensure efficient specialist contracting is that it is fiercely competitive. Given certainty and the authority to make detail decisions, specialist contractors have to be efficient to survive. In a recent study of specialist contracting, Gray and Flanagan (1989) found that, in many cases, between 10 and 15 specialist contractors are invited to bid for the same work package. In these circumstances the successful specialist contractor must concentrate absolutely on achieving efficient production if he is to make a profit against his very competitive price. To achieve this, the design of the work is fully agreed before work starts in the factory or on site. If designers change their minds once manufacturing or construction has started, the cost and time penalties for the developer can be very high.

Managers in US specialist contractor firms concentrate on creating conditions on site which allow fast, efficient construction. This is a key consideration in their decisions about detail design. Construction is kept as standardized and as simple as possible to minimize problems. The US specialist contractors provide their own site facilities, plant and equipment. They negotiate with other specialist contractors to ensure coordination of details and smooth working on site. They recognize that they are totally responsible for their own performance, and once the scope and nature of their work is agreed they expect little further input from designers or construction managers. Consequently, US specialist contractors are self-sufficient and confident in their own abilities. They are characterized by a very positive can-do attitude to any problems that arise. Figure 6.8 shows a typical US specialist contractor at work. Site management is of a high quality and carries total responsibility for the complete work package and all its support services. Site foremen are given great authority and responsibility. They work together to ensure that the project programme is achieved. An important element in enabling this to happen is the US habit of trading favours on site. One foreman will cut holes for another in return for use of the other's hoist or scaffolding. They build up an understanding of how far they can trust each other and what it is sensible to trade. The overall effect is

Figure 6.7 *Prefabricated cooling towers delivered to site in just two pieces*

that most small, irritating interruptions to smooth progress simply do not occur. The foremen avoid the problems.

US site management is helped by very flexible labour employment policies. If necessary, managers can hire and fire competent workers part-way through the day, thus minimizing the high costs of surplus labour. A worker is normally allowed 30 minutes to collect his tools and leave the site. He takes his money with him and it is then up to him to look for another job. This allows work-load variations to be dealt with easily. Site activities are supported also by a very efficient off-site materials and component supply infrastructure. In many cases

(a)

(b)

(c)

Figure 6.8: *(a) The cladding specialist contractor on Crate and Barrel's new flagship store on Chicago's Golden Mile provides his own access platforms. (b) The cladding specialist contractor provides his own mobile platforms and lifting equipment. (c) The unusual design provides many construction challenges which are sorted out on site as they occur*

site managers can rely on same-day or next-day delivery of standardized components. Equally, purpose-made components are assembled off-site into truck loads or half-truck loads which can be called up day by day.

The US specialist contractor system is geared to high productivity. This is achieved by placing the total responsibility for production in the specialist contractors' own hands. Designers and construction managers create an overall framework which provides strategic coordination for the specialist contractors' work, but the details are delegated to where the action and the information needed to make day-to-day decisions coincide.

Project management

Project management on big US development projects relies heavily on the professionalism of designers, managers and specialist contractors. Each knows his own business, and the project management system which has evolved is tailor-made to allow them to concentrate on applying their knowledge and skills efficiently.

The project management system provides clearly defined roles for the main actors. The developer initiates the project, establishes its main objectives, finds the land, air-space and finance and selects the designer and construction manager. They in turn concentrate on strategic issues. The designer decides what is to be constructed by designing the overall appearance and performance in just as much detail as is needed to define everything he regards as crucially important. This includes selecting the key materials and components. The construction manager decides the key features of the construction method and manages the overall programme and budget. These strategic decisions provide the framework for the tactical phase. This is the province of the specialist contractors. They design the details of every part of their individual work-packages, decide how the work is to be manufactured and constructed, and then make and assemble the finished product.

The overall project management structure is simple and effective. It is well understood by experienced participants and it enables them to concentrate on directly productive work. In the main, coordination within the overall strategic framework is achieved by discussion and negotiation between the specialist contractors directly involved. There is normally just sufficient flexibility within the design and construction management targets given to specialist contractors to enable them to find satisfactory answers without seeking extensions of time or more money. Established norms do not provide substantial amounts of slack resources. They challenge specialist contractors to use their established methods efficiently and provide just sufficient profit to enable specialist contractors to stay in business as long as they complete their work quickly. Hence there is a remarkable concentration by every specialist contractor on completing his own work and moving on to the next project.

The main driving force behind the tough, efficient, can-do attitude of the US specialist contractors is the very competitive marketplace. Specialist contractors are forced to accept prices that leave them no choice but to complete work quickly and with the minimum of resources. Designers are equally required by the construction manager, fully supported by the developer, to stick to practical designs. Designers feel themselves under tremendous pressure to work quickly and to stick to budgets. The main pressure that constrains the obvious temptation to cut corners is the need for repeat business. Designers and, even more, specialist contractors rely on their reputations for delivering fast and efficient work to ensure that they will be invited to bid for future projects. Any designer or specialist contractor who gets a reputation for producing poor quality work will go out of business. In fact, the workmanship on much US construction work is mediocre. However, any designer who repeatedly asks for work to be re-done is likely to be faced by great hostility from construction managers and specialist contractors. Designers find it difficult to obtain future work if they develop a reputation for being over-fussy about quality. There is, however, a limit to what will be accepted, and any specialist contractor who over steps that mark so that work has to be re-done will delay the project and so disrupt the work of other specialist contractors. If this happens the whole process can be thrown out of balance. The US project management system is not designed to cope with delays. It is geared for success. Hence, incompetent specialist contractors go out of business quickly.

Equally, designs that create new situations place a strain on US style project management. Sabbagh (1989) provides several examples of this effect which arose during the building of the skyscraper, Worldwide Plaza, in New York. A number of non-standard situations resulted from a decision by the architects, Skidmore, Owings and Merrill (SOM) to add 'a pleasant curvature to an otherwise rectangular building'. This was achieved by introducing an elliptical arcade inside the building, running around the whole of the ground floor. The arcade was to be clad in stone but when SOM's technical team looked at how to deal with the corners where the ellipse met the rectangle they were faced with very complicated non-standard conditions. These would have required a multitude of heavily moulded stones, each needing to be fixed individually. This was recognized as being impractical 'given today's technology and economics'. SOM in consultation with the construction managers, HRH, opted for precast concrete for the complicated parts. So large prefabricated units were designed which combined a high quality concrete coloured to look like stone for the very complicated parts mixed with real granite fixed to the concrete backing for the simpler parts. A further complication was that some of the prefabricated components incorporated steel trusses. The design and manufacture of the prefabricated units was a multi-firm, international operation. Some of the granite was quarried in Brazil, sent to Italy to be cut and then transported to Canada to be combined with the precast concrete or to New Jersey to be fixed to the steel trusses. These complicated non-standard units were the centre of problem after problem throughout the project; so that near the end of the project it was apparent that the project team 'could not control the stone and precast concrete work'. As the developer's agent said 'this is a very difficult complicated job and we lost control of it and once the die is cast there is no way we could throw the contractor out and appoint someone else.' The project finished four months late on a planned 24 month construction period and 10 per cent over budget. Not all of these delays and additional costs resulted from problems caused by the elliptical arcade. Other problems played their part and the fascinating story of Worldwide Plaza provides several illustrations of the difficulties which non-standard details create for the US construction management approach. It also illustrates how these difficulties are exacerbated when specialist contractors from outside the USA are used who do not fully understand the US approach. When it is working well, the US construction management approach produces large and complicated buildings using off-the-shelf components quickly and efficiently. However, the system depends on experienced firms working within the limits of their competence. It is all too easy for developers, designers or construction managers to introduce new demands which have unpredictable, sometimes catastrophic, consequences.

This should teach us that the considerable benefits in efficiency and speed provided by using standard answers depend on sticking strictly to standard answers. It is difficult to retain the benefits once non-standard elements are introduced. The US construction industry as a whole provides for a great variety of forms of construction. However, whenever it adopts answers that fall outside the normal methods of the local industry, it runs the risk of providing another entry in the record of great construction disasters.

7 Practice in Japan

The Japanese building industry delivers reliable quality, on time, with a certainty not matched anywhere else in the world. This performance is the result of decades of steady development based on the principles of mass production: simplify, standardize and systematize. This development is now being extended to embody the principles of just-in-time, which will add speed and high productivity to Japan's already considerable strengths. The almost inevitable result is that Japan will have the most efficient building industry in the world.

The great success of the Japanese building industry depends on long term relationships. Customers, general contractors, suppliers, specialist subcontractors and sub-subcontractors have worked together in tightly knit *families* of firms for decades. These long term relationships are based on trust and a sense of brotherhood. General contractors take responsibility for the well-being of their subcontractors. They set tough standards but help their subcontractors to achieve them. They pay a fair price for work and feel responsible for ensuring that their subcontractors are profitable and have opportunities to grow. In return, subcontractors strive every day to deliver the agreed day's work, complete and exactly to the specified standards. They are willing to try new ways and feel responsible for proposing ways of improving quality, safety and productivity.

Efficiency derives not from competition within the families of firms, but from learning over time how to work together more productively. Small improvements year after year are gradually creating in Japan a tightly structured, thoroughbred building production system.

Although there is competition between the families of firms, this takes place within a carefully structured market. Established relationships with long-standing customers are not challenged, the Government allocates work on the basis of an elaborate market ranking of firms which is up-dated and published annually, but which tends to reinforce the established order; there are many joint ventures and widespread collaboration on pre-competition research. The result is that the market share of individual firms remains constant year after year. It is not correct behaviour in Japan to disturb the home market. Work for a new customer or one who builds occasionally is the subject of fierce competition. Firms will bid low and provide an excellent service in the hope of establishing a new, long term, loyal customer. However, new customers are the exception and it is the long term relationships based on trust that shape the Japanese building industry.

Major construction firms

The most important actors in the Japanese building industry are the major construction firms. Pre-eminent among these are 'the big six': Kajima, Kumagai Gumi, Ohbayashi, Shimizu, Taisei and Takenaka. Bennett *et al.* (1987) describe how the big six play a leading role in establishing the methods of the industry and representing its interests to Government. Also the major, international-sized Government projects within Japan are shared between the big six, usually on a joint-venture basis. However, there are many other construction firms of various sizes from very large to small.

The Japanese approach to building projects is most clearly evident in the work of the big six and so this chapter concentrates on them and their work. The six are all large, each employing in excess of 10 000 engineers, and provide comprehensive design and construction management services. Indeed, they routinely find land, arrange finance, produce conceptual designs and detail designs, manage the manufacturing and construction processes, and repair and maintain the buildings they produce. They do whatever a customer needs, quickly and within that customer's pre-stated budget.

Their most important investment is in people. They recruit university graduates and train them in the company's methods. They provide lifetime employment, take responsibility for their employees' families, their health-care, pensions and general welfare, and pay high salaries plus generous profit-related bonuses in return for absolute loyalty and commitment to the firm.

They have consistent systems, based on tried and tested methods of working, which are used throughout the company. Staff at all levels are encouraged to search for ways of improving established methods by meeting regularly in quality circles. New ideas, speculation and individual brilliance are encouraged and supported in the firms' research institutes. By structuring innovation and research in this way the Japanese major construction firms have combined steady, reliable efficiency with change. When a new and better method is identified, either as a result of ideas developed within a quality circle or as a result of research and development, it is discussed widely with all those likely to be affected. Only when there is a wide understanding of the change is it introduced. Then it becomes part of the agreed, consistent standard approach of the firm until a further new and fully considered better answer is found.

The key, crucial responsibilities of the major construction firms are detail design and construction management. They will not undertake a project unless they produce the detail design and manage the whole process from the conceptual design stage to completion.

Conceptual design

In Japan most conceptual designs are produced by architects employed by the major construction firms. There are design consultants of whom the largest is Nikken Sekkei with just over 1000 professional staff. Most are much smaller. A customer may employ a design consultant to produce the conceptual design for a new project. This may be developed into fine detail before it is handed over to the construction firm. Alternatively, the customer may include the conceptual design stage in the work of his construction firm. This is the more usual arrangement.

The conceptual design stage provides the major weakness of the Japanese approach to building. Most of the modern buildings in Tokyo are dull, reflecting the solid middle-class values that permeate Japanese society. Even the best Japanese architects design buildings, for construction within Japan, which are unimaginative in comparison with the best European designs. Japan's culture and systems do not encourage individual brilliance, or allow the careful working out of the deep and detailed design integrity which characterizes the best European architecture. It is significant that the very best work of Japanese architects is to be found overseas.

Japanese buildings look competent and well built. Their designers are likely to describe themselves as engineers who have taken a specialist course in architecture as part of their engineering degree. The results are predictable and rather boring buildings. This is recognized in Japan and a growing number of new buildings are being designed by some of the best European designers; Richard Rogers, Norman Foster, Renzo Piano and Arup Associates are prominent among these.

Detail design and construction planning

The groundwork for Japanese productivity on site is established during the integrated detail design and construction planning stage. Everything is planned to an extent which is unmatched throughout the rest of the world, and nothing is left to chance.

The design is complete in every detail before manufacturing and construction begin. The details produced by the construction firm use materials and methods which are familiar to their subcontractors. There is extensive use of standardized details and specifications. For example, structural steelwork connection details are standardized. These cover steel-to-steel connections as well as fixings to curtain walling, floors, services and other elements. Consequently, a very consistent approach is used on all buildings. One standardized specification document is widely used throughout Japan. It is called the Japan Architecture Standard Specification (JASS). Various government bodies produce their own specifications and there is a separate document for small projects, but these draw heavily on JASS. The overall effect is that constructability, based on standardized methods which draw on well practised skills, is designed into Japanese buildings during the detail design stage.

Beyond this remarkably well ordered approach to detail design, the construction method is also established and planned before manufacturing and construction begin. This planning is very detailed. It makes use of networks, bar charts and construction method drawings. These are used to provide strong visual images to help the planners think clearly about every aspect of the construction process. Figures 7.1 and 7.2 show examples of methods in common use.

Detail design and construction planning are made easier by the Japanese reliance on long term relationships. The construction firms know their subcontractors through having worked with them for decades. They can therefore select design details, choose methods of construction and determine the sequence and timing of every activity with considerable confidence that their programmes will be achieved. Certainly they can be totally confident that the subcontractors will try very hard to deliver good quality work, exactly in accordance with the programme, in return for the sum of money included in the project budget.

The confidence of knowing that their plans will be taken totally seriously by manufacturers and constructors encourages Japanese detail designers and construction planners to consider every aspect of the work. The use of standardized details and a consistent specification allows the detail design stage to be concentrated on searching for the most efficient total production method. Each task is considered, to ensure that it is comfortably within the capabilities of the subcontractors. Work which can be prefabricated is included in the manufacturing process. Generally, prefabrication does not cut across the established boundaries of a manufacturer's work. Thus, where aluminium curtain-walling is to be factory glazed, the glazing is done by the construction firm's normal glazing subcontractor in the aluminium curtain-walling subcontractor's factory.

Prefabrication is considered at a fine level of detail and commonly includes construction aids. Figures 7.3 and 7.4 illustrate the use of prefabricated construction aids. The result is that, whenever a worker needs access to any part

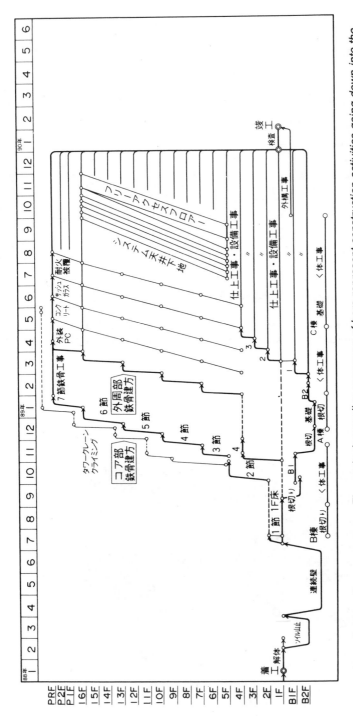

Figure 7.1 *Construction programme. The early descending sequence of bars represent construction activities going down into the basement and the subsequent ascending sequence of bars represent building up from the lowest basement to the roof*

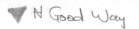

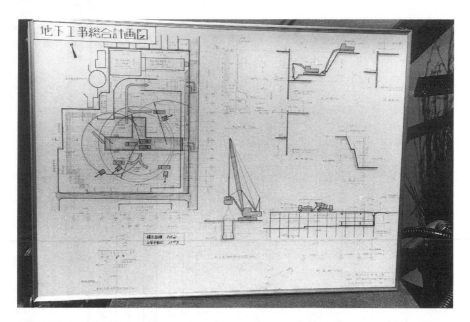

Figure 7.2 *Construction method. Each stage of the construction process is explored graphically by sticking images of the construction plant to be used onto the production drawings*

Figure 7.3 *Brackets and lugs to provide access or help in positioning steelwork are commonly welded on in the factory.*

Figure 7.4   *The ladder used to provide access to a steelwork junction fits into lugs welded on in the factory*

of the structure, the means of providing this will have been planned and incorporated in the manufacturing process.

On sites where there is room for pre-assembly, the benefits of working with a complete detail design are further exploited. Figure 7.5 illustrates a remarkable construction site which used large (18 m × 6 m) pre-assembled floor units comprising steel beams and floor decking. The size of the units is impressive but even more impressive, is that when each one was lifted into place the air handling ducts located under that unit were already in place. Not only this, but hung under each unit was a bundle of the duct connection pieces needed to infill between the units. Similarly, on top of each unit when it was lifted into place was a bundle of the decking pieces needed to complete the floor. So the maximum possible use was made of each crane lift. In this and similar ways the number of construction activities is reduced to as few as possible and each is made as simple as possible.

The detail design and construction planning is carried out by specialists in the construction firm's headquarters or regional office. The project manager who will subsequently be responsible for the construction process is involved in these preliminary stages. Consequently, he has a deep understanding of the task he will manage long before work begins on site. He has the opportunity to think about every construction activity, to simplify it and to ensure that his subcontractors will not be faced with unexpected new challenges or unplanned tasks.

Manufacture and construction

The Japanese manufacturing industry is generally the most productive in the world. The particular Japanese genius is in managing very complex manufacturing processes. In a relatively simple process, for example steelmaking, Japanese and US productivity levels are approximately equal. However, in more complex processes which involve many separate steps, for example producing motorcars, Japanese productivity is more than double that in the USA.

Construction of complete buildings is a very complex process, arguably the most complex undertaken by any industry. Indeed, such is its complexity that it has not yet been turned into a completely integrated production process. The Japanese are closer than anyone else to achieving total integration in construction. This is undoubtedly encouraged by knowledge of the hugely successful Japanese approach to managing complex manufacturing processes.

Figure 7.5   *Pre-assembled floor units in position on the new Tokyo City Hall*

There is ample evidence throughout the Japanese building industry that the integration of detail design and construction planning, allied to technology which has been steadily standardized and simplified is beginning to create total production systems of remarkable efficiency. Figures 7.6 and 7.7 illustrate a simple case of just-in-time methods in action on a small hotel extension in the back-streets of Tokyo. This is remarkable simply because the depth of planning necessary to make a very slick operation possible was applied as a matter of routine to a small unremarkable building project.

The construction operation began with the arrival on site of a lorry loaded with steel beams. It parked in a predetermined place at a predetermined time. The tower crane was ready to unload the beams, which were arranged on the lorry in the right sequence and the right way round for lifting directly into their correct position in the building. Two steel fixers waited to receive the beams as they were lifted into place. The beams fitted exactly. Hung on each end of each beam was a canvas bag which carried all the nuts, bolts and washers needed to secure the beam in place. The beams came complete with a safety wire fixed above them so that subsequent activities would take place in safe conditions. Each beam took about 10 minutes to fix and that part of the work was then complete leaving a precise and safe structure for the following trades to build on.

The efficient, planned and orderly system of production already in place in Japanese building is merely one stage in a drive towards creating a fully integrated just-in-time approach. The long term targets of Japan's steady innovation are undoubtedly major new industries of the twenty-first century which will produce intelligent building components and construction plant.

Figure 7.6   *A steel beam being fixed on a small building project in Tokyo*

Figure 7.7 *A steel beam being fixed on a small building project in Tokyo*

They will operate on a global scale and are most likely to be based in Japan. The full implications of these projected developments are described in Chapter 16.

Project management

Japanese project management focuses on the end product, the completed building, and seeks to eliminate any activity which does not contribute directly to its production. As we have seen, this begins during an integrated detail design and construction planning stage. The project manager works with specialist departments at headquarters or in the regional office to produce a complete plan of action for the manufacture and construction. This defines and specifies everything which must be done to complete the building safely, on time, and to the specified quality. It provides complete drawings, a detailed method statement, a detailed programme for all the necessary activities and a project budget. The budget is based on detailed measurement and pricing of the work. However, pricing is constrained by the budget agreed with the customer during conceptual design and the prices subcontractors will expect for their work.

The project manager's plans depend on experienced technical advice from specialist departments (which in all the major construction firms includes a large, well equipped and very competent research institute) and on his knowledge of the capabilities and prices of his subcontractors. Like much else in Japan, prices are very stable. Inflation is low and prices for different kinds and categories of work vary little from established and widely known figures. Thus there is little opportunity to reduce costs by haggling with subcontractors. Cost reduction is achieved by efficient construction. There is therefore every incentive for the project manager to prepare thoroughly before he moves on site.

It is on site that the project manager comes into his own. He is totally responsible for the project; all orders and instructions emanate from site. The project manager has a large, well educated and experienced team to help him. Figure 7.8 illustrates a typical site project management organization. Their task is to put the agreed plan into effect. The extreme detail of pre-construction planning enables the project management team to arrive on site knowing exactly what they must do to complete the building. As far as humanly possible, nothing is left to chance. However, construction is inherently uncertain and this too is allowed for and reflected in the normal daily pattern of work on a Japanese building site.

A day on a Japanese building site

An important feature of the Japanese building industry is that it is possible to describe a day on a typical site. This is because practice is remarkably consistent throughout Japan.

The working day begins at 8.00 am, but workers have been arriving since soon after 7.00 am. This allows them to change into their working clothes and be lined up in subcontractor teams ready for work precisely at 8.00 am. The formal day begins with 10 minutes of exercises to music played over the national radio. The exercises are learnt at school and practised daily throughout Japan. Then the workforce is briefed on the overall day's work by the construction firm's project managers. They describe the main activities which will take place on site, major deliveries, safety priorities and any other points which need particular attention. Figures 7.9–7.11 illustrate a typical 8.00 am meeting. It usually ends between 8.15 am and 8.20 am. At that time, having prepared physically and mentally for the day's work, the subcontractor teams move to their workplace.

Each team then holds what is known as a *toolbox* meeting. This takes place around a chalkboard on which is written the tasks their foreman has agreed they will complete in the day. This forms a kind of personal contract, which it is a matter of honour to perform. So the purpose of the toolbox meetings, illustrated in Figure 7.12, is to agree exactly how the team will achieve the day's work. Work begins at about 8.25 am, by which time each man on site knows exactly what he is to do during the day and where it fits into the overall plan for the project.

Work takes place in a steady orderly manner until 5.00 pm. However, if the agreed day's work is not complete by that time, work continues until it is finished. There is an hour's break for lunch at 12.00 noon.

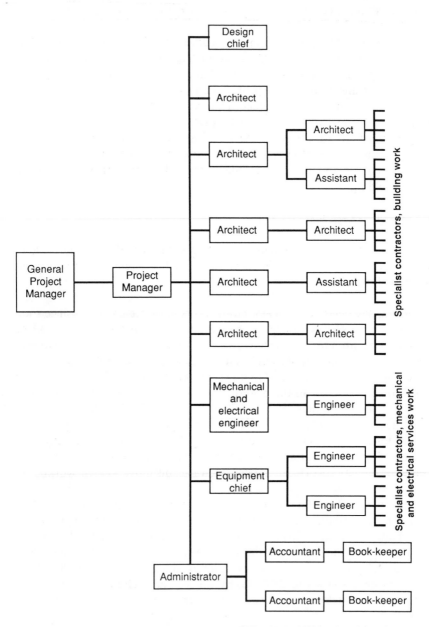

Figure 7.8 *Project management team for a $60 million (1990 prices) hotel constructed by a Japanese construction firm. The terms 'architect' and 'engineer' in this figure describe the educational background of the site managers concerned*

Figure 7.9 *The sub-contract teams line up at 8.00 am every morning*

Day-to-day coordination and control is planned at a coordination meeting which takes place at 3.00 pm every day. All the subcontractors' foremen and the construction firm's project management team meet to review progress and plan the next day's work. First, any problems which have arisen during the current day's work are discussed and resolved. Then the next day's work is considered. The basis for this is the overall programme prepared before work started on site. Discussion can therefore concentrate on coordination issues; the flow of

Figure 7.10 *The 8.00 am meeting begins with an exercise routine which is learnt at school*

Figure 7.11   *The project manager briefs the workforce on key features of the day's work*

materials onto and around the site, the removal of rubbish, the use of cranes and the number of men in each work area are typical examples of subjects discussed.

When problems are raised, everyone present focuses absolutely on finding a solution. Possible answers may be suggested by anyone. Suggestions are taken seriously and considered in turn before a selection is made. When a reasonable consensus has been reached the project manager announces the decision, which is then accepted by all. One of the project management team keeps a record on a chalkboard of all decisions made. At the start of the meeting, the board contains the current pattern of work as agreed at the equivalent meeting the previous day. As changes are made, the old information is rubbed out and the new written up.

The most impressive feature of the 3.00 pm meetings is that everyone concentrates on agreeing the best way to complete the planned work. Time is not spent in discussing contractual issues, there is no mention of claims or extra payments or the need for extra time. There is tremendous pressure, applied by the foremen on each other, to maintain work exactly on programme. The concentration that characterizes these meetings is evident in Figures 7.13 and 7.14.

Slack is built into programmes in various ways. Work is planned to be undertaken by one subcontractor for each trade or specialism during five and a half days a week, in one shift. In addition work is planned in discrete periods of time. So, for example, each two week programme is designed to be independent

Figure 7.12 *A toolbox meeting*

and to include some slack time. When problems arise the slack is used to bring the project back on time by the end of the two week period. If necessary, men will work late into the night, seven days a week. When a problem is more serious, a second shift will be worked. This may involve introducing a second subcontractor or in an extreme case a third. The aim is to keep the project exactly on programme; when this proves impossible, the aim is to return it to the original programme as quickly as possible. The overall aim which must be

Figure 7.13 *A coordination meeting*

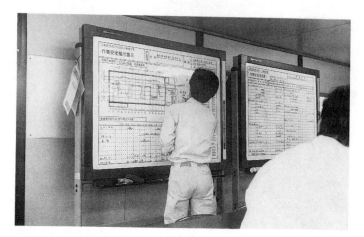

Figure 7.14   *A member of the project management team records decisions made at the coordination meeting, in this case using a hard plastic board with a built-in photocopier rather than the traditional chalk-board*

achieved is to deliver an absolutely complete building exactly on the agreed completion date stated in the contract. It would be a matter of extreme dishonour and a great commercial embarrassment to any major construction firm to complete a building even one day late. They would lose face and lose business.

All of this is understood and totally accepted at the coordination meetings. This produces real teamwork, despite the involvement of many separate firms. The result is that the meeting takes no more than 20–25 minutes and provides a clear and detailed resolution of any immediate problems and a plan for the next day. At the end of the meeting the project manager reads out the agreed decisions, highlights key points and encourages the foremen to be diligent in their work.

The main chalkboard is hung on site at the place where the workforce assembles at 8.00 am each day. This allows everyone to see a short description of the current work plan. The foremen update their own workboards at the end of the day from notes taken at the 3.00 pm coordination meeting. The individual chalkboards are hung in the relevant workplaces ready for the next day's toolbox meetings. Figure 7.15 shows the traditional chalkboards which are used as a key management tool in Japanese building. They have been replaced on some bigger projects by hard plastic boards with built-in photocopiers to provide instant copies. An example of such machines is shown in Figure 7.14. This is a nice example of the Japanese genius for combining tradition with new technology, of simultaneously achieving continuity and change. It is fully in keeping with this key strength that a day on a Japanese building site always has

Figure 7.15 *Chalkboards in use on a Japanese building site*

the same structure. Yet within that overall, consistent framework, the construction firms produce all the variety of Japan's built environment.

Quality

In the trilogy of quality, time and cost, Japan puts quality first. Japanese customers are very demanding. They expect new things to be perfect and to work properly. These tough standards are applied to buildings. As a consequence, Japanese building project managers put considerable emphasis on reminding every worker of the importance of getting work right first time.

Quality in Japanese building begins, as with most of their strengths, with the use of tried and tested methods. Designers and construction managers know the performance of the details, components and systems they use and so appropriate quality is designed and planned into Japanese buildings. This does not mean the highest quality everywhere; it means that a knowledgeable, experienced choice is made of the right quality for each part of the end product, as shown in Figure 7.16. In most cases this is a decision to use a well established answer. When a new solution is essential, the construction company's research institute will be called in to work with the design team, which in such cases is likely to include specialist subcontractors, to test and develop a robust answer. However, generally, detail design uses answers already familiar to the subcontractors who will manufacture and construct them.

Figure 7.16   *Building elements of an appropriate quality: high quality front and basic quality side elevations*

The Total Quality Control Systems introduced by the major construction firms are now well developed and provide detailed procedures for all normal forms of construction. Quality is measured continuously by means of detailed, rigorous and carefully planned tests. The starting point is contained in manuals produced by the construction firms themselves. These describe standard tests for all the elements of buildings in considerable detail. For example, the test schedule for the fabric of a $60 million (1990 prices) multi-storey hotel comprised 30 A3 sized project-specific pages cross-referenced to a 60 page A3 sized standard company manual. Mechanical and electrical services were dealt with separately and equally thoroughly. In addition, several unusual or complex areas of the design were analysed in detail on drawings which show the specific tests to be applied to each part of the work.

As construction proceeds and the planned tests are carried out, a detailed photographic record is made. With concrete work, for example, each concrete pour is photographed together with the relevant work chalkboard. Then a copy of the board is photographed alongside the dial showing the test results. The pairs of photographs are then stored side by side in books which are kept on site as a record. Every activity and its tests are photographed in the same detailed manner.

The photographic records serve to reinforce the daily emphasis given to quality at all the site meetings, especially the toolbox meetings. So culture, company procedures and steady consistent emphasis by project managers all work together to leave no room for doubt about the absolute importance of quality.

Japanese buildings generally work exactly as designed when they are handed over to the customer. Should any defects occur subsequently, the construction firm puts them right straight away. They cannot afford to leave a regular customer with a faulty building. They are paid for work properly involved in maintaining and repairing their buildings, but beyond that the costs of keeping customers happy are absorbed. This total responsibility derives not from contractual liabilities but much more from a sense of honour combined with a mature commercial awareness. It also, in part, explains the Japanese emphasis on quality in design, manufacture and construction. Any failures in these earlier processes are likely to cost the construction firm dear at a later date.

The other major justification for giving a high priority to quality is simply that the Japanese have recognized that getting work right first time is essential for high productivity and fast construction. Re-working, altering work already done, making good defects or simply having to return to a workplace to complete work left unfinished, all cost money, waste time and destroy motivation. The Japanese understand, at least as well as anyone else in the world, that an emphasis on quality creates a virtuous cycle which leads to efficiency and high salaries and profits.

Safety

Safety and quality go together. It is difficult to motivate workers to produce steady consistent quality when they are working in dangerous conditions. Equally, if poor quality work is accepted by project managers, they will find it difficult to persuade their workers to take safety matters seriously. Safety, like quality in Japanese building projects, is designed and planned into the construction method. Safe access to all workplaces is planned at the detail design stage. Provisions for this access, as far as possible, are prefabricated into structural elements. In a steel framed building, lugs and brackets are welded onto columns and beams and even safety wires are attached to these major components in the fabrication factory. Then when workers need access, as Figure 7.17 shows, easy, quick and safe provisions are already in place.

Building sites are rendered inherently safe by the use of sheet steel and plastic protective screens fixed on scaffolding to enclose the perimeter of new buildings. The scaffolding, as Figure 7.18 shows, provides safe access to the exterior face of the building while the protective screens, shown in Figure 7.19, provide protection against the weather and reduce the risk of workers or objects falling

Figure 7.17   *Safety provisions welded on in the factory*

off the building. The vast majority of Japanese new buildings use protective screens. Occasional exceptions are made for major new buildings on open, clear sites. The protective screen helps to create a controlled, predictable working environment. This is reinforced by an emphasis on keeping sites clear of rubbish and generally tidy. Materials are stored in clearly marked areas and their distribution around the site is planned with safety in mind. Indeed the remarkable effort put into planning everything means that the workforce is not faced with unexpected and therefore potentially dangerous situations.

Within this very controlled environment, Japanese project management systems place great emphasis on safety. In part at least, this is because construction firms with bad safety records run a real risk that major public and private sector clients will decide not to award them further projects. It also derives from the previously described understanding that in project management all the virtues, good quality, time, cost and safety, cluster together.

The Japanese project management's emphasis on safety takes the form of training for new recruits and regular updates for experienced workers, weekly and monthly meetings to discuss safety issues, regular inspection by safety officers, daily and weekly routines for cleaning and tidying the site, and constant reminders of the importance of safety. Figure 7.20 shows examples of the safety slogans and special posters evident on all building sites. Safety is emphasized every morning at the 8.00 am meeting and the wearing of safety equipment is

Figure 7.18 *Access scaffolding*

enforced rigorously. Unsafe areas of the site, for example where formwork is being taken down, are marked with clear warning signs, forbidding entry.

Even with all the attention given to safety, construction remains a dangerous business; injuries and death are far too common. Overall, the Japanese building industry's safety record is not good, but it is improving under the effects of safety programmes introduced in the early 1970s, and the record of the major construction firms on building projects is now very good.

Cost control

Cost is important in Japanese construction project management, but it is not of overriding importance. It is understood that, provided the planned quality and time are achieved, cost will automatically be right. The aim is to build up to a defined standard, not down to a cost.

There is great stability in Japanese costs and so, given the consistent, standardized approach to technology, there is no need for narrowly specialized cost specialists. Thus there is no quantity surveying or cost engineering profession in

Japan. Instead, experienced customers, construction firms and trade subcontractors know building costs. Estimating is simple; the work is measured and priced at the established and accepted unit rates.

Contract sums for the major construction firms' projects are usually negotiated with the customer. Negotiation usually takes place with the customer stating his needs, his budget and the required completion date. Negotiation then takes place within that framework, with the construction firm doing its best to give the regular customer exactly what he wants.

Customers are provided with a priced schedule of quantities of work by the construction firm. A typical schedule of quantities of work for a multi-storey, city centre office building contains some 1200 separate priced items. Each item includes a brief description of the finished work. The manual measurement of work is rapidly being replaced by computer-aided methods, including the automatic generation of data by computer-aided drafting systems. Cost estimates are produced by head office estimating departments staffed by engineers. In the main, they will spend three or four years in the estimating

Figure 7.19   *Protective screens are used to surround building sites*

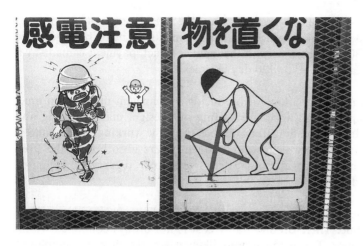

Figure 7.20   *Safety slogans displayed on sites*

department as part of their firm's general policy of circulating staff between departments. Consequently, in estimating, they follow company procedures, using straightforward quantity related estimating methods and company standard unit rates appropriate to the established methods of construction.

The same approach is used for projects subject to competitive tenders. Consequently, the tender period is long, usually two to three months. Tenders are normally invited from three, four or five contractors.

Payments to construction firms are made as pre-specified stages of the work are completed. Payments are made in full, that is without deducting retention. However, it is normal to pay labour costs in cash but to pay for materials by 90 or 120 day cheque. Although called a cheque, the particular financial instrument used is a guarantee to pay on the future date specified. This effectively introduces a large retention.

Project managers use the priced schedule of quantities of work as a budget to guide negotiations with subcontractors. Great trust is placed in the construction firm by the regular subcontractors. Tenders are not asked for; instead, the project manager tells the subcontractors the price allowed in the project budget for his work. It is very unusual for a construction firm to enter into a subcontract which exceeds their budget.

As work proceeds, interim payments to subcontractors are calculated once a month by the project management team using the schedule of quantities of work as the basis. Site-based book-keepers check the calculations and record the payments against the project budget. Actual payments are made by head office between 10 and 30 days later; as with the main contract, payment is made by a combination of cash and 90 or 120 day cheques.

The agreed contract prices allow for producing a competent building on time. This includes implicit allowances for sorting out design, manufacturing and construction problems including, for example, overtime working. Discrepancies in consultants' drawings, which occur frequently, are absorbed in the fixed contract price. The primary aim of cost control is to keep everyone happy by sticking to agreed prices.

However, a higher priority is given to the quality of the end product and to completion on time. Therefore inevitably cost is not always contained within agreed contract sums. This is much more likely where the client has employed design consultants who have produced an awkward or unusual design. In such cases extra overtime, extra working days or additional subcontractors may have to be employed. Everything is done which is necessary to complete the work properly on time. In all of this the construction firm looks after the interests of their subcontractors and so they may themselves face a loss.

When one of the major construction firms does make a loss on a project for a regular customer, the outcome is discussed at a senior level between the two firms. If the construction firm has finished on time, produced a good building and acted professionally in achieving this satisfactory outcome, the customer, conscious of their long relationship, will normally mitigate the loss either on the current project or on a future one.

Specialist subcontractors

The major construction firms in the Japanese building industry are supported by a vast army of subcontractors, sub-subcontractors and so on down to small teams of self-employed operatives. Figure 7.21 shows the typical relationships in Japanese building projects. However, the structure is much more complex than Figure 7.21 implies. Taking the supply of materials as an example, Figure 7.22 illustrates the complex set of relationships likely to exist. Similarly, Figure 7.23 illustrates the multi-layered structure of Japanese contracting.

All the direct construction work is undertaken by subcontractors who directly employ key workers, take responsibility for training and provide technical design advice. However, they have created flexibility for themselves by using sub-subcontractors to undertake much of the direct construction work. The contractual relationships and the degree of support provided from above are

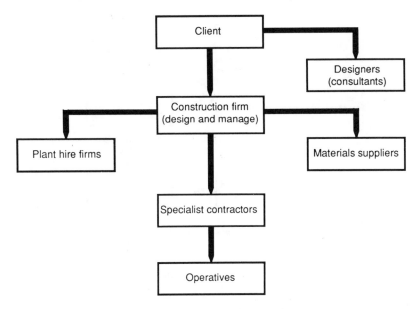

Figure 7.21 *Relationships in Japanese building projects*

less formal and less certain at the lower levels than at the top. It is the base of the structure which has to bear the brunt of economic change. Bankruptcies and unemployment are not uncommon. As a consequence, the major firms at the top of the structure enjoy great stability.

The specialist subcontractors typify the Japanese approach to business. There are two categories of subcontractors, the installation arms of major manufacturing companies and specialist subcontractors. The first category are at least equal in status within a *family of firms* to a major construction firm. They are involved in design, manufacture, installation and maintenance of a wide range of increasingly sophisticated components. Their role is of growing importance on the world construction stage.

The second category of firms ranges in size from small labour-only teams of workers to large firms. Most site work is undertaken on a labour-only basis with the major construction firm arranging for the supply of materials and components. Many of these labour-only firms enjoy a paternalistic family relationship with one construction firm. They depend on the 'father' firm for work. Many of the specialist subcontractors have worked for one construction firm for decades, and in many cases they work only for the one firm.

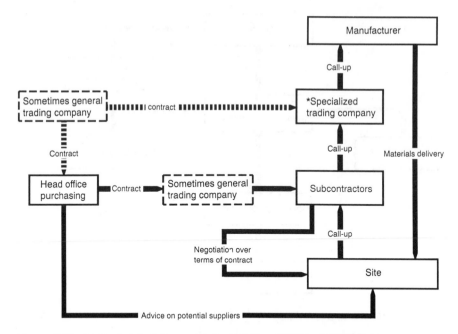

Figure 7.22   *Typical materials supply structure*, subsidiary of manufacturer*

This special relationship means that contracts are given by the construction firm on terms which both parties know to be fair. Conflicts do not arise about payment or claims for additional expense. Very little paperwork is generated. The subcontractor can concentrate on the technical and engineering issues rather than on cost checking everything.

In return for this trusting approach, the construction firm goes to great lengths to provide continuous employment and, indeed, to help his subcontractors to be successful. Construction firms monitor the performance of their subcontractors to ensure that their performance is steadily improving. Each exclusive subcontractor is required to report his financial performance and work capacity at the end of each financial year. Twice a year the construction firm's project managers evaluate all subcontractors and their foremen. This evaluation covers the quality of the work, completion on time, ideas for cost savings, safety record and quality of management. Foremen are evaluated on their general capability, safety-consciousness and cost-consciousness. The reports are reviewed by a subcontractor evaluation committee within the construction firm. Some subcontractors and foremen are commended for their performance. Any failures are discussed at a senior level and actions designed to put the matters right are agreed. Repeated failures will result in reduced work and even loss of exclusive status.

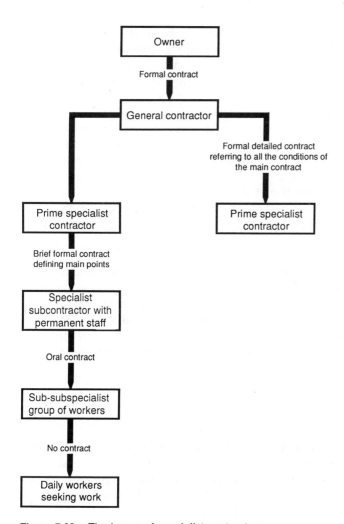

Figure 7.23 *The layers of specialist contractors*

Exactly the same style of relationship governs the subcontractor's employment of his workforce. Typically, the subcontractor will employ new operatives straight from technical high-school. They undergo a five year apprenticeship during which time they learn *on-the-job*. Their practical experience is supplemented by talks given in the evenings by experienced craftsmen. The talks cover the craft and the culture of being a Japanese building worker. The whole process aims to produce complete craftsmen.

At the end of five years the new craftsman will be employed by one of the subcontractor's exclusive sub-subcontract teams. They are employed on a piece-work basis and are organized by an experienced craftsman. After two years of such employment, the craftsman may form his own sub-subcontract team.

Throughout the whole multi-layered structure of Japanese contracting, between 50 and 60 per cent of the firms have an exclusive working relationship with a father firm. The rest work for several firms and are used by them to provide flexibility to meet varying seasonal demand and changes in the overall level of demand for building work. Right at the bottom of the structure are seasonal workers. They comprise less than 5 per cent of the workforce. Most of them work in agriculture for a large part of the year and go into the cities in the winter months, live in dormitories provided by the subcontractors and work on construction projects.

In many ways the impressive stability and certainty of Japanese building rests on and is dependent on the floating sub-subcontractors and seasonal workers who absorb the uncertainty of the marketplace. This, combined with a salary system in which about a third of total remuneration is paid as a profit-related bonus and so allows labour costs to be adjusted rapidly without strikes or redundancies, gives Japan's building industry the confidence to invest steadily in its own future.

Innovation

People working, naturally think of different ways of carrying out their tasks. Some of these ideas would produce benefits, some disbenefits and some would merely provide a change. Typically, the flow of ideas builds up to a peak as a new skill is learnt and practised. Then, as the worker develops his skill to a mature state, the flow of new ideas reduces to a trickle.

The Japanese use quality circles to foster and sustain the flow of new ideas about work, to evaluate them and to ensure that beneficial ideas are put into practice. The result is that the agreed standardized approaches to work steadily become more and more efficient. Wasted effort is identified and reduced to create a thoroughbred production system.

Quality circles are used throughout the Japanese building industry. All groups of workers meet each week for about one hour to discuss their work. Problems are considered, ideas for improving the product or working methods are discussed, and those which promise to provide real innovation are identified. These promising ideas are considered in detail at subsequent meetings of the quality circle. The circle leader can ask for technical advice or even commission research from the firm's research institute, in order to evaluate a potential innovation. When an idea appears to provide benefits, its implementation is considered by the quality circle. They discuss the implications with other workers likely to be affected and, when a consensus in favour of a new idea has been established, the quality circle plans its introduction and then puts their innovation into practice.

Each quality circle is required to report to their superior at six month intervals on the ideas they have considered and the innovations they have introduced. The reports are an important element in annual staff appraisals. Membership of a successful quality circle reflects well on an individual.

Quality circles serve to channel good ideas in a productive manner. Without them, better ways of working arise but are either forgotten or introduced too soon without full consideration and so there is a high probability of failure because of inadequate thought. Quality circles also serve to remind experienced, mature workers of the continuing need to review their products and methods. But, most importantly, they enable routine, normal work to concentrate on applying established, widely understood methods uninterrupted by one-off individual changes. There is a time and place to express good ideas and a time and place for steady, efficient, orderly work. The Japanese approach provides both.

Research and development

In the same way that quality circles provide a home for ideas about improving current working methods, company research institutes provide a place for workers to explore big new issues. These may deal with original design concepts, new technology, improved engineering or different construction methods.

The major construction firms have large, well-equipped research institutes with staff of 250–350 people and annual budgets in excess of $50 million (1990 prices). They undertake planned programmes of research for the company. They do research commissioned by public and private sector customers into specific problems. A further very important responsibility for the research institutes is to solve problems that occur on the company's projects anywhere in the world. In addition, staff in the research institutes are encouraged to spend up to 30 per cent of their time in pursuing their own research ideas. The result is a rich mixture of fundamental and applied research and development work.

The construction firms' research institutes commonly work in collaboration with each other and with companies from other industries. These include communications and electronics firms, plant and equipment manufacturers and component manufacturers. Indeed, one important strength of Japanese research is that it brings together researchers from many companies and many industries to identify new and original combinations of technology. This approach is already producing exciting ideas in computer-aided design and management, robotics and intelligent buildings.

The research institutes produce a stream of ideas for new products and methods, ensure that construction is in touch with the best industrial research, and provide a positive marketing bonus. Investment in research demonstrates a real commitment by the company to its products and to the future. It allows clients to consider design alternatives, all of which have been researched and tested to rigorous standards. In addition, the research institutes provide a proper outlet for creative, original thinkers who emerge within the company. When their ideas are fully researched and developed they provide a significant addition to the company's range of products or its methods of working. Natural researchers are not left in frustration to fiddle with the mainstream production system. The Japanese approach channels their important talent into producing significant, controlled steps forward.

Lessons from Japan

Japanese building demonstrates the advantages and the weaknesses of adopting a consistent standardized approach to construction project management. By ensuring that workers throughout the industry are properly trained for their work and as far as possible ensuring that they are not faced with uncertainty about what they are expected to do or when and how they are to do it, the Japanese building industry succeeds in delivering buildings exactly on time, completed exactly to specified standards. Although fast building is not normally a high priority (certainty is preferred to high speed), Japanese construction firms can build quickly when the need arises. The Japanese approach also has long term benefits, since by providing controlled outlets for workers' innovative ideas and for those who wish to undertake research and development, the building industry succeeds in steadily improving its products and its performance. Productivity is now impressive by world standards, but differences in accounting conventions, problems in establishing exchange rates that reflect purchasing power parity, and differing interest and inflation rates make it difficult to make any firm judgements on costs. Certainly salaries are high, the cost of living is high, land costs are the highest in the world and, on the basis of simple comparisons, building costs are some 20 per cent higher than in the UK. However, this difference is reducing under the influence of different rates of inflation and Japan's steady improvement in productivity.

It is possible to say, therefore, that Japan's approach to building has the potential to provide good quality buildings, fast construction, high productivity, high salaries and competitive total costs. It also provides a well established, secure basis for further advances. Having adopted the basic principles of manufacturing, Japanese building is well equipped to work with major industrial companies in inventing a high-technology component-based building industry for the twenty-first century. The implications of this are discussed in Chapter 16.

So Japanese building has great strengths, but what are the disbenefits of its approach? By far the most significant is the lack of variety in the buildings in Japan. They are well built and work properly, but they are dull. More importantly, they lack the depth of individual design quality which is characteristic of the best European design. It remains to be seen whether this weakness can be overcome and just-in-time technology can deliver buildings which are as much in sympathy with human values as those produced by individual designers and craftsmen.

8 Practice in Europe

Europe's building industry is shaped by the diverse and historic cultures it serves. As a consequence, there is not one European building industry but a multitude of separate national and regional industries. Each comprises a distinctive pattern of roles and relationships.

There are powerful forces which are tending to remove some of the differences between Europe's separate building industries. These include the European Community's programme of legislation leading to the completion of the internal market by the end of 1992. These political pressures are reinforced by technological factors. As building components become more sophisticated and rely on high-technology manufacturing, producers need ever bigger markets. There is already, as a result of these technological forces, a developed European market for a number of types of building components. These tend to be high value, low weight products which require high capital investment and for which transport costs are relatively insignificant. Further pressures towards the emergence of a common industry emanate from the activities of US and Japanese clients and contractors. They tend to see Europe as a single market-place and act accordingly. As local consultants and contractors are drawn into projects influenced by US and Japanese methods and styles, the various individual national approaches are modified in consistent directions.

A final very important and relatively new force which is pushing Europe's building industries towards greater common ground is the effect of very large projects. There is already a European market for the consultants and contractors able to handle mega-projects like Canary Wharf, Broadgate, Euro Disneyland and the Channel Tunnel. Indeed, for certain areas of knowledge and experience, the market is global rather than being confined to Europe. The needs of mega-projects transcend local methods and procedures. Such projects inevitably have a very high public profile and one consequence of this is that the approaches adopted are widely discussed and imitated throughout many of Europe's individual building industries. So there are powerful forces at work which appear likely to produce a truly European building industry at some time in the future.

In the meantime, for all except the very largest of projects, Europe consists of many relatively small and very different national building industries. They do however have one feature in common and it is this distinctive characteristic which provides the focus for this chapter. In Europe, the practice of architecture as a cultural, aesthetic activity which dominates building is more highly developed than in the USA or Japan.

Architecture

Architecture is building design enlightened by culture, style and a sense of place. Design is a particularly human activity. Simon (1969) described design as the distinguishing feature of all professions. It is the act of creating a new answer. Broadbent (1973) clearly sees design as having a basis in the arts, sciences and humanities. Also, it has a conscious and subconscious dimension. It is this above all which ensures that design will remain a human activity. Machines can help, but final choices need human judgement. The deep reasons for this were well expressed by Garry Kasparov after he had trounced the most highly rated chess playing computer. He said 'it does not have fantasy, intuition or imagination.'

Good architects have these in abundance. They create a sense of surprise by doing something unexpected within a familiar pattern. Like all artists, they extend our understanding of the world and of ourselves. Great architecture creates rhythms that we recognize and then adds variations within them which surprise and delight us.

All this is common ground throughout the great majority of Europe, yet the way architecture is practised varies dramatically from country to country. For example, France and Germany are neighbouring countries yet their approaches to architectural practice are about as different as they could be.

Architects in France

In France architects are responsible only for the conceptual design. Meikle and Hillebrandt (1990) describe how they produce the sketch design and some of the more detailed drawings, but not the working drawings. They are not involved in selecting contractors or in monitoring construction work.

This detached role derives from the centuries old view in France that architecture is a liberal profession grounded in the fine arts. France was the first country in Europe to establish a central organization for architects when, in 1671, Colbert created a Royal Academy of Architecture to provide a suitable artistic background for the reign of Louis XIV. At the Royal Academy in Paris architects were trained to design palaces and great public buildings.

After the French Revolution, Napoleon recognized the need for a different approach for the military and more utilitarian public buildings required by the

Republic. In 1795 he created the *Ecole Polytechnique* to provide scientific and general education for civil engineers. This effectively separated engineering from architecture. For educational purposes, architecture found its home with other fine arts in the *beaux arts* system. Entrance to the schools of architecture depended on artistic ability expressed in draughtsmanship and the ability to produce elegant designs. Architectural education in France was not at all concerned with practical technical or managerial abilities. It is fortunate for French architects, that this narrow education system produced only some 180 graduates each year. This small elite profession found sufficient employment in the preservation of historic buildings and the design of grand buildings. However, it was out of touch with up-to-date technology and had little interest in the social requirements of buildings. These practical details were left to others. Despite major reforms, French architects continue to play a role which is relatively detached from the mainstream of the building industry.

In 1968, arising out of a major and long-running debate among government officials, engineers and architects about the need to change the approach, architectural education was reformed. The *Ecole Nationale des Beaux Arts* was closed and 22 new *Unités Pédagogiques d'Architecture* were established to join the *Ecole Spéciale d'Architecture* in Paris and the architectural department of the *Ecole Nationale Supérieure des Arts et Industries* in Strasbourg. There are now some 13 000 students studying architecture at these schools. As a result the profession in France has grown from 8 400 in 1968 to over 25 000 in 1990. This remarkable growth has not yet been translated into a broader role for the profession. As a consequence, many architects engage in non-architectural work and more are unemployed or underemployed. This suggests that the historic patterns of architectural practice will take a long time to change since they are deeply ingrained in the working methods of the building industry which has grown up around them.

In France the building industry, in response to the architects' concentration on conceptual design, is dominated by building engineers. The architects' sketch plans and such detail drawings as they choose to produce are turned into working drawings by *bureaux d'études techniques*. These are large building engineering design firms, typically employing several hundred staff. Many are owned by contractors or industrial firms. Others are owned by banks or insurance companies, while in the public sector they are often integrated within customer organizations. They provide a wide range of services in addition to their primary role of building engineering design. In a typical building project they produce specifications and working drawings in sufficient detail to invite competitive tenders from specialist contractors.

The small role played by architects has allowed the building engineers to flourish and to play the key roles in the French building industry. Building engineers have a very rigorous scientific and technological education which enables them to enter a variety of careers. In building they undertake building design, structural design, services design, project management and construction management. They make no sharp distinction between professional and commercial relationship and so there are relatively few independent consulting engineers. Building and civil engineering are closely integrated in practice.

The dominant role of the building engineers mirrors the position and status of engineers in France generally. The best students compete to attend *Les Grandes Ecoles* and, having graduated, go on to 'own the country' by filling most of the top jobs in both the public and the private sectors. In the traditional French building industry the building engineers, in the *bureaux d'études techniques*, have created very competent firms able to provide a wide range of design and management services. It is they who provide the strategic organization for the specialist contractors.

The traditional pattern of contracting in France is *lots séparés*. That is, the letting of separate contracts to each trade or to groups of trade contractors. Each contractor has a direct contract with the client and has no legal relationship with the other contractors. The number of separate contractors varies greatly with the complexity of the building.

Overall project supervision is generally provided by the *bureaux d'études techniques*. However, day-to-day coordination is provided by appointing one of the contractors as *pilote*. He is responsible for coordinating and monitoring the work in progress on site, and for ensuring that working and shop drawings are available at the right time.

The *lots séparés* approach enables the customer and his advisors to select firms best able to provide the required trade skills. Also, it allows an early start to construction work by, for example, placing a contract for the foundation work before the rest of the building is fully designed. An important feature of the French approach to selecting contractors is that it is normally based on specifications and sketch drawings. Consequently, the contractors invited to tender are expected to state the design details they propose using. Thus competing bids are not necessarily on the same basis. It is therefore not necessarily sensible to accept the lowest bid, and the laws governing public sector building projects permit acceptance of the tender which is most advantageous. This approach allows contractors to use design details and therefore construction methods which best suit their knowledge and skills.

The *lots séparés* approach requires careful planning and strong management of the construction work by the *bureau d'études techniques* and the *pilote*. This is because problems can arise if any one contractor delays operations on site. In these circumstances, the other contractors have no obligation to help put things right and so the knock-on effects of one delay could become very serious.

A number of contractual arrangements are in use to overcome this problem. There is some use of general contractors and it is not uncommon for the separate contractors to enter into a group contract. There are various forms of *groupement* in which contractors may be jointly responsible for the whole project or simply join together to enter into a single contract within which they each retain their separate responsibilities for their own trades. However the *lots séparés* approach remains the most widely used. One important factor in allowing it to continue and to be successful in providing the basis for a building industry which clients generally find satisfactory is the French system of obligatory insurance.

The *Spinetta* law of 1978 introduced obligatory insurance to provide three guarantees: a one year guarantee of perfect achievement; a two year guarantee of satisfactory functioning; and a ten year guarantee of the *décennal* responsibility.

The *responsibilité civile décennal* falls on everyone involved with building projects who has any contractual relationship with the customer. It covers architects, engineers, trade contractors, manufacturers and indeed everyone contributing to a project. It covers any failure of the structure of new buildings, alterations and repair work, and the land on which the buildings stand. Because any one of the organizations involved with a project may be held responsible for a fault, all must insure under the *décennal* responsibility. However, litigation to determine who is in fact responsible may take years and so there is also compulsory insurance for customers, except for some exempted public sector bodies, which is known as *dommage ouvrage* cover. This is always on a project basis, whereas the other participants may have blanket insurance cover. The *dommage ouvrage* cover ensures that the customer will always be able to obtain the money needed to repair any faults that emerge. Both the original owner and his successors are covered and there is, by law, no excess, in order to ensure that repairs can always be carried out.

The effect of the obligatory insurance provisions is that customers are not drawn into the internal disputes of the building industry over liability. They are provided with an effective 10 year guarantee for their new buildings. The system is expensive and various estimates of the total additional cost range from three to eight per cent.

The operation of the building construction insurances is closely linked to the *bureaux de control.* For the great majority of projects one of the *bureaux* is employed direct by the client. It looks at and checks the working drawings and inspects the work on site. The employment of a *bureau de control* is compulsory and insurance will not be granted without their involvement for buildings where it is judged the safety of the public may be at risk. The overall effect of the wide use of *bureaux de control* with the strict insurance system has led to a building industry which produces a reliable standard of construction and is slow to innovate. This has undoubtedly suited the traditionally educated architects. It is also arguable that it has helped France to remain a civilized, pleasant country where, for example, Parisians can justifiably take a pride in their city.

Architects have traditionally enjoyed a high social status in France. However, largely because of the rapid growth in their numbers, they are finding it more and more difficult to have their work adequately rewarded. This is in contrast to the building engineers, who enjoy both high social status and high financial rewards. This is paradoxical given that in France architecture is a protected profession. No buildings above $180 \, \text{m}^2$ of floor area can be built without plans signed by an architect. Perhaps as a consequence nearly all smaller buildings, including most private houses, are designed by building engineers. At the other end of the spectrum, many of France's prestigious, innovative buildings are designed by foreign architects. Major examples include the Pompidou Centre, the Gare d'Orsay, L'Arche de la Defense and L'Opera de la Bastille. So, at a time when unemployment among architects hovers around 20 per cent and their salaries are reduced to levels not much above that of the traditionally poorly paid nursing profession, the role of the independent architectural practice is tightly restricted.

Further pressures on French architects' traditional role are emerging from a steady growth in general contracting. Mainly through mergers, five very large contractors have emerged: Bouygues, GTM Entrepose and Dumez, SOBEA, Spie Batignolles and the SEA group. They are able to provide a complete service from inception to completion. It seems certain that these firms, which are all among the biggest in Europe, will exert an increasing influence on the French building industry.

So on balance the narrow role traditionally adopted by French architects appears to have locked the profession into a minor role except in respect of medium sized, traditional buildings. The dominant roles are increasingly played by the more broadly based building engineers. This is very much in contrast to the position in neighbouring Germany.

Architects in Germany

The historical development of architecture in Germany is similar to that in France with one important difference. That is that the education of architects and engineers shares common roots. Biggs *et al.* (1990) describe how the resulting role of the architects and indeed the structure of the building industry is very different from that in France.

Formal architectural education started in the late seventeenth century in the Arts Academies of Berlin and Dresden. The architect was seen initially as an artist and was trained to meet the demands of the aristocracy. In Germany, as in France, over the next century this was seen to be inadequate for a growing number of public buildings, and in 1798 the Building Academy of Prussia was founded in Berlin. Technical subjects dominated and students studied both architecture and engineering.

The period of common education for all building professionals was relatively short lived and by the middle of the nineteenth century the education of architects and engineers began to be separated. However, both have remained within the same educational institutions. The two disciplines have developed in parallel with a great deal of overlap between the separate courses. As a consequence, as Haenlein *et al.* (1989) describe, today in Germany architects and engineers are educated in *Universitäten* and in *Fachhochschulen*.

The *Universität* or university courses combine research and teaching. The mainly scientific basis of the courses aims to establish a fundamental knowledge base so that graduates can identify new problems in the industry and develop new answers. The university courses concentrate on scientific principles substantially informed by theory. Students are expected to *pace* their own studies, so that when they graduate into practice they will be able to take responsibility for tasks which cut across established fields of activity and develop these scientifically.

The *Fachhochschule* or polytechnic courses combine practice and research. Graduates are expected to be able to apply the knowledge gained, immediately they enter practice. Students are taught established, proven methods of practice. Staff must have a successful track record in practice and indeed many combine teaching with work in practice. The polytechnics produce about 2750 architectural graduates a year compared with some 1200 university graduates. Together these two streams make up a powerful and highly esteemed profession, which numbers some 60 000 members.

Architectural practices in Germany provide a very complete and very thorough design and management service. This includes preliminary planning and negotiation with local authorities, scheme design, estimation of costs, production of specifications and working drawings, planning the construction activities, selecting contractors (usually by organizing competitive tenders) and supervising the construction.

The comprehensive service provided by architectural practices is entirely provided by staff who qualified as architects, aided, of course, by assistants and administrative and secretarial staff. However, individual architects specialize in specific areas of the work. Thus some German architects are specialists in conceptual design, others in various aspects of technology, while yet others concentrate on the management and cost control aspects of construction. The strength of this arrangement is that all the specialists share a common educational base and since they share the same one professional name and work in the same one firm there is no tendency for interprofessional rivalries to develop.

Another factor which makes for consistency and harmony is that the German building industry is characterized by very thorough formal laws and procedures which cover every aspect of building work. The rights, responsibilities and fee scales for architects and engineers are described in specific rules in *Honarordnung für Architekten and Ingeniure* (HOAI) which is incorporated in Federal Government law. The control of development is similarly precise. Local authorities produce land-use plans which, once approved, are binding on the authority, in the sense that if an application conforms to the plan it must be approved. That is, provided the proposals meet all the relevant legal requirements. The granting of a building permit covers all these requirements, including planning, building regulations and infrastructure requirements. Consequently, applications for approval are very detailed and must include full drawings and detailed technical calculations. There are also precise standards for building materials and components published by the *Deutsche Institute für Normung* (DIN). The DIN also produce standard forms of building contract conditions. These are really codes of practice and are widely used. The *VOB Verdingungsordnung für Bauleistungen* provide the basic contractual conditions for construction works. They contain detailed rules for open and selective tendering, negotiating a direct contract award, and the content of specifications and drawings, as well as a very full set of construction contract conditions. Every conceivable situation and circumstance is, as far as humanly possible, made the subject of an explicit rule.

In the substantial majority of building projects, the construction work is organized on the basis of separate trade contracts direct with the client. This can mean as many as 30 independent contracts on even a simple building project. Although the architect undoubtedly plays an important role in coordinating the work of the separate trades, the success of the system depends to a large extent on attitudes of cooperation among all parties. An important factor in ensuring this is the very local nature of construction in Germany. Contractors depend on their reputation within the local community for future business. Consequently, they concentrate on meeting clients' demands for high quality and actively seek the overall success of the projects with which they are involved.

This philosophy has produced some excellent contractors and it is undoubtedly the case that the best of the German specialist contractors are among the very best to be found anywhere. Gartner, for example, is undoubtedly one of the best curtain walling firms in the world. Through sophisticated and long term research and development they have developed an excellent curtain walling system. Their designers are comfortable working together with the world's best architects in designing curtain walling systems for great buildings wherever they are required. Gartner produce comprehensive working and shop drawings, construct and test prototypes, and manufacture huge prefabricated panels which frequently incorporate sophisticated services and controls. They install their curtain walling on site and are happy to maintain it. This total service is provided by directly employed, salaried operatives which Gartner have trained and expect to employ for their whole working life.

Although Gartner are undoubtedly exceptional, German architects can rely on competent, high-quality detail design, manufacturing and construction work from specialist contractors. One very important factor in creating this happy situation is the depth of education and training throughout German industry. In building this includes, for the basic workforce, very thorough early training within a system which produces reliable, well-qualified craftsmen. This combines on-the-job training and classroom work provided by *Berufsschulen* or part-time vocational schools. The in-company vocational training for young people is governed by federal regulations. Teaching at the *Berufsschulen* is similarly regulated by individual state laws. Trainees have to take a final examination on completion of three years' training in order to obtain a recognized occupational qualification. This is a prerequisite for employment at standard wage rates as a *Geselle* or journeyman. This in turn leads on, after several years of working as a journeyman and the passing of a further government examination, to qualification as a *Meister* or master craftsman. Formal education and training for most German workers does not stop at that point; they are provided with a wide range of forms of organized learning. Continuing professional advancement and updating are seen as a normal part of being a master craftsman. This serious and professional attitude to work is a major factor in enabling the German specialist contractors to continue to operate the separate contracts approach on even very complex and sophisticated buildings.

There are, however, some large and successful general contractors in Germany. Many grew on the basis of work overseas, particularly in the Middle East's construction boom of the 1970s. As that market collapsed, general contractors sought new markets overseas and at home. In the main, they have concentrated on highly complex projects for major commercial and public customers. These typically include hospitals, airports, television installations and large scale civil engineering projects. An interesting recent trend is for general contractors to engage in the maintenance of these sophisticated structures. Since they often need continuous and systematic maintenance, the work provides a basis for long term relationships with important customers.

In the main, general contractors work on the basis of designs provided by independent architects. Nevertheless, they are willing and able to provide a full design and build service. Alternatively, they may take responsibility for developing a conceptual design produced by a customer's independent architect. There is also some evidence of the emergence of firms offering a construction management service.

These challenges to the traditional approach perhaps raise some doubts about the long-term role of the independent architect. However, all the hard evidence points to a secure future for the profession of architecture in Germany. Certainly it is held in high esteem. Competition for places on architecture courses in the universities is intense, making it one of the most difficult subjects to enter. In common with other German industries, the building industry produces good quality products efficiently. Buildings in Germany work properly and satisfy their mainly solid, middle-class owners. It is therefore reasonable to conclude that the German approach to architecture, which combines art, science and technology, has served both the profession and the nation well.

Local architecture

France and Germany provide examples of dramatic differences in the role played by architects. In France, with its *beaux arts* tradition, the architect plays a narrow, almost remote role. He provides the overall concept and leaves the technical detail and actual construction of buildings to others. In Germany, with its total faith in science and technology, the architect is master builder. He does everything except the actual construction. As Figures 8.1 and 8.2 illustrate, the overall pattern of the traditional approach to building project organization is, apart from the role of the architect, very similar.

In both France and Germany, architects design for a specific building user. The customer may be an individual, a firm or a public body, but in the vast majority of cases they build knowing who will occupy the building. The *development culture*, seeing buildings as tradeable commodities, is in its infancy. Office blocks are built for a specific organization, houses remain in the same family's ownership for generations, and the retail and leisure revolutions which have so shaped USA building are only just emerging.

The main effect of buildings being very specific is that architecture is local. It is grounded in the methods and skills of local specialist and trade contractors. At

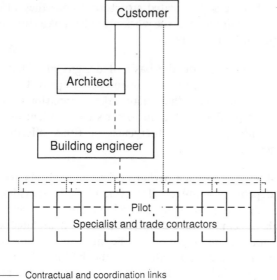

Contractual and coordination links
Coordination links
Contractual links

Figure 8.1   *Traditional building project organization in France*

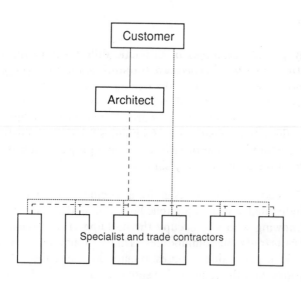

Contractual and coordination links
Coordination links
Contractual links

Figure 8.2   *Traditional building project organization in Germany*

its best, European local architecture produces remarkable buildings. Two widely reported examples are the Scandinavian Airlines System (SAS) head-quarters outside Stockholm shown in Figure 8.3 and the head office of the third largest Dutch bank, Nederlandsche Middenstandsbank (NBM) in Amsterdam. Both are arranged to provide individuals, groups and departments with a sense of identity and ownership by giving users private spaces which can they shape to their own ways of working. The buildings also provide spaces that encourage users to socialize and meet to discuss key decisions and generally to interact in comfortable and productive ways. Communal spaces lead off internal streets, so that meetings take place, not in formal committee rooms, but in spaces more like cafes or restaurants. Both provide much natural light and ventilation through opening windows. Their shapes avoid the rectangles and squares of ordinary office buildings.

The effect on the workers in these two important buildings is dramatic. Productivity is some 20–25 per cent higher than in ordinary air-conditioned, high-rise office blocks, largely because the workers feel healthier, and are able to work effectively for a greater part of each day, and there is less absenteeism. These benefits derive from the concern to create a sense of place, with which people can identify, which is such an important strength of European local architecture. It depends, as Figures 8.1 and 8.2 suggest, on close links between architects and master craftsmen. It depends on respecting human scale and human needs for places which provide tranquility and inspiration. It depends on creating beauty which echoes the familiar, attractive features of local styles but also adds something new.

It is perhaps not surprising that in Britain, which is at the crossroads of the European and US traditions of development, the right approach to architecture and building is the subject of fierce debate. There is great concern about the kinds of building which should be produced and about the kinds of project organization best fitted to produce them.

Building in Britain

Architects in Britain play a role unlike that in any other country. It has been described as being based on an arts and crafts tradition which therefore involves large numbers of architects working on every design detail and supervising their construction. In November 1989, the *Architects Journal* invited a number of well established British architects to identify good products. A very representa-tive view was expressed by one well known practitioner who said 'I suppose I try to avoid using products as such ... mainly because there is nothing on the market that is exactly what I want'. He went on to describe how on a recent project he had the door handles carved out of wood on site in order to get the qualities he wanted. When pressed to name his favourite product he finally decided on paint. But even then he nominated a make of paint which provides a range of stainers (full strength dyes for use with emulsion paint), which allow considerable individual choice of colour.

The British architects' attention to every detail combined with a reluctance to use standard or established designs produces great variety in quality and performance. Britain has produced a remarkable number of the world's acknowledged great architects. Yet the performance of the profession overall has provoked stinging criticism from HRH the Prince of Wales (1989) who has a well founded concern for the appearance and condition of the kingdom he will eventually inherit. The approach adopted by British architects has also provoked steady and well informed criticism from its most experienced customers.

(a)

(b)

(c)

Figure 8.3 *(a) SAS Headquarters, Stockholm. (b) The internal street. (c) Shops and cafes line the street*

They rightly criticize the whole building industry for inefficiency. An influential study by Slough Estates Limited (1979), a very experienced international property company, found that industrial building in Britain was slower, the design process was more complex, and construction was less efficient than in other countries. A number of subsequent studies have added to these criticisms. To improve matters, major customers have given a lead in using a wide range of alternative forms of building project organization. As a consequence, the British building industry is a hot-bed of competing ideas about the right approach to architecture and building project organization.

General contractor approach

For nearly two centuries in England and Wales and about 50 years in Scotland, the most common building project organization has been based on a general contractor approach. Figure 8.4 illustrates the main lines of coordination in this traditional approach. It reached its heyday 20 years ago, an event marked by the publication of the Royal Institute of British Architects' (RIBA) Plan of Work.

The approach is dominated by the architect's wish to control all aspects of design. In its classical form the customer first commissions an architect. The architect establishes the project brief and produces an outline scheme design. He will usually be helped in this process by engineering design consultants and quantity surveyors, whose employment the architect recommends to the customer. Once the scheme design is recommended to the customer, the quantity surveyor produces a cost plan which describes how the customer's construction budget will be spent. The cost plan is arranged in design elements. Thus it provides a cost target for each member of the design team.

A typical design team comprises separate firms of architects, structural engineers and services engineers. Increasingly, it also includes specialist contractors who provide design advice to the architect about the sophisticated, industrialized technologies which form a large proportion of today's buildings. The architect, at least acording to the RIBA Plan of Work, manages this fragmented design process. The main communication vehicle is working drawings, which are passed back and forth between the independent designers. There are also project meetings at which the design is reviewed and decisions about the next stages of the process are debated and agreed. Experienced architects produce formal drawing programmes and appoint internal project managers to maintain progress.

As design decisions are made, the cost implications are estimated by the quantity surveyor and related to the agreed cost plan. When cost over-runs are identified either the design or the cost plan is altered. By incorporating contingency allowances in the original cost plan, design teams can usually work within a sensibly agreed budget. However, it is not uncommon for the original brief, the design concepts or the budget to be altered during the development of

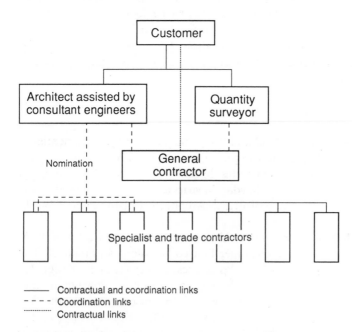

Customer

Architect assisted by consultant engineers

Quantity surveyor

Nomination

General contractor

Specialist and trade contractors

———— Contractual and coordination links
– – – – Coordination links
············ Contractual links

Figure 8.4　*The British general contractor approach*

the working drawings. This inevitably involves the customer in hard decisions and generally tends to delay the project.

The next stage in the classical RIBA Plan of Work approach is for the quantity surveyor to produce bills of quantities. This is a very detailed measurement of all the items of work needed to produce the building as designed by the architect and engineers. The result is essentially a quantified specification which, together with the working drawings, defines exactly what is to be built. However, the involvement of specialist contractors in the design process complicates this neat sequential process. The problem is overcome by including prime-cost sums in the bills of quantities against which the architect can subsequently nominate the firm he wishes to undertake the work. Obviously, he will normally nominate the specialist contractor who has proved to be most helpful during the design stages. So the bills of quantities used to invite competitive tenders from general contractors are a mixture of traditional trade contractors' work, measured out in fine detail, and fixed lump sums, against which a specialist contractor will subsequently be nominated by the architect.

The bills of quantities together with sufficient of the working drawings to enable the nature of the required work to be envisaged are sent to the general contractors selected to submit competitive tenders. They price the bills of quantities item by item and add in the fixed prime-cost sums to arrive at their total price. They usually seek competitive tenders from the trade contractors they expect to employ as subcontractors if they are successful in being awarded the contract. The general contractors' lump sum tenders are submitted to the architect. He normally asks the lowest tenderer to submit his priced bills of quantities. These are checked by the quantity surveyor to ensure that there are no errors in the calculations of the total price and to confirm that the structure of prices provides a sensible basis for the customer to enter into a contract. It is generally the case that the general contractor submitting the lowest tender is awarded the contract.

The contract is essentially an agreement to build all the work described in the bills of quantities for the contract sum under the supervision of the architect. The Joint Contracts Tribunal (JCT) forms of contract for use with bills of quantities, which are the most widely used forms, allow the architect to vary the work and to condemn any which he regards as unsatisfactory. The contract also provides for the quantity surveyor to value the work each month and for the architect to certify interim payments by the customer to the general contractor.

To a very large extent, general contractors subcontract the direct construction work which is included in the bills of quantities as measured items to their own choice of specialist contractors and work which is the subject of prime-cost sums to specialist contractors nominated by the architect. During construction there are project progress meetings on site chaired by the architect. The meetings consider any problems which have arisen, but primarily provide the means for the architect to keep the customer informed about progress. When the work is complete, the architect issues a certificate that this is the case and the customer is given possession of his new building. The quantity surveyor prepares the final account, which takes account of the prices for work by nominated subcontractors and uses the individual rates in the bills of quantities to value variations ordered by the architect.

The approach is widely seen as confrontational, complicated, slow and unfair to the contractors. Since the JCT contracts are negotiated by a large body, representative of all the key interests within the building industry, the forms of contract have over the years become increasingly complicated as they incorporate amendments designed to deal with one or another unacceptable feature of the approach. The latest JCT forms of contract are immensely complicated and remain biased in favour of the industry's own internal processes rather than protecting the interests of customers. In addition to these weaknesses in the process, its separation of detail design from direct construction knowledge and experience is widely thought to have led to Britain being provided with a poor standard of buildings. Not surprisingly, many customers and many contractors have experimented with alternative approaches. In parallel with this, the professions have fought back by attempting to constrain the worst excesses of architects, engineers and quantity surveyors.

Professional response

Many of the building professionals' initiatives aimed at creating a more effective general contractor approach have come from quantity surveyors. This is not surprising, as a bulk of their fee income results from the production of bills of quantities used to select general contractors. Some of the earliest initiatives can now be seen to have made the industry's performance worse. However, more recently a mature approach, enlightened by an understanding of management theory, has led to real improvements in the traditional general contractor approach.

One of the early ideas was to produce approximate bills of quantities. The overall concept comprised producing bills of quantities based on early design decisions filled out with hypothetical quantities of work, which it was hoped would bear a close relationship to the work actually required. Quantity surveyors exercised a fair degree of skill in anticipating the subsequent decisions of architects and engineers. Also the liberal use of prime-cost sums allowed design decisions to be delayed, while still producing a lump sum contract price.

The benefit was that work could start on site much earlier than if the bills of quantities were based on a complete design. The key central problem with the approach was that it diverted general contractors' attention away from planning and controlling the construction work efficiently. With approximate bills of quantities, their best interests were served by concentrating on getting paid the highest possible price for the work actually required by the architect. This led inevitably to sterile disputes over whether or not specific items of work were the same as those described in the bills of quantities. Claims for extra time and extra money became endemic. Meanwhile, actual construction performance deteriorated, as the best minds concentrated on the paper battle and left the real work to muddle through as best it might.

The most important initiatives by the professions in response to this totally unacceptable situation have been, first, for the professional institutions to reaffirm the need to complete the design before inviting tenders, and second and in support of these exhortations, to cooperate in developing a coordinated approach to producing the project information required to invite sound tenders. The Coordinating Committee for Project Information, as described in Chapter 5, is sponsored jointly by RIBA, the Association of Consulting Engineers, the Royal Institution of Chartered Surveyors and the Building Employers Confederation. It produced a coordinated set of conventions which seeks to help architects, engineers and quantity surveyors produce drawings, specifications and bills of quantities which are complete and easy for general contractors to use. There is now a great deal of evidence that providing general contractors with complete design information at tender stage and not varying it during the construction stage is an approach that works well for relatively simple, individually designed buildings which use well established technologies. It has also become clear that for other types of project, or where the customer needs an early completion date, the general contractor approach is not the most appropriate. The alternatives fall into two broad categories: design-and-build, and construction management.

Design-and-build

The simplest and most obvious way of overcoming the divisive fragmentation of the British building industry is for customers to buy new buildings from contractors who both design and build. The development of this approach was severely handicapped by RIBA rules which forbade architects to work in responsible positions in any form of contracting firm. With one or two notable exceptions, this meant that design-and-build contractors either employed unqualified architects or subcontracted the design to an architectural practice who generally felt uncomfortable being employed by a contractor. As a consequence, design-and-build became associated with second-rate design. The few exceptions were provided by good architects who resigned from RIBA in order to create design-and-build firms. The RIBA rule no longer exists and the design-and-build approach is increasingly widely used. Also, it is gradually overcoming its reputation for producing only second-rate design.

The growing importance of the approach was marked in 1981 by the publication of a JCT with contractors' design standard form of contract. It is a very good contract, which provides customers with a useful range of approaches. The key to this flexibility is the statement of the *client's requirements*. This can be as brief or as detailed as the customer wishes. It states all the things which the customer specifically wants in the finished building and leaves the rest to the contractor to design in accordance with established good practice. Pain and Bennett (1988) report a study of the JCT:1981 contract in use which found at one extreme a statement of the *client's requirements* which consisted of a single sheet of paper. In effect it asked for some 240 local authority staff to be provided with new office accommodation on a given piece of land by a specified date within a stated overall budget. At the other extreme, Pain and Bennett found the contract being used with a statement of *client's requirements* consisting of a full specification and working drawings. Whatever level of detail is provided, the contractor is responsible for completing the design and the construction work, and for delivering a fully complete building to the customer.

The design-and-build contractor may simply be selected by the customer and the basis for a contract negotiated between the two parties. Alternatively, the contractor may be selected on the basis of competitive bids. These comprise design proposals and lump sum prices from several contractors. Once one of the bids is accepted or the customer negotiates an acceptable agreement, the contractor has sole responsibility for the project.

The design-and-build approach works well where the customer can fully and clearly specify the building he requires. Obviously, the simpler the building the easier it is for the statement of client's requirements to be comprehensive. Given that, the customer's main task is one of quality control. He must take the necessary steps to ensure that the building produced for him is satisfactory.

Customers using design-and-build for the first time often seek advice from architects, engineers or quantity surveyors in framing their statement of requirements and in negotiating with a single contractor or in inviting competitive bids. This consultancy advice may continue throughout the project to help the customer exercise his quality control responsibilities. Given this help from experienced professionals or given an experienced customer, design-and-build delivers a range of relatively simple building types reliably and quickly at a sensible price. In addition to providing a unified management system, design-and-build brings construction expertise to bear on design decisions.

Construction management

Construction management provides an alternative way of bringing construction knowledge and experience into the design process. In contemporary British practice there are two distinct forms. These are illustrated in Figures 8.5 and 8.6. In Britain, management contracting appeared before construction management. Indeed Marks and Spencer, with the construction firm Bovis, have been using many features of the approach since 1927. However, it is usually accepted that the first British management contracting project was the Horizon Factory built for John Player and Sons in Nottingham in 1971. It brought together two of the British building industry's very best firms, Arup Associates as designers and Bovis as management contractors. As well as pioneering the use of management contracting, the project provided a prototype for the modern flexible industrial building. It provides large column-free spaces with very heavy floor loadings, walk-in service floors above and below the main production floor, high security and an integrated energy plant. All this was achieved within an elegant and well considered design, produced speedily and economically.

It is not surprising, with this excellent start, that management contracting has grown rapidly in Britain. In two decades it has become the established approach

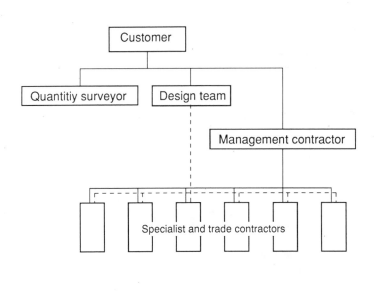

——— Contractual and coordination links
– – – · Coordination links

Figure 8.5 *The British management contracting approach*

for large and complex projects where an early completion is important and the customer wants to be involved in the design process.

The original aim of those who introduced management contracting was to align the contractor's interests with those of the customer; in other words, to create a role which is essentially that of a professional consultant. In doing this it was recognized that the main construction responsibilities are carried by the specialist contractors. It was therefore considered sensible for them to carry the construction risks. Given this background, it was necessary to create a new role. This was achieved by management contractors being paid a fee to manage the physical works in the customer's best interests. In addition, they were paid the actual costs of the work of the specialist contractors and of the so-called preliminaries items of establishing and managing the construction site. The construction manager in essence was liable only for his own professional managerial competence, in the same way as the other consultants involved.

However, many customers and more particularly their consultants were uncomfortable with the idea of contractors, whom they were used to treating at arm's length, acting as trusted professional advisors. Consequently Bennett (1986) found that quantity surveyors continued to be employed to play their traditional monitoring role as cost consultants reporting directly to the customer. It was also found to be impractical to place substantial liabilities on small

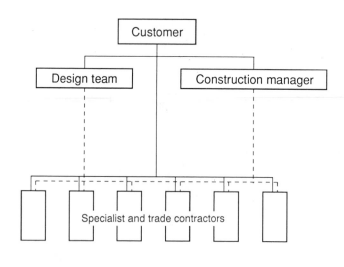

——— Contractual and coordination links
- - - Coordination links

Figure 8.6 *The British construction management approach*

specialist contractors. Consequently, in practice, customers had to bear some of the risks traditionally carried by contractors.

This approach held good until the early 1980s when, following a downturn in demand, many management contractors were forced by customers and their consultants to accept substantial contractual risks. These include: liability for design errors made by specialist contractors: liability for damages which the customer is unable to recover from specialist contractors for such matters as faulty workmanship or materials, defects in the finished building and delays; and liability for the effects of a default by a specialist contractor. In addition, many management contractors were required to agree a fixed price for preliminaries, much of which is of uncertain scope and content.

Inevitably, with the return of contractual risks, came a return to an adversarial approach by management contractors. They had little choice but to look after their own interests and so the original aims of cooperation and flexibility were no longer achieved.

It was against that background that US style professional construction management came to Britain. As Figure 8.6 illustrates, the approach provides an essentially simpler project organization. All the parties to the project enter into direct contracts with the customer. The construction manager is clearly and unambiguously a consultant and not a contractor. The specialist contractors have a design and construction responsibility founded in direct contracts with the customer.

Construction management gives the customer a very significant role. This includes the unavoidable responsibilities of establishing the overall project objectives, appointing the key project participants, making key decisions on whether the project is to be allowed to continue and in what form, and arranging the project finance. In addition to these responsibilities which apply in all projects, with construction management, the customer must also provide the overall leadership for the project. This has to be done in an unusually detailed manner. The customer is in direct contract with all the main project participants and they look to him to provide a sense of direction. The customer must establish the project values and then be consistent in giving time and attention to quality, cost, time or whatever he has decided should have the highest priorities. These responsibilities derive from the *team of equals* approach which characterizes construction management.

Both management approaches, management contracting and construction management, leave the design team with an uncluttered responsibility for designing the end product. This is sensible given the size, complexity and speed of the projects best suited to the approach. Design on such projects is difficult because it requires the knowledge and experience of many consultants and contractors. The difficulties arise from the sheer scale of the task of managing the flows of information between many separate designers working in parallel. Given good information, the best British designers produce world-class designs. However, fast-track methods on large complex building projects are incompatible with the British architect's wish to be closely involved in all design decisions. Even the best designers find themselves forced to accept second-best designs because of time pressures. Also, design effort is wasted as incompatible decisions made in parallel go undetected for several days or weeks.

The problems stem from using US methods, which as we saw in Chapter 6 depend on excellent specialist contractors who are comfortable accepting responsibility for coordinating the detail design and the construction work. Britain has too few specialist contractors, with this all-round competence, to create a competitive market of the kind which supports construction management in the USA. British specialist contractors have developed mainly in the context of the general contractor approach. This provides them with substantial support from architects' very detailed designs and from general contractors' detailed management of construction sites. As a consequence, on the massive Broadgate project in London shown in Figure 8.7, which has led the way in the

Figure 8.7   *Broadgate Square, London*

use of construction management in Britain, the customer has needed to adopt a policy of deliberately fostering potentially good specialist contractors and also using firms from mainland Europe and the USA. The separate trades approach of Europe produces good specialist contractors and they have found it easier to fit into the construction management approach than many of their British competitors. Similarly, the US specialist contractors' all-round competence has stood them in good stead, especially when working on phases of Broadgate designed by American architects.

The main lesson from the past decade of using management contracting and construction management in Britain is that both approaches make great demands on customers, designers, managers and specialist contractors. Given good people throughout the project organization, difficult projects can be designed and constructed quickly and efficiently. The committed involvement of the customer is very important in achieving excellent performance. This is most directly provided in construction management, which provides a straightforward and logical set of roles. When the customer is unable to play a totally committed central role, management contracting provides a good alternative. It is, however, dependent either on the design team and the management contractor trusting each other or one of them, in the final analysis, being clearly in charge of the project. In Britain, as Figure 8.5 suggests, this has tended to be the designer.

There is one further approach used in Britain which helps to throw light on the relationships between building projects and the organizations who design and construct them. This is called the design-and-manage approach.

Design-and-manage

Design-and-manage brings the design team and management contracting responsibilities together in a single contract. The customer is provided with a single point of responsibility for the delivery of his new building. Construction expertise is available during the development of the design. Thus the planning of construction can begin early and potential construction problems can be anticipated and designed out. Equally, the specialist contractors can be selected early so that they too can contribute to the design. As with management contracting, the client pays a fee to the design-and-manage consultant plus the costs of the preliminaries items and the actual prices of the specialist contractors' work.

The approach has been used with great success by Marks and Spencer. For each of their recent new stores, they have caused a consortium comprising a full team of design consultants and a management contractor to enter into a single contract to design and manage the construction. The results have been a dramatic improvement in team working and a better than 50 per cent reduction in the time taken to complete the whole project.

As Figure 8.8 illustrates, design-and-manage creates a project organization which is very similar to the traditional approach in Germany. Indeed, design-and-manage brings together in a consortium all the roles played by architects in Germany. Its Achilles' heel in Britain is likely to be a shortage of specialist contractors competent to play the full role which the approach demands. However, given experienced designers and management contractors with established networks of good specialist contractors, the approach is likely to be used on a growing scale. It gives Britain an approach which could allow the European tradition of competent architecture to be married to the US market-based traditions of competent management.

Architecture's challenge

It is no surprise that it is in pluralistic Europe that the great issues facing architecture are being debated most fiercely. Buildings provide the backdrop for most human activity. They should help us live in harmony with the cultures and societies that surround us. Today we are living through a period of enormous scientific and technological advance. A whole new range of tools from electronics, bio-technology and solid-state chemistry are opening the way for entirely new buildings.

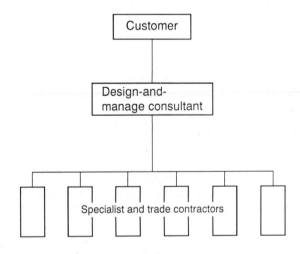

———— Contractual and coordination links

Figure 8.8   *The British design-and-manage approach*

The same new discoveries are changing the work of the people who occupy and use buildings. This change is unpredictable and rapid. Consequently, most buildings outlive the specific organizations they were designed to house, so flexible buildings will survive longer than those which are based on an unchanging form. Yet people need a sense of permanence. Buildings should help us to live in harmony with the past, present and future.

Great architecture creates patterns which give us pleasure. The need to impose patterns on the rich mix of data which our perceptions feed into our brains is instilled deep in the human mind. However, as our knowledge increases we need to be challenged by complex and contradictory cocktails of increasingly subtle patterns. Superficial beauty satisfies children of all ages, but the cultured and educated mind needs a richer mix of images and associations. Harmony in Europe comes from variety, from seeking richness of meaning rather than simple clarity of meaning. We can see this in St Mark's Square in Venice, in the Piazza della Signoria in Florence, and in the area around Kings College, Cambridge in England. Good modern examples include I.M. Pei's glass pyramid in the forecourt of the Louvre in Paris and the rich variety of the totally up-to-date urban designs by Peter Foggo of Arup Associates for the buildings that make up Finsbury Square shown in Figure 8.9 and Broadgate Square in London shown in Figure 8.7. All these examples combine artistry with craftsmanship. What is new is the variety and machine-based nature of modern

Figure 8.9 *Finsbury Square, London*

crafts. Great modern architecture needs to be guided by a love and understanding of machines, as well as of people. It must resolve conflicts between ethics, culture, science and finance. Architecture will inevitably be the work of teams.

Construction project management has a major role to play in creating buildings and environments which use science and technology to enhance human values. It needs to create organizations that allow talented, multidisciplinary teams to work together effectively. By harnessing the wealth of knowledge which we already have about the behaviour of people and materials, by continuing to research the behaviour of buildings as total social-technical systems, and by bringing all this understanding together in effective project teams we can create beautiful, healthy and efficient natural and built environments which give us all more individual control and greater choice.

9 *Universal principles of construction project management*

The first part of this book, in Chapters 1–5, described key management concepts. The second part, in Chapters 6–8, described important examples of current practice. It is now time to impose a pattern on this rich mixture of ideas about construction project management. This is the task of the third part of the book, which begins in this chapter. We begin with a powerful idea proposed by Mintzberg (1979). He suggests that efficient organizations achieve a self-consistent balance between their task, their environment and their internal structure. Consequently, the various features of construction projects discussed in the first two parts of this book cluster together in coherent, efficient systems. Mintzberg further proposed that these gestalts or clusters of tightly interdependent relationships are few in number. Mintzberg's theories of organization apply to construction projects since there appear to be just three distinct systems of construction project organization.

The three gestalts are idealized systems of organization. No actual project is likely to display all the characteristics of any one of the ideal types. However, the theory is that the closer managers can force their projects into the pattern of one of the idealized systems, the more efficient it will be. Since each is a tried and tested system, it must be viewed as a whole and practitioners should remember that changes in any one element are likely to have repercussions in other parts of the system.

It must also be emphasized that any real project is far more complex than the following descriptions. The three gestalts constitute a theory, a way of simplifying the real world and therefore of helping us to understand it. We cannot comprehend all the rich mix of data provided by something as complex as a construction project. We have no choice but to abstract key features from the great diversity of the real world, if we are to make sense of it. The following three gestalts are based on a rational simplification of reality; in other words, they constitute a theory. They provide a framework to help construction project managers think about their work.

The three gestalts are programmed organizations, professional organizations and problem-solving organizations. The descriptions of these three gestalts are firmly based in theory but necessarily describe phenomena which exist in the real world of practice. However, it is important to remember that the gestalts are theories. That is, they do not describe current practice, rather they provide ideals for practitioners to use as a guide in making their decisions. The descriptions refer to current practice, but this is merely to help practitioners locate the gestalts within their own experience.

It is interesting that Mintzberg (1989) sees his gestalts as occurring relatively rarely in practice. He now sees real world organizations as subjected to seven forces: direction, which when it dominates leads to entrepreneurial organizations; efficiency, which leads to machine organizations; proficiency, which leads to professional organizations; learning, which leads to innovative organizations; concentration, which leads to diversified organizations; cooperation, which leads to missionary organizations; and competition, which leads to political organizations. When one of these forces dominates in an organization, the related gestalt emerges in a pure form. However, most real world organizations, in Mintzberg's view, are faced by several, if not all, of the forces and so mixed organizational forms are normal. Mintzberg, however, is writing about complete firms undertaking many projects. These inevitably take many diverse forms because they have to undertake a wide range of tasks and deal with a variety of environments, and because they are shaped by arbitrary events over long periods of time. Construction projects, on the other hand, are small enough and short term enough to make it possible and appropriate for them to adopt the pattern of a pure gestalt. Hence the three gestalts provide a relevant guide for construction project managers.

Programmed organizations

Programmed organizations are so called because their work is highly rationalized. As a consequence, the organizations set up to deal with individual projects are very simple. However, they form part of much larger organizations which take full responsibility for the design, manufacture and construction of standard buildings, bridges or other standard constructions.

In its ideal form, a programmed project organization is an integral part of what is essentially a manufacturing firm. Such firms produce complete buildings or other constructions using a standard system of construction, designed and developed in-house. Ideally the construction system consists of prefabricated elements, which can be constructed on site in different ways to produce a variety of visually different but essentially identical constructions.

Efficiency depends on providing manufacturing with a steady flow of work. Ultimately this will allow the benefits of just-in-time manufacturing to be realized. This in turn will allow new constructions to be delivered fast, for a fixed price, and to a guaranteed quality. However, the variable demand for construction and a widespread belief that buildings should have an individual and distinctive appearance make it difficult to ensure a smooth flow of work for the manufacturing process. Firms providing standard constructions adopt various strategies to overcome the dichotomy between the dictates of the marketplace and manufacturing's need for consistency.

Ideally, firms providing standard constructions standardize the complete design, manufacture and construction process. However, to meet the various requirements of local markets, many adopt a less than fully standardized approach in some stages of the complete process. Thus some firms exercise direct control over the development and finance stage and act as speculative developers. Some do this on the basis of joint-venture arrangements with the owners of under-used land or air-space. This helps to reduce the capital investment required by speculative development. Other firms simply accept that customers make the initial decisions about development and finance and rely on marketing to persuade them to use a standard construction. Some firms exercise direct control over the conceptual design stages. That is, they help customers to produce their brief and develop an agreed conceptual design. Others accept that customers and their design consultants wish to decide what should be constructed without being constrained by the limitations of any specific standard form of construction. Such firms rely on marketing to persuade customers and their design consultants to accept that a standard form of construction provides a satisfactory means of realizing their concept.

Firms providing standard constructions must retain control over the detail design stage. Without this there is no system. So the absolutely minimum requirement for a construction project organization to be regarded as a programmed organization is that it uses standardized detail designs.

Manufacturing provides the next stage and in practice firms providing standard constructions deal with it in one of three distinct ways. The first option is not to manufacture. This approach relies on buying in the components required for any particular project using whatever buying power the firm can assemble to obtain good terms and influence what is manufactured. All firms adopt this approach to some extent. The differences lie in the stage which the elements have reached in the complete manufacturing and construction process when they are bought. Firms who do no off-site manufacturing themselves will either buy in large prefabricated elements or else use general materials and components and accept a labour-intensive and probably complex construction process.

The second manufacturing option is for firms providing standard constructions to produce key elements themselves and buy in the rest. A common form of this approach is to limit direct manufacturing to internal elements, leaving the exterior free to be constructed of whatever materials and forms customers and local authorities require. This approach is used by many of the successful firms who are in the business of providing building systems. It allows great variety in the superficial appearance of the end product yet allows a high degree of standardization internally. It therefore allows the system to serve a range of markets by using local materials and styles for the public face of buildings. It also allows customers to combine a distinctive image with at least some of the benefits of standardization. In these ways the partial manufacturing option enables building systems to serve a reasonably wide market and so helps ensure the steady flow of orders needed for efficient manufacturing.

The third manufacturing option is to produce completely prefabricated constructions. Many of the earliest building systems, especially those providing mass housing, adopted this approach. The results generally were awful. This was because the manufacturing technology available in the 1950s and 1960s imposed a rigid, standard form and appearance on the end products; all too often quality control was inadequate; and in many cases designers' fascination with production problems blinded them to the needs of users and blunted their aesthetic sensibilities. Manufacturing technology has now developed, as we saw in Chapter 4, to provide both variety and efficiency. Total quality control is an integral part of these modern manufacturing processes. Additionally, a greater public concern with all aspects of our environment has forced designers to take account of the interests of everyone likely to be influenced by their constructions. It is therefore realistic to look forward to the emergence of excellent systems based on large prefabricated elements. There are, for example, signs that the completion of the internal market of the European Community by the end of 1992 is encouraging some firms to acquire the design and manufacturing capability to produce complete systems. In the UK, a good example is provided by Condor's acquisition of Elemeta, who produce curtain walling, and Jorden Engineering, who pioneered the production of prefabricated toilet pods, to add to their own successful steel framed, dry envelop, Kingsway system.

The three manufacturing options give rise to three matching construction options. These are, first, to adopt a rationalized, labour intensive approach of constructing the end product from many small elements. This approach essentially uses a restricted range of craft skills in a standardized, consistent manner. Second, and at the other extreme, construction can consist simply of installing large prefabricated elements in accordance with detailed procedures learnt by general, semi-skilled labour. The third option is to adopt some combination of rationalized craftwork and fully predetermined semi-skilled work. This option fits most naturally with the manufacturing option which combines in-house manufacturing with the buying-in of components. However, it is not restricted to this one manufacturing approach and in practice most systems employ a range of skills in construction.

Whichever construction strategy is adopted, the ideal arrangement is for construction to be undertaken by as few separate teams as possible. Their work should be as simple and repetitive as possible, so that it can be learnt in a few weeks of on-the-job training. This should be supplemented and reinforced by very short in-house courses which provide initial induction to the work; instruction on quality control and safety matters; and instruction on how to use quality circles or, more accurately, innovation groups to capture and build on their own good ideas. Basic construction teams producing standard constructions are normally led by experienced working foremen who deal with any non-routine information needs that arise in the work of their teams and lead by example. Efficient construction requires an absolutely consistent sequence of work for the teams. Ideally, they will each work independently of the others, make a single visit to each separate construction site and totally complete their work during that one visit.

The management of construction is straightforward when these ideal arrangements are created. Once work in the ground is complete and a robust foundation is provided for a standard construction, management becomes completely integrated with the basic work. Procedures and targets provide all the information required by construction teams. Provided that each team completes its work as planned, coordination is implicit in the construction system. However, when the ideal arrangements fail, a simple management hierarchy is needed on site. At low levels of difficulty this may simply be a travelling site manager. He will be on site at the start and finish of each construction team's work. In between these events he will be available at the end of a personal, mobile telephone if difficulties arise in the work of any team. At higher levels of difficulty it may be necessary to provide a full-time site manager. He may also require some site-based support. In extreme cases, where systems depart significantly from the ideal construction arrangements, substantial management hierarchies may be needed to coordinate manufacturing and construction. This is very likely to be the case where the construction system relies on bought in components and rationalized craftwork. In this case, site management may be responsible for: calling up components as they are needed and buying some general components or materials; calling up the labour and machines as they are needed, recruiting labour-only subcontractors and hiring machines locally; monitoring and if necessary replanning the programme and budget; instructing and even perhaps training the workforce; and managing all the day-to-day activities on site. The more these tasks are made the responsibility of site management, the fewer are the benefits of standardized constructions compared with the alternatives.

The ideal arrangement for a programmed organization is for the design and manufacturing processes to deal with all the problems, leaving construction as a simple, automatic process. The key to efficiency lies in using a well developed system of detail designs which is closely integrated with the manufacturing process. Ideally, manufacturing is automatically driven by the choice of design details. The more this is achieved the greater the potential efficiency.

Detail designs should be developed quite independently of individual projects. This should be seen as a continuous process of slow but steady improvements, ideally based on well thought-out ideas from innovation groups operating throughout the firm. Major changes should come from long term research and development which aims to improve the product as well as raising the quality and productivity of the complete process.

In current practice, standard design details tend to inhibit conceptual design. In particular, designers' freedom is often constrained by rigid dimensional structures which are necessary to create an efficient manufacturing system. Project designers, therefore, are forced to rely on a canonic approach to design. However, as just-in-time philosophies become fully adopted in component manufacturing, they will allow project designers more freedom to use other forms of creativity.

The way in which conceptual designers are employed varies among the firms providing standard constructions. Some employ conceptual designers as direct employees. However, most subcontract conceptual design to independent consultants. This allows the firm, irrespective of where their products are to be located, to draw on deep knowledge and experience of local design issues and regulations. It allows customers to use a favourite designer. It also provides the firm with potentially rich sources of new ideas about different ways of using their system of construction. On the other hand, independent conceptual designers are a source of uncertainty, especially when they are given a role which in any way continues into the detail design stages. Therefore the greatest efficiency undoubtedly comes from in-house designers who fully understand the limitations and the strengths of the firm's system of detail design and construction.

Figure 9.1 lists the key features of the ideal process for a programmed organization. In their ideal, developed form, programmed construction project organizations rely almost entirely on procedures and targets. A good construction system, even in a relatively early stage of development, is likely to need in addition only a simple management hierarchy and the subprofessional training of semi-skilled workers. Figure 9.1 lists the options available at each stage of the process. As more of the less than ideal options are used, the appropriate project

	Development and finance	Customer's brief	Conceptual design	Detail design	Manufacture	Construction
Ideal	Internal speculative development perhaps as joint-venture with land owner	Internal designers in agreement with customer	Internal designers	Long-term development independently of individual projects	Integrated manufacture of all components	Simple, self-controlled by internal semi-skilled, well trained teams
Options	Use marketing to provide a steady stream of orders from customers	Independent designers employed by firm	Independent designers employed by firm		Manufacture only major (usually internal) components	Mixture of semi-skilled and rationalised craft-work plus site management
		Independent designers employed by customer	Independent designers employed by customer		Buy in all components	Rationalised craft-work plus elaborate site management

Figure 9.1 *Key features of processes in programmed organizations'*

organizations need to use more and more of the basic set of coordination devices.

Construction system firms

In contrast to the simplicity of programmed project organizations, the firms that own standard construction systems usually require far more elaborate organizations. At the top is a board of directors primarily concerned with long and medium term strategic issues. They are responsible for broad financial issues, decisions about the purchase and development of land, and decisions on new product ranges and choice of markets, as well as determining the overall shape of the firm. Middle management is characterized by functional specialists. Development, estates, marketing, design, project management, manufacturing, research and development, finance, purchasing and personnel are all likely to give rise to separate departments. Basic work is undertaken by a wide range of professionals and subprofessionals. All the coordination devices are likely to be used in managing these large, complex organizations.

Any firm that enters into contracts to supply customers with complete constructions has the potential to develop into the ideal form of programmed organization. Achieving this requires considerable capital investment. Initially, this investment is in marketing and detail design development work. As this bears fruit, it can be extended upstream into land acquisition and development and downstream into manufacturing and training for the construction teams. In this way a complete, vertically integrated organization gradually emerges. The legal relationships between the various activities varies from complete ownership by one firm, through various forms of joint venture, to independent firms organized by a network of long term agreements. Whatever legal form is adopted, the key feature of programmed organizations is an ability to enter into contracts with customers for the provision of complete constructions.

Relations with customers

Programmed organizations provide the simplest role for the customer. He merely states what he needs and ideally enters into one contract which guarantees a good quality construction, at a fixed price, delivered on a specified date in the near future. His remaining task is to ensure that he receives everything in the completed product to which he is entitled. The most effective way of doing this is to insist on a long guarantee from a substantial firm. Alternatively, the customer can check the product stage by stage as it is manufactured and constructed. This is more expensive, but may be sensible if the customer does not have total confidence in the firm providing the construction. The extra costs and extra work involved in checking the work of a firm are substantial disincentives to customers. Should they judge that independent quality control is essential, they are likely to insist on low prices to make the total bargain attractive. Obviously, customers are more likely to feel confidence in substantial, well established firms. In the early days of creating a successful programmed organization, there are therefore likely to be benefits in offering customers a comprehensive insurance policy. To make a real impact on marketing, this should ensure that irrespective of the firm's own fortunes, customers will be able to put right immediately any defects that arise in say the first 10 years of use of their new facilities. This would serve to signal to the firm's customers, and equally importantly to its employees, the absolute importance of quality and reliability. Provided they can offer robust, long term guarantees and reliably good quality, in addition to fast delivery, firm prices and some conceptual design flexibility, programmed organizations will always have a substantial share of the world's construction market.

Professional organizations

The second type of gestalt is professional organizations. They are so called because their work is based on using professional skills and knowledge within the boundaries of established technical rationality. Professional construction project organizations depend on the existence of some form of traditional construction. That is a form of construction where designers know the performance they will achieve from using any particular combination of design details. Also, the local construction industry knows the nature of the work required to manufacture and construct any particular combination of design details. Local contractors know the sequence of specialist contractors required, the effective construction methods, and the plant and equipment needed, and can predict the resultant costs and times with confidence.

Given this definition, the actual form of any particular local traditional construction varies from time to time and place to place. It exists whenever and wherever there is some form of construction, whether based on traditional craft skills or sophisticated industrial processes, which is well established locally. This means it is taught to designers, managers, manufacturers and constructors as part of their initial education and training. It is recorded in textbooks and its use is implicit in public standards and widely used procedures.

Traditional construction in the developed world provides a comprehensive set of construction elements. It provides competent, robust detail designs for all the junctions and fixings required within individual elements and between elements. Its performance is well understood. It has been tested and researched over many years. Government regulations control its application in predictable ways. Yet traditional construction allows considerable design freedom. All well developed forms of traditional construction give designers considerable scope to choose the sizes, shapes, configurations, textures and colours of the end product. They allow a range of different performances to be provided. They allow great architecture. They allow challenging technical problems to be solved and above all they provide competent, reliable answers.

The great strengths of traditional construction are achieved with very simple project organizations. Provided that customers accept the limitations and designers respect the disciplines implicit in traditional construction, manufacturing and construction are straightforward, efficient processes. Specialist contractors analyse designs and programmes provided by design consultants, agree the exact detail designs to be used, manufacture or buy the required components, and construct the various elements of the finished product for a fixed price, and do all this within the stated programme. The European traditional separate trades approach to construction project management provides a clear example of professional organization. It depends on the existence of two kinds of firm.

The first type of firm necessary for professional project organizations to perform satisfactorily is design consultancies which produce designs, programmes and budgets. On individual projects they deal directly with the customer to define the overall parameters of the project in terms of function, quality, time and cost. That is, they help to produce the customer's brief. Next, the customer's brief is given expression in a conceptual design and outline programme and budget. For a professional project organization to be effective, the conceptual design must take account of the limitations of the locally established traditional construction. Design is therefore most likely to be based on an iconic approach. That is, using tried and tested forms because they are known to work. However, provided that the design does not create new situations for specialist contractors, designers may be more creative. They may adopt an analogical approach to design and so use an existing form merely as a starting point and then develop it further to create new shapes or styles. However, once designers move away from well established forms, it is difficult not to slip into creating problems for the specialist contractors. There are always temptations to push an initially good idea just a little too far. These temptations place a great responsibility on design consultants to produce, in agreement with the customer, a realistic programme and budget. It is all too easy for a design consultant, perhaps because they are over-impressed by the virtues of their own design, to be optimistic about the likely costs and times. Once a design strays outside the bounds of established traditional construction, problems and inefficiencies are almost inevitable. When this happens, customers are misled and resources are wasted either in abortive design work or in solving problems during the construction stages. So the first requirement for professional project organizations is competent and honest design consultants.

These characteristics are equally important in the third stage of a design consultant's work. This follows on from the customer's agreement to the conceptual design and outline programme and budget. It requires the design consultant to produce sufficient drawings and specifications to allow all the required specialist contractors to understand their part of the manufacturing and construction work. In parallel with this, the programme is further developed so that each specialist contractor understands exactly when his work is required. Similarly, the budget is analysed into sufficient detail to enable the customer and design consultants to judge how much they can afford to spend on the work of each specialist contractor. Once all this detail design work is complete, the specialist contractors can be selected.

As in the initial stages of design consultants' work, it is important that the development of the design details is carried out honestly. The chosen details must take account of established normal practice and avoid creating new situations for the specialist contractors. They must be realistically evaluated in reporting to the customer, so that he is not misled into sanctioning the start of construction on the basis of a design he cannot afford or which cannot be constructed within his timetable. Given competent and honest design consultants, the completion of the detail design stage sets the scene for the specialist contractors to carry out their manufacturing and construction work.

Specialist contractors are the second of the two types of firm essential for the proper operation of professional project organizations. They need to be competent to use the information provided by design consultants to manufacture and construct their own elements in accordance with the designers' intentions. They must also do their work in such a manner that it fits in with that of all the other specialist contractors.

These two requirements mean, first, that specialist contractors must be knowledgeable and experienced in traditional construction. Second, they mean that there must be a number of well established procedures. These play several roles.

Procedures are needed, first, to coordinate the flows of design and programme information from design consultants to specialist contractors. It is important that the specialist contractors receive information in a predictable form. It should define all the details which are important to the designers but leave the specialist contractors free to exercise their specialist knowledge and experience in the most efficient manner.

Second, there need to be procedures to deal with specialist contractors' development of the design. Depending on the particular form of the local traditional construction, specialist contractors may produce further detail design drawings, specifications, shop drawings, manufacturing and construction programmes, and construction method statements. Also, some decisions may be left to site based craftsmen. Established procedures should ensure that the design consultants are aware of all the specialist contractors' design decisions. In addition, they should provide an opportunity for the designers to check that these decisions are consistent with their own designs.

Finally, procedures are needed to coordinate the work of the separate specialist contractors. These tend to develop on the basis of custom and practice so that each specialist leaves his work in the manner expected by the next. In this way, coordination is achieved with very little direct contact between specialists. For example, the traditional method of constructing a window in a load-bearing brick wall is coordinated automatically. The bricklayer leaves the brick opening in the manner expected by the carpenter. The carpenter fixes timber grounds ready for the joiner, who installs the window frame in the manner expected by the ironmonger and glazier. The ironmonger fixes the decorative ironmongery and the glazier fixes the glass and both leave the window in the manner expected by the painter. The painter treats the timber and putty, removes the decorative ironmongery, paints the whole window and refixes the ironmongery to leave the complete element as the designer intended.

Provided that each specialist contractor does his work in the established traditional manner, it is not necessary for them to meet or communicate with each other. Coordination derives from the implicit procedures of normal practice operating within the framework of the design and programme produced by the design consultant. In addition, the design consultant is responsible for checking that the specialist contractors' work is of a satisfactory standard, reporting on progress to the customer at regular intervals, and resolving any problems that arise during manufacture or construction. Finally, the design consultant is responsible for certifying that each specialist contractor's work is completed satisfactorily and agreeing their final accounts.

Coordination in professional organizations

Professional project organizations in their simplest form rely on the basic set of coordination devices plus an information system. Procedures, as we described earlier in this chapter, provide a basic framework of coordination between all the firms involved in any one project. Management hierarchies provide a large part of the coordination within professional project organizations. These include the relationships inside individual firms. During the design stages there is within the design consultancy firm: at the head of the project organization, a lead designer; at a second level, specialists in various aspects of design, programming, costing and the procurement of specialist contractors; and, at a third level, draftsmen, specifiers, planners, estimators and other technicians. During the manufacturing and construction stages the design consultancy firm's internal organization is simpler as much of its work is finished. However, during the same stages, specialist contractors' internal management hierarchies include top level management providing overall strategic direction, a second level project coordinator, several third level foremen, and a fourth level of craftsmen and labourers. Also during these later stages the relationship between design consultant and specialist contractors is hierarchical. This is often supplemented by appointing a lead specialist contractor to provide day-to-day coordination on site and supply any common site services or equipment. When a lead specialist contractor is appointed, the management hierarchy has three distinct levels: design consultant, lead specialist contractor, and other specialist contractors, in addition to the levels which exist inside the separate firms.

Professionalization is the key distinguishing coordination device of professional organizations. Both design consultants and specialist contractors apply the knowledge and skills they acquired during their formal education and training. As described in Chapter 5, in order to ensure that the project objectives remain paramount, as individual professionals make their day-to-day decisions, the work needs to be guided by a carefully controlled system of targets. They are first established in customers' briefs and are gradually developed through the separate sequential stages of projects so that each firm involved knows the performance they are expected to achieve.

The basic set of coordination devices is likely to be adequate for only the easiest of projects which use traditional construction. More typically, a formal information system is needed to help coordinate the work of all the separate firms involved. This provides information on the progress of each element through each of its stages. It keeps track of the actual performance of each firm against their programme and budget. It maintains the formal records of quality control. It records the effects of variations ordered by the customer or design consultant. It records the effects of problems that arise between the work of separate specialist contractors. In general terms, the information system provides coordination by monitoring the project in order to identify any departures from planned progress. However, when problems are found, there are no particularly effective mechanisms for finding solutions. The basic form of professional organization relies on the self-regulating structure implicit in professional education and training. Regular progress meetings provide data for the information system but often do little more than record problems after they have become apparent to everyone involved. It requires a particularly forceful design consultant or leading specialist contractor to maintain a traditional construction project on its planned course. Where the traditional and simple form of professional project organization shown in Figure 9.2 has survived, in for example Germany, its success depends on unusually broadly educated designers and unusually competent craftsmen.

In general, the approach provides pleasant, varied, human environments produced slowly, to a reasonably consistent, good quality. It tends to achieve varied levels of productivity, and overall its performance in terms of time and costs for the customer is unpredictable.

There are in practice a number of important modifications of the basic form of professional project organization. These all in one way or another seek to retain the strengths of the approach, but at the same time enable it to deliver completed constructions faster or more predictably. Two of these modifications serve to demonstrate their general nature and also to illustrate the strength of the relationship between efficient professional project organizations and the use of traditional constructions.

General contracting

The most common modification of the traditional professional project organization is to appoint a general contractor. This is a firm which specializes in managing manufacturing and construction. They therefore employ buyers,

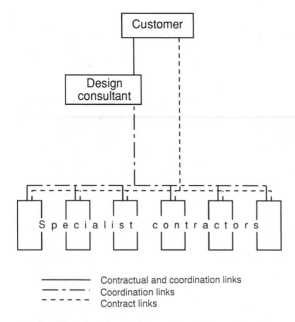

Figure 9.2   *Basic professional project organization*

estimators, construction planners, specialists in plant and equipment, site managers, industrial relations experts, safety officers, quality control inspectors and many other management specialists. Their role is to provide dedicated professional coordination to the work of the specialist contractors. In doing so they are taking over part of the traditional role of design consultants.

The great attraction of the approach is that the general contractor absorbs much of the uncertainty inherent in the traditional approach by entering into a contract with the customer to complete the whole of the manufacturing and construction work. General contractor contracts usually require the delivery of a competent construction, in accordance with the design consultant's detail drawings and specifications, to the reasonable satisfaction of the designer, for a fixed contract sum, by a specified date. The specialist contractors retain responsibility for the actual manufacture and construction. However, their work is coordinated by the general contractor and they are employed by him as subcontractors. It is also sometimes the case that craftsmen responsible for early or key elements are employed directly by the general contractor.

Thus we see that the general contractor approach places responsibility for coordinating manufacture and construction with a firm which has a primary interest in these stages of the total process. The general contractor also has a direct financial interest in the efficient execution of these stages. Once the contract sum is agreed, if nothing else changes, his profits depend on minimizing his costs. He also has a direct financial interest in the timely execution of the work, since general contractor contracts provide for damages to be paid to the customer for late completion. The traditional basic approach does not provide the same direct interest or incentives for designers in their role of coordinating manufacturing and construction. Consequently, the general contractor approach tends to place specialist contractors under relatively high pressure to complete their work at the lowest cost and in the shortest possible time. This provides a positive force to seek higher productivity. It does not necessarily, however, lead to a similar search for higher quality. Since the design consultant retains his role of approving the manufacture and construction on behalf of the customer, the approach has considerable scope for conflict. Also, although it provides the customer with reasonable certainty of completion on the agreed date, and compensation if this is not achieved, it is a slow approach. This is because a complete design must be produced before a general contractor can be selected. For example, the opportunity of appointing specialist contractors for the groundworks and foundations early, before the rest of the design is complete, is not available without substantial modifications to the approach. Also, selecting the general contractor provides an extra step in the overall process. So, everything else being equal, when customers want an early completion, the traditional approach is likely to be faster than the unmodified general contractor approach.

However, the greatest weakness of the general contractor approach is that it separates the designer from responsibility for coordinating the manufacture and construction. Any problems that arise during these stages must be sorted out by the general contractor. He may well consult the designer, but his contractual responsibility is to produce a competent construction based on the information provided by the designer. Under most forms of general contractor contract, he is not relieved of this responsibility by errors in the design. The long term effect of designers losing their responsibility for coordinating manufacture and construction is that designs have become less practical and more difficult to put into effect. In other words, they depart from established traditional construction. This in turn makes it difficult for general contractors to predict their own costs and meet customers' completion dates. So the overall effect of designers' lack of practical manufacturing and construction experience is to make general contracting riskier.

In response to this unsatisfactory state of affairs, general contractors have sought to limit their contractual responsibilities to producing exactly what is shown in the design information used in calculating the contract sum. Given this contractual provision, designers' lack of practical manufacturing and construction experience creates opportunities for general contractors to request additional design information and claim extra payments for the revised details. For similar reasons, any variations to the original design required by the customer or the designer tend to be expensive. This is mainly because the general contractor owns all the relevant information about the practical problems of manufacture and construction and the associated costs. By comparison, the customer and his design consultants are in a weak position in negotiating the costs of variations, as indeed they are in agreeing the cost effects of additional design information supplied to the general contractor after the contract is signed. Almost inevitably the price to the customer increases, especially when the general contractor's own costs are higher than the contract sum.

The overall balance of forces at play within the general contractor approach make it a good approach for some types of customer. They include those who need the assurance of a firm contractual commitment to costs or time before they sanction manufacturing or construction work, and customers who do not require a fast overall completion of their project although they may seek rapid completion once a general contractor is appointed on the basis of a complete design.

Given these objectives the general contractor approach works well, provided customers exercise three disciplines. First, they insist that their designers stick to well established traditional construction. Second, they insist that the design is complete before the contract sum is agreed with the general contractor. This means that the designers will not make any further design decisions. In other words, any gaps in the design information will be filled by the general contractor at his own cost and therefore are allowed for in the agreed contract sum. Third, the customer does not allow any variations to the design which forms the basis of the contract.

This very disciplined approach allows general contractors to concentrate on planning and controlling the manufacturing and construction work efficiently. It provides considerable certainty for the customer. It gives design consultants a limited role and equally restricted practical experience. It may result in strong general contractors or strong specialist contractors. This depends on the particular form of traditional construction. The more it is based on site manufacture and construction by craftsmen, the more likely it is to produce strong general contractors. Conversely, the more it is based on capital intensive prefabrication in factories, the more likely it is to produce strong specialist contractors.

When the three customer disciplines are relaxed, the weaknesses described earlier begin to surface. Problems inevitably follow, whenever designers do not use traditional construction, do not complete their design work before the contract sum is established or vary the design during the manufacture and construction stages. In these circumstances general contractors find that it is not in their best interests to plan for efficient construction. They must concentrate on developing a flexible site organization, with low fixed costs, which can adjust to design changes and variations. They must also ensure that they monitor all the customers' and designers' instructions so that they are paid in full for all the work they are actually required to undertake. They find that it pays them, at least in respect of individual projects, to employ experts in negotiating contractual claims. The experts earn their keep by searching for errors in the design information and then maximizing the recorded costs of remedying the problems they find. This does nothing for the efficiency of the construction industry but does tend to maximize short term profits for general contractors. It is an approach that invariably produces very dissatisfied customers. Therefore it does not provide a sound approach on which to build a long term business.

The effect of these long term market pressures is that mature general contractors seek to impose the disciplines of good practice on customers and design consultants. The major construction companies in Japan provide the most obvious example. They are not, however, the only example; general contractors in the USA traditionally displayed the same approach. The essential strategy of mature general contractors is to develop long term relationships with major customers by providing effective guarantees of the performance of their products. By dealing immediately and without question with any defects that arise in their constructions, they build customer confidence. They give this assurance in return for control of detail design. This is achieved without limiting design consultants' initial decisions. Designers remain free to develop their designs to whatever level of detail they and their customers feel is sensible. The general contractor, however, retains the right to review the complete detail design to ensure that it fits comfortably within the competence of the local specialist contractors. The Japanese construction firms go so far as to produce a complete set of new drawings for each project. The design consultants have no significant role beyond the point at which their design is handed over to the general contractor. This provides general contractors with considerable control over detail design. They therefore consistently use the current local traditional construction. In return customers get constructions completed on time, at a fixed cost, to a reliable standard. In other words they get certainty, which is a very effective way of encouraging them to buy the construction industry's products.

So we see that successful general contracting depends on the use of traditional construction. Pushed to its logical conclusion it leads to narrow and generally feeble design consultants. A logical further development is for general contractors to take over the initial design and so become design-and-build contractors. These trends are generally resisted by design consultants. One interesting approach to this rearguard action provides the second major modification of the traditional professional project organization.

Quantity surveying

Quantity surveying emerged first as a distinct profession in the nineteenth century in Britain. Initially, quantity surveyors undertook the relatively straightforward task of measuring the construction work required to implement architects' designs for new buildings. Their work produces bills of quantities which are quantified specifications. Bills of quantities are used to obtain competitive bids from general contractors on an absolutely consistent basis. In essence, the general contractors simply state their unit price for each item of work, multiply it by the quantity of that item, and sum the totals to calculate their bid. The priced bills of quantities of the successful general contractor, usually the one submitting the lowest bid, becomes the basis of a contract with the customer. In other words, the general contractor contracts to construct what is described in the bills of quantities in return for the total sum calculated therein. Subsequently, the unit prices are used by the quantity surveyor to calculate the effects of variations and any other changes to the design. These are incorporated in the final account prepared by the quantity surveyor, on behalf of the customer, in negotiation with the general contractor.

The basic quantity surveying tasks constitute an integrating management role. Its purpose is to coordinate the work of the design consultants and the general contractor on individual projects. The use of bills of quantities as the basis of general contractors' contracts is fundamental to the basic quantity surveyor role.

Inevitably, over the years, detailed procedures have grown up around the use of bills of quantities. Most important among these are standard methods of measurement. These are rules that define which items of construction work are to be measured as separate items in bills of quantities. Standard methods of measurement also define exactly how each item is to be measured and described. The result is predictable bills of quantities which are well understood by all local general contractors. The bills of quantities approach works well, provided designers stick to traditional construction. This is because general contractors have relevant knowledge of their own costs for familiar forms of construction. Therefore they can commit themselves to unit prices for individual items of work with a reasonable degree of confidence that their total costs will not exceed their bid. Once designers depart from traditional construction, so that general contractors are faced with unfamiliar design details, priced bills of quantities are unlikely to provide an equitable basis for contracts. The inevitable result is that general contractors will seek to undermine the contract bills of quantities by claiming that they do not fairly represent the required work. When this happens, a great deal of time and effort is wasted in negotiating over the proper price. On the other hand, given designs that use familiar forms of construction, bills of quantities provide distinct advantages. They save the costs of several general contractors all measuring the same design in order to calculate competitive bids. They provide a consistent basis for bids so that the general contractor who is most efficient, or at least cheapest, at building the particular combination of items of work described in the bills of quantities is most likely to be awarded the contract. Also, bills of quantities provide an open basis for a contract. The customer has produced on his behalf a full and clear statement of the work he requires and the general contractor states the unit prices for which he is prepared to undertake that work. Both parties have a detailed knowledge of the financial basis of their agreement before they enter into a contract. Priced bills of quantities therefore provide a robust basis for the financial administration of contracts.

Bills of quantities have other effects. They have given quantity surveyors detailed knowledge of construction prices. Also, from their experience of negotiating final accounts with general contractors, they have detailed knowledge of construction costs. This knowledge is now commonly used to provide a design cost planning service. Cost planning enables customers to decide on their total budget, with the advice of a quantity surveyor, before any design work is commissioned. Design work is then undertaken within a cost plan aimed at achieving the agreed budget. The cost plan is administered by a quantity surveyor who estimates the likely price for design proposals as they are produced, compares them with the allowance in the cost plan, and works with the designers to maintain the design within the customer's budget. Cost planning reduces the risks faced by customers. Without cost planning, designs often result in bids that are too expensive. As a result the customer has to find more money than he intended, redesign is needed or projects are abandoned. In any case, time and money are wasted. Good cost planning avoids these problems.

With the emergence of cost planning, quantity surveying has developed into a role that spans the complete design, manufacture and construction process. This has several consequences. The most important of these is that design consultants have retained control of detail design. The mechanism for this is simply that quantity surveyors require a complete detail design on which to base bills of quantities. Therefore, in the UK, general contractors have no design responsibility. Design consultants make all the detail design decisions. This is the case even when approximate bills of quantities based on hypothetical designs are used to enable early manufacturing and construction work to begin before a complete design has been produced. The approximate bills of quantities establish a financial basis for a contract. So, when the design details are subsequently decided by the design consultants, the quantity surveyor uses the contract unit rates to calculate the administratively correct price. No matter how ingeniously they are used, bills of quantities represent detail design decisions by design consultants which must be put into effect by general contractors.

The obvious danger of design consultants making detail design decisions but having no responsibility for coordinating the manufacturing and construction work is that they depart from traditional construction. Designers generally have not resisted this temptation and, as a direct consequence, in the UK building industry, there is now no well established form of traditional construction. The results of this unhappy state of affairs are: considerable inefficiency and administrative complexity; weak, claims-orientated general and specialist contractors; the emergency of some outstanding architects; and a large quantity surveying profession. In a few specific local situations these trends have been resisted by strong quantity surveyors who have gained the confidence of major customers. They have been given the authority to ensure that designers stick to well established design details, complete the design information before contract sums are established and do not thereafter vary the design. This in turn creates the predictable conditions that allow general contractors to price confidently and so concentrate their efforts on planning for efficient work. Thus, in these specific local situations, the quantity surveyor's traditional role of integrating manager is beginning to acquire many of the project management responsibilities formerly carried out by design consultants. The progression from integrating manager to project manager is common with ambitious and talented individuals. It is interesting to observe the same natural human ambition at work within a whole profession. However, these developments have a larger significance. They are one strand among several key changes, all of which appear to be taking professional construction project organizations back to their roots.

Modern professional organizations

There are powerful changes at work which, taken together, logically lead to the re-creation of the classic, professional construction project organization in a modern form. The most important of these changes is the growing importance of specialist contractors. This is an inevitable consequence of the industrialization which is now a significant feature of many forms of construction. This changes the status of specialist contractors because it is often only they who understand the performance of their own technologies. Consequently, designers need to consult specialist contractors during the design stages. It creates obvious organizational problems if specialist contractors, who form part of the design team, are required to become subcontractors to whichever general contractor happens to submit the lowest bid based in part on design information provided by the specialist contractors themselves. It is possible to arrange this, but it does not provide a basis for efficient organizations. In practice the specialist contractor's position within general contractor based project organizations has become ambiguous. For example, as a member of the design team he deals directly with the design consultant. However, as a member of the manufacturing and construction team he should, as a subcontractor, deal with the design consultant only through the general contractor. A variety of contractual devices exist to regulate the complex relationships that arise. However, they all add extra processes and costs to management arrangements which are already complex.

The emergence of industrial-based specialist contractors who are strong and competent in the design, manufacture and construction of their own technologies should remove the need for the extra management effort provided by general contractors. It certainly does not justify making project organizations more complex. The work of modern, industrial-based contractors can be coordinated effectively and efficiently by competent designers, provided that they stick to established design solutions. Therefore the emergence of strong specialist contractors needs to be matched by the development of well rounded, widely competent design consultants. These need to combine knowledge and skills which in the UK are spread among independent designers, quantity surveyors and general contractors. Such firms already exist in some parts of the world, most notably the German architectural practices. However, even in the UK, some of the best design consultancy practices now combine the work of architects, engineers and quantity surveyors in one firm. They are thus recreating the well rounded, widely competent design consultancies which are a distinguishing feature of the traditional form of professional construction project organizations.

The main differences between the emerging modern form of professional organization and the traditional form are the greater formality of the control procedures and the greater sophistication of the information systems used. Quality, time and cost are planned early in projects and progress is monitored by specialists in these topics who are supported by good information systems. This enables customers to establish briefs and work with design consultants in developing a suitable design, in the realistic expectation that subsequent contracts with specialist contractors will serve to achieve their defined objectives of quality, time and cost.

Provided design consultants use established forms of construction, specialist contractors' involvement during design is limited to routine matters. It consists of general commercial and technical advice on the availability and performance of established design details, which is provided as a normal part of specialist contractors' marketing. This is generally a satisfactory arrangement. However, when designers depart from well established designs and so require specialist contractors to undertake substantial project specific calculations, it is unrealistic to expect them to provide their services free. In this case the specialist contractors should be employed as design subcontractors and paid a fee in addition to their normal employment as contractors for the manufacturing and construction work. That is, they enter into two separate contracts, one with the design consultants and the second direct with the customer.

The reason for this apparently clumsy arrangement is that the professional construction project organization requires the specialist contractors to be appointed on the basis of a lump sum contract with the customer. Other arrangements are possible which involve various forms of cost plus contracts, but they add extra administrative work and involve a series of negotiations which inhibit and complicate the relationships between customers, design consultants and specialist contractors. So a lump sum contract is by far the most effective way of employing specialist contractors in professional construction project organizations. However, it is not sensible to attempt to establish a lump sum contract if the design consultants have not finished their design work. This is because, as the design is finalized, the basis of the contract will almost certainly be invalidated, leading in turn to claims and confrontation between the customer, designers and specialist contractors. These problems can be avoided by having the specialist contractors act as subcontractors to the design consultant until the design work is complete. Then the classic form of professional construction project organization, which requires customers to enter into separate contracts with all the specialist contractors for the manufacture and construction, can be adopted.

This still leaves the case of customers who want to use traditional construction but also want to enter into a single contract for the manufacturing and construction work after they have agreed the design. Such customers have a simple choice. They can appoint a general contractor. In doing so they must accept that there is some duplication of effort involved in the general contractor learning the design and establishing relationships with specialist contractors when the design consultant already possesses the relevant knowledge. The alternative for customers who want a single contract for the manufacturing and construction work is to trust their design consultant. That is, the design consultant produces an agreed design in the normal way and then employs the specialist contractors as subcontractors and coordinates their work. There are several ways of establishing the price for the design consultant's total service. The most straightforward is to pay a normal fee for the design stage and then to negotiate a lump sum for the manufacturing and construction stages using bids from specialist contractors as a basis. Other methods exist, including the design-and-manage approach described in Chapter 8. Whichever approach is used, many customers will trust a design consultant to undertake this total role but also employ an independent quantity surveyor to look after their financial interests. So, compared with the modern, basic form of professional project organization, customers who choose to employ a general contractor or to trust a design consultant with a larger role and employ a quantity surveyor obtain more formal certainty and administrative simplicity but incur additional costs. It seems likely, therefore, that in practice a number of effective forms of professional project organization will coexist. Each will appeal to certain customers. The basic form shown in Figure 9.2 remains the model against which all the variants should be judged. Its main characteristics and those of the most important alternatives are shown in Figure 9.3.

Problem-solving organizations

The third type of gestalt is problem-solving organizations. These are organizations which produce innovative constructions efficiently. They are called problem-solving because they are set up to find answers to customers' needs which cannot be met by established answers.

There are many reasons why established answers are not acceptable to some customers. Their needs may be unusual and no good answers exist. They may want better answers than the local industry's norms. They may want better quality, faster construction, more reliable performance, or some other specific improvement to current normal practice. Alternatively, they may simply want a distinctive construction which looks different from any other. Projects sometimes adopt new and original designs because the design consultant wished to produce a distinctive construction. Customers need to ensure that this happens only with their express agreement, because new designs and original concepts

	Customer's brief Conceptual design	Detail design	Coordination of manufacture and construction	Manufacture and construction
Traditional basic form	Design consultant	Design consultant	Design consultant	Specialist contractors in direct contact with customer
Modern basic form	Multidiscipline design consultant	Multidiscipline design consultant in cooperation with specialist contractors	Multidiscipline design consultant	Specialist contractors in direct contact with customer
Design and manage	Design consultant, management contractor consortia	Consortia in cooperation with special contractors	Consortia	Specialist contractors as subcontractors to consortia
General contractor	Design consultant	Design consultant	General contractor subject to design consultant's approval	Specialist contractors as subcontractors to general contractor
Quantity surveyor	Design consultant plus quantity surveyor	Design consultant plus quantity surveyor in cooperation with nominated subcontractors	General contractor subject to design consultant's approval and quantity surveyor's agreement	Specialist contractors as subcontractors or nominated subcontractors to general contractor

Figure 9.3 *Characteristics of major forms of professional project organizations*

tend to be very expensive the first time they are manufactured and constructed. This is true even when it emerges that with practice and repeated applications a new answer is cheaper than current ones. Prototypes are always expensive.

New forms of construction need flexible project organizations. The reason is that it is impossible to predict the skills and knowledge, and therefore the firms, which will be needed at each stage until progress is made on preceding stages. Problem-solving projects gradually unfold, stage by stage, rather like life itself. The only form of construction project organization that fully meets the need for flexibility is the construction management approach. As described in Chapter 6, this encompasses in practice two different approaches. In the UK, they are called management contracting and construction management, but elsewhere they are both commonly called construction management. It is useful to have separate terms for different approaches. The remainder of the description of the problem-solving gestalt refers to the approach which, in the UK, is called construction management.

The only theoretical difference between the two approaches is that specialist contractors are subcontractors of management contractors while in construction management they have direct contracts with the customer. The second approach, often called professional construction management, provides a clearer basis for the description of the third gestalt, to which we now return.

A customer, having decided that he will commission a new and original construction, must first appoint a designer and a construction manager. These should be separate firms so that experienced professionals can be appointed to concentrate on the difficult task of creating an original design. Also, experienced professionals can be appointed to concentrate on the equally difficult task of managing the manufacture and construction of a prototype. The knowledge and skills needed for these two distinct tasks tend not to coexist to equal levels of brilliance in single firms. The networks of contacts needed to create new forms and new design details are different from those needed to realize them efficiently. Wise customers, embarking on the exciting, unpredictable, risky business of buying an innovative construction, ensure that they have independent advice both from an excellent and experienced designer and from an equally competent construction manager.

The twin headed nature of problem-solving project organizations leads them to adopt a matrix structure. This is the best arrangement for the design stages. It will also need to continue into the manufacturing and construction stages if the required work has not been fully defined during the design stages. In these circumstances there remains a need for the flexibility inherent in matrix structures. Also essential is their ability to force problems into the open, where they can become the focus of a concentrated search for answers.

A matrix structure clearly identifies the customer as the final arbiter in all major project decisions. In effect, it puts the customer into the position of chairman of the project organization. Generally, the designer and construction manager cooperate and reach agreed decisions. Where there is disagreement over a design issue the designer's view should normally predominate, and vice versa for manufacturing or construction conflicts. However, both should take a stand on issues which they think are important even if the subject lies within the other's primary competence. It is at such points that the customer must exercise his authority by making a decision, having first listened to the differing points of view.

Customers may decide to play their essential role in various ways. They may be involved with their projects on a day-to-day basis or alternatively exercise their authority at arm's length. In the first case they become an integral part of the project organization, involved in all decisions of any consequence and present at most project meetings. In the second case the customer receives formal joint reports from the designer and construction manager as distinct stages are reached. The formal reports describe progress, identify problems and a short-list of potential answers, and define the work and objectives of the next stage. The customer receives the reports, makes any necessary decisions and leaves the designer and construction manager to direct the project to the next stage and the next report. In practice, experienced customers operate in a variety of ways between these alternatives, depending on their own interests and their degree of trust in the designer and construction manager. Irrespective of the way individual customers choose to play their essential role, problem-solving project organizations inevitably move through a series of short stages. It is good practice for the project organization to define each stage and obtain the customers' formal approval to the planned work and its objectives. Early in the life of a problem-solving project, the stages are short and the definitions of what needs to be done tend to be vague and general. Later it becomes possible to see further ahead with greater confidence. Stages become longer, formal reports less frequent and more certain. As this process unfolds, the project organization must be kept under review. To take an extreme but by no means uncommon situation, it may emerge that a project which began as a problem-solving one can adopt an existing answer. When this happens, the project organization needs to be simplified by reverting to a professional organization or even, in a really extreme case, to a programmed one. The construction management approach provides this degree of flexibility. It does so because all the firms that make up any one project organization have direct contracts with the customer. Also, at least early in projects, they are all employed as consultants on a time-related basis. That is, they are paid directly for the resources they provide. Consequently, if it becomes apparent, because of the way a project has developed, that a particular firm's contribution is complete, the customer merely terminates their contract and pays for the resources used prior to that point in time. It is only when the direction a project will take becomes clear that it is sensible for customers to enter into lump sum contracts for specific and defined elements of work.

This flexibility, early in projects, allows the project organization to include a great variety of firms who may make a contribution to finding good answers. Major innovative construction projects commonly draw on the work of university departments, research institutes, scientists, technologists, experts, artists and philosophers, as well as architects, engineers, specialist contractors and construction managers. All can be brought into the project by means of direct contracts with the customer. All work within the matrix structure formed by designers and construction managers. There is of course a general tendency as manufacturing and construction begin for the majority of firms who make up the project organization to be specialist contractors employed to produce a specific element of the end product. Their work initially may well involve developing new answers and new methods. However, eventually, decisions must be made as to exactly what is to be manufactured and constructed. As these final decisions are made, the project organization should become more formal and stable. At this stage its main features form the classic construction management project structure shown in Figure 9.4. It must of course be remembered that the organization structure shown in Figure 9.4 merely

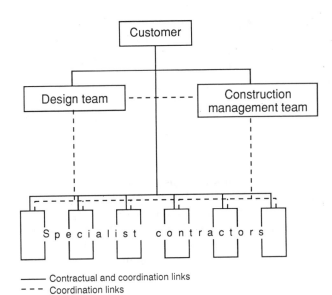

Figure 9.4   *Classic construction management project structure*

illustrates the principles of the relationships within problem-solving projects. On all except the very smallest of projects, real life organization structures are much larger. They form a complex hierarchy in which the interests and responsibilities of customer, designer, construction manager and the specialist contractor teams involved with the various project elements are all represented at every level. Figure 9.4 illustrates the basic unit from which problem-solving project organizations are built. Real life project organizations comprise many such units, each one grouped around the work required for one element of the project.

As such organization structures become larger, the degree of formality tends to increase. However, the character of most of the work in project organizations set up to produce innovative constructions is, as their name implies, problem-solving; that is, searching for new and original answers. Heirs and Pehrson (1982) describe the four essential steps in formal problem-solving by organizations. They provide a basic structure for the work in innovative construction projects.

The first necessary step is to define the question to be answered. This should be stated as clearly as possible, including identifying the criteria that satisfactory answers need to satisfy. Second, a number of possible answers should be proposed using a variety of creative techniques. Designers are likely to use pragmatic and analogical design methods in their search for new forms and original details. Construction managers may well use brainstorming and similar techniques designed to free the thinking of groups from existing answers and help them to find new ideas. The aim of the second stage of problem-solving is to identify a number of possible answers. Third, the two or three most promising of the answers are evaluated. They should each be judged against the criteria identified during the first stage. They should be considered in the context of the project as a whole. The strengths and weaknesses of each should be listed, particularly taking account of the consequences on other elements of the project. Finally, a decision should be made. This may be to select one of the answers reviewed at stage three. It may be to adopt a combination of elements drawn from several of the potential answers. It may be a decision to evaluate more of the answers identified at stage two or to search for more potential answers. When none of these options appear attractive, the original question may be reviewed. Alternatively, a different team may be commissioned to search for an answer. Indeed, in major projects it is common in the early stages to set the same problem for two or three teams to work on simultaneously. Answers are then presented by each team in turn, in front of the others, so that subsequent discussion can provide a more rounded, deeper understanding of the likely source of a good answer.

It is wise to adopt the four-stage problem-solving approach in a formal manner. This ensures that all involved with the various elements of a project know the nature of their current work. In this way, answers are not adopted too hurriedly nor is creativity inhibited by premature evaluation. The four-stage approach is universally effective, being based on the way the human brain itself searches for answers. It is helpful to make the process explicit for problem-solving in teams and in fact this is often true also for individuals. Since the four-stage process is universal, it applies to each of the stages. Thus, in defining the question at stage one, it is sensible to propose a number of possible formulations of the problem to be solved. The best should then be evaluated in terms of their clarity, the extent to which they encourage creativity, and similar criteria. Only then should the question to be tackled, be selected.

A problem-solving project consists of several parallel series of small problem-solving stages each of which comprises the four steps. Each stage within one series helps to define subsequent stages in that series. However, the separate series join and rebranch in a complex pattern. When a project is going well the series tend to coalesce and the stages become progressively more certain. As this happens, the firms that need to be involved settle into a predictable pattern and the project organization can adopt greater formality.

However, if the task of a problem-solving project appears not to be simplifying with the passage of time, this should be the signal for a major project review. At such a time, all decisions already taken should be thrown open to question in a wide-ranging search for a clearer way forward. Such a crisis review is best entrusted to a high level taskforce. The crisis review and use of a taskforce is an example of the strategic monitoring of projects' progress which is a key responsibility of customers and their senior consultants. They need to evaluate their project regularly. They should check the current objectives of each team and assure themselves that all are necessary to meet the customer's defined objectives. Any which have strayed from the overall aims must be modified. In some cases a team's work will be seen to be no longer needed. They must be removed from the project. Equally the customer and his senior consultants need to check that there are no gaps in the overall project organization. However, even when projects are going well, the coordination of problem-solving work is such that it is likely to require all the coordination devices described in Chapter 5.

Coordination in problem-solving organizations

There are likely to be a number of project specific procedures developed in parallel with the project itself. These will control the form and frequency of meetings, the records of decisions that must be kept, and the nature of reports which must be produced. At later stages there are likely to be procedures that coordinate safety, industrial relations, welfare and similar specialist contractor matters which have implications beyond the work of one firm. It may well be impossible to use existing procedures because of the new situations which must be faced and perhaps also because firms new to the industry are required to produce some elements of innovative constructions. In addition to project specific procedures, each firm involved will bring their own normal procedures with them. These need to be reviewed to ensure that they are compatible with the overall needs of the project organization.

Distinct management hierarchies will exist in most of the teams brought into the project organization. These may need to be modified from that used on simpler projects in order to take account of the need to search widely for answers. However, for the reasons described earlier in this chapter, the project structure, at least initially, is a matrix. Therefore the overall management structure is twin-headed and not simply hierarchical. As projects move into their later stages and become more certain, and as increasing weight is given to manufacturing and construction, the matrix may evolve into a simple hierarchy headed by the construction manager. The designer's role in these circumstances becomes one of monitoring the work of the specialist contractors to ensure that it conforms to the agreed designs.

The third of the basic set of coordination devices is professionalization. Obviously many of the teams that make up problem-solving project organizations are professional. However, the need for new and original answers requires them to use established answers as a basis for reflection-in-action. Also, multidiscipline teams may be used to cut across established professional boundaries and so encourage wide-ranging searches for innovative answers. So professionalization provides relatively little coordination within problem-solving construction project organizations.

Similarly, targets must necessarily be general and fuzzy. Certainly, in the early stages of problem-solving projects, only short term targets can be used to coordinate the work of separate teams, which may, as described earlier, deliberately be duplicating or even triplicating each other's work. Equally there are likely to be gaps between answers devised independently so that progress will inevitably be hesitant and unpredictable. Targets can provide general guidance and create a sense of direction, but like professionalization they are necessarily relatively weak in problem-solving organizations.

Information systems are necessary to provide a record of progress. As it becomes possible to establish firmer targets in the later more certain stage of projects, so information systems can provide useful coordination by highlighting exceptions from planned progress. Initially, however, they merely provide a record of the current status of each element of the work.

Lateral relations provide the most important coordination device in problem-solving organizations. The overall matrix structure is itself the most highly developed form of organization for lateral relations. However, the other forms of lateral relations are likely to occur as teams meet together to discuss progress and search together for answers to difficult problems. There are likely to be liaison roles and integrating managers, especially linking design and construction management decision making processes. Taskforces are common and provide the right answer for specific intractable problems or major crises. Problem-solving organizations are characterized by meetings, both formal and informal. They are not only solving the problem of producing an innovative end product, they are also concerned with finding the right form of organization to coordinate their work. Problem-solving project organizations need to reinforce decisions which provide a clear picture of the way forward, by introducing greater formality into the organization. Thus more coordination is provided as it becomes possible to establish procedures, set targets, use control information systems, simplify the organization structure into a hierarchy, or require professional teams to adopt established, technically rational answers.

Management within problem-solving organizations is difficult and challenging. They do, however, provide the right approach for the most difficult of construction projects. They are necessarily expensive because they have to tackle new situations and it takes time and talent to find genuinely innovative answers. Such projects point the way forward for the industry. Indeed, at their best, they provide inspiration for all humanity. They must be taken totally seriously and entered into only as the result of a clear, well considered decision that a new answer is appropriate. It is wasteful to allow projects to drift into a problem-solving mode. Given a properly designed project organization, innovative constructions can be produced efficiently. Everything else being equal, they are not as cheap as standard or traditional constructions but they can deliver excellent value for money provided they result from clear choices by the customer.

The gestalts in practice

We have now described three distinct gestalts. Figure 9.5 lists distinguishing characteristics of each of them. It should be remembered that they are ideal forms of construction project organization. They exist as theories to help construction project managers think about their work. They provide guidance on the direction which project organizations in practice should take as the nature of their task becomes clear.

In general, customers should use a programmed organization unless it is clear that no standard construction meets their needs, in which case they should use a professional organization unless it is clear that established traditional construction will not meet their needs. In this third case, customers should establish a problem-solving organization. When they are uncertain which of the three situations they are in, they should establish an embryonic problem-solving organization, in effect as a taskforce, to produce a report on the nature of the project. This small, flexible organization may need to take the project through several stages before it becomes clear whether it should be developed into a problem-solving project organization or make way for one of the other forms.

As we argued at the start of this book, the choice of an appropriate project organization is crucial to the success of construction projects. We also argued that the choice depends on the nature of the product, its environment and the overall objectives of the customer. We further argued that these independent variables can be expressed from a management viewpoint in terms of complexity, size, repetition, uncertainty (which is composed of variability and interference), speed and economy. There is no simple one-to-one matching between the gestalts and these key project variables. However, there are limits to the range of values each variable may assume if either a programmed or a professional organization is adopted. Figure 9.6 illustrates the general nature of these relationships. It shows that projects are likely to need to adopt a problem-solving organization as they become more complex, larger, include more variety and face more uncertainty. Such projects have difficulty in meeting tough objectives in respect of speed and economy. Programmed organizations work best with projects which are simple, small (unless there is a high degree of repetition) and certain, but can meet tough objectives in respect of speed and economy. Professional organizations tend to occupy the middle ground in respect of all the key variables. They are efficient when faced with moderate complexity, medium size, moderate variety, moderate levels of uncertainty and moderately tough objectives in respect of speed and economy. They provide a reliable middle-of-the-road approach which should, for the foreseeable future, suit a majority of customers.

Organization	Programmed organization	Professional organization	Problem-solving organization
Product	Standard construction	Traditional construction	Innovative construction
Characteristic work	Automated, well practised skills	Technical rationality	Reflection-in-action, problem-solving
Coordination	Basic set of coordination devices	Basic set of coordination devices plus information systems	Primarily lateral relations plus basic set of coordination devices and information systems
Detail design	Standard	Established	Innovative

Figure 9.5   *Characteristics of project organization gestalts*

The relationships shown in Figure 9.6 provide a robust framework for strategic decisions on construction projects. Having identified a project with one of the gestalts, efficiency requires that subsequent decisions respect the initial choice. Construction project organizations should be given every opportunity to perform well by ensuring that their task is consistent, and remains consistent, with their project management system. The three gestalts described in this chapter provide a basis for customers, designers, managers and specialist contractors to work together to provide this consistency.

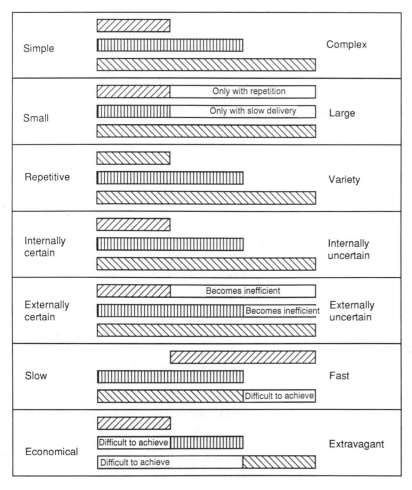

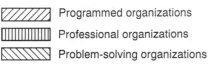 Programmed organizations

Professional organizations

Problem-solving organizations

Figure 9.6 *Relationship between gestalts and key project variables*

10 *Competitive products*

Construction produces a great variety of products: buildings, bridges and other brainwaves by which mankind modifies its physical environment. The theory described in Chapter 9 explains how the nature of these products helps to determine the appropriate form of project organization. However, while appropriate project management systems are necessary, they are not sufficient to ensure an efficient construction industry. The industry needs other attributes for it to be fully efficient. Important among these are competitive products and competent people. The first of these, competitive products, are discussed in this chapter and the next chapter describes the steps which can be taken within individual projects to ensure that construction is provided with competent people.

Competitive products mean those which customers wish to buy. That is, they are competitive with all the alternative uses for potential customers' money. There are two requirements for competitive construction products. First, they should provide good value for money. Second, customers should find it easy to relate to the products available. That is, they should know the range of products available, understand how they can serve their objectives, and be easy to buy. In other words they need to be marketed properly. However, unless products provide good value for money, marketing is a hollow activity.

Value for money

Construction generally has allowed its prices to rise faster than the general rate of inflation. Most capital goods industries have succeeded in reducing the real price of their products. They have done this by establishing efficient production processes and by harnessing the creative forces of steady innovation and research and development. Construction needs all three elements if it is to reverse the trend of providing ever worse value for money.

The essential starting point for creating better value for money is to establish a design, manufacture and construction process based on tried and tested methods. Efficiency depends on competent people working at tasks they understand. This in turn means that the majority of the industry's products should be well developed standard or traditional constructions. These, however, are merely the starting point; the industry cannot stand still. Construction needs the value for money which it provides to be improved steadily by means of innovation. This is really effective only when it is driven by practical ideas from workers throughout the industry, channelled through innovation groups. So the basis for competitive products must be standard and traditional constructions which are made better, year after year, by steady innovation.

This conclusion does not deal with innovative constructions and research and development. These two things need to be linked. Bennett *et al.* (1989) suggest the need for concept buildings. These are exciting designs which are undertaken with the deliberate aim of experimenting with new methods and forms of construction. They are set up like research projects with wide-ranging, multi-disciplinary teams of customers, designers, managers, specialist contractors and researchers. Concept buildings have agreed research objectives in addition to customer's briefs, proper measurement of the performance of the processes and the end products, and rigorous evaluation of the outcomes. The overall aim is to bring together new ideas from many sources in a search for genuine steps forward in the industry's products. There is every reason to apply the ideas of Bennett *et al.* for concept buildings to the work of the whole construction industry. That is, the industry should plan its own future by using concept constructions.

Whatever pattern of work the construction industry adopts, and we shall return to this issue later in this chapter, real, long term value for money comes from meeting users' needs. So we begin our consideration of how construction should approach the task of marketing its products by concentrating on users' needs.

Users' needs

Competitive products are those which satisfy users' needs. This view may be regarded as being at odds with the fact, which this book has consistently recognized, that effective construction demand is channelled through customers who may or may not be the users of the constructions they commission. Clearly the construction industry must market its products to customers. However, the deeper truth is that, unless these products satisfy the needs of users, in the long-run there will be far fewer customers than could or should be the case. Therefore, to maintain a substantial and healthy market, the construction industry needs to ensure that its products satisfy users' needs. This places great responsibility on designers to understand, first, the diverse needs of the world's population and, second, how these can be met by modern construction technologies.

Individual designers need to develop specialized knowledge of specific types of users' needs and the related technologies that serve to meet them. They need to be able to produce designs efficiently, based on the best current practice. In addition, they need a scholarly awareness of general, strategic developments in users' needs and technologies so that they can propose useful new construction products.

Hasegawa (1988) provides an excellent example of the imaginative extension of current answers. He describes how the competitive strategies of the Japanese construction industry are based on analysing users' needs and studying emerging technologies. The results provide lessons for designers everywhere. Hasegawa takes a positive approach to creating demand for construction. He believes that construction firms should stir up dormant demand wherever it is to be found. This means, for example, helping customers to create businesses which will require construction work. It means knowing what is worth building based on knowledge accumulated from working with customers from a variety of backgrounds. Just as financial advisers develop an early knowledge of trends by working with customers from different companies and institutions, and use this to invent useful new financial services, so construction firms should develop construction services to meet latent demands.

New services are most likely to result from the deep knowledge that comes from concentrating on one type of construction. For example, houses, or rather homes, are the core of human activities. There are many different latent demands for the construction of homes. The most important is the need to provide homes for the poor in the developing world. One approach to solving the problem of the world's poor, homeless peoples is to link solutions to generous technology transfer strategies. In other words, designing and building homes for the Third World need to be accomplished in a manner which educates and trains their users and creates self-sufficient communities. Achieving these difficult tasks requires construction firms to work in cooperation with development agencies, research and development institutions, and wise men who understand local cultures and traditions. The aim is to create demand for construction, but this is best done in a manner which provides long term, sustainable benefits for very poor users.

At the opposite end of the wealth league, construction firms should be active in debates about the kind of communities needed by information-rich societies. Such communities are likely to provide private houses linked to information networks so that doing office work, educational studies, banking and shopping from home will become common. Modern communities also need to provide places for people to meet and socialize. There also needs to be easy access to nature, challenging leisure activities, rich cultural experiences and efficient transport systems. All this should be achieved with style and wit, so that each village and town has a clear identity. These new communities will depend on the emerging technologies of electronics, biotechnology and new engineered materials to make them virtually self-sufficient in energy and basic raw materials.

Similarly, imaginative and well researched ideas are needed for all types of construction. To give credibility to their new ideas, construction firms need to become experts in using constructions. The aim should be to help customers to obtain the maximum value from their construction facilities. For example, if the customer is a hospital owner, designers should be able to propose ways of helping the doctors to be efficient, and know the best ways of operating all the hardware of a modern hospital, of linking it to the communities it serves and of providing effective software systems to aid the management of the total facility. Or if the customer operates a leisure centre, designers should know the local market for leisure activities well enough to be able to propose a range of facilities to complement what already exists. They should understand the total life-cycle costs of their proposals, know the best sources of training for instructors, and understand how to market a new leisure complex. Knowledge of how to use new constructions can be marketed in two distinct ways. First, it should be used to generate demand for new construction work. It should also be used to provide services that assist the businesses of customers. These may include: maintaining and operating a new facility, recruiting or training staff, promotional activities aimed at the general public or close neighbours, and acting as project managers for the fitting out and commissioning of new facilities.

The provision of totally integrated and efficient hardware and software for all types of users requires a daunting range of knowledge. There are two important factors which help to make this a realistic aim. The first is that modern design, for all except the simplest of products, inevitably requires teams of specialists. These include designers who specialize in individual elements. Obvious examples are structural engineers, services engineers, civil engineers, landscape architects and external cladding consultants. Multidisciplinary design teams also need specialists with the range of knowledge described earlier in this chapter, about the needs of narrow and specific categories of users. However, such teams also need generalists who can integrate the work of all the specialists to create a coherent and stylish end product. So the sum total of the knowledge of all designers is vast, yet individuals can sensibly specialize in a relatively narrow and therefore manageable subject area.

The second important factor, which helps to make it feasible for designers to provide expert advice to a wide range of customers, is that the vast majority of users share common needs. Broadbent (1973) suggests that 70 per cent of human activities in general can be accommodated satisfactorily in rooms of about 150 sq ft (14 m^2) and about 85 per cent in rooms of under 200 sq ft (18.5 m^2). At least this is true provided the rooms are square or at least nearly square and are not locked into any specific use by services, fitted furniture or built-in equipment. This idea is based on extensive research into the actual use of rooms and users' stated preferences. It means that buildings comprising rooms of between 150–200 sq ft (14–18.5 m^2), with the addition of sufficient toilet facilities, a secure entrance and circulation patterns which can be rearranged either to facilitate or to inhibit movements between the spaces, will satisfy most users' needs. Other needs tend to require larger spaces and very specific equipment and services. There is therefore merit in arranging buildings into long-life, high quality general spaces plus specialized spaces in which the performance is dictated by the nature and life expectancy of the specific use. A further refinement of this design strategy is provided by linking Broadbent's (1973) ideas to Duffy and Henney's (1989) analysis of modern office buildings, described in Chapter 1 of this book.

Duffy and Henney see office buildings as comprising long-life shells, medium-life services, short-life scenery, and sets which are rearranged very frequently. Applying this idea to general spaces suggests a need for robust building shells providing spaces of between 150 and 200 sq ft (14–18.5m^2). They will use largely passive means of providing the basic human needs for fresh air, a variety of good quality lighting, dry, warm and hygienic spaces, reasonable quiet and views of the world outside. This background, general environment, ideally, will have tiny energy requirements. It will rely on the inherent properties of the materials of the external envelope and internal space dividers to provide for the basic human needs. In addition, users will be able to add finishings, furniture, fittings, task lighting, ventilation, computers, telephones, televisions, and other comfort conditioning and information systems to create a micro-environment to suit their individual and specific needs. This flexibility will be provided by plug-in units which can be programmed to match individual idiosyncrasies and by using loose, general purpose furniture. As advances in technology and changing patterns of activities make the plug-in units obsolete, they can be thrown away or sold as second-hand and replaced with newer models. As changing uses make one arrangement of furniture inconvenient, the chairs and tables can be moved.

The strategy of producing a majority of general spaces based on robust general shells and space dividers, individual plug-in units and loose furniture will tend to maximize the long term value of new constructions. It also allows designers who concentrate on the design of general spaces to serve the needs of a wide range of customers. They will need to be supplemented by specialists in the design of very specific spaces. Although some of the specific spaces will have a long life and so should be designed to appreciate in value, many will have a short useful life and so can afford to be wilful, arbitrary, fashionable and fun. The designers of all three categories of spaces (general, specific long-life and specific short-life) need to understand users' needs and so be able to help customers to ensure the efficient use of the constructions they provide.

Shaping customers' expectations

Although a deep understanding of users' needs is essential for the construction industry to produce competitive products consistently, the industry must also sell its ideas to customers. An important part of achieving this necessary marketing is to shape customers' expectations about the industry's products. Doing this, as we shall see, inevitably causes changes to the products themselves.

Modern, successful industries devote considerable efforts to educating their customers about the performance of their products. The motor car industry for example provides a great deal of detailed technical information about the costs, speed, comfort, safety, handling characteristics, servicing and life expectancy of their products. As a result, car buyers know what questions to ask of salesmen and have some understanding of the kind of answers they should receive. By comparison, the construction industry tends to leave its customers in the dark. Debate about construction in the general public media tends to focus on superficial issues and major failures. The result is that many potential customers feel alienated and actively seek to avoid dealing with the construction industry unless this is absolutely unavoidable.

The industry's poor image is unnecessary because construction has an enormous and undervalued potential to raise the quality of life enjoyed by its customers. As has been demonstrated by the motor car industry, all that is needed to generate demanding customers is good published information about the performance of specific categories of products related to users' real needs. For construction, this requires careful systematic measurement of those characteristics of constructions in use which are of real interest to users and customers.

Taking office buildings as an example, because good work has been done in identifying the key characteristics, the following measurements help customers to demand better value. They are based on extensive research by two firms, DEGW (Duffy, Eley, Giffone, Worthington) and FRA (Facilities Research Associates Inc.), published by Davis *et al.* (1985). The key characteristics are:

1 *Change in headcount.* Is the total number of people to be accommodated in the organization stable or changing?

2 *Attract or retain workforce.* How important is it for the organization's success to ensure that highly qualified staff who are hard to replace feel satisfied enough not only to join the organization but to stay?

3 *Communication of hierarchy, status and power.* How important is it for people to recognize clearly the differences in rank, status and power within the organization?

4 *Relocation of staff.* How frequently are people being physically relocated from one workplace location to another inside the office?

5 *Maximizing informal interaction.* How important are informal and spontaneous interactions and face-to-face communications between staff?

6 *Human factors in the ambient environment.* How important to the organization is the quality of lighting, air-conditioning, temperature, acoustics and furniture comfort?

7 *High status image to the outside.* How important is the organizational image presented to visitors from the outside?

8 *Security to outside.* How important is protection of information and other valuable objects from outsiders?

9 *Security to inside.* How important is the protection of information from insiders?

10 *Connecting equipment and changing location of cables.* How important is it to the organization to be able to connect different pieces of equipment to each other and/or to relocate cables to virtually any location within the building?

11 *Adding or relocating environmentally demanding equipment.* How important is it to the organization to be able to add or relocate environmentally demanding equipment to virtually any location within the building?

12 *Protecting hardware operations.* How important is it that operations are not interrupted, even for a moment, or for data to be protected against loss, delay or misrecording due to problems with computer hardware or related equipment?

13 *Demand for power.* How important is the need for high electrical power capacity and good vertical and horizontal on-floor distribution?

14 *Telecommunications.* How dependent is the organization on both internal and external telecommunications?

Each of the 14 key characteristics can be measured in terms of the needs of a specific organization. They can also be measured in terms of the facilities provided by an existing building or a set of design proposals. DEGW and FRA relate the measurements of an organization's needs to the facilities provided by a building to create a framework for a customer, users, designers and managers to work together effectively. A good approach is to bring this group of interests and responsibilities together for a series of structured workshops. The aim is to develop a deep understanding of the customer's problem or the opportunity he has identified and of possible answers. Ideally everyone present is encouraged to think creatively about each of the 14 key characteristics. Such workshops can produce unusually penetrating customers' briefs and lay the groundwork for genuinely efficient and relevant conceptual designs. The key to this success is that the customer focuses on the issues he knows best, and design proposals are presented to him in terms which are directly relevant to his own interests. Using this approach in interactive workshops provides opportunities for designers and managers to help customers to expect more from new office buildings. Ideas for more productive environments, for greater flexibility, for more individual control or for better value can be explored in what is essentially a learning process. The workshop approach allows a few talented designers and managers to shape the expectations of customers. However, they necessarily do this one customer at a time.

There are other isolated examples of excellent research and development. In the UK in the 1940s and 1950s the Ministry of Education, in extremely tight economic conditions, carried out a series of projects which explored new ways of satisfying the emergent educational needs. These projects shaped the customers' demands in the UK's massive school building programmes of the 1960s and 1970s. More recently, Stanhope Properties plc in two landmark developments in London, at Broadgate and Stockley Park, not only anticipated changes in the accommodation needs of the financial services and high-tech industries but also, through a programme of user-based research and effective marketing, succeeded in persuading initially sceptical customers that more sophisticated buildings were, indeed, exactly what they wanted.

These, and other, isolated examples show what can be achieved by careful study and measurement of the performances of new construction products. Provided the measurements concentrate on the interests of customers and the needs of users, they will be effective in shaping customers' expectations. The construction industry needs extensive published data for all types of buildings, bridges and other constructions. However, the starting point is most likely to be individual projects or programmes of projects. It is therefore incumbent on all construction project managers to help customers to demand higher performance and better value from their new constructions. This is, however, merely a starting point and the aim must be to establish clearly delineated ranges of products which are widely recognized and understood by potential customers.

Product range

As Chapter 9 describes, it is important for customers and their advisors to agree the type of end product which any individual project is intended to produce.

However, the classification in Chapter 9 into standard, traditional and innovative constructions is concerned with the industry's internal technology, not with marketing its products to customers. Modern marketing places great faith in brand names to help customers identify specific products. A brand name may be used to identify the products of one company or to distinguish between different products produced by the same company. It can also be used to provide a clear identity for products produced by several companies. The obvious example is Airbus, which is produced by a group of French, German, Dutch, Belgian, British and Spanish aircraft companies.

Brand names increasingly relate to the total package provided by a company or group of companies. That is, they relate to the products and the services which support customers' use of them. Brand names help customers to recognize products. When confronted by the pack, a brand named product stands out as one offering something distinctive. It also ensures that customers associate brand names with appropriate messages, including information on technical sophistication, quality, reliability and the standard of service to be expected. It seems likely, therefore, that the creation and maintenance of brand names will help make the industry's products more coherent to potential customers.

However, the first task for the construction industry in making its products better understood is to identify those which fulfil distinctly different functions. Then, within each function, the industry needs to help customers to distinguish between products that provide distinctly different performance and quality. In the world of transport, for example, there are obvious and widely understood differences between aeroplanes, boats, horse-drawn carts, motor cars, lorries, vans, bicycles, submarines, space craft and helicopters. In addition there are reasonably distinct differences between types of motor car. Limousine, family saloon, hatchback, sports car, grand tourer, beach-buggy and estate car all conjure up distinct images. They imply differences in performance and quality which are reflected in the products of many different manufacturers. This consistent labelling helps potential customers to decide what they wish to buy.

The same clarity does not exist for many of construction's products. There are, to some extent, exceptions in speculative housing, civil engineering and heavy engineering. However, the situation facing customers wishing to buy a new building is far from clear. Dominant function alone is a poor guide. A university building, for example, could mean almost any conceivable combination of functions, performance and quality. Similarly, hotel, office, hospital, studio, bank or almost any other dominant function description tells us virtually nothing about any one specific building.

Earlier in this chapter we identified the existence of generalized spaces, specific long-life spaces and specific short-life spaces. It is likely that further research into the latter two categories will identify useful subcategories. In other words, it is likely that the building industry produces a relatively small number of distinctly different generic functions. Perhaps less than 20 categories would serve to meet the needs of more than 99 per cent of users. It would be of tremendous benefit to the industry and its customers if these categories were clearly identified, described and given consistent names. The improvement in customer understanding would of itself serve to increase the demand for construction's products.

Each of the less than 20 generic functions needs to be provided for by products that give a range of performances and qualities. The size of any specific range will depend on the potential market for the generic function it serves. Thus, for example, generalized spaces will be served by a large range of products. We can expect to see the emergence of *starter, regular, club, executive, classic* and *royal* general spaces or at least some equivalent set of terms, which describe a distinct and widely understood performance and quality. All will serve the same generic function but cater for different sectors of the market. Prices will reflect perceived differences in the value to customers of each model. In other words, prices will no longer be based on unit costs plus a percentage mark-up for profit and overheads. The industry's financial management will become truly market-driven. Costs will be driven down to equal value minus profit; otherwise, as in any other industry, producers will go out of business. The long term benefit of these developments is that they will cause the market for construction to grow. They will do so because they give the industry a coherent language to discuss its products with potential customers and at the same time force the industry to become efficient. As a consequence construction will become more interesting to customers, and appear less risky to them, so there is a realistic hope that it will become fashionable to buy the latest construction model.

Leading producers

A common language which the industry shares with its customers and which reflects an ideal pattern of construction products, as well as producing demanding customers, ought to lead to the emergence of strong firms based on distinct strengths. Some customers do search for the very best practitioners at present, but in the absence of a clear basis for identifying relevant experience the results are often disappointing.

Obvious examples of distinct strengths include the small group of firms who design, construction manage, manufacture and construct high-rise, *regular* buildings in Chicago. The large Japanese construction firm's ability to deliver *club* and *executive-class* buildings absolutely reliably is another distinct strength. Many individual European architectural, engineering design practices produce *classic* constructions, which is also an important and distinct strength. None of these have travelled totally effectively for one of two main reasons. Either the specialists concerned have been commissioned to produce something which functionally or superficially matches their expertise but is in fact fundamentally different. Or they have not taken a complete system with them and the alien elements have made their work difficult. US designers and construction managers working in the UK provide an example of the first misfit. This has not produced happy results because the standardized buildings on which US productivity depends are fundamentally different from the arts and crafts based buildings which the UK is used to. An example of the second type of misfit is provided by UK designers working in Japan. This has created uncomfortable situations because both the UK designers and the Japanese contractors need to have control of detail design to be able to operate in their normal manner. The first misfit arises from concentrating on the process and the second from concentrating on the product. Both are important and in any one project they need to be matched to each other.

Distinct strengths emerge when product and process are in tune. It takes time to achieve an efficient match between the two, which is why the industry needs a clear common understanding with its customers of what it should concentrate on producing. As we have discussed, a common understanding is of no practical value without a common language to express that understanding. Hence the need for clear product ranges produced under brand names. It will be the firms that own major brands which will emerge as the leading producers of constructions in the 1990s.

We can predict the general nature of these firms on the basis of Ohmae's (1990) analysis of the nature of modern successful companies. He focuses on the three crucial fixed costs of any major business. They are manufacturing, research and development, and creating and maintaining brand names. In construction, because of the complexity of the product, manufacturing and construction are subcontracted. This is inevitable and is unlikely to change. Research and development is best provided by means of a combination of internal resources and subcontracting to universities. Branding can also be supported by consultancy advice, but a key advantage of a brand name is that it helps to provide internal coherence. However, as Olins (1989) makes clear, brand names have to be treated with respect and care. He uses MG as an example of a brand name whose integrity was not respected and so it just withered away and died. In the old days, MG had a worldwide reputation for sporty style. Now the MG name has been used as a badge on a variety of indifferent machinery: cars such as the MG 1300, the MG Metro and the MG Maestro. In this way the MG name has been distorted and trivialized. Without respect and understanding, the name that was once worth millions in annual profits is quietly rotting away. This example, and there are many other similar stories, tells us that sustaining brand names must be a direct, internal responsibility.

This analysis of how construction is likely to deal with its essential fixed costs suggests that the industry's leading producers will fall into two broad categories. The first arises where a class of products is best provided as standard constructions. In this case the brand names will be owned, and the research and development needed to ensure that the products remain competitive will be undertaken by firms who own construction systems. Where a class of products is best provided as traditional constructions, the brand names will be owned and the supporting research and development undertaken by modern professional firms. This leaves the case of innovative constructions, which as we discussed earlier in this chapter are essentially research and development projects. It seems likely therefore that they will not be brand named, except when they act as a prototype for a new model within a range of standard or traditional constructions. In these circumstances they are accurately described as concept constructions.

Concept constructions

The industry needs concept constructions to provide test-beds for new design, manufacturing and construction ideas. The purpose of concept constructions is to experiment with ideas, which if successful will lead to the introduction of dramatic new products.

The initiative and probably much of the funding for concept constructions will come from firms who own brand names. Some will produce concept constructions as part of their research effort. After the research is complete, the construction can be used by the firm to house part of its own activities, sold or demolished. An alternative approach to initiating concept constructions, proposed by Bennett *et al.* (1989), is for leading firms to prepare proposals for possible concept constructions; that is, generalized ideas for new methods or new construction forms that potential customers may decide to support. The proposals may come initially from various sources. Some will need joint work by interdisciplinary teams of designers, managers, specialist contractors, research institutes and universities. Others may come from talented individuals with good ideas. Whatever their source, it is likely that most will need the support of leading firms to get them to a state where customers can take them seriously. The aim should be to provide attractive packages which customers can think about and, if they so choose, discuss with enthusiastic teams.

A classic example of the flair and style required was provided by Richard Rogers' Royal Academy exhibition 'London as it could be'. This bold scheme aimed to rescue an important and potentially beautiful area of London from the motor car and return it to the pedestrian. The area involved has two main axes. One runs from Trafalgar Square to Waterloo Station and the second runs along the Thames embankments between Westminster and Blackfriars Bridge. The main features of the scheme, including a river bed road tunnel, a riverside promenade worthy of a great capital city, floating islands and the first pedestrian-only crossing of the Thames since Brunel's suspension bridge was demolished to make way for the present massive, visually obstructive Hungerford Bridge, are well described in Rogers (1988).

The aim of proposals like Rogers' 'London as it could be' is to persuade customers to put bold ideas into practice. An international superstar of Richard Rogers' reputation clearly does not need the support of a brand name to sell his ideas. Indeed, his name itself fulfils many of the functions of a brand name. Certainly, it is associated with a distinctive range of products. However, firms which own established brand names will help talented designers with smaller reputations, but with exciting ideas, to have them turned into reality. The incentives for the firms are, first, that mere association with concept constructions will add glamour to their brands. Consequently, they will devote part of their marketing budgets to funding the construction of brilliant designs. Second, and more importantly, concept designs are likely to provide a rich source of substantial marketable improvements to established products.

There may perhaps appear to be a contradiction in the idea that an industry dominated by firms primarily interested in standard and traditional products will provide the funds for concept constructions. However, every major industry which provides real variety and original design has at its heart an efficient, well tuned production system. It is this which pays for and sustains the production of properly researched new ideas. The apparent contradiction comes from the fact that new ideas can come from anywhere. The classic example is Steve Jobs' and Steve Wozniak's creation of Apple in a garage. As Sculley (1987) reports, these two brilliant young college drop-outs would probably have been unheard of but for the third member of the team, Mike Markkula. He brought a broad business talent to bear on the others' precocious talent. It was Markkula who wrote the original business plan and found the venture capitalists who put up the money needed to transform Jobs' and Wozniak's dreams into reality. It was he who put together, nurtured and ran Apple as a viable company. Jobs provided brilliant, charismatic, visionary leadership, Wozniak created a leading-edge personal computer, but Markkula turned these two talents into a viable commercial force.

So it is in the world of construction, where many talented designers are wasted through lack of commercial realism. Firms with a brand name to foster will need to search out and encourage designers who can give their products a distinctive quality. So the apparent contradiction is no contradiction at all. For concept constructions to flourish and play their proper role of experimenting and creating brilliant new models for the whole industry, it is first necessary to create an efficient industry based on competitive products.

11 *Competent people*

The construction industry needs competent people at all levels if it is to be fully efficient. This requires the industry to recruit people who have a broad education based on the arts, sciences and humanities, or in practical terms design, engineering and management. It requires new recruits to be provided with practical training which combines on-the-job experience with formal skills training in short intensive courses. It requires all members of the industry to be kept up to date with new knowledge and skills and where necessary retrained. It requires that all construction projects are managed in a manner which supports the industry's education and training policies.

The need for education and skills training is well stated by Porter (1990) on the basis of extensive research in ten major and successful countries. Within each country Porter's research team looked at the most successful industries and at the factors necessary for that success. In his judgement, based on what is one of the largest management research projects ever undertaken, education policy is fundamental to the capacity of any industry to achieve competitive advantage. Any industry which is failing to recruit people with a good general education is in serious difficulty. But good general education alone is not enough. The skills that lead to competitive advantage are specialized. They require specialized masters and doctoral courses at the highest level, but equally they need vocational colleges providing training for all the specialized skills of the industry. The vocational colleges, in particular, are likely to be ineffective unless they are run in partnership with industry, so that trainees can see the immediate relevance of their formal studies. There need to be clear links between education, training and practice. While this is essential for the industry's basic workforce, it is important at all levels to produce the deeply rooted competence which underpins all competitive industries.

Education for life

Traditionally, and in stable societies, education taught young people the established conventional wisdom. They learnt the culture and traditions of their nation, which generally included respecting the views of their teachers and elders. They learnt the specific basic skills which would equip them to enter the established professions and crafts.

Since the 1950s it has been recognized in education that society is subject to change. This is occurring at all levels. Indeed so deep rooted is change that the primacy of the nation state itself is in question. Many of the key questions facing the world can be tackled only internationally; drugs, defence, terrorism and the environment all require cooperation across national boundaries. On the other hand, many issues can be dealt with only at a very local level; housing, health, petty crime, regional transport and basic education need debate between the people directly affected. It is at this local level that nationalism, perhaps better called tribalism, is an enduring force. So the twin forces of supranational groupings and local tribalism will change many of today's nations. Given the scale of change in the *real world*, it is patently inadequate to teach merely traditional values. Developments in technology are an even more potent force for change. In the last hundred years, technology has increased life expectancy dramatically and allowed most people to choose how many children they will have. This has changed and indeed continues to change the age structure of society. Technology also makes us all better informed than ever before. We are bombarded with blips of information from all around the world through a high proportion of our waking day. With this access to information comes a widespread wish to be involved in the decisions that affect our lives. Democracy is, in 1990, breaking out all over the world, so change is seen as endemic. Education in many countries has responded by focusing on encouraging children to express their own individuality. However, in all too many cases the initial response went too far and structured education was abandoned altogether in attempts to create child-centred learning situations. No nation is yet rich enough to provide the resources needed to make this a practical approach for all its people. Neither is any nation rich enough for unstructured learning to be the right approach for the majority of its people.

It is now recognized that modern society depends on a mixture of stability and change. Both are needed and it is becoming ever more widely recognized that neither traditional education nor its *flower-power* successors provides an adequate preparation for life. A better way forward is suggested by the new theories of chaos, which are beginning to cause science generally to acknowledge that many phenomena which have been seen as chaotic in fact have a pattern. They have an underlying structure which behaves in a reasonably predictable manner for long periods but then, without the underlying structure changing, suddenly behaves unpredictably. The world's weather is the classic example, but the same general models help us to understand the behaviour of stock markets, large organizations and difficult construction projects.

In a chaotic world, education needs to teach people to respect and understand the underlying systems of society. This includes teaching people to question and develop the systems but not to overthrow them, ignore them or assume that they do not exist. However, because many of society's systems have a chaotic tendency, education must also teach people to deal with turbulence. Crises will arise and people must improvise. So education must teach people to take responsibility for working with others, to find a way through crises, back to stable systematic conditions.

Construction project management requires precisely this mix of skills. It needs respect for standards and procedures. It needs steady, intelligent questioning and development of its systems. It also needs people willing and able to solve the problems which inevitably arise in enterprises as complex as construction projects. Crisis management requires problem-solving skills and a broad education. Breadth is essential since good answers may be found in design, engineering or management.

Construction project managers, as such, do not have any direct responsibility for primary, secondary or undergraduate education. They will hope, and as private individuals may seek to ensure, that education provides for the majority of people who are happier, and therefore learn more, when they are working with their hands. They will hope that education will instil a healthy respect for the environment and for construction's central role in shaping it to mankind's ends. They will hope that graduates from vocational colleges, polytechnics and universities will want to enter the crafts and professions of modern construction. However, once graduates enter the industry construction project managers have direct responsibilities for their further education. Specifically, they are responsible for ensuring that everyone involved with their projects, especially their direct employees, has available formal courses to deepen and widen their knowledge and skills. Today, education is for life. It does not stop when paid employment begins.

As a direct reflection of the broadening of education demand, the ways of delivering education are expanding. Television, video, personal computers, tapes, discs, individually tailored textbooks and many other communication media are being used to complement and supplement more traditional forms of education. Evening classes, modular courses, part-time courses and other patterns of teaching which enable students to combine a full-time job with formal education are in ever increasing demand. Construction, with its large, mobile and generally under-educated workforce, stands to benefit from these general developments. However, this will happen only if all managers actively encourage their employees to seek further education. By far the most effective way of doing this is to link rewards to formal appraisal systems, to link appraisal to skills training and to link skills training, to readily available formal courses.

Skills training

The construction industry needs, at all levels, a skilled and up-to-date workforce. This provides a great challenge for training, as new technology changes the nature of construction work. Modern technology generally requires greater technical understanding and less reliance on manual skills. In the future this change will accelerate as information technology and robotics relieve the monotonous and arduous nature of manual work and allow more human energy to be devoted to creativity and innovation.

It is important for the future health of the construction industry that technological changes are used to society's advantage. This will be achieved only by a cultured and well motivated workforce led by men who are comfortable dealing with problems which mix technical, social and cultural issues and who know from direct experience the hard work and dedication needed to provide consistent high quality and productivity.

All of this requires individual workers to have the encouragement and opportunity to learn new skills and update existing ones. Since the work of the construction industry comprises projects, the direct responsibility for training lies with construction project managers. Certainly they need support from specialists in training. This should include advice on available courses and the most effective ways of linking them to practical work. It should include simple, robust systems of recording the skills acquired by individual workers. It should include training packages, which generally should have a strong visual content, to support on-the-job training. However, the primary responsibility for ensuring that everyone involved with their projects has the opportunity of receiving relevant training rests squarely with construction project managers. There is no avoiding the increasingly widely recognized fact that training is the direct responsibility of managers in industry. Neither government nor the educational establishments can know the skills needed by industry as well as industry itself. Equally, managers directly responsible for the industry's work are in a far better position to define the skills required than are training specialists from head office. The specialists can help once the needs are identified, but the initiative must lie with the front-line construction project managers.

Managers are helped in their training responsibilities where there is an industry-wide scheme which gives everyone a recognized standard document that records his current skills achievement. This is best based on skills testing against defined measures of ability. The old time-serving basis of apprenticeships had great strengths, but the diversity of skills needed today and the rate at which they change requires a more objective qualification which can be updated at regular intervals. This applies to all levels of skills, including professional qualifications, which cannot be regarded as a once-and-for-all preparation for a lifetime's practice. Continuing professional updating and development is essential and is effective only if it is tested and the results recorded on each individual's licence to practise.

An effective scheme of certifying skills will recognize distinct levels of achievement. As we discussed in Chapter 2, higher levels of achievement necessarily develop distinct languages. It is important that the measurements which underlie such schemes recognize that higher levels are not based simply on more knowledge and more skills than the lower levels. They are based on a different kind of knowledge and skills. Higher levels equip practitioners to take a broad overview of lower levels, not to understand or be skilled in all the detail of lower level work.

Skills testing, at all levels, needs to be modular because the specific skills needed are dependent on the type of project in which an individual chooses to work. For example, in terms of basic construction work, new industrial and commercial building tends to require a few rather narrowed traditional craft skills and an increasing range of specialized engineering fitters. In retrofit projects, where an existing building is refitted, there is a need for a wide range of traditional crafts. In new mass housing, general semi-skilled labour undertakes highly rationalized tasks. Their work often produces an industrialized interior which is then encased in an external skin which relies on traditional craft skills. Maintenance work requires multi-skilled operatives who are trained to identify defects, diagnose and carry out simple remedies, and refer major problems to specialists. Thus the emerging pattern of skills includes: the traditional crafts, sometimes in their original form, sometimes narrowed and deepened, and sometimes narrowed and combined with parts of other crafts; semi-skilled and skilled trade specialists, including machine operators, assemblers and fitters working either in factories or on site; and workers with multiple skills which may combine craft and industrial trades. A very similar pattern, driven by exactly the same factors, has emerged for professional practice. Designers and managers specialize in specific sectors of the industry's work and so their work in some cases is concentrated into a deep specialism and in others broadened beyond the traditional bounds of separate professions. While there is no doubt that good ideas flow across from one sector to another, the wise construction project manager employs, for each distinctly different task, people with directly relevant experience. This is much easier where a recognized, nationally administered scheme exists which provides objective measurements of the level of skills achieved by each worker.

The aim of any national scheme should be to provide one single form of qualification certificate based on the standards of competence required by the industry it serves. This will facilitate entry into and progression in employment, further education and training. The qualification certificate should state the level of performance achieved in work-related activities and the level reached in the skills, knowledge and understanding, both practical and theoretical, that underpin such performance. Certificates should relate to distinct levels of achievement which encompass all of the basic work of the industry. The higher levels of qualification will indicate a greater breadth of competences attained, work which is more difficult and theoretical, higher levels of skills, ability to undertake specialist activities, ability to plan and control work, ability to apply competences to a wider variety of situations, ability to innovate and cope with non-routine activities, and ability to supervise and train others.

Individual firms need to provide clear career patterns which link responsibilities and rewards to levels of achievement. Ideally, career patterns should create one single ladder of opportunity. It should create no class barriers or divisions. It should not designate some levels as professional and, by implication, others as less than professional. The construction industry needs a totally professional workforce. It also needs first-class specialists and first-class generalists. Therefore the single ladder of opportunity must provide for outstanding specialists, be they designer, project manager, manufacturer or constructor, as well as outstanding general managers. All must have an equal chance of reaching the main board.

Individuals entering a firm should know the steps they must take to progress up the ladder of opportunity and have the assurance that support and opportunities exist for ambitious, talented and energetic people to rise to the top, irrespective of where they first entered the firm. Given this, individuals will freely invest their own futures in the work of the firm. Personal ambition directed by coherent leadership remains the prime motivating force in construction, as in every other walk of life.

Where a modular skills-testing scheme linked to a clear ladder of opportunity does not already exist, construction project managers can and should encourage its emergence by insisting on clear, robust evidence of the achievements of everyone involved in their projects. They will in effect be creating their own project based scheme because it is good practice and also in the hope that it will become infectious and spread to the rest of their firm's projects. Irrespective of the existence of a formal scheme, construction project managers should back up their concern for the performance of their workforce by regular appraisals for all the teams which make up their project organization. Every team involved should have at least one formal appraisal during their work on a project. This should be repeated at six monthly intervals if they are still working on the same project.

Appraisal

Appraisal by construction project managers has several objectives. It allows each team to stand back from the day-to-day pressures of the current project and review their achievements and failures. It gives them a chance to think about the factors that have shaped their performance and to search for ways of working more effectively in the future. At the same time, appraisal allows managers to form a balanced judgement on the abilities of their teams. However, perhaps more importantly, it causes managers to review their own achievements and failures with the aim of identifying improvements which will help their projects become more effective.

Formal appraisals collected together from many projects provides a robust basis for firms to evaluate their own performance. They also help to ensure that their regular subcontractors are competent, up to date and providing appropriate services and support. They also provide an important means of checking that project objectives and values are clearly understood and being acted upon.

Appraisals also identify training needs; that is, specific individual needs and newly emergent general needs. Put another way, appraisals reinforce individuals' responsibility for their own and their team's performance and for keeping their skills up to date. At the same time, appraisals provide an effective way of checking that the support systems which enable individuals to do these things are in good order.

Team appraisals should deal with total performance in relation to project objectives. Thus, in addition to reviewing quality, time and cost performance, appraisals should look more generally at a team's contribution to the project. Contribution at formal meetings, efforts to cooperate in solving problems, ideas for cost savings, safety record, industrial relations record, the condition of the team's workplaces and the accuracy and timeliness of their record-keeping should, depending on the project priorities, all be considered. Appraisals should also look at the number of new ideas proposed and introduced. They should review the overall style and performance of the team manager as well as appraising his team as a unit.

Appraisals should primarily look forward. Although they are based on past achievements, their output should be a plan of agreed actions. Such plans range widely, but an important element in most is agreement on the specific training needed both in the short and medium term.

Training

Training needs to be both general and specific. The general element instils an understanding of construction and its place in society. It helps to build a team approach to projects so that individual specialists have an understanding and respect for the work of others. To a large extent the development of a broad understanding and mutual respect is the task of all levels of undergraduate education. However, training needs to reinforce and sustain these positive team attitudes. Good ways of doing this include job rotation, where individuals spend their time working in a series of different roles. Reavens' (1982) ideas for action learning as a means of training individuals and of solving organization problems provide one especially effective form of job rotation for people with some practical experience. His scheme involves a group of five or six people drawn from different departments. All are moved to one of the others' departments, typically for three months, and given a current practical problem to solve in addition to normal work responsibilities. The group comes together regularly to discuss the problems they have been set and the emerging answers. They are guided in the discussions by an experienced tutor but to a large extent members of a group teach each other. Where the problems require knowledge or skills not present within the group, the tutor will ensure that suitable specialist advice or training is provided. Action learning often helps people to develop surprisingly rapidly. The success of Reavens' approach is in no small part due to its reliance on the excellent principles of making individuals responsible for identifying their own training needs and linking training directly to practical experience.

Another effective way of developing a broadly based team approach is through joint study by multidisciplinary groups. Studies of unusual, difficult or very successful projects can all provide a good basis for effective training. Looking at other industries or construction in other countries can also provide bases for rapid learning. Provided that such studies have clearly defined and jointly agreed objectives, the interaction between participants from different backgrounds often provides the most valuable teaching. Hordyk and Bennett (1989) describe a very productive multidisciplinary study of the Japanese steel construction industry which illustrates the strengths of this form of training. The study enabled a group of very experienced UK steel construction practitioners to observe Japanese practice at first hand. The group visited customers, design studios, engineering offices, factories and construction sites where the UK practitioners could identify and then form judgements about features of Japanese practice which differed from their own normal approach. Each member of the group was challenged to identify changes which they intended making to their own practice when they returned to the UK. The statements of the individual action plans, recorded by Hordyk and Bennett, provide ample proof of the value of purposeful joint study.

Training also needs to provide for specific skills. These include generic skills such as typing, using spreadsheets, analysing statistics, negotiating, report writing, team building, public speaking, interviewing and being interviewed. They also include new developments within individual specialisms. In the main, training for specific skills is available in short courses, individual training aids or books. Where knowledge has not been formalized in this way, conferences, discussions at professional institutions or trade associations, or the news media may provide the only publicly available information.

In all these cases, both general and specific, construction project managers should actively encourage everyone involved with their projects to identify their own personal training needs. Then managers, if necessary with the advice of training specialists, should match the needs to the courses available. Managers should give absolute priority to ensuring that their staff have all the time they need to attend courses, ensuring that people are properly briefed before they go on a course and debriefed immediately on their return. The aims of the briefing and debriefing are to emphasize the importance of personal development, to establish how the course contributes towards this for the individual, and to ensure that training received on courses is put into practice. A second debriefing some months after a course, to check that the course has proved to be useful and that the new skills are being applied, is equally important in ensuring that training is effective.

Perhaps the most important formal role within properly integrated training schemes is that of mentor. It is part of the responsibility of every experienced worker to provide guidance for younger people. This is most effective when mentors are appointed on a one-to-one basis for every young person. These one-to-one relationships are outside of and in addition to any formal management structure. Mentors provide training in specific skills and knowledge but they are just as much concerned with the culture of work. They teach a young man to be a good craftsman, a good designer or a good manager, but they also help him to recognize the responsibilities that come with his growing maturity. That is, they teach him to become a good man. It is of course also one of the joys of teaching that mentors learn from those they help. Mentoring in practice is a two-way process or else it is not working properly.

Another very important training ground which is integral with good working practice arises in the work of innovation groups. As a work group meets regularly to review its own methods and products in the search for practical innovations, so they will identify gaps in their knowledge and skills. It is fundamental to the proper working of innovation groups that the firm provides resources to make good these deficiencies. In this way individuals or the group as a whole may decide that they need training to make the work of the innovation group more effective. This may include training in statistical techniques, quality control procedures, computing or research methods. Equally, they may identify a need for training in a specific direct work skill. Whatever the needs, provided a group is pursuing innovation seriously, firms should place a very high priority on providing the training they want. Nothing is more motivating to an employee than the clear knowledge that his employer is eager to invest in his development.

Practical vision

Practice provides the framework for education and training. As such, practice should be a motivating force which encourages people to develop their own abilities. To do this it must provide a vision which people are prepared to pursue. At a basic level, this means that construction must provide realistic opportunities for people to become rich. There must be clear career paths to the top of the industry, and the rewards for those who work hard and are talented and lucky must be worthwhile. But material rewards and the visions they generate are just a base. Construction needs more.

Since construction is centrally involved in the biggest issue currently facing mankind, there is every good reason for the industry to create a clear vision of the world's environment. It would be a great advantage to the whole industry if it could persuade society that construction is not part of the problem but is a central, crucial part of the answer to creating a healthy, stimulating, enriching environment. Achieving this will be helped by concept constructions which provide bold models of self-sufficient, environmentally neutral communities based on using information rather than consuming vast quantities of energy. It will be helped by joint programmes of research into construction and the environment. It would be further helped if every new construction project produced, at an early stage, an environmental impact statement which set out the balance sheet of resources and waste expected to result from the new facility. In other words, the industry will need to become an effective watchdog with a practical concern for the total quality of life. Finally, it will need media personalities who explain construction's role whenever environmental issues hit the headlines. In all of this the industry will have three direct aims: to improve the planet for our children, to increase the demand for construction, and to make it easier to recruit talented, idealistic young people into construction. There are other possible bases for a motivating vision for construction, but a deep practical concern for the environment is going to be the most effective for the foreseeable future.

As far as creating a competent workforce is concerned, a clear focus on the environment is likely to have two distinct but closely related effects. First, a genuine concern for the world's environment will present the construction industry with a very wide range of tasks. The industry will need to understand problems expressed in cultural, scientific and social terms and be able to translate them into practical design, engineering and management solutions. It will need to help in developing a language which allows these translations to take place and so enables interdisciplinary and public debates to be effective. So the industry needs scientists, artists, philosophers, economists and sociologists as well as its established professions.

The second effect of construction demonstrating a genuine concern for the environment will help the industry to meet this need. This is because an environmentally sensitive industry will attract a wide variety of talented people who want to make the world a better place. These will include graduates, at all levels, who have followed a traditional course in architecture, building, construction management, design or engineering. They will include graduates who have followed a broadly based construction course, aimed perhaps at producing a modern-day master builder. They will also include graduates from many other disciplines who find that construction provides a challenging, exciting, worthwhile career.

There are many practical reasons why construction should seek to recruit a wide variety of graduates. It increases the number of potential entrants to the industry by providing access to people who wish to pursue a career in construction but made a poor choice of undergraduate course. It gives the industry direct access to a wide variety of viewpoints and therefore increases the potential sources of answers to problems. It allows the industry to be represented by people who know something of the language of major customers. It gives the industry a better chance of recruiting talented graduates from, at least in the developed world, a reducing number of young people. However, non-cognate graduates present the industry with difficult training tasks and some difficulty, at least initially, in devising productive work.

The more the industry adopts a distinct pattern of standard, traditional and innovative work, the easier it will become to make effective use of people from a variety of backgrounds. This is because standard constructions give rise to many routine tasks which can be defined in procedures and therefore learnt quickly. Traditional construction gives rise to some such tasks. It is these which provide a practical training ground for new recruits, whatever their backgrounds. New entrants need intensive training in narrow standardized work. They then apply their new knowledge, initially under close supervision from a more experienced person, in straightforward situations. A pattern of short intensive courses in gradually less structured and more demanding tasks, interspersed with periods of practice, should continue for at least three years. Ideally, during this time, entrants will experience a variety of types of project and a range of roles within those projects. Entrants from cognate courses may move through initial training modules rapidly or even bypass them altogether. However, experience in other industries suggests that within three years the subjects which practitioners studied as undergraduates are of minor consequence compared with the quality of training and experience they have received.

There is an important and obvious objection to the idea that all entrants to the industry should begin their practical experience on standard or traditional constructions. This is that such an approach will stifle creativity. There are several answers to this criticism.

First, creativity in construction must have a practical basis. That is, it must be grounded in an understanding of the established work of the industry. New forms and methods of construction often use established answers as a point of departure. Just as all great artists must first master their basic crafts, so great designers must first learn what already exists and become fluent in their use of standard and traditional constructions. Similarly, creative managers, manufacturers or constructors need to understand the established basis of their business before they can take it in new directions.

Second, talented and creative graduates will rapidly force their way onto a fast-track career path. In recognition of this, construction project managers need to give attention to identifying high flyers and providing opportunities for them to soar.

Third, a model of construction in which a high proportion of its work is provided by excellent standard and traditional constructions in no way excludes innovative or concept constructions. They will draw on small, creative firms, the studios of international superstars, design boutiques and management gurus. Many such firms provide the intensive, ruthless, heady environment essential for some of the most brilliant people to be trained and then for their talents to flower and flourish. They must remain an integral part of any great construction industry. Their role is to question established methods and to provide leading-edge models of possible ways forward for the industry. Society needs their talent to be given full reign. However, it also needs a competent, efficient construction industry which provides everyone with a decent built environment. That requires standard and traditional constructions as well as innovation and creativity. Without that clear delineation of products, which must be reflected in skills training and in practice, the great majority of society will be poorer. So the need for creativity, at all levels, will not be squeezed out by providing training for competence. Depending on their character and talents, individuals will find a wide range of niches within a modern construction industry.

It is during their initial three years in the industry that people develop specific interests. These should play a large part in determining career paths. Some will require further specific training. Others may require concentrated experience in particular work situations. The industry needs to be sufficiently flexible to be able to provide tailor-made career paths which match the interests and the values of their best people. Firms unable or unwilling to do this will simply lose their talented staff. As Olins (1989) tells us, the most important audience for firms in the future is going to be their own staff. Good people will stay only so long as they find that the public vision that motivated them to join a firm corresponds with their day-to-day work experiences. In simplistic terms, it will, for example, be counter-productive for a firm to voice its concern for the environment unless its workforce is trained to recognize environmental problems and given the authority to act in defence of endangered species or the health of our air, water and soil. Consistency of image and performance is becoming ever more vital to achieving any kind of lasting success because integrity is a key factor in any firm's and any project's ability to retain well motivated, competent people. Such people have no need to accept work that conflicts with the things which they personally know and value. So construction's future and the success of major construction projects depends on the industry's leaders creating an exciting and honest vision.

Figure 11.1 illustrates the steps described in this chapter which will help to produce and retain competent people. The same pattern of steps applies to all levels of achievement. The important responsibilities for construction project managers within this process are to know the achievement levels of the people involved in their projects, to encourage them to improve both the range and depth of their skills, to provide relevant training and experience, and to ensure that people have the chance to apply and practices new skills.

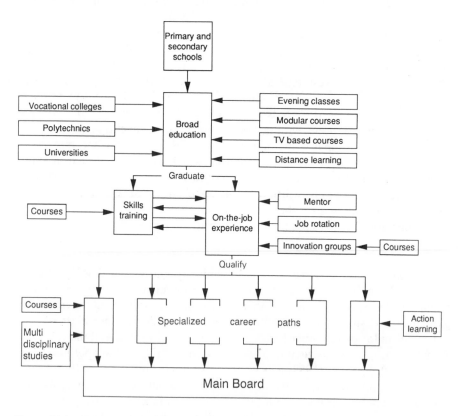

Figure 11.1 *Educating and training competent people*

12 *Project management models*

A construction industry in which the process and product of individual projects are closely in tune with each other, which produces and markets competitive products and is blessed with competent people, is achieving excellence. In other words, the framework of ideas described in Chapters 9–11 provide the basis for construction to become one of the world's glamour industries. The full realization of this potential requires the framework of ideas to be applied consistently by the whole industry. Achieving consistency between objectives and methods within this overall industry-wide framework is the responsibility of construction project managers.

Construction project management is difficult. This is because construction projects are more complex and uncertain than most other human undertakings. In order to understand their work, construction project managers need clear, simple models of their projects. They have to be clear and simple because these are the only kind which the human mind can comprehend at any one point in time. However, the complexity of construction projects means that managers need a number of such models. Good practice consists of thinking about projects with the aid of a repertoire of models. Each on its own is simple, but together a well developed repertoire of models helps experienced construction project managers to understand complex and uncertain projects. Experienced practitioners are people who have built up a large memory bank of the patterns assumed in practice by each of the models which they find useful. Also they know which patterns *feel* right and which signal a problem.

A large and effective memory bank of patterns can be developed only through practice. Formal courses, including reading books, like this one, are the best way of identifying useful models. Additionally, simulation techniques in, for example, case studies and management games can speed up the pattern learning process, but there is no substitute for practical experience. Also, experience on successful projects is more useful than experience on disasters. This is because projects can go wrong in hundreds of different ways and the causes and effects are virtually impossible to identify accurately. There are, however, far fewer ways in which things go right. It is the patterns that arise when things are going well which experienced managers learn thoroughly.

This chapter begins the task of developing large and effective memory banks of the patterns of success, by identifying models of construction projects which managers are likely to find useful in thinking about their work. The ideas behind the models are, to a large extent, described in earlier chapters. Therefore this chapter takes the theory as given and concentrates on providing a checklist of good practice for construction project managers.

Networks

The first useful model is the network. Much modern management literature, either explicitly or implicitly, is about networks. Peters (1987 and even more so 1990) provides important examples. The term network is used to describe systems of human interactions. They may be formal or informal. They may or may not be widely distributed geographically. They may be wholly contained within one firm or they may serve to connect individuals in many firms. They are found in all walks of life, including the world of construction projects.

A network is any collection of people who interact frequently because of a shared interest. Networks are informal in the sense that they develop because individuals choose to interact with others. However, they frequently go with the grain of the interactions required by formal organizations. Thus they facilitate formal work. They emerge much like the patterning in the human brain, which is formed by deepening frequently used connections between neurons. When people interact frequently and successfully, it becomes an instinctive habit to continue to interact. In this way effective networks grow up and develop naturally, simply because they are useful. The development of networks is greatly facilitated by modern information technology. The creation of an information network tends either to reinforce an existing human network or to lead to the creation of a new one. It is helpful to keep in mind the link between the technical and social phenomena of networks. It provides one means for managers to encourage the emergence of specific human networks.

Construction projects consist of many networks. It is helpful for construction project managers to think about their project as a network and also to recognize the existence of personal networks and try to work with them.

Project networks

Project coordinators are needed by every firm which becomes involved in a construction project. Some project coordinators combine the role with other responsibilities. Others are committed full time to project coordination on several projects or on just one. Yet others make up a project coordination team fully committed to one project. The precise staffing arrangements which are appropriate depend on the difficulty of an individual firm's work within any given project. The people carrying out the project coordination role within separate firms often carry different job titles. This is unhelpful and it is good practice for every firm on every project to nominate one person as their project coordinator. Construction projects are coordinated by this network of named project coordinators.

Figure 12.1 illustrates a project network. It is a useful model for construction project managers to have in mind as they approach their responsibilities on a new project. It is based on the idea that firms have an internal operating core which works in a consistent manner, largely irrespective of the nature of individual projects. It is the responsibility of project coordinators to feed the operating core with a steady, predictable stream of work which is comfortably within its competence. In other words, they act as a boundary controller, solving problems, either on their own or by communicating with other project coordinators, and so not allowing any interruptions to the smooth working of their own firm's operating core.

The model assumes circumstances which encourage firms to concentrate on developing efficient operating cores. That is, they can invest in training and capital equipment. They can develop long term relationships with suppliers. They can create a dedicated core which concentrates on building efficient teams and robust, stable sets of standards to guide their basic work. In these circumstances it becomes sensible and feasible to establish and foster innovation groups and to undertake research and development. In other words, the model assumes that productivity and reliable quality, which in turn lead to high profits and high salaries, come from an efficient operating core which is insulated from uncertainty.

The creation of the desirable situation, assumed by the model, requires project coordinators to understand the capabilities of their own firm's teams and then ensure that they are provided with conditions which enable them to work effectively and profitably.

Earlier chapters contain much advice which is relevant to project coordinators' boundary control responsibilities. This includes tuning into the local industry and local power structures. It includes getting to know powerful neighbours and understanding the general environment of each new project. It also includes doing everything possible in the design stages to create easy, predictable tasks. That is, fitting work comfortably within teams' established competence; designing large independent tasks; and providing time and space for teams to work without interruption.

Project coordinators should seek to establish tough challenging targets in agreement with their teams and then provide well considered contingency allowances. An allowance for contingencies for each team should be based on

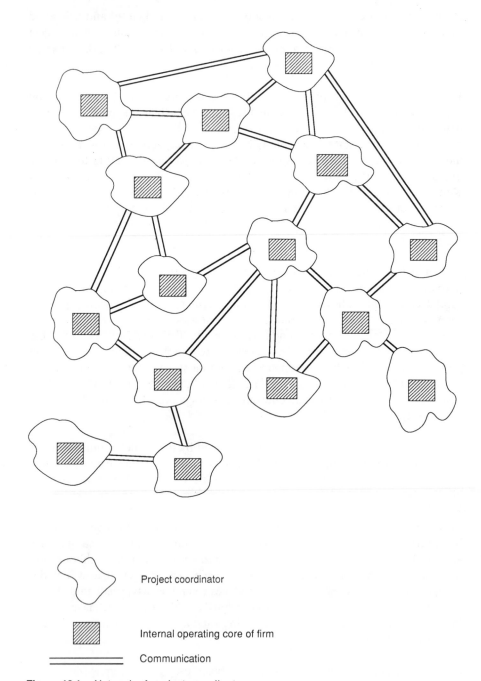

Project coordinator

Internal operating core of firm

Communication

Figure 12.1   *Network of project coordinators*

an evaluation of interactions with the work of other teams and with the project environment. It should also explicitly recognize the likely effects of any aspects of the work new to the team. This evaluation will identify a number of risks faced by each team. When the possibilities of taking action to avoid or to insure against all these risks have been considered, a contingency to cover those which remain should be calculated and provided. The aim is to create an objective for each team, comprising tough targets for the separate parts of their work plus well considered contingency allowances, which overall allows just sufficient slack to cater for the inevitable day-to-day problems of construction. The main benefit of this approach is that it removes the need for claims for extra payments or extensions of time. It gives teams no excuses not to concentrate on productivity and quality, delivered on time.

As the work progresses, project coordinators should continually remind teams of their targets. They should manage the contingency allowances with great care, treating them as a last resort, to be used only for intractable problems. Every effort should be made to meet every target. Achieving time and quality targets should be seen as absolutely essential and worthy of extraordinary efforts.

Project coordinators should, during the execution of work, actively resist the imposition of changes to the required work. They are always disruptive. They tend to be contagious; once one is accepted, others follow. It is almost always cheaper and quicker to complete work as planned and then, if necessary, alter it afterwards by means of a new and separate project.

A further important aspect of operating an effective project network is to have regular progress meetings between all the project coordinators. A good pattern is to hold weekly meetings. It is essential that project coordinators take these meetings totally seriously. Their aim should be to report honestly that their team's work is absolutely on programme. When it becomes apparent that this is not the case, they should explore a range of solutions to whatever problems are causing the failure, if necessary with other project coordinators, before the next progress meeting. The aim in these circumstances is to report, at that next meeting, that problems exist but that they can be solved within the firm's own resources. It is only when really serious problems arise that a project coordinator should accept the need to report a failure with which he is unable to deal and so needs help. That is, in the terms used in Chapter 6, category C situations should be unusual. As such, any that do arise can be given full attention by the whole project team.

In preparing for progress meetings, and even more in the immediate lead-up to a key decision point, project coordinators need to be alert for signs of problems. They should look for small warning signals; these may be changes in the pattern of behaviour of key people, an increase in the variability of their team's productivity, or a change in the firm's or the project's environment. Anything that makes them feel uneasy should be checked. Problems must be treated absolutely seriously, all failures investigated, and permanent robust answers found while the situation is still fresh in everyone's mind. The aims must be to meet every key date or else sound a clear, urgent, early warning that a crisis has occurred; and to develop the basis for more efficient, trouble-free project organizations for the future.

Personal networks

All of this is much easier to achieve when project coordinators are used to working together than it is when a project faces them with a multitude of new relationships. Therefore experienced project coordinators put considerable effort into developing personal networks and ensuring that as far as possible they are used to form the organizations set up to handle the projects in which they are involved.

The main benefit is that they are familiar with all the project coordinators with whom they will work. They know how they will behave, how to approach them, what deals will be possible, and generally can operate on the basis of trust. This makes for great efficiency and low levels of risk, which is a state of affairs which works to everyone's benefit. Customers obtain good value for money, firms make good profits, and individuals can have good salaries. Therefore it makes excellent sense for project coordinators to devote time and effort to building long term relationships with project coordinators in other firms. Essentially this means building and maintaining a network of key people who can be trusted.

Trust comes from working together over time and being consistently honest. It comes from a history of favours given and returned. The behaviours that serve to create trust are discussed in more detail in Chapter 14. For the moment, it is sufficient to recognize that good project coordinators consciously seek to build personal networks and that wise construction project managers build their project organizations out of well developed personal networks. These models, for that is what personal networks and project networks are, provide useful pictures for construction project managers to keep in mind in planning their work.

Hierarchies

The formal structure which connects teams together to establish a project organization forms a management hierarchy. Most projects require a single management hierarchy but, as we have seen, the most difficult projects require a double management hierarchy or matrix structure. Establishing and maintaining the formal management hierarchy is one of the prime responsibilities of construction project managers. Consequently the characteristics of appropriate project management hierarchies have already been described, in Chapters 2, 5 and 9. Many of the key features are illustrated in Figures 2.4 and 5.4.

Hierarchies are one of the oldest, most firmly established and useful models of organizations. They can be applied to many features of projects in addition to the formal management structure. Any aspect of projects in which the basic units are grouped into larger units, which are themselves grouped into even larger units and so on, forms a hierarchy. Indeed, it is good practice to consider whether all aspects of projects can be usefully regarded as forming hierarchies. When they can, it is often useful to match them exactly to the formal management hierarchy. In this way there is a consistency about the whole project which greatly simplifies its management.

Obvious examples of project features which can be matched to the formal management hierarchy include programmes and budgets. Both are structured in levels which deal with the whole project at the highest level and with the work of individual teams at the lowest level. There is every good reason to match these structures exactly to the project's formal management hierarchy. Doing so gives every manager his own programme and budget, which have the same formal relationships with those of other managers as exist between the managers themselves.

Programmes

Taking programmes as an example, we can begin by recognizing that there is a natural rhythm about the human perception of time. It is arranged for good practical reasons in a hierarchy of days, weeks, months and years. The hierarchy continues into decades, centuries and millennia. However, it would be a very unusual construction project which could make any practical use of these higher levels of the hierarchy of time.

We established in Chapter 1 that the basic unit of work in construction projects is days-work for teams. This should be the basic unit of project programmes which is the direct responsibility of level 1 teams to put into effect. The group of teams working on the same one element during any one stage of a project form the basic management units for the next level in the hierarchy. This is level 2, which in the terms discussed in Chapter 2 and illustrated in Figure 2.4 is competent to make local decisions. The hierarchy of time suggests that the right time-span for level 2 decisions is one week. That is, the team of first line managers responsible for one element within one stage should work together in planning days-work for their teams, within an overall time-frame of one week.

When it becomes apparent that they will be unable to achieve a programmed week's work, they must send a warning signal to their manager.

The next level in the formal management hierarchy provides coordination for complete projects on a monthly basis. The level 3 managers are, at any one time, each responsible for one project element within one stage. The level 3 planning units of work should be programmed to take one month to complete. That is, the team of level 3 managers should work together in planning weeks-work for their teams of first-line managers, within an overall time-frame of one month. When it becomes apparent that they will be unable to achieve a programmed month's work, they must send a warning signal to the level 4 and 5 managers. It is the responsibility of level 4 managers to gather information, including warning signals, filter it and pass it to project management, at level 5, in an appropriate form. One of top management's prime responsibilities, aided by managers carrying out staff functions, is to prepare, monitor and maintain the overall project programme. They should plan in broad stages, each designed to take one month to complete. Project management should see it as a personal failure if their project is not complete, exactly as planned, within one year.

The hierarchies of concepts that link the formal management structure to the project programme are shown in Figure 12.2. The management hierarchy implicit in these concepts is illustrated in Figure 12.3. The rigid linking of time to project management hierarchies may appear to be arbitrary. It is, however, based on the natural structure of efficient human organizations and the way in which mankind has agreed to view time. There is no good reason for the construction industry to operate on a different basis from the rest of the human race.

Taking the judgement that the natural time for a construction project is one year as an example, it is common knowledge that many construction projects take much longer and some are completed in a few months. Therefore, on the face of it, the linking of the agreed human view of time to project programmes appears to be impractical. However, the certainty arising from a consistent approach makes it worthwhile to adopt one common pattern of linking time to project hierarchies. In practice this is not difficult to achieve.

Projects which cannot be completed in one year should be subdivided into subprojects, each taking one year. That is, projects taking more than one year should be treated as mega-projects comprising several distinct projects. Such distinct projects within a mega-project (or subproject within a project) are likely to require the project management hierarchy illustrated in Figure 12.3. This in turn means that mega-projects (or projects which are divided into subprojects) require additional, level 6 and perhaps even level 7, management. A mega-project may take several years but ideally is made up of projects each taking one

	Formal management hierarchy	Hierarchy of time discretion	Planning unit of work
Level 5 (top management)	Project manager	Year	Project stages
Level 4 (middle management)	Staff managers	Year	Projected stages, elements and week's work for teams
Level 3 (middle management)	Project coordinator	Month	Project element and week's work for teams
Level 2 (first-line management)	Team manager	Week	Week's work for team
Level 1 (basic workforce)	Team	Day	Day's work for team

Figure 12.2 *Hierarchies of construction project management and programmes*

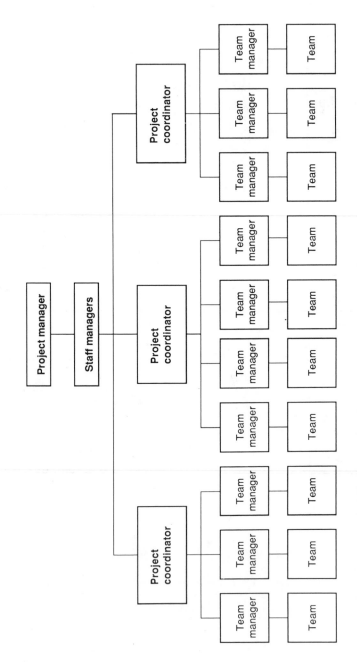

Figure 12.3   *Project management hierarchy*

year. For example, the Broadgate mega-project in London took five years to complete 17 projects, each of which took about one year. Broadgate required two levels of management above the five level project management hierarchies. Level 7 provided the overall vision for the mega-project and level 6 provided the long term strategy within which the 17 separate projects were carried out.

Projects which can be completed in less than one year may well require less than the full five levels of the project management hierarchy illustrated in Figure 12.3. They may well be able to be managed efficiently with no staff support for the project manager. In an even simpler case, a project coordinator may be able to take responsibility for what is colloquially regarded as a project; and so on down to an activity which can be undertaken by a single, unsupervised craftsman. There is, however, little point in dignifying very small scale construction work with the title of project. Certainly in the world of theory it is unhelpful.

So we see that the rigid linking of the five level model of project management hierarchies to a time-scale of one year is not arbitrary. Similar justifications exist for the rest of the hierarchy of time discretion of days, weeks and months. There is no doubt that forcing real life projects into this rigid framework will require a degree of ingenuity. However, the benefits of having every team and every manager throughout the industry working to one consistent approach to programming are enormous. It provides a basis for the whole industry to develop robust, consistent units of work. Programming construction work will become simpler and more effective. Control can be exercised within an industry wide framework of responsibilities and reporting procedures. Each manager will know the time-frame that applies to his own work. He will know when to deal with problems and when to refer them to his manager. Many of these benefits can be obtained by applying a consistent hierarchy model to individual projects. Thus the model is useful for all construction project managers. However, it would be even more useful if it were applied consistently to all projects.

Budgets

We have thus far dealt only with project management structures and programmes. The same hierarchy model can, and indeed should, be applied to project budgets. This requires the overall project budget to be subdivided into targets for each stage, element, team, weeks-work and days-work.

The consistent pattern of stages, elements, teams, weeks-work and days-work gives rise to a great variety of specific targets. Each team can have a budget target set in its own terms and indeed, at the level of days-work, they will set their own targets. We may find, for example, on a building project in the design stages, that initially the elements consist of spaces and groups of spaces within and around the building. Later the appropriate elements consist of the main physical elements of the finished building. During the construction stages the appropriate elements, as we described in Chapter 3, consist of the major stages of establishing the site organization systems, substructure, structure, external envelope, internal subdivisions, concealed fittings and services, finishes, exposed fittings and services, decoration, and commissioning. During the manufacturing stages, the appropriate elements, depending on the amount of design work and prefabrication involved, may be the main physical elements of the finished building or construction stages. Within these various patterns of elements, each group of teams employed by one firm will have an overall budget embodied in the contract sum for their work. However, this must be divided among a variety of cost heads, including a budget target for each separate team arranged in units of weeks-work. The targets should all be expressed in money and in terms of direct production targets. This helps teams to understand where their own work fits into the whole project and also the financial consequences of failure to meet their production targets. Figure 12.4 shows the hierarchies of concepts which link formal management structures to project budgets.

So we see that hierarchies provide a powerful and useful model for many of the formal aspects of construction project managers' work. To obtain the full

	Formal management hierarchy	Budget targets
Level 5 (top management)	Project manager	Project stages
Level 4 (middle management)	Staff managers	Project stages, elements teams
Level 3 (middle management)	Project coordinator	Project element, teams and week's work
Level 2 (first-line management)	Team manager	Teams and weeks-work
Level 1 (basic work force)	Team	Days-work

Figure 12.4 *Hierarchies of construction project management and budgets*

benefits and to ensure that a consistent pattern is embedded deep in the *mind of the project*, managers need consistently to match the project procedures and language to the formal management hierarchy.

Procedures

Teams bring procedures with them when they join a project. These are their normal standards of work and ways of doing things which they will adopt in the absence of any strong pressure to behave differently. As far as possible, it is sensible to allow teams to use their established norms and methods. Therefore, in forming a project organization, wise construction project managers seek teams who will bring with them procedures that match the overall pattern of work it is intended to adopt. Indeed, wise managers seek to appoint networks of teams who are experienced in using robust clusters of procedures which match the needs of their projects.

The other important set of given procedures are those imposed by government, public utilities and other official guardians of the public interest. It is obviously necessary for the project organization to know all the requirements of the official procedures. They often impose major constraints on the sequence and timing of major stages of construction projects. For example, a public concern about the effects of earthquakes and hurricanes in Japan has led local government to require absolutely complete and detailed design information to be submitted for approval before any construction work can begin. This major constraint has been used to advantage, since, as Chapter 7 describes, Japanese planning of every aspect of manufacture and construction is remarkably detailed and even more remarkably effective. So, in this kind of way, publicly imposed constraints and requirements can be turned to advantage, but only if they are identified early and built into project plans. This means that the work to which they give rise should be clearly allocated to specific levels within the formal project management hierarchy. Ideally, the given procedures of teams and public agencies will be sufficient, without the need for further project specific rules. However, even within a well developed set of procedures, as described in Chapter 5, there are likely to be some requirements for project decisions about procedures. In checking the given procedures, construction project managers are likely to find the model of hierarchies especially useful. For example, they should check that procedures exist to handle conflicts between people within each level of the hierarchy. These will deal with minor routine matters at level 2 but with more substantial issues at level 3 and so on.

Then, construction project managers should review the operation of the given procedures for higher levels issuing instructions. It is important, for example, to draw clear distinctions between formal instructions and informal advice, questions and comments which lower level managers and teams have the discretion to consider, act on or ignore as they see fit. Also, in this context, construction project managers should consider whether the rules adequately determine the precise circumstances in which a local decision should have priority over higher level instructions.

Next, construction project managers should review the operation of feedback thoughout all the hierarchical levels of their project. They should consider whether its timing matches the hierarchy of time discretion shown in Figure 12.2. Where appropriate feedback, even if it has to be rough and ready rather than precise and accurate, cannot be made available in time to be effective, procedures to provide formal checks and tests of the work are needed. Where the given procedures do not include such safeguards, project specific procedures are necessary.

Construction project managers should also consider whether the given procedures will provide them with an adequate range of feedback. They need direct links into all the project grapevines. They need to ensure that staff managers are aware of local decisions. They should also consider whether all the *specialized computers* of the project are working on one common information and decision stream and, if not, they should think about the possible consequences of this inefficiency. They should review the procedures used by staff managers in filtering and combining feedback from multiple sources. They should especially check that there is no ambiguity in their own procedures for setting the tone of the project. They should test the procedures that provide for fast-track warnings to act through the formal hierarchy. They need to ensure that the whole warning system is working and that everyone fully understands their responsibilities for activating it. Construction project managers should also consider whether the given procedures provide feedback from all the studios, offices, factories, storage depots and sites where the project work is being undertaken.

Finally, construction project managers should review the procedures for providing long term feedback from their projects to future projects. That is, they should accept responsibility for ensuring that their own firm's and public databases and information systems are up to date with the direct experiences arising from their projects.

Hierarchies provide, in these various ways, a powerful tool for reviewing given procedures and deciding when and where project specific procedures are needed. Generally, the latter should be few in number and, as far as possible, supportive of the given procedures. Beyond its important role in reviewing and checking, the formal project hierarchy should form the overall structure for the procedures which are to be used. That is, the responsibilities arising from procedures should all be allocated to specific levels within the hierarchy in a manner which is consistent with each individual manager's and team's scope of work and time-frame.

Language

Chapter 2 describes the importance of project managers thinking and speaking in the language of project managers and craftsmen thinking and speaking in the language of their own crafts. Subsequent chapters describe more of the subjects and time-scales which different levels of language need to reflect. It is important for construction project managers to encourage the use of appropriate languages at each of the levels in their project hierarchies. For example, the overall project objectives need to be expressed in different terms for staff managers, a design coordinator and a team responsible for excavating the foundations. Staff managers are concerned with trade-offs between quality, cost and time. They need to check for internal consistency between the planned process and the intended product. They need data on the patterns of interference and variability. Generally good staff managers talk about abstract and relatively long term concepts. Design coordinators need to understand all the subtle and complex issues raised by design. While they must keep the customer's objectives in terms of function, quality, cost and time firmly in mind, they must also understand and respect the individual designer's own ambitions for the project. These may deal with aesthetic, technical, cultural and social problems. As a consequence, design coordinators tend to talk about highly abstract concepts concerned with current design decisions. In contrast, the team responsible for excavating the foundations is likely to be concerned about immediate, practical issues. These may include how many cubic metres of muck must be shifted each day, how much they will be paid, and the type and model of the equipment they will drive. It is important for construction project managers to recognize these differences and to respect and encourage everyone involved to be confident and expert in their own business and their own language.

It is equally important for construction project managers to build a common project language. The aims of creating a common language are to make communication throughout the project more certain and efficient. It should be designed also to build a project team spirit. That is, to get people's commitment to the project by giving them a sense of belonging and of being an insider because they know the language of the project. Finally, the common language must enable superiors to give commands in a crisis.

Given these objectives, common project languages need to be short, simple and direct. It helps if they include an element of insider humour and they should serve to express the project values and myths in graphic, memorable terms. A common language must provide the words by which the project manager sets the tone at important stages of his project. Suitable subjects for the common project language include: the name of the project and its customer; the style of the end product; the major separate physical parts of the end product; the separate stages of the overall project process; the key meetings; the key decision points; the main people involved in the project; formal reports which record measurements of performance against the key project objectives; major items of plant and equipment; offices, stores, canteens and other buildings which house the site workforce; and any other things or events of wide concern within the project. The language should be recorded in graphic posters widely displayed around the studios, offices, factories and sites where project work is underway. For example, a diagram of the end product with its style made clear and its separate physical parts graphically identified, which is widely distributed, perhaps made into a letter heading or a postcard or incorporated in project note pads, will serve to make the project memorable and establish an important part of its language. Personalized safety slogans, statements of current performance against key objectives and similarly important messages from specific managers, displayed in site offices and workers' lounges and changing rooms, can all serve to build a common project language. Induction courses for people joining the project should be couched in the common language. A small, colourful project handbook should be given to everyone joining the project. It should explain the project in the common language and do so with style and wit. In short, every opportunity should be taken to build and reinforce a simple and graphic project language. This will, by definition, cut across the levels of the project hierarchy; yet, in doing so, it should serve to identify the levels and explain their roles and responsibilities.

Developing a hierarchy

The steady, consistent development of one consistent hierarchy which runs through many aspects of a construction project is expensive. It requires time and effort from managers, it requires them to think about their work systematically, and it needs investment in forming a totally coherent organization. These costs are justified and in any case can to a large extent be shared between projects.

The costs of developing robust hierarchies can be shared between projects by firms which are in the business of providing construction project management. Many of the elements of hierarchical approach can be used on many projects. For example, the overall structure of the hierarchy should be consistent. Equally the job descriptions, the pattern of meetings, the structure of programmes and budgets and many other elements should also be consistent. Sharing development work between projects helps to reduce the costs of good and consistent management.

A more important factor in deciding to apply a coordinated hierarchical approach is the overwhelming evidence from practice, which tells us that projects which are not clearly structured and so allow inconsistencies within their overall organization, deliver low productive and erratic quality. It may be, as is discussed in Chapter 8, that local market norms allow poor management to remain competitive. Such a situation undoubtedly makes it difficult for individual firms to break out of deeply ingrained bad habits. The necessary initial steps will increase their short term costs, they will need the support of designers and specialist contractors willing to change with them, and they will need customers willing to take a long view. So improvements that go against the grain of a local construction industry are hard to achieve but the benefits, in terms of competitive advantage, for those who succeed are huge.

Therefore, whatever decisions are made by firms and by individual construction project managers about the practicability of applying hierarchies to their projects, the model provides an important aid to thinking about construction project management. There are very few projects, indeed probably none, which do not apply the principles of hierarchies to some aspects of their work. The main message of this section is that it is an advantage if this is done explicitly and consistently.

Processes

A third useful model for construction project managers is provided by thinking of projects, and stages within them, as processes. The basic form of a process is shown in Figure 12.5. It consists of the simple sequence of inputs being incorporated into a project or stage, the inputs being processed, and outputs being produced. Depending on the subject to which the model is applied, the outputs may provide the inputs to other parts of the same project or they may be exported into the general environment. We encountered the model shown in Figure 12.5 in Chapter 3, which describes general characteristics of systems. In using the process model to aid thinking about construction projects, we are explicitly drawing on systems thinking.

All construction projects involve the basic process of establishing the customer's brief, designing the product, manufacturing components, and constructing the product. The basic work must be planned and its execution controlled. This is

Figure 12.5 *Universal model of processes*

the task of construction project management. Figure 12.6 illustrates the relationship between the basic operating subsystem and the management subsystem of projects. The two subsystems are connected by flows of information. That from management consists of instructions and decisions. It tells the operating subsystem what work it must do and provides answers when problems arise. The flow of information from the operating subsystem to management provides feedback. This is information on progress and requests for further information and decisions. So even within the closed system of Figure 12.6 both the management subsystem and the operating subsystem fit the model of input : process : output.

However, construction projects are not closed systems. They take place in environments with which they interact. The management subsystem's interactions with its environment result in flows of information, finance and rights over land or air-space. The information flows concern official authorizations and any informal support needed for the project to go ahead. They include general knowledge about the political, economic, social and technical environments which may hinder the project or help it be successful. They include information about the project which managers hope will help it be accepted by neighbours and other powerful actors in its environment. The flows of finance are primarily those needed to pay for the work of the operating subsystem and are provided, therefore, by the customer. However, he does so on the advice of the management subsystem. It is its ability to influence the provision or withholding of finance which gives management its ultimate authority over the

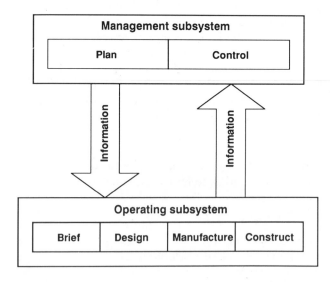

Figure 12.6   *Main subsystems of construction projects*

basic work of projects. There are additionally flows of finance back into the environment, for example, rent, interest on and repayments of borrowed money, and fees for official authorizations. The flows of property rights are to obtain control of the site before construction work begins and return it to the customer when the project is complete. So we see that the management subsystem fits the model of inputs : process : outputs. Since the inputs and outputs affect the environment, the management subsystem is an open system. This means, for example, that it requires feedback if it is to remain under control. So construction project managers need good intelligence on the current and likely future states of their environments, especially those parts which provide inputs to or receive outputs from their projects.

The operating subsystem also interacts with its environment. This results in flows of information and tangible resources: physical, human and energy. Each team undertaking basic work needs knowledge about its own marketplace and about developments in relevant professional domains. They will each, to some extent, also add their own project experiences to the general pool of knowledge from which they draw the information needed for their particular project role. However, the operating subsystem's primary responsibility is to obtain tangible resources and process them into the end product. The necessary men, machines, materials and energy come from the project's environment and they become the end product which itself forms part of the greater environment at the completion of the project. Projects also produce pollution, rubbish and waste which find various ways into the environment.

Figure 12.7 illustrates the subsystems or processes and flows of information and tangible resources which make up a universal model of construction projects and their environments. It shows the operating subsystem interacting with the project environment. However, the project network model, described earlier in this chapter, suggests that efficient organizations use boundary control units to insulate their operating core from direct contact with the project environment. Therefore Figure 12.7 shows the management subsystem wrapping itself around the operating subsystem to imply that its inputs and outputs should be managed. The earlier description tells us that they are managed by a network of project coordinators.

Milestones

The universal process model can usefully be applied to every stage of construction projects. It is a prime responsibility of construction project managers to identify and manage the definition of separate stages. Stages are separated by key decision points. That is a point in time, often called a *milestone*, at which the customer receives specific information about the current state of his project. Figure 12.8 lists the information which should appear in a milestone report. On

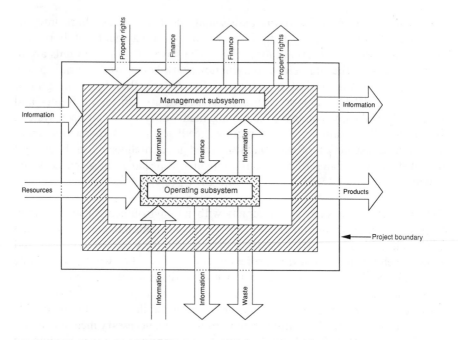

Figure 12.7   *Universal process model of construction projects and their environments*

Stage just completed
Objectives achieved
Success = cost of stage : value added to project
Level of variability and interference experienced
Consequences of organizational changes introduced
Current state of project
  Function
  Quality
  Programme
  Budget

Next stage
Objectives
New teams entering the project
Environmental factors needing special attention
Organizational changes proposed
Lead activity
Success criteria
  Measurement of costs
  Measurement of value added

Figure 12.8   *Milestone report contents*

the basis of a careful review of that information, the customer authorizes the next stage.

An important part of the authorization process is to define the criteria for establishing the success of the next stage. As discussed in Chapter 3, these criteria should, as far as possible, be measured in terms of the costs of all the inputs to and the value of all the outputs from the processes which constitute the next stage. Therefore the information presented to the customer at each milestone should include a statement of the costs incurred and the value added by the stage just completed. In addition, it should state the cost and value targets for the next stage, including defining exactly how these will be measured.

Key decision points or milestones often signal the need for significant changes in the project organization. This is because, as projects move through time and the end product is defined and then realized in ever more definitive detail, the project organization also evolves. This evolution should be planned and controlled by reviewing the project organization in the light of the likely demands of the next stage, and if possible of all the remaining stages, at every milestone.

This is because a milestone may signal: a significant change in the nature of the work; that different features of the environment demand attention; the need for new teams to be brought into the project organization; that some of the project objectives should be given a different emphasis; that new procedures should be introduced; or that the management subsystem should be expanded or reduced. Equally, a milestone may signal the need for a change in the tone of the project.

The most significant milestone change is when a project changes from a problem-solving mode, in which the teams that make up the project organization are employed essentially as consultants, to stages concerned with the disciplined execution of a plan by teams employed, as contractors, to produce a specified product. The point at which this change occurs varies considerably from project to project. Figure 12.9 suggests that there is a pattern to these variations which is structured by the characteristics of the end product. That is, the change from problem-solving to disciplined execution is determined by whether the project aims to produce a standard, traditional or innovative construction.

Standard constructions reach the major milestone between problem-solving and disciplined execution very quickly. With a decisive customer, the initial definition of the problem and selection of a fully defined answer may take a few hours. At the other extreme, an innovative construction may remain in a problem-solving mode right up to the point at which the customer enters into

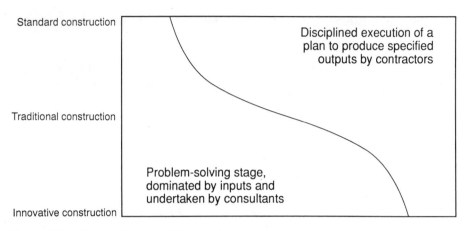

Figure 12.9   *Major milestone within construction projects*

contracts for specific elements of the end product. In the case of a very difficult project, even that point may never arise and the basic workforce may be employed as consultants to help explore the problem in the hope that a solution will emerge. Although the major milestone usually signals the most significant change in a project's organization, all milestones have the potential to make it appropriate to make some change.

Construction project managers should therefore review their project organization as each milestone approaches. At this time it is sensible to check that the project as a whole is becoming more certain. There should be fewer crisis meetings and less management paperwork. Productivity should be steadily increasing, variability should be reducing, and the environment should be springing fewer surprises. The customer's involvement with the project should be settling into a planned and predictable pattern. Generally, the project should feel as though it is settling down. The overall aim should be to resolve all problems in the design and manufacture stages so that construction on site is a simple, automatic process, in which management is integral with the technology, and in which the required work can be executed productively to high standards. When these things are not happening, the construction project manager needs to identify the causes of the problems which are inhibiting efficiency and act to eliminate them or reduce their effects. Such actions will almost inevitably change the project organization. Proposals for changes identified in this way, together with any needed to undertake the next stage of the project, should form part of the report to the customer at the next milestone. It is good practice to introduce no more than one or two changes at any one stage. These should be based on wide discussions and agreement throughout the project organization. This is essential in all modern free societies so that, when the changes are introduced, they are acted upon and not made the subject of debate, rumour and opposition. Newly introduced changes should be monitored to ensure that they are understood, working properly and having the intended effects. Where they are not producing benefits, even after careful attention from top management, they should be reversed. Generally the initial discussions throughout the project organization serve to eliminate unproductive changes, but if an error is made it should be put right quickly. A report on the consequences of the major changes agreed at the previous meeting, beneficial or otherwise, should be included in the information provided to the customer before each milestone is reached.

Another important function of the milestone reports is to identify the lead activity for the next stage. This is the activity which dictates the tempo of the work. As described in Chapter 1, Bennett and Ormerod (1984) identified brickwork as the lead activity in projects that use load-bearing brickwork to provide the main structure. It is also suggested, in the same chapter, that structural steelwork provides the lead activity in projects with a steel frame. In the early design stages of building projects, it is often the architect's work which provides the lead activity and, as the design develops, the lead passes at different stages to structural engineers and service engineers.

Since the lead activity sets the overall tempo and indeed tends to dictate the general style and method of projects, it is sensible to concentrate on providing it with as predictable an environment as possible and ensuring that it has adequate resources to complete its work in accordance with the overall programme.

As with the just-in-time philosophy, concentrating on lead activities helps to focus attention where it will have the most effect. The benefits spread to the other teams whose work interacts with that of a stable, predictable lead activity. Problems that stand in the way of lead activities should therefore be taken totally seriously and analysed in detail, one at a time, by considering all the inputs, processes and outputs involved. The construction project managers should ensure that the answers adopted are permanent and irreversible. They should become part of the future normal way of working of the teams concerned. Thus construction project managers' efforts have the maximum effect, not only on their own current project but also on future ones. That is a proper aim for all construction project managers.

Streams

Milestones are static. They mark boundaries between stages of the overall project process. It is useful to think about clearly defined stages, but it is also helpful to think about continuous streams which flow through the project.

It is, for example, good practice to review the complete process which results in each main category of materials or components being put into their final position in the end product. Reviewing each step in the design, manufacture and construction process can serve to identify economies. It can equally well serve to highlight potential problems. It may identify the possibility of eliminating or overlapping steps in the overall stream of activities. Alternatively, it may highlight a need for additional resources to overcome bottlenecks. In all events, the activity of tracing the one continuous process through all its stages is likely to make it easier to manage. This is the common effect of all rehearsals, even purely mental rehearsals of future physical actions.

Another stream which it is useful for construction project managers to think about is formed by the actions which must be taken by each item of major construction plant. Thinking, for example, about all the work to be done by a hoist or a tower crane throughout all stages of the construction process is likely to make the actual work easier. It may reveal the need for tough procedures to control the use of the plant. It may suggest the need for a team to work on distributing materials before the normal working day begins. It may make it clear that materials and components will need to be packaged and delivered to site in a specific and unusual manner.

A further stream is formed by the work which must be carried out in each distinct workspace. Thinking about each separate workspace and all the activities it must house provides another useful rehearsal for construction project managers. In doing this, it is especially helpful to think about boundary control processes. It is good practice to divide construction sites into clearly defined and distinct workspaces and allocate each, at any one time, to just one team. Doing this may require physical barriers and warning notices. It may also require clear procedures to firmly establish teams' 'ownership' of their workspaces.

In thinking about streams of work through workspaces, managers should consider: actions necessary before control of a space is handed from one team to another; actions necessary before teams accept control of a work space; the physical conditions needed to enable each specific type of work to be accomplished efficiently; and the support needed during the carrying out of each type of work. Undertaking such a review may reveal the need for temporary works, including services, screens, heating or specific protection. It may suggest special rubbish collection and disposal provisions. It may identify useful management or technical checks which should be introduced.

There are many other processes in construction projects which benefit from being thought of as a continuous stream running past the milestones. It is also, as we suggested earlier, equally beneficial to think of distinct stages of projects divided by milestones. Both types of process model are helpful and construction project managers should make a habit of applying them regularly so that they become well practised in their use.

Model repertoire

We have now described three categories of models: networks to aid thinking about informal and lateral interactions; hierarchies to aid thinking about formal and vertical interactions; and processes to aid thinking about the development of projects through time. These three categories of model provide a sufficient basis for construction project managers to develop their own ways of thinking in a structured and systematic manner. Individual managers will develop, through practice, their own repertoire of well used, familiar models. They may combine aspects of networks, hierarchies and processes. They may use entirely different forms of model. The only criteria they need satisfy is that the individual manager finds them useful in planning his work.

In developing their own approaches, construction project managers should remember that, generally, the criterion of utility is more fully satisfied with simple, clear models than it is with very complicated or subtle ones. This in no way conflicts with the fact that construction projects are complex. It merely reminds us that the human mind is most effective when it concentrates on one well defined problem. This means that in practice, construction project managers cannot think effectively about whole projects but must instead focus, at any one point in time, on just one aspect. In this way, each model in their repertoire will prove to be useful in dealing with particular categories of problems. So, by using a range of models, each selected to aid thinking about a specific current problem, construction project managers can and indeed must, if they are to be effective, use simple, clear models to help them plan complex projects.

13 Control through communication

Control is fundamentally important in management; indeed, a sensible working definition of managers could be: people who control the work of others in order to achieve planned objectives. In practice, managers often draw a distinction between planning and control. Planning is deciding what should be done and control is checking to ensure that it is done properly. Yet in Chapter 3, when we discussed controlled systems, the two activities were linked into an integrated process which is illustrated in Figure 13.1. It comprises: setting objectives; deciding on an action aimed at achieving the objective; taking the action; observing its effect; comparing the effect with the objective; deciding on a new action, which may be to repeat the first action, also aimed at achieving the objective; and so on in a controlled loop. The actions decided on within this integrated process can take many forms, including selecting a new objective. This may be because the first proves to be impractical or because it has been accomplished by earlier actions. The actions can also include subdividing overall objectives into smaller, separate objectives for individual teams or

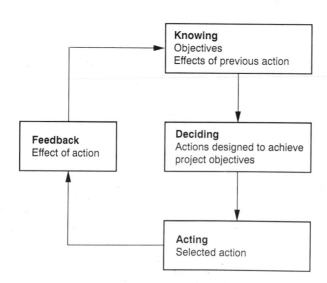

Figure 13.1 *Universal model of planning and control*

separate stages of projects. In other words, setting objectives, or planning, is one kind of action. Most actions are designed simply and straightforwardly to put the agreed objectives into effect. However, the overall process may identify a need to modify work already carried out because it fails to meet the objectives. That is, the process may need to exercise control. So we have to regard the diagram in Figure 13.1 as a universal model which encompasses both planning and control.

One important aspect of this universal model is that it is implicit that the process it models exists to achieve overall objectives which are given to it by some higher authority. In the context of construction project management, the overall or higher level objectives are defined in customers' briefs. Once these overall objectives are given, planning is logically indistinguishable from control. So we see that, once a customer's brief is given to a project team, the process described by the model in Figure 13.1 cycles around and around until the objectives are achieved. In doing so it draws no sharp distinction between planning and control. It simply does what is necessary to achieve the overall given objectives.

Planning is often associated with long term and large-scale activities, while control is used to refer to short term and small scale subactivities. That is, the terms are used to distinguish between strategy and tactics. Certainly construction project managers need an overall plan of campaign and they need to deal with immediate crises. They need, in other words, to be pragmatists with a clear vision. However, the way they think about and decide on appropriate actions cannot be divided usefully into planning and control. Indeed, a sensible view of control is that it is nothing more nor less than short term planning. That is, faced with an immediate problem, we plan an appropriate action and put it into effect. If we have made a good decision, the problem is solved and our project is back under control. Equally, the purpose of planning is to control the activities with which it deals. Probably the sole benefit of drawing a distinction between planning and control is to help to emphasize the superiority of careful, well thought-out decisions, or planning, over short term expediency, or muddling through, which is what control degenerates into in the absence of good, thoughtful management.

In Chapter 12, construction project models were described as being useful to construction project managers in planning their projects. This use of the word is intended precisely to emphasize the superiority of careful, well thought-out decisions over short term expediency. Similarly, linking the word control with communications, in the title of this chapter, is intended to emphasize the importance of a wide involvement in and understanding of project decisions if they are to be implemented efficiently. Control in modern organizations is most effective when it is based on self-control by well motivated people who share a common vision of their joint objectives. Therefore managers, in order to exercise control, must influence the values of those for whose work they are responsible. They do this by communicating. Therefore this chapter is about communication within the universal model of planning and control illustrated in Figure 13.1.

Communication

Communication requires, as described in Chapter 2, the five steps of source, coding, medium, detection and decoding. That is, it comprises transferring knowledge from one human brain to another. It is one of the two primary tools (negotiation is the other) available to all managers, including of course construction project managers. Communication provides information which is nothing less than the lifeblood of project organizations. Therefore managers need to give attention to creating circumstances which encourage effective communication throughout their projects. They are, of course, also responsible for initiating some specific communications.

Figure 13.1 provides a good basis for identifying the various types of information which construction project managers need to consider. The figure illustrates three distinct categories of information. First, information is needed about objectives; that is, the definition of the end product including specifying any aspects of the process of producing it or any effects on its environment which the customer wishes to constrain. There is usually little difficulty in identifying and communicating primary objectives, but secondary objectives or constraints often emerge only after a project has hit a sensitive issue. It might, for example, emerge part way through a project that the customer had assumed that no tropical hardwoods or goods from South Africa would be used. Consequently, secondary objectives, of which these are two not uncommon examples, can all too often create a degree of uncertainty. Also, difficulties arise where there are conflicts between objectives. It could occur, for example, that the only way to achieve the particular effect demanded by a customer for his own office uses tropical hardwood and goods from South Africa, both of which he refuses to allow onto his project. A further important feature of objectives is that they are developed throughout projects into increasingly detailed descriptions of the end product and the constraints within which it must be produced. In other words, Figure 13.1 represents a whole hierarchy of processes which fit the same model but at different levels of detail. The characteristics of uncertainty, conflict and continuous development make it necessary for construction project managers to give considerable attention to the procedures for maintaining and communicating an up-to-date definition of their project's objectives.

The second type of information illustrated in Figure 13.1 is descriptions of the actions it is decided should be taken. The actions required from each team vary from minute to minute, hour to hour, day to day, and week to week. They vary in step with each team's developing objectives, but they also vary with the work situation faced by each team. The particular current situation of any one team is known most clearly by that team. This is why the choice of appropriate actions is best delegated to competent teams who have clear objectives. Trusting competent teams to make good choices of their own actions is hard to do; many managers are reluctant not to 'help' because they feel that they could do the work a little bit better. In fact, of course, managers are not employed to do the direct work but to create conditions that allow their teams to do it. This includes trusting their teams to make good decisions about actions needed to achieve the agreed objectives. However, managers retain overall responsibility for the process and so, in addition to clearly communicating objectives, managers need feedback. This is the third type of information illustrated in Figure 13.1.

Feedback, as we have discussed in earlier chapters, is essential for control. Managers need to give attention to the procedures that provide feedback. They should also check, frequently and randomly, that all the separate parts of their projects have reliable and timely feedback. So we see that construction project managers' communication responsibilities are concentrated on ensuring that teams are aware of their current objectives and that their project's feedback procedures are working effectively. Information which describes the actions it is decided should be taken is best generated by competent teams making their own local decisions. So managers' further responsibility within the process, illustrated in Figure 13.1, is to ensure that projects are staffed by competent teams. This responsibility is discussed in Chapter 14.

Communicating objectives

As we discussed in Chapter 12, construction project objectives can usefully be thought of as forming hierarchies. At the highest level are the overall objectives provided by the customer's brief. At the lowest levels are decisions about a day's work for each team, and within those even finer decisions which determine individual actions from minute to minute throughout the project. Except on the very smallest of projects, no one manager is involved directly in all levels of decisions. For each manager there are objectives which are given; objectives which he determines in discussion with the members of his team; and objectives which he trusts individuals within his team to decide for themselves. Figure 13.2 illustrates this overall structure of decisions about objectives. This section of the chapter is concerned with the vertical communication of given objectives by managers to their subordinates.

Managers communicate all the time in everything they do within their projects. Olins (1989) identifies four components in the way organizations communicate their identity or sense of purpose. Just as we have earlier used the human nervous system to provide a model of behaviour in human organizations, so we can now use organizational behaviour as a model for an individual manager's actions. Olins identifies products as the first communication medium. He argues, for example, that the most important factor in determining the image of Jaguar is the car itself, what it looks like, what it costs, what it feels like inside, what it smells like, how it sounds, and how it starts, stops and goes. It is these qualities which primarily determine the identity of the whole company.

Second, Olins identifies environments as a major communication medium. He uses Harrods as an example of an organization whose identity is largely formed

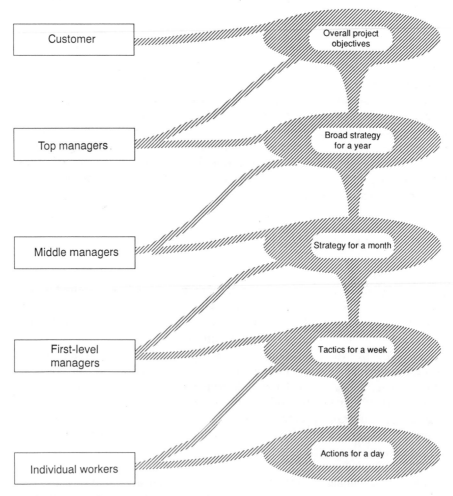

Figure 13.2 *Structure of decisions about objectives*

by the store itself. He argues that the goods sold by Harrods can nearly all be bought elsewhere, often cheaper. They are made distinctive by use of the Harrods logo on packaging, carrier bags and signs; all of which is done excellently. While this use of information techniques helps to reinforce the sense of place, it is the overall feel of the building itself which forms the identity of this great department store.

Third, Olins identifies information techniques as an important communication medium. Information techniques are the ways in which organizations, or managers, formulate and publicize their explicit messages. Coca-Cola is the classic example. A maroon fizzy liquid, little different from thousands of other soft drinks made all over the world, has become the world's greatest-ever brand. In the USA, people drink nearly as much Coca-Cola as they do ordinary water. This phenomenal success has been achieved by the brilliant use of information techniques which have made Coca-Cola synonymous with all the good things in life. There is throughout the whole of Coca-Cola's contacts with the general public a fanatical dedication to ensuring a consistent image. This is created by the way that colours, logo types and overall style are used within local cultures to create a message which is instantly recognizable throughout the world.

Fourth, Olins identifies behaviour as a crucial communication medium in shaping identities. He uses a police force as an example of an organization whose identity is shaped very largely by the behaviour of its individual members. Indeed, it is mostly shaped by the behaviour of the most junior and inexperienced police officers because it is they who have the greatest contact with the public. It is therefore their behaviour which police forces need to keep in line with their overall objectives.

Managers, as with whole organizations, communicate through the products with which they are associated, the environments they choose to work in, the information techniques they use and their behaviour towards other people. These four components need to be consistent with each other and with the intended message, for communication to be fully effective.

This complex and subtle truth is well understood by many of the modern management gurus. Peters (1988), in particular, provides much excellent advice on the multi-faceted approach to communicating objectives which is used by effective managers. We can best describe the sense of this by means of an example. A construction project manager who wishes his project to concentrate on producing a high standard of work needs to ensure that everything he does is consistent with that objective. He should hang copies of workmanship awards won by his previous projects in prominent places in his office. He should encourage teams on his current project to enter competitions which judge the standard of work. He should start every meeting with a review of the standards being achieved. As he walks around the factories where components are being prefabricated, he should ask everyone about the results of quality control tests on their work. He should attend courses on the subject and send copies of his own notes to colleagues, asking how the ideas can be used. His shelves should be full of books on quality control and some should be open on his desk. He must get excited when he sees excellent work, he must reward individuals for producing a good standard of work, and he must spend time on issues concerned with workmanship. When crises arise, the standard of work must never be sacrificed to solve the problem. He should also ensure that project information encourages good work, first, by setting tough but achievable standards and, second, by setting the good example of being well presented, complete and accurate. When these and similar things are done consistently, there is no doubt that this manager wants, above all else, a consistently good standard of work.

It is important to be consistent about overall project objectives. If standard of work is to be given top priority, it must have top priority every day. It does not work to concentrate on the standard of work at one time and then switch to cost cutting or fast construction. Such an approach is merely confusing and serves to ensure that priorities are not taken seriously because 'there is every chance that they will be different next week'.

The overall aim in communicating primary objectives is to create an inspiring vision of what is to be achieved by a particular project. This provides a steady, constant guide for all the teams involved. As they make day-to-day decisions, they know the priorities and so can act with confidence. Indeed, a clear vision is one essential prerequisite for delegation. Without it, subordinates tend to refer problems back to their boss and get him to check their decisions. Given a clear, inspiring vision, teams get on with the job of turning it into reality.

The constant vision provides an overall guide for teams' individual key objectives. These are the one or two objectives to which they decide to give special attention. They should, as Figure 13.2 suggests, be decided in agreement with their manager and be consistent with their given objectives. Obviously, teams must carry out the work they have contracted to do. However, to remain competitive, they should also seek to use each new project to improve one or at the most two aspects of their work. It is these improvements which provide their key objectives. In identifying key objectives teams should agree exactly what special effort they propose to make. This may be to improve on current norms by five per cent, to beat their own previous best performance by at least one per cent, or some other goal to which they commit themselves. Managers are responsible for ensuring that key objectives support the overall constant vision and do not conflict with or put at risk the essential constraints defined in the project information.

The purpose of a constant project vision is to ensure that individual teams' decisions are reasonably consistent and supportive of each other. The project vision should be bold yet sufficiently precise to allow teams to decide between alternative priorities. For example, to aim at producing the best building project in Britain in 1992 does not help teams decide priorities. To aim at producing the fastest rate of production in Britain in 1992 is more helpful. It tells teams that speed is the top priority objective.

Creating an effective project vision requires all managers to act in support of it at every opportunity. They should preach it, discuss it, tell stories about it, and live it all the time. Managers should listen carefully to teams' views on their own key objectives and use misunderstandings and mistakes as opportunities to make the vision clear. In doing this, managers must give attention to the details of their own behaviour. They should check how they spend their own time. They should ensure that they undertake specific acts, which reinforce the constant vision, at least two or three times every day.

Much of the advice provided by Peters (1988) and similar management gurus is based on common sense plus a sharp understanding of modern research into human psychology and sociology. As such, it often conflicts with traditional views because there is a kind of perversity about the human mind which causes good things to cluster together. So, for example, traditional views often assume that aiming for better standards will inevitably increase costs. In practice, as demonstrated most successfully by Japanese manufacturing industries, consistently high standards of work lead to greater productivity and therefore to lower costs. Similarly, becoming more competitive depends on building long term cooperative relationships between customers, consultants and contractors. Higher standards depend on having fewer quality control inspectors by making teams totally responsible for their own work. Greater control is achieved by delegating to competent teams. More success comes from being prepared to accept failure by teams who take responsibility for their own performance. At least, this is true provided that managers make sure that the teams learn from their failures.

Given these apparent paradoxes, how should construction project managers take account of all the advice provided by the modern management gurus? First, they should accept that the general thrust of the advice applies to construction as to all other human activities. Second, they should recognize that construction projects have a relatively short life compared with the organizations in which the gurus have done their research. Therefore their actions need to be dramatic and crystal clear, so that they are effective quickly. However, they should also remember that construction firms are, or at least intend to be, permanent organizations and so can afford to take a longer view. In particular, they can afford to invest in developing their systems and procedures and in training their people. Third, construction project managers should recognize that much of the work of today's management gurus is based on a concern with human issues. Certainly this is essential for construction project managers, but it is not the whole story. To an unusual extent, construction project managers have the opportunity, and indeed the responsibility, for determining the technology they will use. This is because, in theory at least, each new project can use an entirely new combination of technologies. Therefore, as managers, they need to take account of technology's need for standards and consistency at a detailed level as well as giving attention to the needs of people. Taking these three factors into account, the following paragraphs provide some ideas for actions which construction project managers might take in communicating objectives.

Involve the customer in establishing the constant vision and key objectives at all levels. Encourage him to express his views, worries and ambitions at every opportunity so that all his secondary objectives are identified and dealt with early.

Establish what the project aims to be best at and make this the constant vision. Do this early in the project with total commitment from the customer. The constant vision provides the control which enables teams to act with confidence because they know the priorities. Check that the vision is consistent with the overall character of the project. This means in general that standard constructions tend to have visions which are concerned with efficiency, traditional constructions with care, competence and concern for the environment, and innovative constructions with creativity and problem-solving.

Get agreement on one or at most two key objectives for each team. Do this early in their involvement with the project, in agreement with the whole team. Build on their successes on previous projects but make the objectives new, fresh and specific to the current project. Aim to improve on their previous performance. Identify clear objectives which challenge the team to give of their best. Check that the key objectives match teams' roles and time horizons. Finally, and most importantly, make sure that teams are committed to key objectives which are comfortably within their competence. This is essential so that the project becomes embued with success because teams are meeting their objectives.

Establish standards of absolute safety, completion on time and zero defects. Remember that the details are important; do not let small errors go uncorrected. Pay attention to the look and feel of workplaces. Insist that they are clean, tidy and safe.

Create a safety net of slack resources which is used to give teams the confidence to strive for their best performance without fear. Use the safety net sparingly, with justice and good humour. The aim is to set challenging goals, in agreement with teams, which are comfortably within their competence. Therefore they will succeed, feel good about their success and do even better next time.

Improve the norms by asking teams how they plan to do better. Ask managers what they have changed recently. Ask how much they have improved their teams' norms and how fast they are improving. Suggest improvements for teams to think about. This is especially effective during the early stages of their involvement with projects. Take one job and examine it in depth to remove all the obstacles that prevent it from being done better. Do this once every month. Remember that big changes come from lots of little steps in the right direction guided by a constant vision.

Listen to people at all levels. Remember that good ideas come from everywhere; good managers are the ones who recognize them. So carry a card which reminds you to *listen*. Ask elementary questions and keep asking until you understand what is happening. Take notes of good ideas as they arise. Provide feedback to the people you talk with and do so very soon after the discussion.

Get rid of the paperwork. Refuse to read long reports; insist that they comprise no more than one page. It is even better to talk directly to whoever is making the report so that nothing needs to be written as a memo. Make a ritual out of getting rid of a pile of papers which you have refused to read. Invent a ceremony which emphasizes that paperwork is wasteful.

Create a graphic description of the project. Get the designers and customer to create and agree a strong visual image of the project and its objectives. Use it at every opportunity. Use it especially at induction courses for people entering the project for the first time. Use it at seminars in factories producing components for the project. Make sure the project itself is true to its image. Consider what the look of the project says to people. Put the names of key people on the project sign board. Do not just include the names of firms but also name their project coordinators and the first-line managers responsible for each work area.

Take actions early. Do it now. Create a sense of urgency and hustle. Generate a sense of fun, energy and vigour. Try to create clean, hustling work environments throughout the project which enable people to act.

Give clear signals by your behaviour. Be first at work. Walk all the first-line work places and talk to people. Be excited about the project. Be excited about training courses and involved in the follow-up actions. Be excited about success. Cut out all the trappings of office and work from an open desk. Never compromise on the constant vision or key objectives. Remember people learn from your behaviour, so consider the symbolism of your actions. Consider what questions you ask first, where do you spend your time and what is the pattern in the notes you send people. Act the way you want your subordinates to act. Promote people who create excitement.

Spend your own time on key objectives. Discuss them widely and ask questions about performance and goals. Give teams working on lead activities badges to signal that, today, their work is critical. Find examples of teams meeting their objectives and talk about their success at every opportunity. Boast about the achievements of the first-line workers. Check that you are spending at least 50 per cent of your own time on key objectives.

Preach the constant vision at every opportunity. Kick-off each meeting by reminding everyone how the subjects under discussion relate to the vision and to key objectives. Get angry when people blatantly act in ways which are contrary to the vision. Act out the vision, do not just preach. Attend induction courses for new entrants to the project and seminars in factories making components for the project and preach the vision.

Create myths, images and metaphors which reinforce the vision and key objectives. Develop the common project language. Interpret events to imbue them with meanings which explain and illustrate the constant vision. Use examples of what is happening now to bring the vision alive. Collect good news and bad news stories about achievements and use them to build the project vision. Use symbols to reinforce the vision and key objectives.

Publish all information about the project in prominent places. Use clear, simple graphic representations which describe current performance against key objec- tives and the crucial constraints of safety, speed and standards. Put a record of how each team and each firm is performing this month in the project reception area. Remember secrecy is corrosive of human relations and the antithesis of trust. The real test of this is firms' willingness to publish all salaries. If they are fair, that is, outstanding workers, at whatever level, are paid more than ordinary workers, then there is no need for secrecy. If they are not published, everyone will assume that they are unfair.

Give rewards for good work, good suggestions and interesting lessons gleaned from failures. Do it as you walk the job. Remember that whoever gets the biggest car and the biggest salary will become a model of how to act. Give prizes for the best team; do this every week. It is absolutely essential to give recognition for jobs well done. This is the most fundamental and the most reliable form of control action.

Communicating feedback

Having created a constant vision and either one or two key objectives for every team, as well as ensuring that each team knows the work it must do, the standards it must achieve and the constraints it is operating within, construction project managers need feedback which tells them how their project is performing. Every manager needs feedback for himself; he needs to ensure that his team has feedback; and he is responsible for providing feedback for his superiors. Figure 13.3 illustrates the general structure of the flow of these categories of feedback through construction projects.

Feedback serves a number of purposes, all of which should be forward looking. That is, feedback provides a basis for improving performance in the future. The improvements should help each team's performance on the remainder of their current project but, more importantly, they should also aid their long term development and so benefit their performance on future projects. In other words, feedback should help teams to make permanent improvements to their

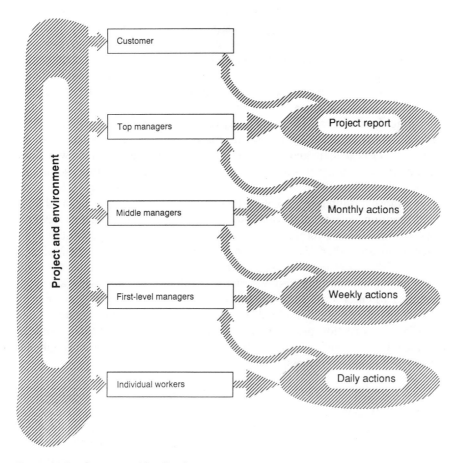

Figure 13.3 *Structure of feedback*

performance. Ideally it should also identify ideas that lead to long term improvements to products and project organizations. Achieving all of these purposes requires very effective feedback. This in turn means the feedback must be honest and available quickly to the responsible teams and managers.

Feedback has to be honest because teams and managers take decisions based on it. Nothing will push a project out of control faster than decisions based on dishonest feedback. It is not just that poor decisions will be made; the greater problem is that dishonest information will discredit the whole feedback system. Once that happens, chaos and anarchy are virtually inevitable. Therefore all construction project managers must act with total integrity in providing feedback and insist on total integrity from their teams. Any attempt to conceal the true situation must be taken absolutely seriously and repeated offenders dismissed from the project.

Feedback must be made available to teams and managers so that they can act to control their work within the agreed targets. Several consequences flow from this obvious but, in practice, all too often ignored requirement. First, the feedback must relate exactly and completely to the key objectives or constraints which it purports to describe. A common type of error arises with cost feedback. All too often the information given to a manager is incomplete. He is provided with readily available information but not warned of other items of cost which will surface in the future. There are many reasons why costs get forgotten. Some occur quarterly or annually and so are missed by monthly reports. Some are complicated to calculate and it requires time to produce an exact answer. Some are subject to arbitrary accounting policies which change over time, sometimes retrospectively. For these and similar reasons cost feedback can all too easily mislead those it is intended to help. The same kind of gap can occur in all kinds of information. For example, measurements of output may include defective work; or it may gloss over the common problem of the last one per cent of a task which is left unfinished when a team leaves their workplace, and then takes 10 per cent of the budgeted time and resources when they return to finish the work. In the midst of their day-to-day work it is difficult for managers always to remember to check for and adjust for all the possible gaps in the information they are given. This is especially true when it tells them that they are doing well. Therefore construction project managers must make sure that their teams are provided with feedback which is complete. That is, it can be related simply and directly to the agreed targets.

Second, feedback should highlight trends. A single report of a deviation from expected performance should be the signal for corrective action only if it confirms a deteriorating trend. However, if it is merely a blip on a pattern of variable performance, any simple corrective action may make the situation worse. Figure 13.4 illustrates the two cases. It may well be necessary to provide training to enable managers to distinguish between a trend and random, yet acceptable, variability. It should be added that although the second case in Figure 13.4 is unlikely to benefit from short term action, it may well benefit from a longer term study aimed at reducing the variability in output.

Third, feedback should be visible and comprehensible to all. It is best recorded in a simple graphic form on a wallchart in the workplace of the team whose performance it describes. The charts illustrated in Figure 13.4 provide an appropriate form of presentation. They are simple, clear and give a graphic picture of what is happening.

Fourth, feedback should be focused sharply on just two or perhaps three clear, simple measurements for each team; and no manager should receive more than three, four or at the very most five categories of feedback. There are several benefits from sharply focusing feedback. It means that the choice of what is measured is likely to be made carefully. Then there can be a realistic hope that measurements will be accurate and the results understood throughout the project. That is, when a problem appears in the measurements, it will be identified early and acted upon. Unless that happens, feedback is largely a waste of resources.

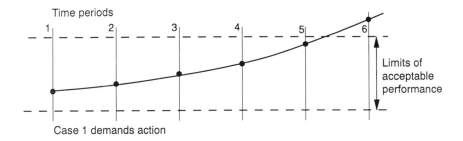

Case 1 demands action

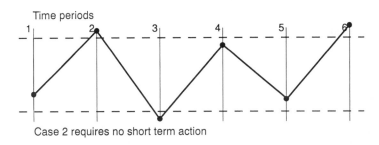

Case 2 requires no short term action

Figure 13.4 *Control charts*

It is useful to summarize the points made thus far on making feedback available to the responsible teams and managers; feedback needs to relate exactly to agreed objectives, it should highlight trends, be visible and easily understood, and it needs to be sharply focused. Given that it is also honest, that is, produced with integrity, the only further requirement for effective feedback is that it is produced quickly.

Feedback needs to be provided comfortably within the time discretion of those receiving it. It is arguable that the most important feedback in construction is that provided for the first line, the argument being that, if the direct operating work is controlled, the whole project is likely to be under control. Since the first line needs feedback on a daily basis and their managers need it on a weekly basis, there is no choice but to provide quick, rough and ready measures of performance. Equally, using manual methods, there is no time available for data to be collected, transferred to a remote processing department, analysed and turned into a formal report. Data must either be collected, processed and presented electronically in real time or it must rely on simple direct manual methods entirely contained within the workplace.

Construction that uses sophisticated prefabricated components is likely to be provided with feedback most effectively by electronic sensing devices incorporated into the components themselves. These can be used to provide feedback on productivity and standards of work for the people working on site. This may be displayed on a screen in the workers' lounge, on portable screens carried by first-line managers or, perhaps less likely, in the workplace itself. In addition, sensing devices built into components can be used to inform factories directly about progress, so that manufacturing and delivery are fully coordinated with construction. Where a high-technology approach is not available, the most effective form of feedback to the first line uses very low technology. A chalkboard or a whiteboard and marker pens in the workplace, which is used to record events as they happen, provides a good basis for effective feedback. Given this, teams can record their own performance as they work. The number of units fixed in position, the results of tests of the standard of work, the weight of waste and rubbish removed from the workplace, and the length and cause of delays are all examples of information which can be recorded as the events it describes happen. What is important is to identify one or two measurements which the team feels are important, which are under their control, and can be recorded unambiguously with the minimum of effort. The measurements should relate to the value of the work produced. In other words, a good standard of work must be measured as better than poor work; higher productivity must be recognized as superior to low productivity; waste must reduce a team's score; defective work and work unfinished by its programmed completion date must reflect badly on a team's measured performance; and good ideas and cooperative attitudes should enhance a team's record. All of these requirements are difficult individually, and taken together they are extremely difficult to meet. The only way of reconciling them is for managers to discuss all the requirements of good feedback with their teams and then agree how their work is to be measured. The aim is to find one or two or at most three simple direct measurements which the team sees as fair, which serve the project's objectives, and which can sensibly form the basis for evaluating the team's performance. Experienced teams who have previously worked on well managed projects are likely to be able to suggest sensible measures. Others will need help, possibly training in the issues involved, and suggestions of the kind of measurements which could be adopted. The purpose of this careful search for the right feedback is to ensure that teams take responsibility for collecting and using it to help themselves to deliver their own work in a controlled manner.

Figure 13.3 illustrates first-line feedback being systematically collected, analysed, filtered and used throughout the project organization. The figure also shows the filtered feedback which originated at the first line being joined, at each level, by direct feedback about the project and its environment. The direct feedback to higher levels tends to be softer and fuzzier than the measurements used at the first line. It consists of impressions about the tone of the project; reports about individual problems and how they were solved; blips of information about events in the environment; and managers' own judgements about progress.

The softer, fuzzier information which is collected should be decided in discussions within each group of managers at each level. Just as each first-line team agrees on the feedback it will use, so managers throughout a construction project should do likewise. In making these decisions they need to consider what measurements of project performance they require in addition to those derived by analysing the feedback flowing up from their own teams. They need to consider what features of their project's environment they should monitor. They should think about all the inputs to and outputs from their part of the overall process. For each of these, they should consider market conditions, factors that affect the availability of resources, and anything else which may alter the nature of their task. In this way, each level of managers will have three, four or five items of feedback which they use to help them control the work for which they are responsible.

The main mechanism for formally collecting together feedback at middle and top management levels is the daily, weekly and monthly progress meetings. The hierarchical structure described in Chapter 12 provides the formal framework for communicating feedback. Thus each day the team of first-line managers responsible for one element within one stage of the project should meet to review the current day's work and to review and then confirm the plan for the next day. Any problems which have arisen should be solved and any necessary new actions agreed. The meeting should be short, taking 20–30 minutes at most and held at one consistent time throughout the project, preferably in the middle of the afternoon.

Each week the level 3 managers meet in the same way to review the current week's work and confirm the plan for the next week for the whole project. This meeting should take no more than one hour and be held at a consistent time, preferably on Friday mornings.

Each month, top management meet formally with the customer to review the current month's work and confirm the plan for the next month. This meeting will be short when the project is going well and much longer when serious problems remain unsolved. Indeed, if the problems are very serious, the monthly meeting may turn itself into a taskforce and so move into an almost continuous sitting, spanning several days. In these circumstances top management, with the customer, may well meet more frequently than just once a month. However, routinely, the monthly meetings should take between one and two hours and be held early on the Monday following the last Friday of each month.

In a fragmented industry, like construction, the creation of effective feedback systems throughout whole projects requires good and consistent management. In particular, top management should encourage and help the firms they work with to develop their own systems. These should fit within an overall framework so that feedback can flow through individual projects in the pattern illustrated in Figure 13.3. The following paragraphs provide some ideas for actions which construction project managers might take in order to create a framework which encourages the communication of feedback.

Require teams to devise quick, rough and ready measures of their work. The aims are to gain teams' commitment to feedback and to find measurements which provide a basis for control well within the time discretion of each team.

Measure degrees of success, not failure. Aim to have at least 90 per cent winners. Given competent teams, a good evaluation system produces 20–25 per cent of the people achieving outstanding work, five per cent who need help and the remainder, in the middle, doing well.

Focus on value. In summarizing and analysing feedback from teams throughout construction projects, managers should concentrate on measuring the value added. Thus they should focus on the quality of the service to the customer; look for increases in the ability of the project organization to cope with problems and so maintain better control; count the number of innovations introduced; and measure improvements in the workforce's skills.

Publish feedback in the workplace. The aim is to provide a simple, graphic, lively presentation which is up to date and taken seriously as a means of informing the whole workforce and of achieving control. It is most likely to be either on an electronic screen or simply handwritten on a board. The presentation should provide one, two or at most three measurements of performance. It is essential to provide teams with information so that they can make decisions rather than wasting time asking managers for decisions. Given information, people ask questions and so refine the information. If published information is wrong, someone will see this and so help to make it more accurate. If it is not published, this feedback on the feedback cannot take place and it is certain that decisions will be based on inaccurate information.

Publish teams' skill achievements. In each workplace put, on a large board, a list of the names of the members of the team which currently 'owns' the space. Against each name list the relevant skills possessed by that individual. Keep the list updated as training and experience expand their capabilities.

Provide training on the meaning and use of feedback. This can be informal and included as one part of an initial discussion with each team of how their work is to be measured and rewarded. It can also include formal training in such subjects as the use of measuring devices, statistical techniques and the interpretation of trends. Wherever possible, formal training should be multi-firm to help build the project team spirit.

Discuss feedback with teams at every opportunity. Take feedback absolutely seriously and insist that it is collected and used to achieve control and to search for ways of improving performance. In doing this, deal straight away with any problems raised by teams. Remember a manager's role is to create the circumstances which enable their first-line teams to be productive. This means removing problems so that they have no excuses for not meeting agreed targets. However, do not take over; advise or suggest but do not give orders that cut across the line of command. You should never undermine a team's manager; always support him in front of his team. Remember you have made the manager responsible for his team, so you must trust him and let him run his own show or else replace him.

Go to the first-liners' parties and invite them to all project functions. The aim is to break through any reservations or 'them and us' attitudes and to build trust based on mutual understanding.

Ask managers questions which force them to know their first-liners. Ask for specific information which managers will know only if they talk to the first line. The aim is to make sure that managers really know what is happening. This means they need to be where the action is taking place.

Ask managers what changes they have made to their team's capabilities, the project organization and the product. Ask what major improvement these changes are directed towards. The aim is to encourage them to use feedback to search for innovations.

Learn from failures. Do not allocate blame; remember, as a manager, you are responsible for everything. Do ensure that teams learn from failures and use them to find better, permanent answers.

Ask yourself, what have I changed? Do this at the end of every day. Consider what you have made better, faster or more efficient. Also, identify the major improvement which the changes you have made are directed towards.

Communicating values

Communication within construction projects should be aimed deliberately at establishing the required tone and values. This requires managers to create conditions which ensure that everyone within their project organization has the opportunity to be well informed about their work. The essential philosophy behind this approach is that construction, at least in the developed world, is undertaken generally by well educated and well informed people. Television in particular has made everyone widely informed about the world they inhabit. Given this wide general knowledge, it would be madness not to give the whole workforce good information about their own work. Certainly, if managers do not provide good information about the project's objectives and the way they affect the work of individual teams, they cannot reasonably complain if workers develop their own private objectives which are contrary to the best interests of the project.

The style and content of communications should seek to breed trust and cooperation throughout the project. Trust takes time to build up. It requires a history of promises kept, delivery dates achieved, targets met and complete honesty. It requires managers at all levels to trust their teams. This means doing away with petty rules, setting spending limits sky high, and agreeing realistic, achievable targets.

Spending limits provide a good example of the approach needed to construct quickly and efficiently while at the same time building up the competence and skills of the people involved. It is axiomatic that everyone should have a clear budget either as a key objective or as a constraint. Budgets should provide targets which give teams a better than 90 per cent chance of success. This is because the aim is to produce winners not losers. Certainly targets should challenge teams and managers to give of their best, but it is futile to set targets which are widely regarded within the project as being unrealistic. Given achievable, challenging targets and teams' commitment to those targets, it is arguable that no spending limits are needed. They simply get in the way of action. It is better to trust competent people to check informally with their manager before making a decision which involves any large expenditure. However, most financial directors will feel uncomfortable without spending limits. Any which they successfully insist on setting should be very high. Peters (1988) suggests limits which at 1990 price levels are equivalent to first-line worker, £250; first-line manager, £2000; level 3 manager, £25 000; and level 4 managers, £50 000. On large projects these limits should be increased. The aim is to encourage workers at all levels to act, even if they make mistakes. Workers who make mistakes are a problem only if they do not learn from them and so repeat the error. In these circumstances, people should expect to be dismissed from the project or in the very least be given their own very specific spending limits. It is a good idea to treat any individual spending limits like a no claims bonus on insurance policies. That is, they can be increased by continued good performance. However, most people, given real responsibility and trust, perform responsibly and well.

A further important part of enabling and encouraging first-line teams to act decisively is to give them the authority to call on expert advice and help, as and when they need it. This helps to establish the primary importance of the first line, or front line as it might more accurately be called. The whole point of the project organization above the first line is to enable the basic operations it carries out to be executed efficiently. Making experts available to the first line, on demand, demonstrates top management's commitment to this crucial point. It also serves to emphasize the responsibility of the first line for acting. If they meet a problem which they are unable to tackle, they have the right to call in the experts. Even when an expert is called to a relatively trivial problem, discussing it may reveal something of greater significance. In any case it is good for experts to spend time at the first line even if, on the face of it, they are asked to look at small issues.

In this context, the term expert refers to any manager within any of the firms associated with the project who has developed a special interest, experience or expertise in a subject. These will often be level 3, 4 or 5 managers. Equally, it maybe an individual from a research institute or university who works frequently with one of the project firms. With modern information technology, such experts can be consulted at very short notice. In the near future it will be possible to use an inexpensive video camera to send live pictures of the project situation down a cable to anywhere in the world. In this way experts can in effect be brought to the first line at a few minutes' notice. Given that facility, the only sensible place to put the authority for seeking expert advice is with competent first-line teams.

Given competent first-line teams, the purpose of communications within construction project organizations is to inform them of the work they must do and to remove any obstacles which stand in the way of the efficient, productive, fast and accurate execution of that work.

No sharp distinction has been made, in this chapter, between planning and control. The emphasis has been on communication which seeks to influence decisions. A construction project consists of a vast and complex collection of decisions which build up in finer and finer detail over long periods of time. Each is intended to have some effect on the finished product. Some are decisions which have a major influence, some are merely the short term working out of the consequences of an earlier strategic decision, while others modify or even reverse earlier decisions subsequently found to be in error. Within this great collection of decisions, plans, which are essentially a mental rehearsal for the actions they contemplate, should be alive and growing with the project. They should involve everyone in the project in debate and discussion in order to secure agreement on action. Control should be implicit in the normal working methods used in putting plans into effect. Feedback which links control and planning should form an integral part of all meetings, discussions and actions. The theoretical distinctions between planning, control and feedback become blurred in the practical process of first thinking carefully about what is to be done and then doing it. The important distinctions are between the constant vision, key objectives and constraints. Provided teams know these and direct their actions towards realizing the vision, meeting the objectives and staying within the constraints, project communications are effective and the planning and control system is in good shape.

14 *Negotiation and trust*

Construction project managers need to ensure that their project organizations are made up of competent teams. The previous chapter describes actions which managers can take to inform teams about the work they are to do and to provide them with feedback on their performance. This, as the model in Figure 13.1 illustrates, leaves teams to decide for themselves on the detailed day-to-day actions they will take. That is, by recruiting competent teams, managers can trust them to act sensibly in carrying out their defined work. However, managers are responsible for coordinating the work of all the separate teams and so they may on occasions need to persuade them to agree to take one course of action rather than another, in the interests of the project as a whole.

Bringing teams into a project organization and then ensuring that their actions fit within the project as a whole requires negotiations to take place. These fall into two distinct categories. First are negotiations which lead to a major bargain. That is, the agreement which brings a team into a project. It specifies in as much detail as possible what work the team must do, the constraints they must work within and what they will receive in return. It is usually embodied in a formal contract of some kind. The second category of negotiations are those which lead to subsidiary transactions. These are agreements which settle any details of work and rewards which are not fully specified in a team's major bargain. They are mostly concerned with day-to-day matters, but may occasionally need to deal with a large issue either because of changed circumstances or because of an error in the major bargain.

Negotiations should be a search for an agreement in which both parties feel they have done well. Particularly within construction projects, which depend on cooperation, it is important not to regard negotiation as a kind of contest in which one party wins and the other loses. The aim of mature negotiators in construction is to reach win : win agreements. The reason is simply that, if a firm believes it has been forced to come into a project on poor terms, it will try to make up the loss during the course of the project. This provides no basis for an effective project organization. Equally, there is no merit in construction project managers being over-generous in order to create a happy team. There are two almost certain consequences. First, the customer will become dissatisfied when he discovers that he is paying too much for his project. Second the firms who have been treated generously in their major bargains will become greedy and ask for more in the subsidiary transactions. Therefore construction project managers have little choice but to be good negotiators who are skilled at finding win : win agreements which build mutual trust throughout their project organizations.

Negotiating

The basic model of a negotiation comprises two parties who have an interest in agreeing a transaction. The transaction consists of an exchange of valued things or services. Negotiation is the process by which the two parties agree the rate of exchange. Figure 14.1 illustrates the position at the start of a negotiation. It shows two parties, A and B, who are about to negotiate the price for something. They do not know what attitude to price the other party will adopt, so during the negotiations each attempts to discover how far the other is prepared to move over the price, while at the same time concealing the limits of their own position. The two parties have different effective preferences about the outcome. Effective preference means the limit to which a party to a negotiation is authorized to go. In the case in Figure 14.1, A has the authority to pay up to £5000 while B has the authority to accept as little as £3000. Thus there is considerable scope for agreement and good negotiators are likely to agree a price of £4000. When they do so, there is no reason for them not to think that they have done well.

Figure 14.2 illustrates a slightly different situation involving the same party A and a different party B. A is still authorized to pay up to £5000, but the new B is not authorized to accept less than £4800. There is still some scope for agreement but in this situation, again assuming competent negotiators, A is likely to have to agree a price of £4900. However, the negotiations are likely to be difficult because the limits of the two parties' positions are close together. Consequently,

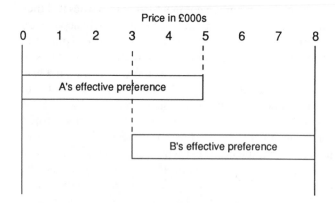

Figure 14.1   *Negotiating case 1*

they have little room for movement and so each is likely to be trying to push the other beyond their limit. In other words, it is harder for the second B, with the shorter effective preference, to reach an agreement. However, when he does reach an agreement, he obtains better terms than the first B, who has a longer effective preference.

The two figures illustrate a general principle about effective preferences. This is well described by Kuhn (1976) and it tells us that our power to reach agreements is directly related to the length of our effective preference; and our power to obtain good terms is inversely related to the length of our effective preference. Conversely, our power to reach agreements is inversely related to the length of the other party's effective preference; and our ability to obtain good terms is directly related to it. In plain language, if we are greedy we will find it difficult to obtain things but when we do it will be on good terms. It follows also that, if we negotiate with greedy people, we shall find it difficult to reach agreement and when we do it will be on poor terms, from our own point of view.

It must be remembered, however, that the act of negotiating incurs costs. In the context of a construction project, the costs of adopting a strategy based on short effective preferences are likely to be considerable. Negotiations will take longer and be tougher. That is, they will absorb a large amount of management resources. Many of the negotiations entered into will fail to produce agreement. Those which do produce an agreed transaction are likely to leave teams feeling they have obtained a poor deal which they must attempt to redress during the project. Against this kind of background the management of a project is likely to be very difficult. As we argued earlier in this chapter, this does not mean that construction project managers should be generous in negotiations. Such a strategy is likely to have even worse outcomes. The only approach which is fully effective in the long term is to be tough but fair.

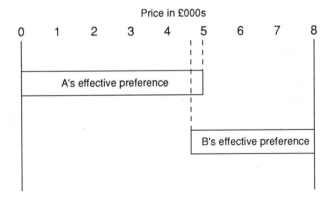

Figure 14.2 *Negotiating case 2*

There is good research which describes the overall structure of effective negotiations, and further research which identifies the types of behaviour adopted by effective negotiators. Taken together, these two sets of ideas provide a good basis for construction project managers seeking to adopt a tough but fair approach to negotiation.

Negotiation structure

The structure of negotiations is commonly described as a series of stages. However, in practice, negotiations do not form a single, consistent sequence of stages. They move back and forth between the stages as arguments are put, proposals are made, and negotiators withdraw to reconsider their position. Therefore descriptions of the structure of negotiations are best seen as maps which help negotiators to recognize where they are within a negotiation and remind them of the stages they need to move through in order to reach agreement.

Kennedy *et al.* (1980) provide a good description of the structure of negotiation. Their complete scheme consists of eight stages: prepare, argue, signal, propose, package, bargain, close and agree. For most negotiations in construction this can be simplified into four stages: prepare, discuss, propose and agree.

Prepare

Preparation is arguably the most important stage of negotiation. The negotiator who knows the facts, understands the issues and has thought carefully about his own position and that of the other party is much more likely to find a good agreement than one who is ill-prepared.

Construction project managers should look on preparation as a continuous activity. They should keep themselves informed on the firms and the teams they deal with regularly. They should know whether they form part of a growth industry, what the current level of demand is, whether they have many local competitors, what is the state of their order book, whether the firm is growing or shrinking, what is the general morale of their staff and so on. It is sensible for firms to maintain formal information systems which can comprise a series of simple box files, or their electronic equivalent, in which copies of firms' annual reports and other formal publications and snippets of information from the trade press or general media can be collected together with information gleaned first hand. It is especially useful to keep notes of previous negotiations, including comments on the approach adopted by the other party. Simply browsing through the files regularly helps managers understand some at least of the behaviour of the firms and teams with whom they deal. Certainly a careful study of their own information should be part of the preparations for any major formal negotiation.

The most important part of preparation is defining the objectives of the negotiation. This is, first, identifying all the things you want. These should be realistic demands which ideally you will get. Second, you should identify all the things which you *must* get. That is, things which are essential if any agreement is to be reached. A good way of identifying your bottom line is to consider what happens if you fail to reach agreement. What is the next best alternative? Having defined the best and the worst outcomes, the third task is to consider the various positions that lie between them. This is where agreement is most likely and so good preparation involves establishing a sensible range of options. For example, payment terms may vary considerably and so make a fairly wide range of total prices acceptable. It is easier to negotiate confidently if these implications have been worked out. Having explored a range of objectives, the next step is to allocate priorities to them. It is important to know where concessions can be made and which things really are crucially important. In other words, focus on defining your real interests and avoid adopting any fixed positions at this stage.

Having established their own objectives, the wise negotiator next considers what the other party is likely to want. Again it is sensible to consider what they might ideally like to get, what they must get, and what they probably expect to settle for. It is important to remember that these assumptions should be tested in the discuss stage of the negotiation.

In the prepare stage it is sensible to consider what things you could offer to the other party which are likely to be valuable to them but are cheap for you to provide. These might include early payment, access to a computer-aided design system, use of standing plant and equipment, use of site offices and storage, complete control of defined workplaces, use of a rubbish collection and removal system, beds in a workman's hostel, and places on internal training courses.

The next part of preparation is to consider the information needed in the negotiation. Identify exactly what you need to know in order to decide whether any proposed agreement is or is not acceptable. It is often useful to know how well the other party's firm and its individual teams are performing and whether this is better or worse than normal for their part of the industry. You will need to identify and check all your assumptions about their position, to identify their strengths and their weaknesses, and to establish exactly what they want from the negotiation and how badly they want it.

Having identified the information you need, also consider what information you want the other party to have and any which you would prefer them not to know. The aim of this part of the preparation is to consider how you can structure the other party's expectations. For example, if you let them know that you have a cash flow problem, they should deduce that it will be futile to ask for early payment. Equally, they may be encouraged to ask for a discount in return for credit. So you need to balance the possible responses and, in this particular example, decide whether it is in your interests to structure their expectations by providing information about your own cash flow problem. You should also decide what you want to know in return for any information which you offer. In the actual face-to-face negotiations you should insist on getting some information from the other party in return for any you give. As we shall see, it is one of the basic principles of negotiating not to give anything away for nothing.

Having decided how information is to be used in the negotiation, the next step is to plan an overall strategy. This must deal with the form of the negotiation, whether it will comprise face-to-face meetings, telephone conversations, an exchange of letters or some other communication medium. The strategic plan should establish who will conduct the negotiation on your behalf. Ideally, in face-to-face negotiations, each party is represented by at least three people. The first of these is a leader who conducts the negotiation and therefore does most of the talking. The second is a summarizer who keeps track of progress and is ready to summarize the point reached in the negotiations when asked to do so by his leader. Also, the summarizer should help his leader when he is in any difficulty. He should in no sense take over the negotiation, but should create time for his leader to think, by providing a summary of the point reached. The third person in the team is an observer who watches the other party's negotiators in order to establish exactly what is happening. He should try to judge whether they are a united team, which points are really important to them, which issues worry them, and what are their real reactions to arguments, proposals and offers. It may also be necessary to include experts within a negotiating team to provide first-hand knowledge of specialized subjects.

During the preparation stage, the leader should check that each member of the negotiating team knows their own role. In particular, he must make it clear that he is conducting the negotiation and will call on colleagues as he needs their help. It is good practice for any team member who wants to help his leader to suggest that he asks for a recess. In this way any doubts or differences within the team are sorted out behind closed doors and never in front of the other party.

The final part of a negotiating strategy is a statement of what you intend should happen. The structure of negotiations described in this chapter provides the overall framework. However, as described earlier, this does not unfold in a single consistent sequence. Therefore, as a major negotiation progresses, it is necessary to keep track of the stages reached and to decide exactly what role the next stage is intended to play. Then it is helpful to consider exactly what you will try to do during that stage: whether you will ask questions, offer information, make proposals or do something else. Equally, you should consider what the other party may do and how you will respond. In doing this you should also decide on the right overall approach. Are you going to adopt a 'take it or leave it' attitude; are you going to try to frighten the other party by describing the worst possible consequences if he fails to agree; are you going to open with very high demands in order to restructure his expectations; are you going to press hard for a minor part of your claim at the start, in the hope that by subsequently backing down you will get agreement to a much more important part; are you going to claim that you need someone else's authority before you can agree; are you going to claim that certain actions are against company policy; are you going to refer to competitors' offers; or are you going to use one of the many other ploys that make negotiating such fun?

The overall strategy cannot be a detailed action plan. The other party may behave differently from the way you expect. Therefore, in formulating your strategy, you should see it as a flexible decision tree. It provides a guide as to how you should act because you have considered a range of possibilities, but it cannot provide a hard and certain script. For this reason it is sensible to carry any notes you need on small cards, each containing just a few words, which you can rearrange as the negotiation proceeds. The cards should be few in number and each contain one simple idea.

The final point to remember about preparation is that it should be reviewed at every recess. This is obviously true of major recesses which cover several days, but it is also important during short recesses in the middle of a single negotiating session. You should check all your earlier assumptions, consider where you have got to in respect of each of your objectives, and consider whether your planned actions are working or need to be changed. You should also consider whether a change in the negotiating team is likely to produce benefits.

Discuss

The next stage is for the two parties to discuss the subject of the negotiation. They each state how they see the situation and describe what they expect to get from any agreement. They talk about their own interests and try to avoid taking any fixed position at this early stage.

Each party will seek information on the other's objectives, interests and priorities. They will test their own assumptions, and try to identify the other's major interests and points on which the other party seems keen to stick. Also, each party will offer the information that they want the other to know.

Generally, after a few minutes of preliminary social pleasantries aimed at establishing a sense of working together to find an agreement, the two parties should check that they have a common understanding of the meeting's agenda. Then each party will open with a statement which, at the very least, describes the things they ideally would like to get from an agreement. These statements should be concerned mostly with each party's interests couched in general rather than specific terms. For example, it is better to state that you need fair recompense for a tower crane left standing idle due to late work by the other party, rather than to insist that you want £10 000 compensation. At some point, of course, you will need to be more specific. That raises the difficult issue of deciding at what level to open. Probably the best advice on the right opening position to adopt in a negotiation is to start from the highest position which is realistic. That means, if the position is challenged, as it very likely will be, it can be justified by reasonable arguments.

As each party states its position, it is sensible for the other to ask questions which seek clarification. It is also good practice to summarize the other's position to make sure that it is properly understood. In doing this it is important not to antagonize the other party. Listen to what they have to say, and make it clear that you have listened seriously and understood what they are asking for. Check that you understand their arguments, ask what their priorities are, ask why a particular point is important to them, ask what you could do to enable them to accept something different, and generally ask open-ended questions which invite more information. Equally, insist on a fair and careful hearing of your own position. Check that it has been understood. Ask which of your proposals they do not like, ask whether there are circumstances in which what you want could be acceptable, ask what is missing from your proposals, and generally continue the policy of asking open-ended questions; that is, questions which cannot be answered by a simple yes or no.

In giving and seeking information during the discuss stage of negotiations, both parties should also be looking for signals. These are less than firm statements which offer the possibility of some movement from the stated opening position in return for some movement by the other party. It tells each party where the other is prepared to search for an agreement. Common forms of signal include the use of the following phrases: as things stand; at the present time; that would be difficult; it is not our normal practice; we could discuss that subject; we could not agree to a 10 per cent reduction; and we cannot complete all the work in six weeks. Wherever possible, skilled negotiators follow up a signal from the other side by seeking more information and signalling that they are prepared to respond positively to movement by the other party. If, however, they do not receive any signals, they signal their own willingness to move and insist on some response. If their signals are ignored, they repeat them more clearly and more explicitly. If they still receive no response, they begin to consider whether the other party is in fact prepared to negotiate.

Signals are important; they indicate a willingness to move on to the next stage of a negotiation. They suggest that the party sending the signal feels that he has sufficient information to make a proposal. When a signal is reciprocated, the scene is set for the next stage.

Propose

The third main stage in negotiations is one in which the parties make and discuss proposals. It comprises a structured search for an agreement. Initially, proposals are tentative. They are aimed at exploring possibilities without commitment on either side. Gradually they become firmer and form more explicit offers. The classic form for a proposal is: 'if you will . . . , then I will . . .'. In each case the row of dots represents some specific action. At the start of the propose stage, when proposals should be couched in exploratory terms, the classic form becomes 'if you were prepared to consider . . . , then I may be prepared to consider . . .'. Initially, proposals are best couched in general terms which can gradually be made more specific. So an initial request for an early completion date can be defined later as completion within six weeks or by asking for a specific date. An initial request for a substantial reduction in price can be redefined, as the propose stage progresses, to a specific percentage reduction or to a proposed new price.

Proposals are very powerful within a negotiation. Provided it is clearly made, a proposal gives the initiative to the party making it. It is often helpful to announce that you wish to make a proposal. This immediately commands attention. The proposal should then be stated in the form: 'if you will . . . , then I will . . .'. As described above, early in the propose stage, a more tentative form of words is appropriate. However, irrespective of the stage, once you have made a proposal, it is best to remain silent until the other party responds. The power of a proposal is that it requires a response. Even if a proposal is rejected, it remains open for the originator to retain the initiative by asking for an alternative proposal from the other party.

The first clear proposal within a negotiation often has a decisive effect on the eventual agreement. Therefore, in a negotiation, as soon as you feel you understand the subject from the point of view of both parties reasonably well, it is good practice to make a proposal. As far as possible it should address the other party's apparent major concerns. Obviously, it will also deal with all of your own interests.

Should the other party make a proposal, you should take it seriously because it provides you with important information. You should never interrupt a proposal. You should never reject a proposal without giving it some consideration. It is good practice to ask questions to clarify exactly what is being offered. It is sensible to summarize the other party's proposals to ensure that you have fully understood them. It helps the process of negotiation if you identify features of the proposal that you like and those which require further movement before you could accept them. It is also very effective to use proposals from the other party as a basis for a new proposal of your own. This demonstrates that you want to work together to search for an agreement.

As the propose stage develops, proposals should begin to take the form of specific bargains. In effect, a proposed bargain is an offer to move from one's own ideal position in return for movement by the other party. Many people in practice find it hard to bring themselves to propose any movement from their preferred position. They are concerned that any movement which they offer will be accepted, but that the other party will not agree to give anything in return. As a consequence, all too often neither party is willing to make the first move and negotiations drag on aimlessly.

In proposing bargains, to avoid the trap of one-way movement, it is essential that the conditions you wish to place on your offer are stated first. That is, the formal 'if you will ... , then I will ...' is used. Then it is not open to the other party to accept your movement without also either agreeing to or proposing some modification of the conditions you have placed on your offer. If he wishes to modify the conditions, it is then open to you to alter your original offer to bring it into line with his proposal.

It is also important in proposing bargains to include everything in your statement. That is, you must list all the conditions which the other party must meet, and it is sensible to include everything which you are prepared to offer at that stage. This is because it is difficult to introduce a new condition once your proposal has been taken seriously by the other party. Adding a new condition tends to look like an act of bad faith; and it can all too easily appear that you are becoming greedy. The most likely consequences are that your proposal as a whole will be rejected and it will be much harder to get the other party to take subsequent proposals seriously. Therefore proposed bargains should be complete so that, if the other party accepts, there exists a full and complete agreement.

Finally, in bargaining it is good practice not to give anything away without receiving something for it. Acts of generosity do not usually teach the other party to be generous. They are more likely to teach him that you are generous and therefore to ask for more. Therefore even tiny concessions, which are very cheap for you to give, should have a specific condition attached to them. It is always worth considering the value to the other party of concessions which you can make cheaply. Consider what he will have to do if you do not give him the particular thing. What will it cost him to make alternative arrangements? Then decide what is a fair price and ask for something in return which matches the value to the other party.

Bargaining is a process of trading concessions; give something in return for something which you value more than the thing you agree to give up. Each new proposal should build on agreements already reached, and it is sensible practice to make your moves smaller and smaller as time passes. This tells the other party that he is going to get very little more by prolonging the negotiation. This is important because bargaining may continue for a long time as the parties try to win a little more from each other. This can be counter-productive. Good agreements may be missed in a search for some tiny further advantage. It is also irritating to the other party if you refuse to conclude a negotiation even though both parties know that the offers on the table are fair and reasonable. Also, it is sensible in building a construction project organization to be brisk, to create a prejudice in favour of making decisions and taking actions. Therefore negotiations should not be dragged out in a search for some further small concession but concluded as soon as a sensible agreement is in sight.

Agree

The final stage of negotiating is to agree. It can of course happen that the only agreement possible is to decide that the parties cannot reach any agreement. They must then use some other means of settling their joint problem. This usually requires the introduction of a third party to act as referee or arbitrator, or resort to the formal processes of the law. These courses of action are usually expensive and time consuming and therefore negotiators should try very hard to find an agreement.

An agreement requires the bargaining to be closed. This in turn requires one of the parties to propose that it should be closed and for the other to agree. The safest approach to proposing a close is to summarize all the points which have been agreed, emphasizing how much movement both sides have already made, and suggesting that it provides a fair basis for a bargain. If this proposal is accepted, the bargaining has finished. If it is not, it is open to the party which has made the closing proposal to ask what they would have to do to make the complete package acceptable to the other party. The response to this question may indicate that the other party is nowhere near agreeing and still wishes to negotiate over major issues. On the other hand, it may reveal that a small further movement will secure agreement. The bargaining may resume for some time while the final points are resolved, but the option exists for the party which initially attempted the summary close to agree to the further movement in return for the other party's acceptance of the complete agreement as now defined.

There are other approaches to closing, but generally they involve greater risks than the summary close. A common approach is to offer a concession in return for agreement. The concession may be designed to resolve some minor or major sticking point in the negotiation. It may introduce a surprise new element which deals with a matter which it is known the other party feels is important but has not formed part of the present negotiation. The risk of course is that the other party mentally accepts the concession but also continues to bargain for more. Another common approach is to introduce a proposal as your final offer or your bottom line. The risk involved in this approach is that the proposal may be rejected and you are then faced with no agreement or accepting the damage to your own integrity which flows from negotiating below what you have described as your bottom line. It is even riskier to attempt to force agreement with a threat. You might for example say 'if you do not agree I will give the contract to your major competitor'. If the other party does not agree, you have narrowed your own courses of action. Even if he does agree, he will probably resent being threatened and this is a poor basis on which to build a project organization. There are other approaches to proposing a close, but generally the summary close is the least risky because, if it fails, it leaves the door open for the other approaches to be used.

Once an agreement is reached, there is one further vital step. This is agreeing exactly and in detail what has been agreed. This step is crucially important. It is best to write down all the points which have been agreed and for both parties to formally agree the written statement. When this is not done, there is almost inevitably disagreement over some of the details of what was agreed. Therefore a formal written note of the agreement is the necessary final step in the structure of negotiations.

Recesses

Recesses do not provide an extra stage in the formal structure of negotiations. However, they are an important part of the whole process. Recesses consist of short breaks in the face-to-face discussions while the teams representing each of the parties meet in private. A recess can be requested by either party at any stage of a negotiation. Recesses are generally under-used in construction negotiations, yet they provide a valuable part of the good negotiator's armoury. One of the important advantages of recesses is that they can be used to interrupt a negotiation which is dragging on aimlessly. In such a situation, a recess can be used to give each party time to reconsider a specific point or to try to formulate a proposal. It is sensible to define the purpose of a recess so that, when negotiations resume, they are likely to do so purposefully.

Recesses can also be used defensively when one party finds itself in difficulty and needs time to think. In these circumstances, it will often be the summarizer who proposes the recess in order to rescue his leader. It is also sensible to ask for a recess after the other party has made a proposal and it has been questioned and understood. The recess provides time to evaluate the proposal carefully and to decide how to respond. During recesses, the observer comes into his own by describing what he believes is really happening in the negotiation. He should be able to identify which points appear to be of real importance to the other side, where they are weak and where strong, where they are bluffing and where in deadly earnest, and generally provide an overall picture of the other party's position.

Also during recesses, the material produced during the preparation stage should be reviewed to see if it can be extended to provide new opportunities or a better picture of the best way forward. This all contributes to the main purpose of a recess, which is to decide on the next steps to take. It is worth deciding very carefully exactly how a negotiation should be resumed because, during the few minutes following a recess, everyone is likely to be paying full attention. Therefore statements made at this time are likely to have considerable impact. In other words, recesses create opportunities to move forward rapidly.

Recesses may occur in any of the stages of discuss, propose or agree. They often signal a movement from one stage to another. This may be progress forward towards agreement or a step back to an earlier stage in order to try a different approach. In either event it is helpful, when negotiating, to be clear which stage has been reached. This helps negotiators to decide how they can steer negotiations forward towards an agreement. It helps them to decide which of the possible next actions is most likely to be most effective. Therefore it is sensible for construction project managers to use the prepare, discuss, propose and agree model or something similar to develop their own simple, clear model of the structure of negotiation.

Behaviour during negotiation

Construction project managers, as with other negotiators, find that in practice they can negotiate better with a clear model of the structure of the process in mind than they do without it. However, this benefit is either enhanced or wasted by the way they behave in negotiations. In describing the structure of negotiations, we have necessarily illustrated the stages by describing various examples of effective behaviour. There are, however, overall patterns of behaviour which cut across the separate stages and which distinguish good negotiators from the less good.

Fisher and Ury (1981) provide clear advice on effective behaviour which all negotiators would do well to follow. Their approach is based on four principles: separate the people from the problem; focus on interests, not positions; generate a variety of options before deciding what to do; and insist that the result be based on some objective criteria.

People

The first important negotiating behaviour for construction project managers to adopt is to deal separately with people issues. It is very important in helping to build an effective project organization to remember that you are dealing with the subject of negotiations and with people. The two should be given separate consideration. This is because it is important to treat people well, even when you need to be very tough on the subject of the negotiation.

Negotiations provide important opportunities to teach the project vision and values to members of the project organization. The way managers deal with potential members and those who are already part of the project organization very largely determines the success or otherwise of the whole enterprise. The negotiations which precede the agreement of a new major bargain provide the best opportunity to build a firm's commitment to a project. That is why experienced construction project managers insist on each firm's project coordinator being involved in the initial negotiations. The style and approach used by the construction project manager sets the tone for all subsequent negotiations over subsidiary transactions.

In the vast majority of negotiations within construction projects, one important aim should be to build long term cooperative relationships based on mutual trust. Thus each new negotiation is smoother and more efficient than the last because it takes place between people who understand and respect each other.

Human relationships are beset with misunderstandings. We attribute attitudes and motives to others which are based on our own fears. We blame others for our own problems. These are important matters and good agreements are unlikely unless the people issues are explicitly dealt with first. This requires each party to work at understanding the other and for them both, eventually, to see negotiation not as a battle of wills between adversaries, but as a cooperative process of solving a joint problem. A good manager will also see each negotiation as an opportunity to help educate the members of his project organization in correct negotiating behaviour.

The best place to start in tackling these responsibilities is with yourself. Negotiators should identify their own feelings and attitudes. Are they angry, fearful, nervous, aggrieved, proud, out for revenge or simply feeling very confident? They should ask themselves why they feel like this, why they have a particular viewpoint, and generally seek to understand their own feelings and attitudes. Then they should do the same for the other party. How are they likely to be feeling and what must they be thinking about the people with whom they are negotiating?

It is good practice in face-to-face negotiations to describe your own feelings and attitudes. It is important in doing this not to blame the other party for your viewpoint but simply to make them aware of the emotional baggage you bring with you. Similarly, it is sensible to encourage the other party to describe how they feel and to explain why they view the problem in the way they do. Create opportunities for the other party to let off steam, encourage them to say everything which is bothering them so that there are no hidden, remaining grievances. All of this information about the other party helps you to understand them and therefore leaves you better able to deal with them as real four-dimensional people separate from the particular subject of the negotiation.

During negotiations always listen carefully to the other party. Ask questions designed to check the meaning of what they have said, summarize the points they have made, and do not be afraid to restate their case in a positive light. If it is clear that you have understood their case, any points on which you disagree are likely to be taken more seriously than if you appear not to have listened to them. Also check that your own communications are clear. Ask questions to check their understanding of your interests. Generally, try to avoid problems developing simply because of bad communication.

In discussions, do not talk about the other party's attitudes or motives unless this is to ask questions to clarify a description they have just given. Talk about your own feelings, your own viewpoint, your own objectives, but do not attempt to tell the other party about themselves. Doing so merely antagonizes them, generates a defensive attitude and reduces the chances of being given an open and honest description of how they really feel. It is much more effective to say 'my firm feels that they are asked to do a lot of extra work on your projects for which they do not get paid' than it is to say 'you always cheat us over payments for extra work'. The first statement opens up the possibility of a discussion as to why the firm feels that way. This may in turn lead to a discussion of how best to deal with the feeling. The second statement, because it is a direct accusation, is much less likely to produce a cooperative response. Generally in negotiating, it is counter-productive to attempt to allocate blame. It is much more productive to state a problem in a way that leads on to a search for a solution.

In searching for solutions to problems in negotiation, it is most effective to work with the other party. When they have been involved in a search for a solution, they will feel that they own the resulting decision. It becomes theirs because they were involved in finding it. Joint working is much the best way of building commitment to agreed courses of action. It is helpful to be explicit about the need for cooperative working. Talk about working together, joint interests and common concerns. Try sitting side by side rather than on opposite sides of a table. All of this helps to find a jointly acceptable solution and also helps to build a project team.

When an answer is found, it is helpful to present it as a fair result in which both parties win. It is often sensible to allow the other party to present the agreement as their own idea. Certainly it is no part of a manager's responsibilities to build up his own ego by claiming the credit for joint work. It is his role to build up the self-confidence of the firms and teams with whom he deals. If this requires a manager to allow the other party to take the credit for a good agreement, so be it.

Finally, in dealing with people, it is very helpful to take opportunities to show your interest and understanding by means of your actions. Small acts of sympathy, concern or generosity can have benefits out of all proportion to any costs involved. So managers should deliberately seek to act in ways that remove the other party's concerns. If they see you as greedy, act generously; if they see you as careless about their interests, show your concern; and generally treat people as fellow human beings with all the same fears, emotions and hopes as yourself.

Interests

It is important in a negotiation to focus on the interests of the two parties. That is, rather than concentrating on defining and defending specific and detailed solutions to the problem, initially at least, describe your interests and encourage the other party to describe their needs, wishes, concerns and fears. It is generally unhelpful to adopt a hard, fixed position based on your own solution to a joint problem. It is much more effective to describe the real interests which any solution must satisfy in order for it to be acceptable.

To take an example, a manager may demand completion of a specialist contractor's work on site in six weeks. The contractor may state that it will take at least ten weeks. However, the manager's main interest may be to create clear work areas for the following specialist contractors, while the contractor's main interest may be to match the work to the capacity of the factory manufacturing the components. If these two parties focus on their positions, they will simply argue over the range of six to ten weeks and probably settle on some intermediate figure which serves neither's main interests particularly well. By focusing on interests, a whole range of solutions are possible. It may be possible to programme the work to release clear work areas in stages and so allow the following specialist contractors to start work. It may be possible to use a second factory and incur slightly higher transport costs. It may be possible to use simpler components which require less work in the factory but allow work on site to begin earlier. So in this example, as in most real negotiations, concentrating on positions serves only to lock the negotiation into a dispute or haggle; focusing on interests opens the negotiation to free-ranging, creative problem-solving.

Focusing on interests requires negotiators to talk about their own interests in specific, practical terms. Talk about what you need for the future. Describe what you have to achieve in detail. Try to make your problems come alive for the other party. Equally, encourage them to describe their interests. If they adopt a fixed position, ask why. Ask how they calculated their solution, exactly what factors did they take into account, and generally try to identify their real interests. Think about possible reasons for the other party not accepting your own proposals. Do they have outside interests which must be satisfied? Who do they report to? Does your proposal enhance their self-respect or their reputation among their peers or superiors? Having done all of this, make sure that the other party is aware that you understand and respect his interests.

Negotiators should be tough in looking after their own interests. This is not incompatible with being generous in their treatment of people. Indeed, treating people well, which includes recognizing their interests and at the same time insisting on the importance of your interests, is by far the most effective approach to negotiations within construction projects. It helps to turn the process away from confrontation and convert it into a cooperative search for joint solutions which serve both parties' interests.

Options

Having turned negotiation into a problem-solving process, it is logical, as we described in Chapter 9, to search for a range of options before any attempt is made to evaluate them, still less to settle on any one particular solution. This is indeed exactly what many experienced negotiators do. They use brainstorming and other creative techniques to produce a list of possible solutions. They look especially for those which will meet the interests of both parties.

It is important to separate the use of creative techniques from the actual process of negotiation. This is especially true when they are used by both parties working together. In particular, it is essential to ensure that everyone is clear that putting forward options does not in any way constitute a proposal, still less a formal offer. It can often help to adopt a distinctly informal style and location and to bring in an independent facilitator. It is helpful for the facilitator to record ideas in full view on a board, as they are suggested. It is also essential for the facilitator to insist that ideas are not criticized during the creative stage. He can also help to free the teams' thinking by suggesting that they adopt different viewpoints. For example, they might think of options which might be proposed by different professions, they might consider the situation they would expect to see next year and ten years into the future, they might think of possible newspaper headlines reporting the outcome of their negotiation, or they might try analysing the problem in detail or devising a process which could lead to an answer being found.

The aims of generating options are to free everyone's thinking about the problem, to create a chance of working together in an informal way, and to produce a list of possible solutions. Once such a list exists, it can be evaluated to identify any options which are worth pursuing further. Ideally, each party will find two or three interesting ideas which they can agree to examine to see if they provide a basis for them to make a formal proposal. In doing this, each party should test the ideas from the point of view of both parties' interests. Then, when the formal negotiations resume, it is reasonable to ask how any proposals made by one party help to meet the other's interests. All of these actions serve to create a sense of cooperating together to find an agreed solution.

Objective criteria

When a specific value has to be placed on a variable within a negotiation, it is unwise to settle it by confrontation in which the strongest will or most intransigent party wins. It is much better to insist that the value be settled by using some objective criteria. These take one of two forms: fair standards or fair procedures.

In establishing the price for construction work, an example of a fair standard might be to use the prices in a well known published price book. An example of a fair procedure might be to base the price on the consultant's or contractor's actual costs as audited and agreed by a jointly appointed independent firm, plus 10 per cent. Common bases for standards or procedures often include some use of market value, reference to a previous similar case, judgement by an independent professional, published standards, normal practice, equal treatment and actual costs. Most variables involved in construction negotiations can be established by use of either a fair standard or a fair procedure. Indeed, many of the clauses in construction contracts serve to establish exactly which standards or procedures should be used in particular circumstances.

It is often useful in a negotiation to seek agreement on the objective criteria which will be used to resolve disagreements. It can be easier to agree a fair standard or a fair procedure than to resolve the main subject of a negotiation. Achieving some agreement is nearly always helpful; agreement tends to be habit forming and so any progress may serve to help unlock bigger issues. However, the great benefit is that objective criteria prevent negotiations getting stuck on petty arguments over matters which ought to be resolved on a largely factual basis.

Practice cooperation

Most of the actions which construction project managers are required to undertake involve negotiation of some kind. In the great majority of their dealings with their customers, important actors in their projects' environments and especially with the teams which make up their project organizations, there is an element of bargaining. This may be as simple as trading small favours, but it often involves substantial matters, with major consequences for the overall success of their projects. All of these interactions are helped by an understanding of the patterns of behaviour used by experienced negotiators.

The prescriptions described by Fisher and Ury (1981) (separating the people from the problem; focusing on interests, not positions; generating a variety of options before deciding what to do; and insisting that the result be based on some objective criteria) provide an excellent framework. Running through these prescriptions is a strong preference in favour of cooperative behaviour. This is quite simply because it is more efficient than confrontation. Although it can be fun to win a good argument, if winning means the other person feels they have lost, this provides no basis for an effective project organization. Construction is difficult enough without the added complication of having to deal with people who are trying to get even because of some wrong they believe they have suffered. In negotiating, construction project managers need to consciously build a sense of trust, understanding and cooperation. So their negotiating behaviour must display these same characteristics.

Adopting this approach is obviously much easier when the firms and people involved already know each other well. It is even easier when they are working together on designs and technologies in which they are well experienced, which is why this book has consistently emphasized the benefits of long term relationships and the use of established answers. Departing from either of these social or technological certainties is an important decision which almost inevitably incurs large additional costs. Departing from both in the same construction project makes management very difficult and requires a patient and rich customer.

Dealing with new kinds of construction or working with unfamiliar teams makes it more important than ever for managers to adopt the behaviour patterns of a good negotiator. Essentially, this means treating people generously. It means not attacking the other party or the positions they adopt. Instead, managers should search for the reasons behind any fixed position the other party seeks to adopt. They should try to discover which of their interests these fixed positions are thought to serve. If the other party attacks you, do not defend yourself but accept the attack as an attempt to solve the problem. Assume that the subject of their criticism of you highlights a major interest and concentrate on searching for answers that meet that interest. Generally, ask questions or make tentative statements which invite their opinions rather than making hard statements or adopting fixed positions. Try at all times to draw the other party into a joint, cooperative search for an agreed solution. Aim to create conditions which will help people to grow, seek to banish their fears and actively provide opportunities for them to feel like winners. However, while it is best to treat people generously, it is not sensible to be generous over the subject matter of the negotiation.

Good negotiators, including good construction project managers, are tough, even hard, on the issues. They state their interests clearly. They insist on fair and objective methods of deciding all of the variables in the agreement. They check their facts, they do not give in to threats, they do not weaken in the face of delaying tactics, and they consistently insist on adopting a principled approach. They know that they need to work with the other party as part of their project organization. Therefore they want an agreement which the other party feels good about and is keen to implement, which at the same time meets all the requirements for a successful project. They should always be sure that neither party is being pushed into promises which will be difficult for them to keep. An experienced negotiator may well be able to persuade a less skilled one to give away too much. However, it is of no help in managing a construction project for members of the project organization to make commitments which they cannot live up to.

Construction project managers who behave in accordance with these prescriptions in their relationships with all the other people involved with their projects will, over time, build around themselves a network of competent teams held together by mutual trust. Such networks provide the very best basis for successful construction project organizations.

15 *General theory*

The preceding 14 chapters have used a combination of theory drawn from many sources and descriptions of contemporary practice to describe a general theory of construction project management. It is presented in a manner designed to provide practical advice for practising managers. However, having reached this point, it is now appropriate to add a formal description of the general theory implicit in the preceding chapters. This must begin by describing the basic elements used in the general theory.

Basic elements

Construction projects need to achieve a balance between the objectives of the customer, the project organization, the nature of the product and the environment. This idea is illustrated in Figure 1.1. We know that construction project managers need models of each of these four key elements in order to manage the direct manufacturing and construction work. The work of creating the models is undertaken by design and management teams. The work of teams undertaking design, management, manufacturing and construction is usefully described in terms of days-work for teams. The whole point and purpose of construction project management is to create conditions that enable the teams who make up project organizations to carry out days-work efficiently.

Efficiency is measured in terms of the output : input ratio for whole projects. The most fundamental practical expression of this ratio is value : costs.

Thus the general theory tells us that construction project managers seek to maximize the value : cost ratio using models of objectives, project organizations, products and environments. Objectives are the independent variable; project organizations and products are dependent variables, and environments provide constraints. In other words, the construction project manager's task is to select the set of mutually consistent models of their project organization and its product which maximize the value : cost ratio and which satisfy the customer's objectives within the constraints imposed by the environment; and then to turn the models into reality.

The relationships between project organizations and products are complex. Each influences the other in much the same ways as do chickens and eggs; and it is just as idle to debate which takes priority. The nature of the product influences the project organization, and the nature of the project organization influences the product. Both influences are strong and both are important in construction project management.

The concept of days-work for teams combines the models of project organization and product, at a practical level, into a single description. The descriptions of all the days-work which comprise a complete construction project are produced by designers and managers in cooperation. In simple projects a single person can be both designer and manager. A complex project requires many design teams and many management teams to produce a description of all the days-work required to undertake and complete it. Whatever design and management workforce is required, their practical work mixes together the theoretically separate models of the project organization and the product. In practice, of course, managers' work is primarily concerned with models of the project organization and designers' work with models of the product. However, as with the chicken and the egg, each is constrained and conditioned by the other and so, except in theory, the two are tightly interlinked. Obviously in the real world project organizations produce products and then leave them. That is, in the real world products and project organizations are separable. It is the models of these things produced during the life of construction projects which are inextricably linked in descriptions of days-work for teams.

Descriptions of days-work specify the work that teams must do to make a contribution towards the production of an element of the product. This is the essential information which teams must have to undertake and complete a construction project. Construction project managers directly manage this information in order to influence the work of the teams which make up their project organizations. They use the skills of communication and negotiation to do so. Figure 15.1 illustrates these theoretical relationships. Like all useful models it is a considerable simplification of the real world.

Some of the more important simplifications include the idea that the customer's objectives are given to the construction project managers and designers in a one-way interaction. In practice the objectives of a construction project result from a rich two-way interaction which may continue throughout the life of a project. However in the final analysis, the fact that the customer has authority over his project, because he provides the finance, means that he can have the final say in determining the objectives. This is what the general theory assumes, as illustrated in Figure 15.1.

A second simplification is the idea that the interactions between the project organization and its various environments can be reduced to two one-way effects: constraints on managers and designers, and interference with teams.

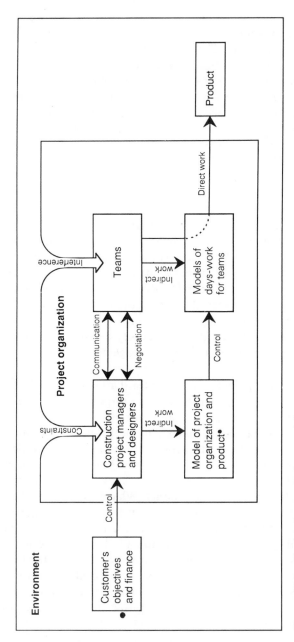

Figure 15.1 *Basic elements of general theory*

This simplification is inherent in the definition of environment which is used in the general theory. Features of what in everyday language are regarded as projects' environments, which managers, designers or teams seek to control in order to modify constraints or reduce interference, are regarded, in the general theory, as part of the project. The environment means those things to which the project organization has decided merely to react, rather than attempt to manage. In other words, in the theory, the interactions between project organizations and their environments are one-way. That includes the important interaction of delivering the product into the environment. It follows from the model's assumption that this is the only output, that the concept of product includes all the outputs of the project: intended and unintended, desirable and undesirable, as well as planned and unplanned.

The third simplification inherent in the model which warrants comment is the idea that teams produce the descriptions of their own days-work. This is carried out under the control of managers and designers. Control is exercised through direct communication and negotiation and indirectly by supplying models of the project organization and product. The nature of this simplification is that it ignores the practical reality that the boundary between those aspects of their work decided by teams and those decided by managers and designers varies considerably. It varies between different projects, but it also varies between different teams within the same one project. Indeed, the particular point at which this boundary is drawn is one of the key determinants of the nature of individual construction projects, from a management viewpoint.

The final important simplification is the idea that managers and designers can be separated from the teams which make up project organizations. Linked to this is the idea that the project description moves through just two distinct stages: models of the project organization and product, and models of days-work for teams. These sharp distinctions are important theoretically but are often difficult to identify precisely in practice. Managers and designers form parts of teams which produce a continuum of models in ever finer detail which are eventually fully realized in the product. What this means is that real world teams are regarded, by the general theory, as managers and designers while they are dealing with customers' objectives and finance, and environmental constraints, while they are producing models of the project organization and product, and while they are seeking to control the work of other teams through communication and negotiation. The same real world teams are regarded as teams while they are producing models of their own days-work and while they are undertaking the direct work of manufacturing and constructing the product. It is perhaps useful to regard this distinction as being between project strategy and tactics. Some real world teams will be very largely or possibly even entirely concerned with strategy, and others entirely or almost entirely with tactics.

Others, mainly middle management teams, will be concerned more or less equally with both. Figure 15.2 illustrates the range of teams' work patterns likely to occur within construction projects.

One implication of this view is that the concept of team encompasses not just the people who make up a team but also the factories, plant, equipment, materials and components they need in order to undertake their work. That is, the concept of team includes everything necessary for the work of teams except project specific information.

The final general point about the model in Figure 15.1 which must be made is that it describes an open system which develops over time. The overall structure of the system does not alter, but the form and nature of the basic elements, which make up that structure, develop throughout the life of a project. The task of construction project managers is to so manage this development that at the completion of the project the product meets the customer's objectives efficiently. Essentially, this means maintaining the appropriate balance between the models of the project organization and of the product in the face of changes in the environment and any alterations to the customer's objectives; and ensuring that these models control the work of the teams which make up the project organization.

Organization and product

Within any one construction project the nature of the product determines the teams required to form the project organization; and the teams determine the nature of the product. This interdependent relationship begins when the customer appoints a team and states his objectives.

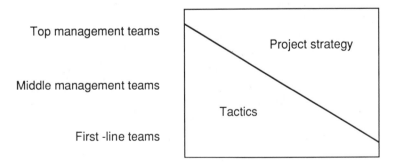

Figure 15.2 *Teams' work patterns*

Customers' objectives influence the appropriate project organization and product. They may do this directly by specifying some features of one or the other. Alternatively, the objectives may exert an indirect influence by establishing constraints within which the project must work.

Once a project has been initiated by a customer, the managers and designers whom he appoints develop models of the project organization and product. They work through a series of approximations. Each successive pair of models is more detailed and precise than its predecessor. That at least is the intention. The difficulty of this task and the uncertainty surrounding it mean that false starts and blind alleys cause progress to be less than smooth. However, despite the existence of irregularities in the progress of construction projects, the overall pattern is of managers and designers producing a series of increasingly detailed and precise models.

The models exist to fill the gap between the knowledge, values and skills already possessed by the teams who will make up the project organization and that required for them to undertake their direct work efficiently. Teams competent to undertake a range of work exist in all local construction industries. Taken together all the teams in any local construction industry possess a wide range of competences. These include management, design, manufacturing and construction competences. The teams tend to cluster together in networks relating to families of products. Figure 15.3 illustrates a hypothetical local construction industry. It shows the firms in the industry classified in terms of their main competency and in terms of the family of products that dominates their work. It also shows three projects, X, Y and Z, at an early stage of development, mapped onto the categories of firms competent to produce the work required by the current version of the product design.

Project X provides a straightforward situation. As long as it is developed within product family E, it will be relatively easy to set up an efficient project organization. It could develop within product family A or C but in so doing would face potential problems with work categories 13 and 14. Competent local firms exist in these two work categories, but they would need to be brought into the product network and their induction would require additional management and design effort. Alternatively, the work giving rise to the need for category 13 and 14 teams could be eliminated from the design. It could be replaced with work from a category which fits within whichever product family is eventually selected. In other words, as the project progresses there are considerable organizational benefits in deliberately ensuring that decisions keep it within one well developed family of products.

Project Y is self-evidently a relatively complex project. As such it does not fit neatly into any product family. Firms competent to provide all the required

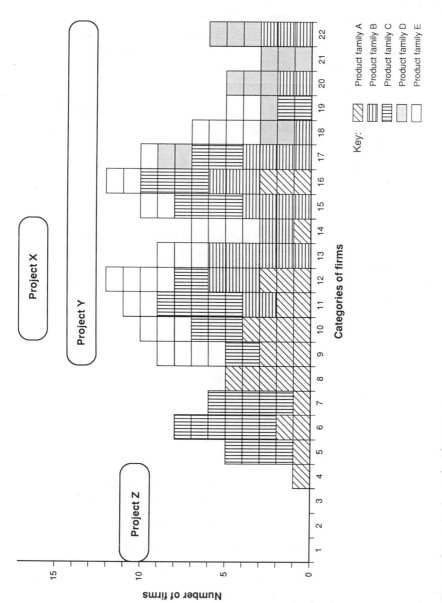

Figure 15.3 *Local construction industry*

categories of work exist locally but special attention will be required to weld them into an efficient project organization. It may be most effective to base the project organization on firms drawn mainly from one product family. Families B and E provide obvious possiblities. The strategic choice facing the project organization is either to modify the design so that the project fits within an established family of products, or to accept the additional management and design costs involved in setting up a project organization comprising teams which are not used to working together.

Project Z, in terms of the local industry, is clearly intended to produce an innovative construction. It will require considerable management and design effort to achieve an efficient project organization. The saving grace is that the project is relatively simple and so the cost premium incurred should be reasonably predictable. Nevertheless, there will be considerable costs in bringing new firms into the local area and welding them into a project organization which can operate efficiently.

Figure 15.3, with its hypothetical industry and projects, serves to illustrate the general nature of the relationships between project organizations and products. The easiest way to identify the general principles at work is to think in terms of the costs associated with the different situations. The term cost is used here in the same way as it is normally used by economists. That is, the cost of anything is equal to the most attractive alternative given up in order to obtain it. Thus costs may be measured in terms of money, time or any other resource.

The general theory assumes that each different category of work has a reasonably stable basic cost. That basic cost arises when an experienced team has the knowledge, values and skills needed to undertake its work efficiently. Such a team has progressed a long way down the learning curve and therefore brings to each new project a well practised approach to its work. So when it is given a clear work space and is not interrupted by other teams it is likely to achieve the basic level of costs.

The basic cost of different categories of work is different. However, within any one category all the experienced, efficient firms achieve the same or at least very similar basic costs.

In addition, projects incur management and design costs. These vary depending on the difficulty of creating conditions which enable teams with relevant experience to work efficiently. Management and design costs depend on the extent to which a relevant product network exists locally. Where one exists, teams bring with them established habits of working that fit neatly together into a project organization which requires the minimum of project specific management and design. Where a suitable product family does not exist, teams must be informed and trained in appropriate methods of working and persuaded to adopt them. All of this incurs additional costs compared with simply using an existing network of teams.

All management and design costs increase with increases in the difficulty of projects. Bennett and Ormerod (1984) describe research which suggests that management and design costs increase geometrically with increases in difficulty. That is, as projects are more complex, bigger, less repetitive, less certain and face tougher customer imposed constraints, their management and design costs increase rapidly. Figure 15.4 illustrates the general character of these relationships added to a plausible pattern of basic costs based on the learning curve. The figure suggests that the total costs of units of construction vary considerably with changes in the inherent difficulty of the project. This is consistent with Bennett and Ormerod's research.

Given the relationships illustrated in Figure 15.4, the strategic decisions faced by the managers and designers appointed to take responsibility for a construction project are to select the degree of difficulty and the related level of costs

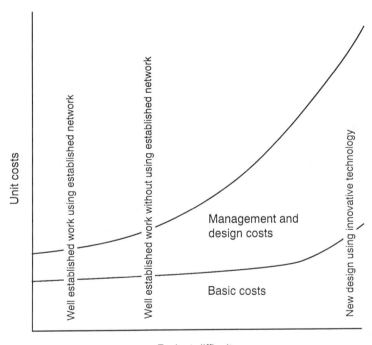

Figure 15.4 *Project costs*

which most nearly meet their customer's objectives. Having done so, their further responsibility is to develop the project in a manner which delivers the product implicit in their strategic decisions. In doing this it is important to remember that Figure 15.4 illustrates a range of essentially different projects, each of which is delivered efficiently. The greater costs associated with increases in difficulty cannot be avoided, for example, by reducing the resources devoted to management. All that happens when too little management is provided is that basic costs rise rapidly and increase the total costs. Similarly, if too much management and design effort is provided, the basic costs cannot be reduced sufficiently to pay for the excessive provision of management resources. Therefore total costs increase. In other words, Figure 15.4 illustrates minimum costs for each level of difficulty. It is the responsibility of construction project managers and designers, in developing their projects, to keep them as close as possible to the optimum mix of basic costs, and management and design costs.

Project development

The overall shape of construction project organizations and the pace at which it is prudent to appoint teams to form them depends on the full set of key project factors described in Chapter 1: complexity, size, repetition, uncertainty, speed and economy. These combine to determine the difficulty of the project. Obviously, they are capable of generating a huge variety of real world projects. Theory, however, for the reasons explained throughout this book, simplifies the real world. Chapter 9 provides one important simplification by classifying project organizations into just three categories: programmed, professional and problem-solving. The classification is related to the use of fully standard solutions or one-off innovative solutions. It provides a sufficient basis to describe the development of construction projects, with two major exceptions. The size of projects and the nature of their environments have direct and separate effects. Consequently, the ensuing description is arranged in three parts under the subject titles which are conventionally used in general management literature: technology, size and environment. This treatment of organization theory closely follows the approach used by Mintzberg (1979). He adds power and fashion as other determinants of organization structure, but the view taken here is that neither a powerful actor nor current fashion should be allowed to overrule the influence of technology, size and the environment.

Technology

Projects begin with the appointment of one or at most two teams: a manager and a designer. Initially they may have available, as project specific information, nothing beyond a very general and vague description of the customer's objectives. From this point, projects develop to produce one of the many different products which could have satisfied the customer's objectives. For this to happen, the initial, general and vague description must be developed into precise and detailed descriptions of the direct work required from all the teams who make up the complete project organization. This progression moves through distinct stages marked by key decision points. The pace of this development is dependent on the form of technology employed in the product.

It is obviously efficient to begin the direct manufacturing and construction work of projects as quickly as possible. Time has costs and so, everything else being equal, the first-line teams undertaking the direct work should be committed to projects early. On the other hand, it is sensible to appoint teams on the basis of a full understanding of the work they are required to carry out. This allows major bargains to be reasonably comprehensive and leaves subsidiary transactions to deal with only minor issues. To achieve this desirable state of affairs requires construction project managers and designers to produce a sufficiently full understanding of the work required from a first-line team for it to provide a sensible basis for a major bargain. Ideally this should define, if not days-work, at least weeks-work in considerable detail. The further a project departs from this ideal, the more management resources will be needed during the execution of the work. This is because, in the absence of a precise and detailed major bargain, the work eventually decided upon must be coordinated with the work of other teams in real time. In other words, the subsidiary transactions become extensive and complicated. Figure 15.5 shows the ideal arrangements and the problems likely to be encountered by projects which depart from them, by committing first-line teams either too early or too late. The figure links the timing to the general nature of the technology assumed by the product design. When fully standard solutions are used, first-line teams can be committed to the project early. When one-off, innovative solutions are used, the first-line teams which will be required cannot be identified until very much later in the life of projects.

The same general principles apply to teams at all levels. They should be committed to projects as soon as their work can be defined within the limits of their natural time discretion. Therefore, in the terms used in Figure 15.5, a complete project organization can be established early where a fully standard solution is used. However, in the case of projects using one-off innovative solutions, it may be unwise in the early stages to commit more than managers and designers at levels four and five; or, in the case of mega-projects, levels six and seven. It is only when these managers and designers have worked out the nature and character of their project in more detail that further teams can be added. The new teams will also need to make progress on their own work before sufficient is known about the direct manufacturing and construction work, to make it sensible to appoint first-line teams. So we see that technology exerts a direct influence on the way in which construction project organizations are developed.

Size

In Chapter 10 we suggested that a construction project takes one year and has a five-level project organization. Mega-projects take longer, comprise a number of projects, and require seven-level organizations. Smaller projects can be regarded as less than full projects and may well require organizations comprising fewer levels.

However, not all one year projects are the same size. Therefore, to maintain the ideal number of levels of management, differences in project size must be absorbed by differences in the size of the teams employed to form the project organization. Figure 5.4 illustrates the existence of this effect. It is based on Woodward's (1965) research into the actual organizations she found in many different industries. She linked the differences in the most successful of the

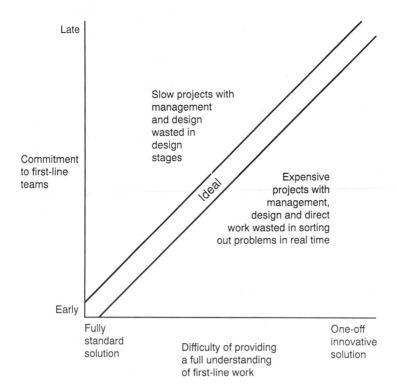

Figure 15.5   *Timing of project development*

organizations which she studied to differences in their technology. However, within each technological group, size also exerts effects which are sufficiently consistent to lead us to the conclusion that project size exerts an influence on the size of teams. Woodward's work suggests that within large programmed organizations (which she found in mass-production industries) the larger teams will be concentrated in the first line; and in large professional organizations (which she found in unit-production industries) the larger teams will be concentrated in the middle management. It is harder to make a simple one-to-one link between Woodward's research and large problem-solving organizations in construction. It is perhaps tempting to draw an analogy between her process-production industries with their large top management teams, and problem-solving mega-projects with their extra levels of top management and a duplication of managers at each level arising from their use of matrix structures. However, innovative constructions employ technology which is entirely unlike that employed in process production. It is much more like that of unit-production. Therefore we must stick to the conclusion reached in Chapter 5, that process production organizations are more likely to provide a directly useful model for the construction industry of the twenty-first century, rather than for contemporary practice. However, one of the roles of problem-solving organizations is to explore possible future project organizations. They are not solely concerned with product innovation. Accepting this, suggests that, in construction, problem-solving organizations may share characteristics which Woodward found in unit production and process-production industries. That is, larger teams are likely to be found both in top and in middle management. This is consistent with the use of a matrix structure in the early stages of problem-solving projects based on distinct responsibilities for management and design.

These ideas are summarized in Figure 15.6. In combination with the ideas in the earlier section on technology, they provide us with a general theory of the influence of size on construction project development. It tells us that, in large projects, large teams appear at the lowest level in the project hierarchy at which teams can sensibly be committed early. Thus, in large programmed organizations where complete project organizations can be committed early, large teams tend to be concentrated in the first line.

In professional organizations, where early appointments are drawn from an ever-proliferating range of distinct construction professions, large teams appear in the middle management level inhabited by these professionals. This arises because it is efficient for the traditional first-line teams to remain at their normal and most efficient size. Large professional projects require more of these first-line teams, which causes the middle management span of control to increase. As soon as it is decided to adopt traditional construction and a professional organization, the middle management level professionals can be committed,

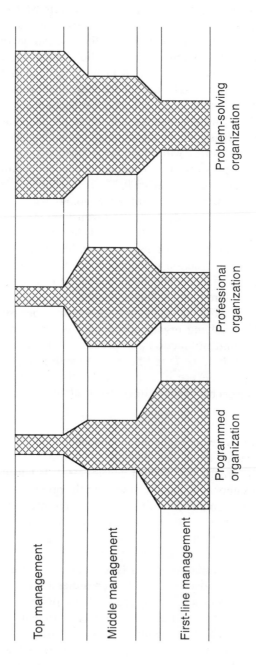

Figure 15.6 *Spans of control in large project organizations*

which is consistent with the theory that large teams will occur at the lowest level where teams can be committed early.

Finally, in large problem-solving organizations, early commitments are restricted to top management. They must undertake a great deal of exploratory strategic work before it becomes clear what type of teams are needed at lower levels. Hence, large teams occur at the top of large problem-solving organizations and are appointed early. However, reasonably large teams occur also in the middle management levels of large problem-solving projects. They do so for the same kind of reasons as large middle-management teams are needed in large professional organizations. That is, first-line teams dealing with new types of work must be small to be efficient. On large projects, many such teams are needed and so middle management is faced by wide spans of control.

Large teams are unlikely to be committed right at the start of projects. The theory does not imply this, but it does suggest that, as project organizations develop and the need for large teams becomes apparent, they will tend to occur at the levels illustrated in Figure 15.6, that is, the lowest level at which it is sensible to commit teams early.

Mintzberg (1979) suggests that size also increases the need for coordination devices. Relating this idea to our previous analysis of the use of coordination devices in construction project organizations, as summarized in Figure 9.5, suggests that we can expect to find in large programmed organizations considerable use of procedures and targets, significant use of professionalization, and some use of project control information systems, in addition to the large first line within the management hierarchy we have just described. In large professional organizations, we can expect to find extensive use of procedures, professionalization and targets, elaborate information systems, and some use of lateral relations, in addition to a large middle level of the management hierarchy. In large problem-solving organizations, we can expect to find extensive use of all the coordination devices.

These effects will be strong in large, complex projects. However, where great size is achieved by means of repetition, the need for increased coordination will be weaker. This is because, everything else being equal, greater size and greater complexity make projects more difficult to manage, and greater repetition makes management easier.

Environment

The environment interferes with the planned progress of construction projects. The less predictable the environment and the greater its potential effects, the more it must be taken into account in managing the development of construction projects. The environment influences construction project organizations in two distinct ways.

First, project organizations should make explicit provision for significant risks posed by their environments. There are a number of different approaches to handling risks. All affect project organizations either indirectly or directly. They can be regarded as being either some form of insurance or direct action to counter the effects of the hostile features of a project's environment.

Insurance has an indirect effect on project organizations. Its influence is that it uses resources which are therefore no longer available to the project organization.

Direct action essentially involves bringing additional expertise into a project organization to protect it from a potential threat from its environment. Obvious examples include: appointing a designer with an established reputation for dealing with difficult local authority planning regulations, as part of a project organization expected to produce a controversial design; appointing a recently retired and much respected trade union official, as part of a project organization expected to face difficult labour relations; appointing a very experienced buyer, as part of a project organization expected to have difficulty ensuring a smooth supply of materials and components; and appointing a leading member of the green movement, as part of a project organization expected to arouse opposition over environmental issues. These internal experts may attempt to manage the threatening environmental feature and so bring it inside the project boundary. Alternatively, they may decide to help the project organization react to the threat and so continue to regard it as an environmental feature. In either case the project organization is made bigger and the internal experts must be taken into account in designing the project's management subsystem.

So the first way in which projects' environments influence their organization is either to cause resources to be expended on insurance, which resources are therefore not available for the management work, or to exert a direct effect by increasing the level of expertise required, which in turn increases the size or complexity of the project organization.

The second type of effect is that, faced with an unpredictable and threatening environment, project organizations should remain flexible and uncommitted for as long as possible. They should keep options open, explore several solutions in parallel, and develop fallback positions in known and established designs. Then, if the environment interferes in some major way, it is easier and cheaper to reform the organization to meet the new situation. In this way projects are less likely to be thrown completely off course by a difficult environment. It is sensible also to give early consideration to potential threats from projects' environments and seek the views of a range of experts as to the probable effects. Such an analysis helps in making judgements about how far ahead project organizations can be committed, without facing unacceptable risks. Both types of direct effect on project organizations incur additional costs which should be evaluated against the costs of insurance in deciding how to respond to a difficult project environment.

Construction project managers' behaviour

The general theory deals with construction project managers' behaviour in addition to the ideas concerned with organization structure described thus far in this chapter. There are two important general ideas about managers' behaviour within construction projects.

The first is that cooperation and trust are more efficient than competition. This requires managers to create conditions that build cooperation and trust within their project organizations. Cooperation and trust come from good experiences in working with others. They take time to build up. Therefore managers need to behave in ways which encourage the development of long term, cooperative and trusting relationships.

The first general idea about behaviour within construction projects in no way denies that competition is necessary to provide a spur to innovation and creativity. However, productive competition takes place between projects not inside projects. Competition between projects requires that customers are able to make informed comparisons between the range of products available to them. Hence managers need to provide good published information about the performance of clearly defined families of construction products.

The second general idea about construction project managers' behaviour is that efficiency in construction projects derives from competent teams working comfortably within their own ability and quite separately, but being challenged to improve their performance norms. This requires managers to encourage the teams that make up their project organizations to undertake training to steadily enhance their knowledge and skills. It also requires managers to encourage the work of innovation groups throughout their projects so that good ideas are channelled into genuine innovation.

Some of the behaviour required from construction project managers depends on consistent support from their firms which extends beyond the life of any one construction project. However, long term strategies directed at improving construction's efficiency are to a large extent implemented through actions taken on individual projects. Therefore all of the requirements listed earlier in this section are legitimate demands on the behaviour of construction project managers. They fall into four main categories: training and innovation, building cooperative networks, satisfying demanding customers, and competition between projects.

Training and innovation

Construction projects cannot be efficient unless the local construction industry comprises competent people who keep themselves up to date and are continually looking for ways to improve productivity and standards. This requires steady long term action from firms to ensure that good training courses exist to serve the needs of all forms of modern construction. As described in Chapter 11, training must be supported by appraisal which is designed to give all workers a clear career pattern. Ensuring that construction has competent and forward-looking workers also requires firms to take innovation groups seriously. This means ensuring that time is made available for all workers to take part in innovation groups. One hour per week during working hours is the right provision. This must be backed up by training to ensure that the time is used productively. In addition, firms need to develop systems which ensure that practical innovations devised by the groups are put into effect and that successful groups are rewarded for good ideas.

The implementation of all of these policies is, to a large extent, a responsibility of individual construction project managers. The long term efficiency of all construction projects depends on managers giving themselves time, and allowing everyone involved with their project organizations time, to devote to preparing for their own futures. It means consistently demonstrating commitment to training by never cancelling or postponing attendance at a course. It means never allowing a crisis, no matter how serious, to be used as an excuse for cancelling an innovation group meeting. It is likely, in a crisis situation, that the group will decide for themselves to use their innovation group hour to consider solutions to the current problem. Equally, the group may well decide that direct attention to the crisis is even more pressing; but managers should never seek to impose such decisions. In other words, it must be clear that innovation group time belongs to the group, not to the manager.

In selecting teams for their projects, managers should draw them only from firms who are committed to training and the use of innovation groups. During their projects they should actively seek to foster project team spirit by organizing inter-firm training in general knowledge and skills relevant to modern construction. Also, they should encourage innovation groups to draw members from several teams with closely related work interests.

A clear commitment to the future health of construction means that project programmes and budgets must make explicit provisions for all the requirements of training and innovation groups. These provisions should be sacrosanct even when faced by customers demanding their reduction or removal. In these circumstances, two possibilities exist. First and ideally, all construction firms are resolute in maintaining their training and innovation groups. The second possibility is that only some firms undertake training and encourage the work of innovation groups.

In the first case, customers will need to be educated in the benefits of a competent, forward-looking industry and made aware of the increased value for their money which it provides. One good way of doing this is to bring customers into training courses and innovation groups, as a way of helping them to understand and use their own construction facilities more efficiently.

In the second situation, where not all firms invest in their own future competence, those that do have an easier task in persuading customers not to cut this investment. Since those which train and innovate become more competent, they can simply undercut competitors who do no training and who fail to capture the good ideas of their workforces through innovation groups.

It must be said, however, that all too often practitioners see investment in the future simply as a cost. They fail to recognize the benefits and so make short-sighted and false economies in their training budgets and do nothing to encourage innovation. This brings us right back to the second idea about behaviour in the general theory; efficiency in construction projects derives from competent teams working comfortably within their own ability and quite separately, but being challenged to improve their performance norms. Since there is very substantial evidence that this is true, it is safe to take the view that training and innovation groups give firms a competitive advantage over those who fail to invest in their own future competence.

Building cooperative networks

In a fragmented construction industry the benefits of training and innovation groups can all too easily be dissipated when teams leave a project on completion of their work. The lessons learnt, especially the organizational lessons, can be forgotten on the next project when teams are faced with new people and new situations. The best way of ensuring that valuable new knowledge and skills are retained is by deliberately building long term, cooperative networks made up of teams drawn from separate firms. As Porter (1990) has demonstrated, efficient firms cluster together and reinforce each other. Such virtuous clusters or networks need to be fostered by construction project managers. They also require action from firms.

Construction firms need to build long term relationships which bring together customers, designers, managers, manufacturers and constructors. It is most likely, since they are responsible for project organizations, that firms providing construction project management, either as a separate service or in combination with other parts of the whole construction process, will take the lead in forming and sustaining networks. Doing this means identifying firms able and willing to work together efficiently to produce a range of distinct construction products. It means continuously searching for ways of improving the performance of networks formed from such sets of firms. This requires, for example, that the construction management firm regularly appraises the performance of the individual teams and then acts to reinforce strengths and eliminate weaknesses so that the network as a whole becomes more efficient over time. Creating cooperation and trust requires networks to work on a completely open-book basis, so that decisions are based on actual input costs, rather than market determined output prices. It means deliberately seeking opportunities for joint activities, both social and directly work-related. It means taking every possible opportunity to build up trust between the firms and never doing anything which breaches that trust. This includes, for example, accepting joint responsibility for the profitability of all the firms involved in any one project and equally joint responsibility for problems. Such an approach is far more efficient than spending time trying to allocate blame or tackling problems by fighting a battle to determine who has the strongest case. Given trust, all firms can accept that everyone involved is doing their best and that solving problems is a common responsibility. Equally, if a project goes very well and generates unexpectedly high profits, they should be widely shared.

As we suggested earlier, this behaviour and these attitudes are most likely to emanate from strategic decisions by firms providing construction project management. It is, however, for individual managers within these firms to give day-to-day expression to these strategies. This means that, like good negotiators, managers must be generous to their teams in encouraging, helping and rewarding them, but at the same time be absolutely tough in demanding excellent work delivered exactly on programme. In return, managers must ensure that the teams which make up their project organizations earn the most important reward of all for their firms, that is, repeat business. Building up long term relationships is a crucially important responsibility of all managers.

These ideas on behaviour do not assume that all teams will behave well, even when they are dealing with excellent customers, managers and designers. Not everyone is well intentioned, and just as society at large needs a police force so managers must deal with wrong-doers within their projects. Individuals and teams who fail deserve a second chance but not a third, fourth and fifth. Managers must root out ineffective parts of their networks. Individuals or teams who fail, who have been given opportunities to improve but who still fail, must be replaced.

Too many construction project managers in practice fail to deal decisively with weak individuals and teams. It is this failure which gives rise to the only real and serious doubt about the value of cooperative networks. This is that, over time, they become too cosy and rather than fostering productivity and high standards they breed sloppiness and inefficiency. The most important check that prevents these bad effects emerging is to ensure that managers have to deal with demanding customers.

Satisfying demanding customers

Construction project managers should encourage the emergence of sophisticated, demanding customers. This is because such customers push industry into ever better performance and ever faster and more imaginative innovation. Lazy, pliant customers have the opposite effect; they tend to allow construction to become slow, sloppy and backward. They allow networks to become corrupted by self-seeking and confrontational attitudes.

Successful and demanding customers should be drawn into construction networks. They should be encouraged to state their real requirements, no matter how far-fetched they may seem in the light of current technology. They should be involved in working out good solutions, they should have standing invitations to project meetings; they should be involved in training and innovation groups; they should attend social occasions; and they should be active in giving rewards for achieving targets and having good ideas.

Most of all, customers must be involved in defining the performance criteria for construction projects. This means that they should help to establish exactly what contributes to value for the customer and exactly what constitutes cost to the customer. How is value to be measured? How are costs to be accounted for? What is the influence of time on these measures? How are they affected by quality and standards? Customers should be involved in answering these questions.

Managers need to be active in encouraging their customers to become fully involved in defining the values, objectives and constraints of their construction projects. Equally, customers should be given every opportunity to follow up and if necessary reinforce the effects of their demands on the whole project organization. Nothing has such a decisive effect on the performance of the construction industry as striving to satisfy well informed and demanding customers.

One very important benefit is that ideas flow into construction from the experiences of successful customers. The Japanese construction industry provides many examples of this synergy. Their application of just-in-time thinking derives from working closely with customers who apply such ideas in their own hugely successful manufacturing businesses. The Japanese development of construction robotics is influenced by long term customers who use robots successfully in their own industries. Similar examples of fruitful ideas emerging from demanding customers exist in other construction industries. As Porter (1990) makes clear, this phenomenon is found in all internationally competitive industries. It is a foolish construction project manager who does not seek the benefits of working with successful and demanding customers.

Competition between projects

The final essential behaviour for construction project managers is that they must compete. Competition between whole construction project organizations provides a major spur to efficiency. Competition between parts of construction project organizations (for example, between architects, structural engineers, foundation contractors or bricklayers) is damaging. It tends to distort project organizations, leads to an emphasis on narrow esoteric goals of little real value to customers, and generally detracts from the efficiency of projects. So managers need to encourage the teams that make up their whole project organizations to cooperate in competing with other construction projects.

There are two levels of competition. First is competition between projects within the same network. This should be friendly competition. Managers should seek to achieve the very best performance but do so in ways which do not damage other projects being handled by their own network. Also, good ideas should be fed back into the network's information systems so that all may benefit. Nevertheless, within these constraints of friendly competition, each manager should strive hard to make his current project the best within the network.

The second level of competition is ruthless. It is an all-out fight to deliver better products, faster, more reliably, at lower costs, and backed up by more comprehensive guarantees and aftersales care than any other network is capable of providing. Competitive products, as described in Chapter 10, are essential for a healthy and efficient construction industry. They arise out of direct head-on competition between construction project managers, their project organizations and the networks of which they form a part, and other managers and organizations in other networks. It is this competition which drives the search for competence and innovation and which encourages customers to be ever more demanding. As Porter (1990) suggests, at its most effective, this ruthless competition is based on intense rivalry, even outright hatred between competing organizations. It forces managers to blow their own trumpets, to boast of their projects' successes and to market their products aggressively. One important consequence is that, in so doing, managers are very likely to create a public image of a vital and exciting industry.

Practice and theory

The general theory described in this chapter deals with the structure of construction project organizations, the way they develop over time and the behaviour of managers within those organizations. Like the rest of the book, apart from Chapters 6–8, it provides a set of idealized models of construction projects. The general theory represents a gross simplification of practice in order to make it understandable. It is intended to help practitioners to make good decisions about their own projects. It is for them to wrestle with the complexity and uncertainty of real world construction projects and, if they wish, to relate them to the general theory for guidance on appropriate decisions. In so doing they will undoubtedly identify parts of the general theory which need revision. It is in this way, theorizing, applying the theories, and then improving them where they prove to be inadequate, that our knowledge grows. It is in the minds of practitioners that the general theory will make its most important contribution to the efficiency of the construction industry. For, as the general theory tells us, success in construction projects comes when we place our trust in competent people working within a clear framework of values and objectives, which they have helped to shape and so feel that they own. Excellence is born in the minds of construction project managers and then grows and flourishes into construction products which the whole industry can take pride in creating.

This book offers one final piece of help. It is to look ahead to the beginning of the twenty-first century. Chapter 16 assumes that the world's economy continues reasonably successfully, without any major, global-scale catastrophies, through the 1990s. With the confidence to look forward, which this assumption provides, the final chapter of the book uses the general theory to roll forward the strong trends already evident in the construction industries of the world's three great trading blocks. It does this in order to describe an ideal global construction industry for the year 2001. In other words, it provides a model for the construction industry's leaders in planning the futures of their own firms.

16 Global construction 2001

The need for the products of the world's construction industries is growing. It is growing because the world's population continues to expand and at an ever faster rate. It passed one billion in 1830, two billion in 1925, three billion in 1962, four billion in 1975, and is expected to be six billion by 2001. The United Nations and the World Bank foresee the possibility of the world's population stabilizing at around ten billion during the course of the next century.

The absolutely minimum needs of all these people are a secure home, clean air and water, wholesome food and safe waste disposal. In addition, they need education and health care. They need places to exercise and play, and places to be alone.

Providing for these simple needs, for the whole population of the world, will require many things to turn out well. Inevitably, construction has a major part to play. Most importantly, this is in helping to create a robust, sustainable basic infrastructure within which every individual in the world has the opportunity to take responsibility for themselves, their families and their local communities.

In parts of the world, mostly in the developed West, there is effective demand for much more than merely satisfying these basic needs. Many people are able to buy comfort, convenience, challenge and entertainment. They have the money to use global information systems and they want to travel the world at speed and in comfort. They have sophisticated houses in beautiful places, they demand health care which keeps them fit and active for at least 80 years, they want education and training which gives them interesting and meaningful work, and they want to live in safe, free communities which are close to nature yet are richly endowed with cultural and sporting facilities and as many other sources of stimulation as man's ingenuity can devise. In other words, each individual wants to stretch his mind and body so that he can fulfil his own potential. How widely it will be possible to satisfy these aspirations is very largely a political question concerned with how the world's wealth is to be distributed and used. Assuming that large numbers of relatively rich people will continue to exist, which seems very likely, construction will face a great diversity of demands.

Construction is deeply involved in realizing the dreams of the world's rich. However, in doing so, the role of the traditional construction industry is shrinking in relative terms. In the rich developing countries, construction often accounts for 20 per cent of gross national product. In rich developed countries it usually accounts for less than 10 per cent; construction's role has been taken over by newer industries producing more sophisticated products.

On the basis of these global trends, it seems likely that by 2001 there will be two very distinct construction industries. The first will be a straightforward development of today's established construction industries. It will depend on the site-based technologies of moving wet, heavy materials into place and cutting and fitting basic general materials and products. Where labour is cheap, the industry will be supported by primitive hand tools and simple equipment to provide access to workplaces. Where labour is expensive, relative to capital, the industry's work will be supported by power driven hand-tools and sophisticated machines and robots.

The second distinct construction industry will be based in factories. Site activities will be reduced to just one simple and minor part of complex and totally integrated production processes. This second industry will become increasingly distinct from the currently established sectors of construction. The relationship will perhaps become as tenuous as that between motor car manufacturers and the construction firms who build the roads on which the cars depend.

Established construction industries

The established construction industry which is likely to remain significant to 2001 and beyond, pretty much in its present form, is divided into two distinct categories. Both of these, in the main, use traditional construction and professional project organizations. The two categories are: local building and civil engineering. The differences between them will become more marked in the future and will very largely be based on the size of projects and of the markets they serve.

Local building

Traditional building construction is, and will remain, essentially local. Every village, town and city in the world needs its own local construction industry. It undertakes the repairs, maintenance, alterations, rehabilitation and small scale infill subprojects and projects required by local communities. These include small scale civil engineering work which will continue to be, as it is now, mixed into small building projects. The need to deal with, and fit in with, the existing built environment will continue to require individual craftsmanship and very local decisions. All of this can best be provided by small local firms organized into professional project organizations using traditional construction.

The general prospects for traditional building construction are for it to become a mature industry. The design, management and construction firms which make up the heart of traditional building construction will change slowly and in the main do so in response to external factors. The development of new materials and components by manufacturers will gradually change the technology employed. The development of information processing systems by the information technology industry will gradually change the working methods of designers and managers. The development of better hand-tools and more sophisticated plant and equipment by manufacturers will gradually change the working methods of the direct construction workers. Increased demands by society generally for greater energy efficiency, reduced pollution and more individual control over internal environments will alter the nature of traditional construction products. Customers wanting better value, higher standards and a faster response to their demands will, in places, push the industry into greater efficiency.

Overall, traditional building construction will remain much as it is now: in total a large industry, but made up of a large number of comparatively small firms. However, this sector of the industry is shrinking as a proportion of national economies and, in many parts of the world, is shrinking in absolute terms. The main factor which determines these characteristics is that this sector of the industry will remain labour intensive. This is so because of the small scale, individual character of work which necessarily has to be undertaken in and around existing constructions. Indeed, where sufficient space exists for a large project, it is likely that different technologies will be used. Thus small, local, traditional construction will remain essentially a low technology industry, based on individual hand craftsmanship, mostly of a simple nature. Except where the work is combined with speculative development, it is unlikely ever to be very profitable or to pay high salaries. It will provide a reasonably safe and steady career for many people around the world. However, its image of heavy, wet, dirty work in uncomfortable conditions will not generally appeal to the most talented young people. It is this poor image, as much as anything, which will cause the small, local, traditional sector of the construction industry to stagnate or shrink. It will make it difficult to recruit adequate numbers of the ambitious people who shape and develop growth industries.

Although it will not become a glamorous industry, where small and local traditional construction is taken seriously, especially where it is supported by good training, it will remain a significant sector of the construction industry. This will be helped by the activities of two important kinds of supporting actors.

The first is professional institutions and trade associations formed to bring individuals or small firms together, to further their own interests and to provide a more effective service to their customers. They will provide design, technical and managerial advice to their members and to their customers. They will publish standards describing good practice, ensure that suitable training courses exist, and operate skills certification schemes to give each individual a widely accepted record of his achievements. They will operate schemes which provide customers with guarantees of the proper performance of their members' services and products.

The second, and probably more important, type of supporting actors are the firms who manufacture the general materials and components used by traditional construction. They will invest in capital-intensive manufacturing plants, and in research and development to produce a steady stream of new and improved products. Where government and trade associations have failed to provide adequate training courses, the manufacturing firms will take initiatives, probably based on a franchise approach, in training and skills certification. They will back this up by providing excellent and well researched design and technical advice. This will increasingly be produced in an electronic form. Their aims, in these supporting activities, will be to ensure that their products are easy to use and are used properly.

Many manufacturers will become very large international firms, and as such will probably come to dominate this sector of the industry. Their main problem in attempting to provide coherent and visible leadership is that they do not produce a whole product in the eyes of the industry's customers. That is provided by the consultants and contractors who enter into direct contracts with the customers. Thus the image of this sector will remain one of a small, low-technology, fragmented industry despite the activities of the massive manufacturing firms.

The small and local sector of traditional construction will exist largely independently of the rest of the industry. When traditional craftsmanship is needed in other types of projects, it will be isolated in a separate and distinct subcontract. Where more sophisticated technologies are needed within a traditional project, they will generally be provided by a large firm drawn from a different sector of the industry. It will tend to have a direct contract with the customer, which will provide terms and conditions similar to those in other consumer industries.

One of the dangers for construction 2001 is that the dull and stolid, small-scale, local, traditional sector will be regarded by the general public as the whole of the construction industry. It is because of this very real danger that the other sectors are most likely to seek to become distinct and very different industries.

Civil engineering

Large scale traditional construction is likely to be restricted to relatively simple infrastructure projects. In the developed world, they will use sophisticated machines and robots to handle traditional materials and components. In much of the developing world, muscle power will substitute for the machines and robots. This sector of the industry will provide the world's major physical arteries (roads, railways, tunnels, bridges, pipelines and cablelines) and mould the physical environment to serve mankind's needs in runways, dams, harbours, storage vessels, reservoirs, wells and mines. This sector of the industry will comprise, much as it does now, large civil engineering consultants and contractors operating on a national and international scale.

The consistent engineering basis of the whole of this sector of the industry gives it a unity and coherence not found in sectors dominated by building. In part, this advantage derives from the relative difficulty and narrowness of the technical problems faced. It is often the case that the technological solution chosen by the designers determines the construction method in considerable detail. Therefore design and construction become one tightly integrated process dominated by civil engineering considerations. By comparison with the technological problems, management is relatively straightforward because projects tend to be shaped by the characteristics of large size and repetition. This advantage is reinforced by the existence of an unusually high proportion of competent managers in this sector. The reasons for this happy state of affairs arise from the long time-scale of the individual projects and the fact that designers and managers are drawn from a single professional base. This in turn means that there is time and opportunity for all of those within the profession who have management aptitudes to be identified and developed. Thus project management responsibilities in civil engineering are usually well handled, provided that customers are prepared to work within the industry's norms.

Historically, governments have provided most of the customers for large, international scale, traditional construction projects. They will retain a major influence on into 2001 and beyond. Their objectives have often been concerned primarily with issues of public accountability and the management of national economies. These do not provide direct or very sharp pressures on the industry to strive for efficiency. For example, projects have all too often been let to local firms in order to protect narrowly perceived national interests. However, the privatization of major utilities in many Western countries in the 1980s and 1990s promises to bring a different emphasis to the work of this sector. The commercial orientation of public-sector customers will present civil engineers with new and more difficult management tasks. They will be faced with more intense competition, as private-sector customers look for the best available deal, irrespective of the national origins of the consultants and contractors they employ. Consultants and contractors will be given tough budgets and pro-grammes by experienced customers who will expect these objectives to be achieved. Customers will be looking for firms able to offer comprehensive construction services, which may include finance, design, management, manu-facture, construction, operation and maintenance.

The large, international projects that make up this sector will continue to rely on traditional construction in the sense that they will utilize the well established work of professional organizations. However, civil engineering technology is unlikely to stand still. International competition will force firms to innovate and to research and develop new and more efficient technologies. There will be increased use of very sophisticated plant and equipment. The products them-selves will also become much more controllable and efficient. They will have sensors and expert systems built into their hardware so that, for example, roads will know the prevailing traffic conditions and so be able to advise motorists on the fastest routes. Public utilities will know the likely patterns of demand and so, by monitoring actual demand and the relevant environments, will be able to adjust production and the capacity of their distribution systems, in anticipation of events. Waste disposal will use biotechnology to recycle energy and basic materials. The energy industries will use smart materials which extract energy from light, air and water.

These and other ideas will be drawn into the industry by means of joint research with firms from the information, computer, chemical and biotechnology industries. These research ideas will be developed in concept constructions, some at least of which will be in space and marine environments. These research and development activities will be undertaken in parallel with the efficient, well established methods of this exciting sector of the industry. They will not be mixed arbitrarily into individual projects but will form separate problem-solving activities tailored to the needs of innovative constructions.

The need for long term investment means that civil engineering will become increasingly concentrated in larger and larger firms. They will to a great extent identify, create and manage their own markets on a global scale. They will recruit and train university graduates. They will build up integrated design, management and construction processes which, especially for the simpler and more repetitive projects, will become very largely automated. They will provide customers with a total service, and will provide and maintain important elements of the infrastructure which supports mankind's use of the world.

Construction project management in civil engineering will in the main operate within professional project organizations. However, a proportion of civil engineering projects will deal with recurring, straightforward problems which will benefit from adopting the methods of programmed organizations. These may include aspects of major road-building programmes, long pipelines or cablelines and similar repetitive constructions. Civil engineering will span the full range of construction types because, at the other extreme from standard constructions, will be projects designed to produce concept constructions using new civil engineering ideas. They will require problem-solving organizations. This diversity will lead inevitably to the emergence of more specialized managers within the civil engineering sector of construction 2001.

New traditional construction

We have now described how the first main sector of the construction industry of 2001 will be much like parts of the industry of today. It will be greatly influenced by two kinds of large firms. The first will research, develop and manufacture the general materials and components which the industry uses. They will also, where a local industry does not provide itself with suitable training, take steps to ensure that their products are used properly and that the industry's customers are provided with a sensible guarantee of good performance. The second kind of large firm in this sector of the construction industry will be the major engineering firms of consultants and contractors who between them design and manage large infrastructure projects. Both categories of firm will operate internationally. They will be self-sufficient, invest in their own futures, and actively seek to create and foster the markets for their products.

The other large scale actors in this sector of the industry will be trade associations, each representing many small, local builders, and the professional institutions representing small, local designers. They will be active in raising the level of competence of their members and in protecting their interests in dealing with customers, suppliers and government. Where the government does not provide adequate training courses they will seek to encourage the setting up of such courses. Where the government does not operate a skills certification scheme, they will run one for their members and supervise the establishing of clearly defined levels of achievement. They will foster and encourage research and development, publish work standards and statements of good practice and, where the law allows it, recommended terms and conditions for their members to use in contracts with customers.

The direct construction work in local building industries will be in the hands of small firms of craftsmen and in civil engineering will be very largely undertaken by increasingly automated machines or robots. Both technologies are properly regarded as traditional construction because they can rely on designers working independently, yet producing designs which are well understood by the local constructors. Both technologies will develop over time due mainly to initiatives by large firms. Consequently, progress will tend to be slow and steady. This is in stark contrast to the second main sector of the construction industry of 2001.

Emerging construction industries

The emerging sector of the construction industry is based on the factory production of sophisticated components. It draws in ideas and technologies from many sources in creating environments fit for the twenty-first century. So diverse are the sources of research, development, design, management, manufacturing, construction, marketing and finance that this sector of the construction industry already has no clear boundaries. However, at the heart of this ubiquitous industry are two distinct kinds of firm. By 2001 they will have developed so that each dominates a distinct sector of the industry.

The first kind of firm is described in Chapter 9 as construction system firms. They enter into direct contracts with customers to deliver complete constructions for a fixed price by a fixed date. The clearest models we have of such firms are those supplying the most important of construction's markets, that is, housing. The volume housebuilders already display many of the characteristics likely to be found, by 2001, in construction system firms providing a wide range of buildings and infrastructures.

The second kind of firm which will dominate a major sector of the emerging construction industry is being formed in today's problem-solving project organizations. In Hasegawa's (1988) words, they will become worldwide system organizers. By this he means construction firms who coordinate different companies, from different industries, from all around the world, to undertake the development of market needs, land use planning, design, construction management, procurement of machinery and components, and the maintenance and operation of the resulting constructions in such a way that customers' objectives are achieved. They will be global firms working alongside the global players from other industries. Indeed, it is entirely possible that some of the most important worldwide system organizers will come from the computer, aerospace or other project-based industries.

Construction system firms

Whenever a market can be created for the products of an integrated design, manufacture and construction process, an opportunity exists for construction system firms. Those that succeed on a major scale will do so by pursuing policies similar to the ones adopted by all global manufacturing firms. These policies are based on understanding their major markets and creating distinctive ways of satisfying local tastes and needs. The successful firms will create brand names which people trust and associate with good quality, reliability and value. They will develop low cost and reliable production systems. They will provide comprehensive services for their customers so that buying, using and owning their products is easy and enjoyable. They will guarantee their products and ensure that, if any defects occur, they are put right without question and without delay.

Marketing is crucial to the success of any construction system firm. They will need to become insiders in all their key markets, so that they fully understand the specific local needs. It is unlikely that they will find the best answers by accepting current practice or copying competitors. Successful firms are those which find something different and distinctive that serves a real need. This means that before a firm decides to enter a new market they should work with experienced and demanding customers. It means spending time with them as they use their existing constructions, and asking questions until basic fundamental needs are identified. All of this must be done very thoroughly. This means, if we take housing as an example, spending time in at least 200 houses in any given market and understanding how they are used and why they are used in that particular way. Only then is it sensible to begin the design of a product and the supporting services for that specific local market.

As Ohmae (1990) suggests, a good strategy is to identify key markets with strong and distinctive traits and develop products to suit them. Thus, in housing, a firm could develop models to suit Japan, California, New York, Paris, the English country town, Switzerland, and so on. Each house model would be designed to suit the specific tastes and style of the local market. It would be tested and developed with the help of demanding customers so that it became a distinctive leading product in the key market. Then it can be sold, not only in the market it is designed for, but also in other markets. In this way it can be sold to all the people who happen to like the Japanese model, the Californian model, or whichever lifestyle and image appeals to them, wherever they happen to live.

Customers have worldwide information sources. They know how other people live. They know what is possible and so, when they see something which is attractive, they demand it. Satisfying well informed, demanding customers in a way that creates long term, stable markets requires more than just hardware. Distinctive products are a combination of hardware and software. This means, for example, that housing system firms will need to create living, vibrant communities. They will need to build neighbourhoods, which give individual families peaceful, secure, good quality living environments, which also have easy access to work, shops, restaurants, leisure and cultural facilities. They will need to support families when they first move into an area, provide them with local information, be active in encouraging local clubs and societies, and create a distinct sense of place which people can learn to love.

Having discovered how to create successful communities, firms also need to ensure that all potential customers are aware of their products. The most effective means of doing this is to create a brand name which is associated with desirable and successful products. Brand loyalty is a very powerful force and may in fact be the only constant factor in a global firm's operations. As manufacturing and construction are increasingly subcontracted to wherever reliable low cost producers can be found, brands in fact relate to constantly changing, multinational collections of companies. In such a world, brand names become the only stable factor to which customers can relate with any real confidence. Successful firms necessarily use the fact that customers develop faith in the quality and supporting services provided by their favourite brands, to build a secure market for their products.

The successful construction system firms of 2001 will be keenly aware of the value of brands. They will have spent years building up their image by advertising and by ensuring that they feature regularly in good news stories. They will employ specialists to ensure that there is a coherence and consistency to their image. All of these activities help to create a market for a firm's products. This is one important half of the secret of success. However, the other half is being able to deliver the products.

The very heart of every successful construction system firm is a finely tuned design, manufacture and construction system. Figure 16.1 shows the key elements in such a system, as it is likely to be in 2001. Sticking to housing as an example, the process is set in motion by a customer entering a showroom to browse through the available models. Figure 16.2 shows various models displayed in what is in effect a showroom for houses in Tokyo. It is an area of land open to the general public on which system house builders display their products. Customers can walk around the houses, browse through catalogues of the options available, and discuss their needs with local designers. Computer-aided design systems are used to help customers visualize possible designs and in effect to walk through their new home and play with different layouts and arrangements.

Once a customer is serious about buying a house, the available land and financial arrangements are matched to his needs. The actual house is designed by the customer and an experienced local designer working together. They work with a computer-aided design system, supported by expert systems which constrain decisions within what the local authority will allow and the firm's technology can provide. They select the style and feel of the house, the finishes, colours and patterns, and all the fittings, equipment, furnishings and controls needed by the family. The outcome is a firm and complete design, a fixed price and a guaranteed date for the customer to move into his new home. This information is then conveyed electronically to the firm's production control office. From this point on, by 2001, the process will be virtually automatic.

The production control office can be situated anywhere in the world. Its task will be to analyse the statement of the customer's requirements and turn it into integrated sets of instructions for manufacturers and site based constructors. In other words, the production office will fit the customer's requirements into their global manufacturing plans, organize the actual manufacturing to take place wherever reliable and low cost capacity exists, and ensure that the construction site receives an organized flow of components and instructions.

The instructions for manufacturing will comprise complete and precise details for all the components required for the house. They will be communicated electronically to the manufacturing subcontractors. This information will be

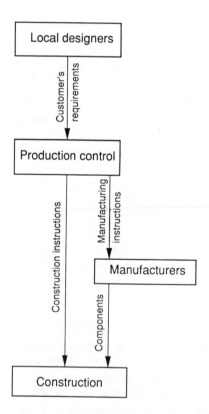

Figure 16.1 *Construction system firms' production system*

automatically checked by the subcontractor and then fed into their automatic manufacturing processes. They will deliver the components to site in the right sequence for the construction programme. Each component will be delivered so that it can be unloaded directly into its correct, predetermined position in the final product. The whole manufacturing and delivery process will be designed on just-in-time principles. These include, in particular, absolutely rigorous quality control which will ensure that defective components are not delivered to site. Also, the construction system firms will devote considerable efforts to monitoring and improving the productivity and standards of their already excellent manufacturers. As a consequence, the manufacturing and delivery process will provide very reliable input to a rapid site construction process.

The instructions for the construction process from production control will be communicated electronically to local construction managers and to the local designer assigned to the customer. The construction manager will organize the preparation of the site. This involves preparing a surface which is connected to the public services and is ready to receive the manufactured foundations and landscaping. The manufactured components will be handled almost entirely by robots supported by a small multi-skilled construction team. The local designer's task will be to check the quality and standards of the product and to ensure that the customer is completely happy with his new home. The actual construction team will usually be a locally based subcontractor, who is fully committed to the construction system firm. The construction subcontractors will be trained, retrained, financed and fully supported by the construction system firm. Some may grow into medium sized firms comprising many construction teams, and in some cases perhaps take over some of the other local responsibilities of the 'parent' firm.

The local representatives of construction system firms, whether direct employees or subcontractors, will be responsible for providing a complete service for customers. They will be tuned into the local political scene, anticipate local changes in fashion, culture and art, understand the economic forces that shape the local communities, and so be able to respond to their customer's real needs. By knowing the market, they will be able to help their firms to add real value to its products rather than simply adding more options, which is the only approach available to firms with poor local intelligence.

The local representatives will also provide an automated maintenance service. Each house will be monitored electronically, not merely as protection against burglars and terrorists, but to ensure that all the parts are working properly. Routine servicing will ensure that the house is running smoothly and efficiently and that the family is getting the maximum value from it. The local representatives will ensure that it is easy to extend or alter existing houses. Finally and to provide a complete cradle-to-grave service for customers' use of their products, the construction system firm will ensure that there is a rapid, convenient and fair market in second-hand houses.

Providing a full range of services in all the world's major markets may be difficult for firms working alone. There may well, therefore, be advantages in forming alliances with other firms who own a complementary range of distinctive products. Two-way agreements can give pairs of firms access to much bigger markets at low additional costs. By using each other's marketing and distribution systems where their own are weak, both firms can obtain a better return on their fixed capital investments.

Construction system firms will need to be flexible in other ways. For example, the needs of local markets may dictate that in places the construction system

(a)

(b)

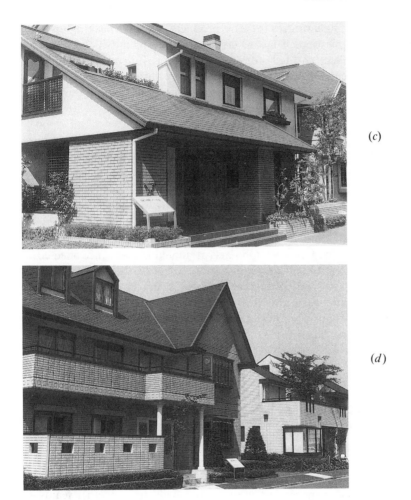

(c)

(d)

Figure 16.2 *Show houses in Tokyo*

firm will have to cater for do-it-yourself home builders in order to create a market. This may require selling basic houses which can be extended and upgraded over time. It may mean providing very easy payment terms. It may mean initially taking an equity share in houses. It may mean providing evening classes for self-build owners. The responsibility of the local organization is to create a market of committed, loyal customers and to do whatever it takes to achieve this essential objective.

A key part of creating customer loyalty is ensuring that they do not have problems with their existing homes. This means that the construction system firms will provide long guarantees for their products. It means backing up these guarantees without question. It means creating situations in which customers feel compelled to collect and tell stories of the wonderful service which *their brand* provides. It means ensuring that the houses are always working properly, so that running costs are low, users are comfortable, and an army of satisfied customers become the firm's major marketing force.

The reason for emphasizing marketing is that in a competitive business, with high fixed costs, the volume of sales very largely determines unit costs and therefore profitability. Ohmae's (1990) view is that manufacturing, research and development, and creating a brand name are unavoidable fixed costs for successful global manufacturing firms. Therefore expanding the total market and increasing their market share are crucially important to covering their fixed costs. Obviously firms must also generate sufficient income to cover variable costs and provide profits. However, Ohmae's argument is that, since fixed costs now predominate, sales volume is essential. In the long run, this can be obtained by housing system firms only by creating good living environments which people really want and need and then telling the world about them. These principles apply to all construction system firms, whatever type of products they choose to produce and market.

Worldwide system organizers

The second sector of the emerging construction industries uses industrialized components to produce individually designed products. At the heart of this part of the industry, by 2001, will be major construction project design and management firms. Some will comprise a single legal entity, and others a network of separate firms. In either case they will own an integrated, largely automated design and management system. They will bring together teams of designers, managers, manufacturers and constructors, drawn from wherever the required talents happen to reside, to tackle challenging construction projects. These separate teams will, in effect, be plugged into the integrated system to create a coherent project organization tailored to the needs of individual projects.

Ideally the teams assembled for any one project will all come from a long-established network of firms used to working together. However, the extent to which this will be possible in specific cases depends on the nature of the project. Indeed, the great strength of successful worldwide system organizers will be their ability to organize teams drawn from diverse backgrounds. While much construction in 2001 and beyond will be produced by firms who regard themselves as part of the construction industry, it is likely that important parts of many major constructions will be provided by firms from outside the industry.

The diversity of the teams which will make up this sector of the industry results from the nature of the constructions it will produce. They will be very sophisticated, high-technology, complex manufactured products. To a large extent they will shape the public's image of construction. They will set the fashion, both in appearance and performance, for other sectors to follow. It is the demands of this leading, trend-setting role which will require project organizations to bring in teams from outside the construction industry. They will help produce buildings, for example, which are able to monitor what is happening both inside and outside themselves and then, on the basis of that information, to create conditions for users which suit their individual needs for comfort and stimulation. The outside teams will help produce buildings in which the layout of spaces can be altered automatically using robots, so that users always have an ideal space for their activities. They will bring automated storage systems into all kinds of buildings, including the home, so that, for example, a wardrobe will record which clothes are worn each day by their owner. The wardrobe can then provide advice on a set of clothes to suit each new day's activities and locate whatever the owner decides to wear. The external teams will bring new materials into the industry, so that external envelopes can act like a human skin in controlling the internal temperatures. External envelopes will go even further in handling light by restricting, admitting or generating the correct amount for the particular activities underway at any one time. Buildings will monitor their own condition, carry out minor adjustments and repairs and, if necessary, call the plumber, electrician or computer operator to remedy a defect. In other words, buildings will become very smart indeed. The external infrastructure produced by this sector of the industry will also become intelligent, self-controlled and responsive to human needs.

Much of the hardware and software which will make these things possible will be researched, developed and produced by firms that fall outside the construction industry. Bringing them together with firms from within the construction industry, to form effective construction project organizations, will pose difficult problems. Firms able to solve these problems are likely to be large, multidisciplinary organizations. Their distinctive competence will be in dealing with firms and teams drawn from many backgrounds and fitting them into a coherent design and management framework. They will be able to assemble multidisciplinary teams to lead project organizations. who are comfortable discussing design and technological problems, who understand management theory and are experienced in applying it in practice, and who can deal with all the political, economic, legal, management, aesthetic and technical issues raised by major, innovative construction projects. It is by no means certain that such firms will regard themselves as part of the construction industry. It is just as likely that they will prefer to be regarded as part of the information or computer industries who happen to employ construction firms as subcontractors.

This is a serious issue for the whole construction industry. If its leading edge is taken over by others, construction generally will find that all its dealings with the rest of society become more difficult and less satisfactory than they could or should be. It would become harder to recruit talented young people, finance would become more expensive, legislation would often work against the industry's interests, the media would portray construction as a low-technology, low-value industry, and construction would in fact become a third-division sector of many national economies.

The alternative is for the leading firms in the industry to invest now in their own long term competence. It means raising the stakes, so that, for example, architecture is taken totally seriously and is not trivialized into superficial arguments about fashion and style. It means understanding the complex interactions between mankind and his built and natural environments. The construction industry must research answers to the violence and poverty which disfigure far too many major cities. It must produce only *green* constructions. It must understand how local communities need to be involved in new construction developments and in running their existing built environment. Where these issues are being mishandled, the industry's leaders must speak out for the environment and the community. It is essential that construction is seen as part of the solution to enabling ten billion individual human beings to live decent, worthwhile lives on this planet.

The leading firms need to learn how to deal with their customers and their critics. They must take the lead in correctly identifying the need for construction and in knowing how to assemble the necessary finance and political support, and then be able to deliver their products reliably. In 1990 the BBC broadcast frequent news items to the effect that the Channel Tunnel, which provides a rail-link between France and the UK, will cost 60 per cent more than the original estimates. It is certain that these reports owe as much to the way that the costs are reported by the Channel Tunnel company, Eurotunnel, as to construction failures. For example, the latest figures include the effects of predictable inflation which were excluded from the so-called original estimates. Nevertheless, the effect of these and similar reports is that the general impression that construction cannot be trusted to handle large, complex projects is provided with further ammunition. This bad publicity simply has to be reversed, so that it becomes normal for major new constructions to get into the news because of their technical ingenuity, their design flair and the success of their management systems.

The construction design and management firms who invest successfully in their own long term competence will become the worldwide system organizers of the twenty-first century. They will form the heart of the fourth major sector of the construction industry of 2001.

Construction industry 2001

The overall pattern of demand and supply likely to shape the construction industry by 2001 is illustrated in Figure 16.3. It undoubtedly provides a greatly simplified and unrealistically tidy picture. However, it does serve to identify important gaps and overlapping interests, both of which provide potential battlegrounds for firms fighting for market share.

The first and most important of these potential battlegrounds is provided by large traditional building projects. As discussed in Chapter 9, modern professional organizations require well rounded, widely competent design consultancies. These are most likely to be provided by ambitious firms emerging from the local building industry for small and medium sized traditional projects. However, in many cases the difficulty of the management task posed by large projects, especially if they are also complex, uncertain and have tough objectives, will make it more appropriate for a worldwide system organizer to be appointed. The local building industry consultants will also face competition for the lead role in large, simple and repetitive traditional projects from construction system firms. Those with flexible systems may well be able to supply satisfactory products backed up by more comprehensive supporting services and larger guarantees, at lower costs, delivered faster than the local building industry is able to provide. The outcome of these battles for market share will vary from place to place. The winners will have a large effect on the character of local built environments in the twenty-first century. This is because there are important forces at work which should serve to make this a large sector of the industry's market.

First, given the pace of technological change, there will often be a sound economic case for large scale development. Second, efficiency requires construction to use good traditional forms of construction. Therefore large, traditional building projects ought to be a substantial sector of the industry's workload. This sector needs to be supplied with both the concern and sensitivity of the best local building firms and the efficiency and broad competence of worldwide system organizers. These needs will be provided in various ways throughout the world. In places, one or the other will dominate; in others, firms will work together in some form of joint venture. The essential conflict which prevents a clear way forward is between the ambitions of designers faced with a large

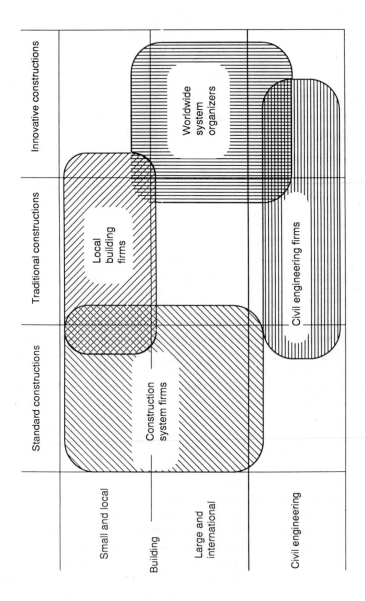

Figure 16.3   *The construction industry 2001*

opportunity and the management requirements for a complete design before manufacturing and construction begin. This basic conflict will ensure that projects in this sector require very experienced and tough customers, if they are not to run out of control.

The other potential battlefields for market share are less important than the large, traditional building project sector. One is the possibility of creating standard constructions for infrastructure projects. The competitors are likely to be drawn from civil engineering firms and construction system firms. The need to fit construction closely to the specific, local physical environment tends to work against standard answers. However, flexible manufacturing techniques are continually rolling back the frontiers of what is possible and so in the long term this may prove to be a more interesting sector than seems likely at present.

The final interesting potential battlefield is that provided by small, innovative constructions. They provide the ideal basis for concept constructions. The particular firms that in practice succeed in this sector will depend to a great extent on the nature and objectives of the innovations introduced. If they are primarily concerned with aesthetic design, the local building firms, specifically architectural practices, will play a leading role. If innovation is more concerned with technological or management issues, local building firms and worldwide system organizers may both be prepared to use them as test-beds for their own ideas or as training grounds for new young staff. In such cases customers are likely to be able to negotiate very attractive terms from firms eager to treat a project as an investment in their own long term competence.

So, in total, construction in 2001 is likely still to be a diverse and fragmented industry. In parts it will rely on the steady application of well established methods and standards. At the same time, in other parts, it will be a hot-bed of new ideas and innovation.

Construction will continue to provide employment for people with a great variety of talents although, for its own long term health, by 2001 the industry needs to have raised the average level of competence of its people to that currently achieved only by the very best. The industry's workforce will continue to be employed by firms of all sizes, from the one man business, right up to massive firms operating on a global scale. These firms will form networks built around the experience of working together regularly on many projects. Within these networks of firms, construction needs to work in a cooperative manner to a greater extent than it generally does at present. On the other hand, the industry's long term efficiency depends on fierce competition between networks of firms producing complete constructions for demanding and well informed customers.

Construction needs a sense of continuity, especially in its search for better productivity and quality, but it also needs to be flexible so that it can respond to rapidly changing markets. An important element in achieving all of these apparently contradictory aims is provided by the firms who work across the boundaries of the main sectors of the industry. They provide an important means of disseminating first-hand experience throughout the industry. Three types of these boundary-crossing firms are sufficiently interesting to warrant a separate description. They are specialist contractors, design boutiques and master builders.

Specialist contractors

Direct construction work in all sectors of the industry in 2001 will be undertaken by specialist contractors. Their important characteristics are already clear and are described in Chapters 6 and 9. The best of them will provide a comprehensive and integrated service encompassing research, development, design, manufacture, construction, servicing and maintenance. Some at least of the specialist contractors will be operating globally in 2001. They will be a major force in shaping construction. Since they serve all sectors of the industry, they will provide an important means of disseminating ideas and encouraging common methods and procedures.

Specialist contractors will undertake much of the industry's research and development. They will be active in finding uses for new materials. They will develop ever wider ranges of ever more sophisticated components. Much of this work will be undertaken jointly with firms from other industries in large scale, pre-competition research. Specialist contractors will have their own research laboratories so that they can play a full part in such work, and also to enable them to keep abreast of contemporary research worldwide. They are likely to have their own test facilities so that project designers can try out new ideas in prototypes and so identify and sort out problems before they can disrupt construction on site.

Specialist contractors will undertake the training of the industry's manufacturing and construction workforces. They will be employed almost entirely on a full-time, salaried basis. Each worker will have a clear career pattern in which skills training is coordinated with practical experience. Appraisal will be broadly based so that individuals are rewarded for their own performance, as well as that of their teams, their projects and their firms. Overall the industry will have a much more professional manufacturing and construction workforce than at present. Careers in the big specialist construction firms will be seen as increasingly worthwhile, as the challenging, high-technology nature of their work becomes more widely known.

Design boutiques and master builders

Although there is an emphasis, in this chapter's description of construction 2001, on large firms, small talented firms will also have a part to play. The construction industry has always provided a home for talented designers and craftsmen who want to be self-employed or to work in small firms. This will remain the case and their natural base is working in local building industries on small, traditional, projects.

In addition, as happens now, some individuals and small firms will develop outstanding or unique talents which earn them a place within large or innovative project organizations. However, these design boutiques or master builders will be the exception, even though their role in construction is important in providing true originality and even genius. Most small firms will need to rely on using well established answers in order to avoid the risk of incurring crippling liabilities if they try something new and it fails. This is not to suggest that some ambitious individuals will not indeed try something new, which succeeds and allows them to turn a small firm into a much bigger one. Good ideas often come from small firms but increasingly it requires substantial marketing and financial resources to realize their full potential. Therefore really successful small firms tend to grow rapidly and are often absorbed by a bigger competitor. There are exceptions: individuals who turn work away rather than lose their independence and freedom of action, which they fear would happen if they got bigger.

So construction will continue to provide employment for a great variety of individuals and firms. However, if it is to play its full part in society in 2001 and beyond, design boutiques and master builders will be interesting decorations in an industry increasingly dominated by big firms. This is made inevitable by the opportunities provided by the technology of flexible manufacturing and information communication systems, and by the demands of society for a safe and healthy environment for everyone in the world. An industry of small firms would be marginalized in the search for answers to the greatest challenge which will face mankind in the twenty-first century. That is, working out how to accommodate ten billion people within this one world. Construction must be involved in finding decent human answers to this crucial question; and that requires real leadership from within the industry backed up by powerful organizations able to manage construction projects efficiently, anywhere in the world.

References

Beer S. (1972). *Brain of the Firm*. Harmondsworth: Penguin.

Bennett J. (1985). *Construction Project Management*. London: Butterworths.

Bennett J. (1986). *Construction Management and the Chartered Quantity Surveyor*. London: Royal Institution of Chartered Surveyors.

Bennett J., Ormerod R. N. (1984). Simulation applied to construction projects. *Construction Management and Economics*, **2**, 3.

Bennett J., Flanagan R., Goodacre P., Gray C., McLaughlin N., Norman G. (1979). *UK and US Construction Industries: A Comparison of Design and Contract Procedures*. London: Royal Institution of Chartered Surveyors.

Bennett J., Morrison N., Stevens S. (1981). *Cost Planning and Computers*. London: Department of the Environment.

Bennett J., Flanagan R., Norman G. (1987). *Capital and Counties Report: Japanese Construction Industry*. Reading, UK: Centre for Strategic Studies in Construction.

Bennett J., Croome D., Atkin B. (1989). *Investing in Building 2001*. Reading, UK: Centre for Static Studies in Construction.

Biggs W. D., Betts M., Cottle M. J. (1990). *The West German Construction Industry*. London: Construction Industry Research and Information Association.

Broadbent G. (1973). *Design in Architecture*. Chichester: Wiley.

Brownlie S. M., Harris F. C. (1987). A review of finance for large-scale construction. *Constructon Management and Economics*, **5**, 2.

Coordinating Committee for Project Information (1987). *Guide to Coordinated Project Information*. London: Coordinating Committee for Project Information.

Davis, Belfield, Everest (1977). Initial cost estimating: the cost of warehouses. *Architects Journal*, **165**, 22, 1037–1042.

Davis G., Becker F., Duffy F., Sims W. (1985). *Orbit 2*. Norwalk, Conn.: Harbinger Group Inc.

Duffy F., Henney A. (1989). *The Changing City*. London: Bulstrode Press.

Fisher R., Ury W. (1981). *Getting to Yes*. London: Hutchinson Business.

Flanagan R., Norman G., Ireland V., Ormerod R. (1986). *A Fresh Look at the UK and US Building Industries*. London: Building Employers Confederation.

Galbraith J. (1973). *Designing Complex Organizations*. Reading, Mass.: Addison-Wesley.

Gray C., Flanagan R. (1989). *The Changing Role of Specialist and Trade Contractors*. Ascot, UK: Chartered Institute of Building.

Haenlein H., Brookes A., Penz F. (1989). *Professional Education for Construction: Overseas Comparisons*. London: Department of the Environment.

Hall P. (1980). *Great Planning Disasters*. Harmondsworth: Penguin.

Hasegawa F. (1988). *Built by Japan*. New York: Wiley.

Hayes R. W., Perry, J. G., Thompson P. A., Willmer G. (1986). *Risk Management in Engineering Construction*. London: Thomas Telford.

Heirs B., Pehrson G. (1982). *The Mind of the Organization*. New York: Harper & Row.

Hillebrandt P. M. (1984). *Analysis of the British Construction Industry*. London: Macmillan.

Hordyk M., Bennett J. (1989). *New Steel Work Way*. Ascot, UK: The Steel Construction Institute.

HRH the Prince of Wales (1989). *A Vision of Britain*. London: Doubleday.

Humphrey N. (1983). *Consciousness Regained*. Oxford: Oxford University Press.

Hutchins D. (1988). *Just-in-Time*. Aldershot, UK: Gower.

Kennedy G., Benson J., McMillan J. (1980). *Managing Negotiations*. London: Hutchinson Business.

Kuhn A. (1974). *The Logic of Social Systems*. San Francisco, Calif.: Jossey-Bass.

Kuhn A., Beam R. D. (1982). *The Logic of Organization*. San Francisco, Calif.: Jossey-Bass.

Lawrence P. R., Lorsch J. W. (1967). *Organization and Environment*. Boston, Mass.: Harvard University Press.

Leopold E., Bishop D. (1983). Design philosophy and practice in speculative house building. *Construction Management and Economics*, **1**, 2.

Lowe J. G. (1987). Monopoly and the materials supply industries of the UK. *Construction Management and Economics*, **5**, 1.

March J. G., Simon H. A. (1958). *Organizations*. New York: Wiley.

Marshall H. E. (1988). *Techniques for Treating Uncertainty and Risk in the Economic Evaluation of Building Investments*. Washington DC: US Department of Commerce.

Meikle J. L., Hillebrandt P. M. (1990). *The French Construction Industry*. London: Construction Industry Research and Information Association.

Miller E. J. (1959). Territory, technology and time: the internal differentiation of complex production systems. *Human Relations*, **22**, 3.

Mintzberg H. (1979). *The Structuring of Organizations*. Englewood Cliffs, NJ: Prentice-Hall.

Mintzberg H. (1989). *Mintzberg on Management*. New York: Macmillan.

NEDC Construction Industry Sector Group (1988). *Faster Building for Commerce*. London: National Economic Development Office.

Ohmae K. (1990). Management briefing. In *Drucker, Ohmae, Porter and Peters: Management Briefings*. The Economist Publications, Report No. 1202. London: The Economist.

Olins W. (1989). *Corporate Identity*. London: Thames and Hudson.

Pain J., Bennett J. (1988). JCT with Contractor's Design form of contract: a study in use. *Construction Management and Economics*, **6**, 4.

Peters T. (1987). *Thriving on Chaos*. London: Macmillan.

Peters T. (1990). Management briefing. In *Drucker, Ohmae, Porter and Peters: Management Briefings*. The Economist Publications, Report No. 1202. London: The Economist.

Peters, T. J., Waterman R. H. (1982). *In Search of Excellence*. New York: Harper & Row.

Porter M. (1990). Management briefing. In *Drucker, Ohmae, Porter and Peters: Management Briefings*. The Economist Publications, Report No. 1202. London: The Economist.

Reavens R. W. (1982). *Action Learning*. Lund, Sweden: Chartwell Bratt.

Rogers R. (1988). *Architecture and Urbanism*. Tokyo: A & U Publishing.

Sabbagh K. (1989). *Skyscraper*. London: Macmillan.

Schon D. A. (1983). *The Reflective Practitioner*. London: Temple Smith.

Sculley J. (1987). *Odyssey: Pepsi to Apple*. Glasgow: Collins.

Simon H. (1969). *The Sciences of the Artificial*. Cambridge, Mass: MIT Press.

Slough Estates Limited (1979). *Industrial Investment: A Case Study in Factory Building*. London: Slough Estates Limited.

Taylor, F. W. (1903). *Shop Management*. New York: Harper and Brothers.

Taylor F. W. (1911). *Fundamentals of Scientific Management*. New York: Harper and Brothers.

Townsend R. (1971). *Up the Organization*. London: Hodder Fawcett.

United Nations Committee on Housing (1965). *Building and Planning: Effect of Repetition on Building Operations and Processes on Site*. New York: United Nations.

Walker A. (1989) *Project Management in Construction*. Oxford: BSP Professional Books.

Woodward J. (1965). *Industrial Organization: Theory and Practice*. Oxford: Oxford University Press.

Index